Patrick Boyde brings Dante's thought and poetry into focus for the modern reader by restoring the *Comedy* to its intellectual and literary context in 1300. He begins by describing the authorities that Dante acknowledged in the field of ethics and the modes of thought he shared with the great thinkers of his time. After giving a clear account of the differing approaches and ideals embodied in Aristotelian philosophy, Christianity and courtly literature, Boyde concentrates on the poetic representation of the most important vices and virtues in the *Comedy*. He stresses the heterogeneity and originality of Dante's treatment, and the challenges posed by his desire to harmonise these divergent value-systems. The book ends with a detailed case-study of the 'worth and vices' of Ulysses in which Boyde throws light on recent controversies by deliberately remaining within the framework of the thirteenth-century assumptions, methods and concepts explored in previous chapters.

Patrick Boyde is Serena Professor of Italian in the University of Cambridge and Fellow of St John's College. He is the author of *Dante's Style in his Lyric Poetry* (Cambridge, 1971) and *Night Thoughts on Italian Poetry and Art* (Cambridge, 1985). *Human Vices and Human Worth in Dante's 'Comedy'* is the third book in his trilogy, which also comprises *Dante Philomythes and Philosopher: Man in the Cosmos* (Cambridge, 1981), and *Perception and Passion in Dante's 'Comedy'* (Cambridge, 1993).

Human Vices and Human Worth in Dante's *Comedy*

PATRICK BOYDE

Serena Professor of Italian in the University of Cambridge
and Fellow of St John's College

CAMBRIDGE
UNIVERSITY PRESS

PUBLISHED BY THE PRESS SYNDICATE OF THE UNIVERSITY OF CAMBRIDGE
The Pitt Building, Trumpington Street, Cambridge, United Kingdom

CAMBRIDGE UNIVERSITY PRESS
The Edinburgh Building, Cambridge CB2 2RU, UK www.cup.cam.ac.uk
40 West 20th Street, New York, NY 10011-4211, USA www.cup.org
10 Stamford Road, Oakleigh, Melbourne 3166, Australia
Ruiz de Alarcón 13, 28014 Madrid, Spain

First published 2000

Printed in the United Kingdom at the University Press, Cambridge

Typeface Janson Text 10.5/13pt *System* QuarkXPress™ [SE]

A catalogue record for this book is available from the British Library

ISBN 0 521 66067 X hardback

Non similiter in omni materia certitudo quaerenda est, sed secundum quod natura rei subiectae recipit.

ARISTOTLE, *Ethics*, I, iii, 4, quoted by Dante, *Monarchia*, II, ii, 7

'Ex omni ligno paradisi comede. De ligno autem *scientiae boni et mali* ne comedas, in quocumque enim die comederis ex eo, morte morieris.'

'Scit enim Deus quod in quocumque die comederitis ex eo, aperientur oculi vestri et eritis sicut dii, *scientes bonum et malum*.'

GENESIS 2.16–17; 3.5

De finibus *bonorum et malorum*

CICERO (title)

Juris prudentia est divinarum atque humanarum rerum notitia, *justi atque injusti* scientia.

JUSTINIAN, *Institutes*, I, i, pr.

Haec exposuimus ut vobis possibile sit summo digito et quasi per indicem ea tetigisse.

Ibid. IV, xviii, 12

Neither in inward *worth* nor outward fair.

SHAKESPEARE, Sonnets, 16, 11

Worth makes the man, and want of it the fellow:
The rest is all but leather or prunella.

POPE, *Essay on Man*, IV, 203

'I wish . . . that her birth were equal to her fortune, as I am sure that her *worth* is superior to them both.'

TROLLOPE, *Dr Thorne*, chapter 46

Contents

List of figures *page* viii
Preface ix

Introduction: the role of context 1

PART ONE Authority, reason and order

1 Dante's authors 11
2 Putting authors to the question 25
3 Division and numeration 50

PART TWO Competing values

4 Aristotelian values through Dante's eyes 77
5 Christian values through Dante's eyes 100
6 A courtly value in Dante's hands 126

PART THREE Arch-vices and the supreme virtue

7 Covetousness 149
8 Pride 174
9 Justice 198

PART FOUR Amid such wisdom ('tra cotanto senno')

Preface to Part Four 227
10 The worth and vices of Ulysses: a case-study 231

Notes 273
Bibliography 303
Index 309

Figures

1 The Tree of the Vices. British Library, Arundel 83, fol. 128 verso. Reproduced by permission of The British Library. *page* 54

2 The Tree of the Virtues. British Library, Arundel 83, fol. 129 recto. Reproduced by permission of The British Library. 55

Preface

This is the third book I have devoted to the study of the interactions between Dante's poetry and thought. It stands on its own and presupposes no familiarity with its predecessors (*Dante Philomythes and Philosopher: Man in the Cosmos*, 1981; *Perception and Passion in Dante's 'Comedy'*, 1993). But given that it is written in the same spirit, and as part of the same enterprise, it may be worth restating two points made in the preface to the second volume. First, the book's main claim to originality lies in the connections it seeks to re-establish between a medieval poem and medieval ideas. Second, the adjective 'philomythical' is occasionally used as a correlative to 'philosophical' in order to signify the kind of creative writing that is open to and nourished by philosophy. Anyone who is curious to know how I conceive the relationship between *mythos* and *sophia* in Dante, or who would like to read my own sketch of his development and his other works, is referred to the Introduction to the first volume.

The editions of Dante's works and the abbreviations used are listed on p. 273 below, at the beginning of the Notes. All unattributed translations are my own. (They are intended primarily as guides to the syntax and the meaning of the individual words in the original text.) It should go without saying that all italicisations for emphasis in classical and medieval texts are mine.

My warmest thanks are due to the colleagues and friends who read the draft during the year in which the book was taking its present form and who gave me their reactions cheerfully, frankly and promptly. Richard Beadle, Joseph Cremona, Meera Frost, Lino Leonardi, Laura Lepschy, John Marenbon and Gianni Vaggi read individual chapters within the field of their special competence. The following were kind enough to read the whole book in draft and to make many suggestions for improvement: Piero Boitani, Peter Brand, Francesco Calvo, Virginia Cox, Simon Gilson, Catherine Keen, Robin Kirkpatrick,

Alison Morgan, Elizabeth Mozzillo-Howell, Christopher Ryan, Max Saint, John Scott and Jill Tilden. My particular thanks go to Robbie Carroll and David Gibbons who not only read and criticised the final draft chapter by chapter, but gave me invaluable practical help in revising the text, finalising the notes, and streamlining the bibliography. All of those named have helped to make the book more accurate, more useful and more readable; but any errors of fact or judgement and the remaining infelicities of expression are of course my own responsibility.

This is also the place to record my debt to the staff of the Cambridge University Press for their encouragement and good advice at every turn, and for their firmness in keeping me to a timetable and a word-limit. My gratitude goes in particular to the editor, Linda Bree, and to the copy-editor, Rosemary Williams.

Introduction: the role of context

The joint squareness of malt

Anyone who has tried to explain a joke to a foreigner, or a family saying to an outsider, will know that it is next to impossible. This truism was brought home to me with particular force by the sentence 'Malt is both square.' Set down on the page like that, the four monosyllables seem both ungrammatical and nonsensical, and it would take about four *hundred* words to show why they were meaningful, good English, and funny, when they were first pronounced. One would have to supply so many facts about the age of the speaker, his relationship to his interlocutor, and the question to which the four words were a spontaneous answer; and one would have to explain so much about the eating habits and material culture of the English middle classes in the 1960s. And yet that terse reply convinced me once and for all that it is impossible to understand any piece of 'real language' without some familiarity with its context.[1]

What is true of a single phrase is true *mutatis mutandis* of a paragraph, a chapter, a book, even a whole œuvre. The context varies in kind and scale. Sometimes (and to avoid confusion, we may confine ourselves to a work of fiction such as the *Comedy*) it is enough to register the words immediately preceding and following the passage to be interpreted. Sometimes we need to grasp the situation, the character of the speaker, and the nature of his intentions (otherwise we should never understand irony). At other times we might misunderstand the meaning or implication if we did not remember the plot of the book, or recognise the genre to which it belonged. At the highest level of all, we need to be broadly familiar with the culture to which the author belonged, by which he was formed, and for which he wrote. This is as true of Dante as of any lesser author. Although it is a matter of definition that a writer who has achieved the status of a classic has in some sense risen above the limits of his time, we shall fail to understand him, or misrepresent the nature of his greatness, if we cannot distinguish what is individual and original in his work from what is typical of the species and genus to which it belongs.

'The past is a foreign country'

In reading contemporary fiction in our native language, we hardly ever pause to think of the ways in which our interpretation is being controlled by our familiarity with this hierarchy of contexts. Perhaps it is only when we *re*-read a novel or play from an *earlier* period that we discover how much we had failed to understand on the first reading because of our lack of such familiarity. The beginning of wisdom in this regard is the recognition that 'the past is a foreign country: they do things differently there'.

L. P. Hartley's much-quoted dictum has a particular relevance for English-speaking readers of Dante. The poem we are trying to understand is twice removed from us – first by the barrier of a language we have learnt late and imperfectly, and secondly by a distance of six hundred years. Nevertheless, Dante himself offers rational grounds for hope that it is possible to become sufficiently familiar with the necessary contexts to come close to his meaning or meanings. He was acutely aware that linguistic and cultural differences in time and place are essentially of the same kind. Everything human, including our language, is subject to constant change because 'man is a highly unstable and variable animal' ('instabilissimum atque variabilissimum animal'). This, he knew, was why there were 'more than a thousand sub-species' of the spoken language in the different regions of Italy he had visited; and this was why a citizen of Pavia would not be able to understand his fellow countrymen if he were to return to his native city after an interval of five hundred years. On the other hand, Dante accepted that human infants can acquire any spoken language whatsoever, mastering both the sounds and the meaning of the sounds they hear simply by listening, imitating, and observing the reactions of their minders. He had learnt Latin at school and knew it was possible to translate from the *grammatica* into the *vulgare* (as he called the artificial and natural languages respectively), or from Greek and Hebrew into Latin. And while he was aware that correspondences are rarely exact, he was sufficiently confident in the possibility of translation for him to compare different versions of the same text and to judge them better or worse, more or less faithful to the original.[2]

The child's innate ability to learn any language by natural means, and the more limited ability of some adolescents and adults to become proficient in a foreign language through conscious study, are both closely related to our capacity to feel our way into the customs, beliefs and rituals of other human societies which are different in place or time. Just as we can learn to understand the words and syntax of Dante's Italian, so we can learn to understand the most important aspects of his culture. Whether the obstacles are linguistic or cultural, all we have to do (to paraphrase Terence) is to be human and refuse to accept that anything human can be alien to us: 'homines simus, et humani nil a nobis alienum putemus'.[3]

'They do things differently there'

For reasons I have explained more fully elsewhere, one of the most important contexts for the better understanding of the *Comedy* is that of medieval philosophy and theology. For many years of his life (in round figures, from the age of twenty-eight to the age of forty-three) Dante regarded himself primarily as a 'Lover of Wisdom', knowing that this was the meaning of the two roots of the word 'Philosopher' (*philos* + *sophia*). During this time he composed verse and prose in the service of the 'Noble Lady' who had come to replace Beatrice as the inspiration and subject of his writing. The greatest differences between the poetry of his youth (much of which is contained in the *Vita nuova*, which was probably completed in about 1293) and that of his full maturity (the *Comedy*, most of which was written after 1308) are to be attributed to the enrichment and redirection of his imagination, which he owed to his passionate study of the highly sophisticated and comprehensive system of thought that has come to be known as scholasticism, and, in particular, to his study of scholastic ethics.[4]

Scholastic moral philosophy is radically unfamiliar to most readers today. Ethics in our time tends to be pluralistic, relativist, tolerant, and anxious to free itself from the preconceptions of the past. Late medieval thought was utterly different. It looked to the past for authority; it believed in objective truth and was correspondingly rigorous in its methodology. It was confident it could distinguish a true good from an apparent one. Setting out from the premiss that goods are different in kind and unequal in value, it attempted to combine all true concepts into a single hierarchical system. They did things differently then. Some introduction is therefore required. And, in essence, this is what the present volume sets out to provide. The *Comedy* will be studied as a poem – as a product of Dante's imagination and literary craft – but the poetry will be set within the context of his own specific pronouncements concerning the nature of right and wrong, and these in turn will be located within the larger context of thirteenth-century thought.[5]

Proportional comparison

Many first-time readers of Dante feel that he speaks to them directly across the centuries, giving a true portrait of the positive and negative sides of human nature, redefining the goals of human life, offering insights that can influence the choices they make in the real world of every day. This book is written in the conviction that Dante can become more of a living force in our time if we restore him to his own, and if we do not search his work for universal truths, but look instead for similarities between him and us, for likenesses between his situation and ours.

It is helpful to think about these likenesses in the way that Aristotle analysed metaphor and simile, that is, by looking for proportional relationships, rather than precise correspondences – for ratios of the kind that a geometrician would express as A:B = C:D. To see what this implies, we may look at a famous metaphor in the *Comedy* which links the words 'wings' and 'oars'. It is used by Dante's Ulysses (in the famous episode which forms the subject of Chapter 10 below) at a point in his narrative when he has persuaded his ageing crew to join him on a final voyage of discovery 'to a world without people behind the sun'.

Commentators on Canto XXVI of the *Inferno* have noted that the image is a revitalisation of its ancient sources, because classical poets had used 'oars' to refer to the action of 'wings', whereas Ulysses turns things round by saying 'we made wings of our oars for the mad flight', 'de' *remi* facemmo *ali* al folle volo'. But the Aristotelian analysis is valid in either direction. It rests on two assumptions about the nature of metaphor. The first is that a metaphor is nothing other than a compressed comparison. The second is that the similarities between the two terms of the comparison may be multiple but far from complete. (In our example, an oar is not made of feathers; wings beat up and down, whereas oars pull fore and aft.) The comparison rests on a series of analogies. Wings are to oars as flying is to rowing, as the bird is to the boat, and as air is to water. The metaphor does not assert a straightforward resemblance between object A and object C. It suggests that the relationship between A and its context B (where A stands for the wing, and B for the bird, for flying, and for the air) is similar to the relationship between C and its context D (where C stands for the oar, and D for the vessel, rowing, and water). That is why the likeness implied or asserted by the metaphor should be expressed in the form: as A is to B, so C is to D (or, more economically, A:B = C:D).[6]

There is infinitely more that might be said about the concept of metaphor. But even this very simple example can serve as a model to suggest how we might transfer the insights gained from our reading of Dante to the lives we lead in the twenty-first century, by restoring him to his own context in the fourteenth. Dante will be more, not less, 'of our time' if we consciously reflect – to take a few examples only apparently at random – that the personal computer, popular television series, democracies of a hundred million people, or an international organisation like the United Nations have no counterparts in Dante's culture, but nevertheless present distant analogies, respectively, with the quill pen, courtly romances, the Florentine republic of 80,000 inhabitants, and the Holy Roman Empire.

The scholastic synthesis of all certain knowledge (*scientia*) – incorporating both what God has revealed and what men have discovered for themselves – is very different indeed from the astonishing range and diversity of sciences studied and pursued in any modern university. But there is an analogy between what *scientia* meant to Dante and what 'science' means today. The thirst for knowledge remains just as much a distinguishing feature of human nature as it was when Aristotle laid it down in the first sentence of his *Metaphysics* that 'all men by nature desire to understand', or when Dante translated that sentence in the opening words of his *Convivio*: 'Tutti li uomini naturalmente desiderano di sapere.'

What Dante might teach us – to take some examples from my earlier studies of the relationship between Dante's thought and his poetry – is not that there are only four elements, or that the earth is at the centre of a steady-state universe which came into existence in 5198 BC. We are not to follow him in believing that procreation is due initially to the activity of the father's seed operating on the mother's passive menstrual blood, while the specifically human faculties are breathed into the embryo by God at about the twenty-eighth week. Again, we are not to accept that individual character is largely determined by influences rayed down from the stars; or that the brain transmits messages to the limbs through gaseous spirits moving along the hollow nerves and the veins and arteries. Those 'facts' are plainly not true.[7]

If, however, we apply the proportional model (A:B = C:D), we shall recognise that Dante took all those 'facts' on trust from the best-qualified experts in exactly the same way as we accept that the universe is still expanding, that the earth is a planet orbiting the sun, that there has been life on the planet for at least five million years, that individual character is greatly influenced by the genes, and that a mother contributes half the genes to the embryo in her womb. We shall see that the essence of the comparison lies in the presumed relationship between natural science and ethics. Dante believed that it is impossible to understand human nature (and impossible therefore to understand what we ought to do in order to live well and to achieve happiness), unless we understand something of the nature of the universe and the matter of which it is composed, the processes of procreation, the formation of character, and how it comes about that human beings can all learn a *vulgare* and a *grammatica* while no other animal can. If we really want to understand 'human vices and human worth' in the way he did, we must think 'proportionally'. That means we must not look for answers in fundamentalist religion, or in simple common sense, but seek to discover what happens at conception, how the human brain differs from those of other animals, why Darwin gave a more scientifically credible account of the origins of man than the author of Genesis, why the structure of DNA gives a better explanation of personality-types than astrology does, and just how thoughts and feelings are really translated into bodily movements.

'Sustanze, accidenti e lor costume'

The context to be discussed in the present book is formed not by the metaphysical, cosmological and physiological ideas that underpin Dante's ethics, but by his moral philosophy considered as a highly structured system which incorporates and gives meaning to each of the distinct concepts of which it is composed. We shall have to grasp the interconnections between the parts and the whole, the whole and the parts. But it is relatively easy to break into this 'hermeneutic circle', because ethics has changed a great deal less than the natural sciences over the past six centuries. As a result, the interlocking concepts of scholastic moral philosophy are more familiar than those in the field of medieval physics or psychology. And it will be possible to round off this introduction with a few words of caution and encouragement concerning the application of Dante's insights to the modern world.

Time and again it will be found that there are 'false friends' among the terms used by Dante. His words survive, but they have acquired different meanings or connotations. Hence it may prove less easy to distinguish between his *justitia* and our 'justice' than between his four *elementa* and the ninety-two 'elements' in the periodic table.

While we have to accept that Dante believed he was dealing in facts, we do not have to commit ourselves to their literal truth. For example, it is not necessary to affirm that there is any such place or state of eternal punishment as Hell before one can learn something from Dante's *Inferno* about the nature of evil, the relative gravity of different crimes, or our apparently infinite capacity to make ourselves and others miserable in the pursuit of happiness. But it is dangerous to pick and choose. To paraphrase John Donne, 'no concept is an island'. And it is unsatisfactory to endorse Dante's representation of the folly of greed while ignoring his treatment of suicide, homosexuality or forgery.

Dante and his culture have no need of an apologist. His treatment of ethics is rich, rigorous and nuanced – far more so than anything taught in the schools or universities of the United Kingdom at the present time. We should study his ethical system sympathetically, seeing it as an astonishing attempt to encompass all the contradictory data of human existence. And we might ask ourselves whether this system does not accommodate the potentially conflicting demands of our complex nature – work, leisure, study, friendship, love, the rearing of a family, political obligations – at least as well as any of its modern rivals or counterparts.

The *Comedy* also challenges us to entertain the notion that there is some absolute criterion by which all values and actions may be judged. It asks us to empathise with Dante's belief in a Last Judgement when we shall be called to account for our actions on earth, and either rewarded or punished eternally. It invites us to share imaginatively in his confidence that we all have a 'concreated thirst' for God. There is no need to subscribe to Dante's convictions as articles of faith before we enter into the world of his imagination. But if we do suspend our disbelief, and exercise the special human gift of empathy, then we shall find ourselves occupying a strange and wonderful viewing-point, particularly if we follow Dante the protagonist through the last stages of his journey in the *Paradiso*. The globe 'that makes us so ferocious' will seem no more than a patch of dry earth. The 'order which all things have among themselves' will appear in the perspective of eternity. We shall see 'all independently existing beings, their attributes, and their relationships' ('sustanze, accidenti e lor costume') 'conflated in a simple light', because we shall have glimpsed the 'universal form of their knot'.[8]

PART ONE

Authority, reason and order

CHAPTER ONE

Dante's authors

'Viaggio, cammino, volo'

The *Comedy* is the first-person narrative of a divinely willed journey through Hell, Purgatory and Heaven, a journey from which the author returns to write his poem 'for the good of the world that lives so ill' ('in pro del mondo che mal vive'). Canto XXVI of *Inferno* contains a first-person narrative put into the mouth of Ulysses in which he relates the ill-fated voyage from which he never returned. Both travellers undertook their journeys to gain understanding of 'human vices and human worth' (the phrase is used by Ulysses); and the realistically detailed stories they tell are of course fictional representations of a purely metaphorical journey towards the 'knowledge of good and evil', which occupied Dante the author for much of his adult life.[1]

During that quest he undoubtedly learnt much from introspection and from close observation of the people he met. His poem is packed with references to himself and to characters and events of his own time. But unlike Ulysses, he did not limit himself to gathering information at first hand. His 'expertise' did not derive simply from the 'experience of our senses'. A very large part of his 'voyage of discovery' was made in his mind and imagination as he read the works of other men. And the purpose of this chapter is to give some account of the earlier 'explorers' who had acted as his 'guides' and of the extraordinarily detailed and accurate 'maps' of the moral universe they had drawn.[2]

The libraries available to Dante were very much smaller than those to which we have access today. But the relative paucity of books meant there was time to read them and to remember their contents (Dante's personal library in the years of his exile must have existed largely on the shelves of his memory). There existed numerous works in the field of ethics which are still regarded as fundamental, and which are astonishingly varied in their provenance and the values they uphold. When

Dante looked at the moral world, his vision was not myopic, monochrome or blinkered.

The same point might be made with an analogy from the law-court. Dante took it upon himself to sit in judgement on human affairs, but he delivered his verdicts only after he had sifted the contradictory evidence of countless witnesses, after he had listened to the eloquent but opposing pleas of many advocates, and after he had studied the conflicting judgements of his predecessors on the judicial bench.

Chief among these predecessors were the great teachers in the 'schools' of the University of Paris between about 1250 and 1280. Like them, and like the whole intellectual culture we call 'scholasticism', Dante's ambitions may be described as both syncretist and systematic. 'Syncretist' means attempting 'to unite or reconcile diverse or opposite tenets or practices, especially in philosophy or religion'; while 'systematic' characterises a body of thought that aims to be comprehensive, rigorous and methodical. Both tendencies may be viewed as a response to the challenge posed by the diversity and wealth of a much-revered inheritance. And the following survey of Dante's 'authors' – who were also his 'authorities' – is intended above all to convey some idea of this wealth and diversity.[3]

The proud Greeks: (a) the soaring eagle

Dante knew no Greek, but he knew that the Romans had recognised the pre-eminence of the Greeks in philosophy and literature, and he was anxious to pay his tribute to the civilisation which had produced the greatest philosopher and the greatest poet of all time.

The poet was Homer, and Dante honours him as the 'lord' who with his 'lofty song' 'soared like an eagle' above all his rivals in antiquity. Homer was the ultimate source of information about the heroes and gods who were involved in the War of Troy and who have marched and counter-marched through the European imagination ever since, providing paradigms of so many human types and so many insights into human behaviour. He had been held up for admiration by Macrobius as a philosopher-poet who had revealed 'the truth of all divine inventions under a veil of poetic fiction'. So it is fitting that Homer should prove to be Dante's authority for two of the most important propositions in his political and ethical thought. It was Homer who anticipated the argument of the *Monarchia* in his assertion that there should be one supreme ruler; and it was he who said that the noblest human being is like the child of a god rather than of a man.[4]

The proud Greeks: (b) the three sects

In the thirteenth century, all the other philosophers of ancient Greece were completely overshadowed by Aristotle (384–322 BC), whose main ideas on ethics will be presented in Chapter 4 below. But a rapid glance at Dante's scattered remarks about four other thinkers will serve to indicate his attitude to the relationship between philosophical thought and day-to-day life, as well as documenting his familiarity with a range of ideas he rejected, and showing the respect in which he held all those who had made an effort to reach the truth.

Plato (427–347 BC), 'uomo eccellentissimo', was Aristotle's teacher. He had explored topics of the greatest interest to Dante, such as the influence of the planets and stars on human behaviour. Aristotle revered him, but dissented from many of his ideas, refusing to allow love for his master to overcome his greater love for the truth. Dante tried to live up to this model.[5]

Like Plato, Democritus (c. 460–c. 370 BC) was admired by Dante because his evident contempt for worldly values proved that he rejected superficial concepts of happiness. For Dante, 'morality is the beauty of philosophy', by which he meant, among other things, that it is right to judge the quality of a man's beliefs from the quality of his life. Personal virtue, however, is not the same as true understanding; and in Dante's view Democritus was wrong in his belief that matter is composed of atoms or that the universe is the product of their chance collisions.[6]

It had been a commonplace since antiquity to compare and contrast the ethical teachings of Epicurus (341–270 BC) and Zeno of Citium (335–264 BC). Epicurus asserted that the human soul dies with the body, and that the highest good is pleasure (understood as 'the absence of pain'): Dante repudiated both views with some vehemence. He was more sympathetic to the ideas of Zeno, the founder of Stoicism, who taught that the highest good lies in the exercise of the cardinal virtues, whether or not this leads to worldly approval or happiness. Dante admired the austerity and integrity of a Stoic like Cato of Utica, and tried to live up to Cato's example in the long years of his exile. But he clearly rejected the Stoic view that moral virtue demands the suppression or eradication of the passions.[7]

Aristotle's followers, the Peripatetics, are also said to have missed the mark by attempting to locate human fulfilment in the 'active life'. Even Aristotle himself, who held that the supreme happiness lies in contemplation, will be consigned to Limbo together with all these thinkers. And yet Dante recognised that all these erring 'sects' had been animated by a common love for truth and goodness, and that they had been striving towards the same goal. Philosophy (he argued in the *Convivio*) prepares our minds to accept the Christian faith; this is the basis of our hope; this in turn is the cause of Christian charity; and 'through these three virtues one ascends to philosophise in that celestial Athens where the Stoics and Peripatetics and Epicureans, by the light of the eternal truth, run shoulder to shoulder in concord and one will'. There are few more eloquent testimonies to the spirit of medieval syncretism:[8]

> Per le quali tre virtudi si sale a filosofare a quelle Atene celestiali, dove li Stoici e Peripatetici e Epicurii, per la luce de la veritade etterna, in uno volere concordevolemente concorrono. (*Con.* III, xiv, 15)

'The noble seed of the Romans': Dante's first masters in philosophy

Dante came to believe that the Romans had been destined by God to rule over the whole of mankind. The 'populus romanus', whom he celebrates in the second book of his *Monarchia*, had fulfilled the prophecy made by Virgil's Anchises in the *Aeneid*. They had excelled, not, as the Greeks had, in sculpture, oratory or astronomy, but in the 'arts required to govern the peoples and to impose the pattern of peace'. They had exercised those 'arts' for many centuries before Augustus established the Empire; and they continued to do so in the West for another five hundred years until the time when Italy was invaded by the Goths and Lombards at the end of the fifth century AD. As thinkers, they themselves were the first to admit that they were not as subtle or profound as the Greeks, but their practical experience of government and their sense of an imperial destiny gave their ethical, political and legal thought a new dimension; and they bequeathed a rich legacy of works which Dante could and did read in the original Latin, and which deepened and refined his understanding of human vices and worth.[9]

Among the moral philosophers, the two most significant for Dante were Cicero, who flourished just before the establishment of the Empire, and Boethius, who lived just after its collapse in the West. They were of unique importance in his intellectual development, because, as he himself tells us, it was in their writings that he first discovered philosophy, when he was seeking consolation for his grief at the death of Beatrice.[10]

Dante must have recognised a good deal of himself in Marcus Tullius Cicero (106–43 BC), whom he calls Tully ('Tullio'). Cicero had been a man of humble origin who took an active part in the political life of the Republic, rising to hold high office at a time when he had to 'defend Roman liberty' against the conspiracy of Catiline. Ousted from power and influence, he dedicated his enforced leisure to spreading knowledge of Greek philosophy in his native tongue, casting his work in the accessible form of the dialogue. From his dialogues Dante quotes with approval a condemnation of riches, arrogance and decadence, stirring examples of valour and magnanimity drawn from Roman history, a definitive defence of old age, and an affirmation of belief in personal immortality – all these ideas being expressed in a fluent and elegant prose which gave Dante a model to emulate when he set himself a similar task in similar personal and cultural circumstances in the *Convivio*.

Dante refers to five of Cicero's works in all, but the one that left the deepest impression on him was the one he read first, the dialogue *De amicitia*. There he found a celebration of disinterested friendship as a supreme value together with a cluster of related ideas that would permeate the prose of his *Vita nuova*. There also he found a model that would help to shape the *Comedy*, inasmuch as the ideas and ideals are not expressed analytically and in the abstract, but form part of a moving, personal account by an historical individual, Laelius, who speaks of his friendship for Scipio Africanus, the greatest Roman of the previous century.[11]

Boethius (480–524 AD) was born in Rome but ended his days as a consul under Theodoric, the Ostrogothic king whose capital was at Ravenna. Dante was to place him not in Limbo (like Aristotle and Cicero), but as a Christian martyr in the Heaven of the Sun. The title of his most influential work – *Consolatio Philosophiae* – delimits its scope very precisely. It does not draw on the revealed truths of the Christian religion; and it has the practical aim of giving comfort to anyone in distress. Boethius tells of his imprisonment on a trumped-up charge (for which he was subsequently executed) and how he learnt to rise above his misfortunes. His book would 'console' Dante not only for the death of Beatrice but also for his sufferings and deprivations in exile (significantly, Dante invokes the example of Boethius in the *Convivio* to defend himself for speaking in the first person in order to clear his name).[12]

In the long run the spirit and shape of the *Consolatio* were perhaps more important for Dante than its content, because its strictly ethical ideas are derived from Plato, Aristotle and the Stoics. But Boethius' narrative of a spiritual journey towards happiness (achieved through successive acts of understanding about the nature of goodness and the nature of love) was to influence Dante over a thirty-year span from the *Vita nuova* to the *Comedy*. So too was Boethius' vision of mankind as part of a universe created and governed by a supreme being, who is identified with the Supreme Good that all existing things are striving to attain in whatever way is appropriate to their nature.[13]

Roman Law

Shortly after the death of Boethius, the Eastern Emperor Justinian (who ruled from 527 to 565 AD) set out to consolidate his military re-conquests by means of a radical overhaul of the law. Sixteen experts were given the task of sifting through the accumulation of statutes, edicts, decrees and rescripts from the past, together with the all-important interpretations that had been given by the great jurists in the period from 100 to 250 AD. By the end of the year 533 they had stripped out repetitions, contradictions and obsolete material – 'il troppo e 'l vano', in Dante's famous phrase – and arranged the surviving material by subject matter into fifty books to create the *Digest* (a work about half as long again as the Bible). The *Digest* was complemented by the *Institutes*, an introductory textbook for students, and by two further collections of earlier and new laws to form the 'Body of Civil Law'. In the opinion of many scholars the *Corpus juris civilis* was the single most important bequest to the Middle Ages from the classical past, and the most distinctively Roman.[14]

By the beginning of the twelfth century it had become an object of renewed study in Bologna and other universities, and by the year of Dante's birth the long task of interpretation and recovery was complete. His lifetime coincided with the work of the Commentators who sought to apply the 'grammar and terminology' of Roman private law to the vastly different context of their own day. For the university student of law in Dante's time, the *Digest* had the same status as the Bible had for the student of theology; and the educated laymen who administered the communes of Northern Italy (including a number of

Dante's fellow poets, and a good many members of his first audience) were trained lawyers who were steeped in its concepts, axioms, terms and procedures. They were confident that the Roman jurists had been able to deduce universal categories and principles from the bewildering complexity of daily life, and that it was possible to apply these categories and principles in such a way that all men could live in peace and harmony under just laws, justly interpreted and justly enforced.

Dante himself did not study make a formal study of the law (or if he began the course, he did not complete it), and there are several passages in his works where he speaks of jurists with hostility or contempt as people who sell their knowledge for a stipend or a fee. But he too could venerate the law as 'Reason written down'. His ideal vision of a universal Empire under a divinely constituted 'sole ruler' (*monarcha*), who is the supreme *legis lator* and *legis executor* for all mankind, owes a substantial debt to the Prologue to the *Digest*. As one reads the *Inferno* – above all the eleventh canto which explains the principles underlying the classification of sins in Hell – one becomes aware that the spirit and some of the details of his analysis are derived not so much from the 'divine law' enshrined in the Bible as from the 'human law' embodied in the *Corpus juris civilis*. Canto XI might even be described as Dante's *Institutes*, his highly personal 'digest of the *Digest*'.[15]

'La bella scola': Horace, Ovid and Lucan

Dante's greatest debt to classical Rome, however, was to the poets who flourished in the hundred years on either side of what he took to be the turning point in world history, that is, between c. 40 BC and c. 60 AD. Four of them are quoted with reverence in the *Vita nuova* and the same four – Horace, Ovid, Lucan and Virgil – will be 'set apart and honoured' in Limbo as members of Homer's 'bella scola'.

Horace is recalled for his *Satires* and verse *Epistles*, which depict some of the follies and vices of late Republican Rome (in *Inferno* IV he is described as 'Orazio satiro').[16]

In the *Vita nuova* Ovid is cited for his *Remedium amoris*, the 'antidote' to the better-known *Ars amatoria*, which had provided the Middle Ages with a uniquely witty and sophisticated account of sexual love. In Dante's other works, however, he figures above all as the author of the fifteen books of the *Metamorphoses* – the supreme virtuoso in the description of how human beings were changed into non-human forms. Most of Dante's references to pagan myths can be traced to the

Metamorphoses; and he was inclined to treat such myths as deliberate allegories or as veiled perceptions of the truth about human nature.[17]

Lucan is coupled with Ovid in *Inferno* xxv because of his description of some particularly repellent metamorphoses, but the ten books of his unfinished *De bello civili* describe a totally different world (the poet was compelled to commit suicide under the Emperor Nero in AD 65 at the age of twenty-six). Dante drew extensively on Lucan's epic as a source of historical information about the struggle for power between Pompey and the victorious Julius Caesar, a struggle which, in Dante's view, had paved the way for the Empire, the coming of universal peace, and the birth of the Saviour. The politics of this decisive civil war are treated without any idealisation and the battle-scenes are horrific. Only one man emerges with dignity and honour – Cato of Utica; and it was from Lucan that Dante derived his hero-worship for this statesman turned soldier. Cato is presented in the epic as the embodiment of Stoic virtue. He asserts that there is but one God. He believes he was born not just for himself or for his native land, but for the good of the whole world. He loves true freedom so much that he prefers death by his own hand to life under a tyrant. One can no more speak adequately of him than one can of St Paul, says Dante; and no man was ever 'more worthy to signify God'.[18]

Statius and Virgil

Two other Roman poets from the first century AD were important in helping Dante to understand the interests and values of pagan, imperial Rome in the period when St Peter and St Paul came to the capital and were martyred there. They were Juvenal (born c. 60 AD), who is still recognised as the most important successor to Horace as a satirist, and Statius (born c. 45 AD), who was the author of two epics dealing with themes from the remote mythological past. (His unfinished *Achilleis* deals with events at Troy, and his *Thebaid* with the misfortunes of Oedipus and Jocasta and the wars between the twin sons of their incestuous union.)[19]

In the fiction of the *Comedy* Dante chose to represent Statius as a 'secret' and 'tepid' convert to Christianity; and the fictional Statius remains on stage for twelve cantos after his appearance in *Purgatorio* xxi. He has a complex role to play, but the most important of his various functions is to pay homage to Virgil. Virgil, we are told, gave Statius 'the strength to sing of men and gods', and the *Aeneid* had been his 'mother and nurse in writing poetry'. A striking phrase in that epic led to a change in his moral life, by showing him that prodigality is a vice no less than avarice. The opening of Virgil's Fourth Eclogue had sown the seeds of his Christian faith by prophesying the descent of a 'new progeny from heaven' at the birth of a Son who would usher in an age of justice and primal innocence. The intensely moving encounter between Virgil and Statius – the former exiled for ever in Limbo, the latter finally on his way to Heaven – is a celebration of the power that Dante himself still exerts over *his* readers, the power of a long-dead poet from an alien culture to 'instruct, please and move' his readers and to bring about a change in their lives.[20]

The historical Virgil was indeed Dante's 'maestro' and 'autore' in writing the *Comedy*; and it is probable that he drew on the *Aeneid* more often than all the other works considered so far. He found in Virgil two overarching visions: the first, of an individual human life portrayed as a hazardous journey to a promised land; the second, of an entire nation playing its role in a divine plan involving all mankind from the beginning to the end of time. (Aeneas undertook his journey from Troy to Italy in order 'to found the Roman race', and the *populus romanus* was to play a part in world history second in importance only to that of the Jews.)[21]

The *Aeneid* also offered Dante a diversified cast-list of exemplary characters among whom there are no outright villains (except perhaps the treacherous Sinon) and where even the hero has many moments of human weakness and uncertainty in the course of his long quest. Several of Virgil's characters reappear under their own names in the *Comedy*, while some of Dante's most memorable creations are based on his prototypes. There are of course profound differences between the two poets in the representation of human vices and worth. But these are all compatible with the fact that Dante sat down to write a counterpart to Virgil's 'Tragedy' (as he called it) – a 'Comedy', which was to be just as much the expression of his own Christian culture as Virgil's had been of that of pagan Rome.[22]

The 'Writings' and the 'Book'

The next group of Dante's authors could hardly be more different from the poets and philosophers of ancient Greece and Rome. They include a charismatic leader, two kings, several 'outsiders', a farmer, some fishermen, a doctor and an intellectual. They wrote from within a pastoral or rural society over a very long period, in very different forms: historical narrative, invective and exhortation, prose-poems, aphorisms, parables, sermons and open letters. In a shortlist given by Dante himself, they are named as Moses, David, Job, Matthew and Paul, and to these we might add Solomon, Jeremiah, Isaiah, Peter and Luke. For Dante and his culture their words were 'Writings' with a capital letter (in Latin, *Scripturae*). Their collected works formed the Bible, the 'Book' par excellence ('Bible' comes from *Biblia*, which is simply a transliteration of the Greek word for 'books'). They enjoyed this special status because the voice that speaks through all of them was believed to be that of the Holy Spirit. In Dante's own metaphor, the authors were no more than 'scribes' who wrote at God's 'dictation': 'unicus dictator est Deus'. The Bible was read aloud in Latin and expounded in the vernaculars from the lecterns and pulpits of every church in Europe, because it was universally regarded as the Word of God.[23]

Among the messages recorded by these 'scribes' are clear instructions on how to lead a good life. Many of these are similar to the precepts offered by the Greek and Roman philosophers; but others can be understood only within the kind of framework to be sketched out in Chapter 5 below, where we shall examine the distinctive values enshrined in 'the life of Christ, including both his words and his actions' – 'vita Christi, tam in dictis quam in factis comprehensa'. For the moment, therefore, it must be enough to make two very simple points about the ways in which biblical teaching differs from that of the pagans.[24]

First, the precepts given are not simply counsels but commands or commandments. Taken together they constitute a 'law', which has unique authority because it comes from on high. Human beings are required to obey the divine law or suffer the inevitable consequences, because God is not simply the Lawgiver, but the all-seeing Judge and the all-powerful Executive. Second, the *lex divina* differs completely from its human counterpart, as codified by Justinian, in that it always embodies the perspective of eternity. God is 'from everlasting to everlasting'; and human beings do not cease to exist when they die. Our conduct in *this* life (and the addition of the simple demonstrative 'this' diminishes the value of all 'earthly' goals and rewards) becomes a matter of supreme importance, since it will determine the quality of the *other* life, an eternal 'after-life'. We shall be judged once and for all on what we did or left undone in the brief span of threescore years and ten. Paradoxically, the achievement of success or happiness as measured by the standards of this world may lead to eternal misery in the next; whereas earthly suffering may be rewarded by heavenly bliss.

Even in this highly compressed account, it would be wrong to leave the impression that Dante took from the Bible no more than a perfect *exemplar*, a set of values, and a code of conduct. The historical books of the Old Testament provided a gallery of complex moral portraits and striking instances of behaviour that was either pleasing or displeasing to God; and these were no less important to him than their counterparts in the classical epics. More significantly, the characterisation of Dante as protagonist of the *Comedy* is influenced by the three main 'actors' in the New Testament – St Peter, St Paul, and Jesus himself. The impetuosity that leads him into error, and the transparent goodness of intention that soon earns him forgiveness, are both modelled on the 'festina et impremeditata praesumptio' and the 'fidei sinceritas' of St Peter, as he is presented by Dante in a remarkable piece of practical criticism in the *Monarchia*. Dante's ascent into heaven echoes that of St Paul (just as his descent into the Underworld is based on that of Aeneas). And his journey to Hell (which he enters on the evening of Good Friday and leaves on the morning of Easter Sunday) is in its way an 'Imitation of Christ'.[25]

Two 'giants' and a 'Colossus'

This rapid survey of Dante's 'guides' through the territory of moral philosophy is now almost complete. He did acknowledge generic debts to later writers, including some from his own thirteenth century. Vernacular poets such as Guido Guinizzelli (whom Dante once cited as 'il saggio') had celebrated the ennobling power of a certain kind of sexual love. St Francis and St Dominic founded two orders of mendicant friars who were to carry the Christian good tidings with renewed fervour into the booming cities of Western Europe. Great teachers – such as St Albert, St Thomas Aquinas and St Bonaventure – had been active in the University of Paris. But they were not Dante's 'authors' in the full sense: they were not 'authorities'.[26]

Dante would accuse the poets of courtly love of muddying the waters they brought to the well (Guinizzelli and Arnaut Daniel will be encountered among the lecherous in Purgatory). St Francis was simply obeying to the letter the commands that Christ had given to his first disciples; while the Parisian theologians and philosophers were engaged in the task of interpreting, reconciling and putting into order the truths they had inherited from the past (as we shall see in the next two chapters). To borrow a famous phrase from Bernard of Chartres, writing in the twelfth century, they were 'dwarfs' perched on the 'shoulders of giants'. They could admittedly see further than their masters, but they did not enjoy the same status.[27]

Before recalling the names and major works of Dante's remaining authorities, however, we must pause to reflect on the vast and ultimately irreconcilable differences between the works that have been presented so far. The heroic world of the Homeric poems was not that of Plato's Athens, and its values were not the same. Similarly, the late Roman Republic produced works very different in ethical content from those of the Empire in the first century AD. The three philosophical sects of the active life were not really 'running towards the same Athens in the sky'. It was anything but self-evident to a majority of the Jews that Jesus was indeed the 'Messiah', the 'Anointed One' (the 'Christ'), whose coming had been foretold by their prophets, or that their Law had been 'fulfilled' in his life and teaching.

In the early centuries of our era, moreover, there had been an apparently unbridgeable gulf between the monotheism of the Jews and Christians and the polytheism of the rest of the Roman Empire. It did not matter to Jews or Christians whether the local gods of the Gentiles were rainmakers, Olympians, natural forces, abstractions, dead emperors who had been raised to the skies, or the new astrological deities from Babylon: they were all 'false and lying'. By contrast, the educated members of the Roman ruling class who continued to worship the ancestral gods in those early centuries were repelled by many aspects of Christianity – its subversive values, its concept of history, its philosophical naïvety, and the stylistic barbarity of its sacred texts.[28]

Until the beginning of the fourth century AD (down to the year 313), Christians were intermittently persecuted and often executed for refusing to worship the pagan gods (a 'martyr' was a 'witness' to the faith). By the end of that century, however, under Theodosius I (379–95), the situation had been reversed and Christianity became the official religion of the Roman state. And the years between toleration and recognition saw the birth of three men who have been revered ever since as the Doctors (that is, 'Teachers') of the Catholic Church. They were Jerome (c. 340–420), Ambrose (340–87) and Augustine (354–430).[29] These men were still 'giants', and it was they who played the definitive role in the long task of assimilating Christianity to classical culture, which had been begun by St Paul.

Of course, much had already been achieved before their time. It is now thought that the canonical scriptures had been defined, and arranged in the two Testaments, during the second half of the third century AD. The Council of Nicaea in 325 agreed on a single Creed which summarised the essence of orthodox Christian belief. But even in this favourable new climate, there was still much to be done in order to fill out the implications of the words and deeds of Christ, and to make Christian ideas accessible and acceptable to those who had been educated in the classical schools, as the three Doctors had been.

Jerome mastered Hebrew as well as Greek and produced the definitive translation of the Bible for the Latin-speaking Western Empire.[30] Ambrose is now remembered chiefly for his hymns (such as the *Te lucis ante terminum* sung by the souls in Dante's Antepurgatory), which proved to be an effective way of spreading sound doctrine. But he was probably most important historically for his role in establishing the allegorical interpretation of Scripture, which was still the norm in Dante's lifetime (a good many of Dante's references to the Bible are not so much to the literal meaning as to one of the commonly accepted 'sovrasensi').[31] The greatest and most influential of the three was undoubtedly Augustine, a Colossus, of whom one might remark, as Jerome said of Paul and Dante said of Cato, that 'it would be better to keep silent than say too little'.[32]

Dante, it must be said, refers to the works of Augustine very seldom and his quotations are almost certainly at second hand. But with his usual unerring instinct he singles out the three most influential texts. The first of these was *De doctrina christiana*, which set out a programme of Christian education, indicating exactly what was to be preserved from the classical curriculum. It is to this work more than to any other that we owe the survival of the Seven Liberal Arts and, in consequence, the copying and re-copying of the pagan works necessary to teach them. The second was the vast and sprawling *De civitate Dei*, which begins with an exposé of the absurdity of polytheism and the inadequacies of pagan philosophy, and goes on to adumbrate the definitive Christian view of world history, starting with the Fall and looking forward to the Second Coming of Christ on the Day of Judgement. The third book cited by Dante is the *Confessiones*. This begins with Augustine's account of his own childhood as the son of a Christian mother in North Africa, his schooling and career as a teacher of rhetoric and his passionate love for his mistress. It goes on to recount his long quest for a meaning in life, which started (as Dante's did) with the reading of a dialogue by Cicero, passed through a prolonged adherence to the dualist teachings of Manes, led him on to the Greek philosophers and brought him, at long last, to a re-discovery of the Christian faith of his childhood (this Father and Doctor of the church was baptised at the age of thirty-three!).[33]

There is no clear evidence that Dante read the *Confessiones* closely. But he was certainly familiar with its contents and with its character as a work of personal 'confession'. He referred to it explicitly in an early chapter in the *Convivio* where he defended his decision to speak directly about himself in order to clear his good name. And so it is probably to Augustine (rather than to Boethius, who is mentioned in the same context) that we owe Dante's crucial decision to set down his conclusions about 'human vices and human worth' by representing his own experiences, errors and faults, and by tracing the slow development of a purer love for the good, which came as the result of a progressive understanding of its true nature. That was Dante's method in the autobiographical *Vita nuova*; and – making due allowances for the fictional form – this would be his method in the *Comedy*.[34]

CHAPTER TWO

Putting authors to the question

New uses for old monuments

Having seen that Dante was typical of his age in his reverence for the wisdom of the past, and even in his choice of authorities, we must now investigate his *use* of those authorities and ask in what ways this use was typical and distinctive of his time. Many later centuries have drawn on the reservoir of classical and biblical culture, but they have channelled the waters to run in very different courses.

The punning title of this chapter suggests that the very notion of asking a 'question' lies at the heart of scholastic methodology. 'Putting authors to the question' could mean (to take examples of Middle English usage from the *OED*), subjecting them to a judicial examination, torturing them as part of that interrogation, or re-phrasing their words to focus on a difficulty or doubt, thus making them the basis of a problem to be debated and decided within the fixed form of a disputation. All these meanings are relevant in some way (even putting to the torture!), and all were present in the Latin word *quaestio* (from *quaerere/quaestum*, 'to seek, to inquire'). This is why the central part of the chapter will be devoted to the reading of a representative scholastic *quaestio*, and why it will end with Dante's metaphorical celebration of a 'quest' for knowledge carried forward by the posing of one question after another.

Some sort of introduction is necessary, however, to provide a context for the example of a scholastic thinker in action, and, given the limitations of space, this can be provided only by resort to circumscription and simile. We shall focus on three distinct ways in which the ancient heritage was re-employed in scholastic culture; and these will be linked and illuminated through an analogy deriving from the architectural monuments of the past.

There are some obvious parallels between the works of Dante's authors and the surviving buildings of classical Rome; and there are parallels, too, between the ways in which these two kinds of 'monument' were pressed into service in the late Middle Ages, which can help us to understand how thirteenth-century scholasticism created something quite new while always deferring to the past. Some of the ancient Roman buildings had been preserved in their entirety, but were assigned a new function (the Pantheon became a Christian church, S. Maria Rotonda, and Hadrian's mausoleum became a fortress, later known as the Castel Sant'Angelo). Others had become ruinous and were treated like quarries from which the individual stones, or even whole columns, could be removed and reassembled in structures of a totally different kind. Finally, a good deal of the marble from the remains was burnt in limekilns to make the cement which would bind these building blocks together.

The *written* 'monuments' were put to similar uses. Some were studied as complete entities, but with little regard to their original context. The majority were treated as a storehouse of weighty paragraphs, which were incorporated and given pride of place in new works. And these 'reclaimed materials' were held in position thanks to a powerful 'mortar' of procedures derived from the logical works of Aristotle and from Roman law.

The three-part analogy is no more than an analogy and is not to be pressed too hard. One of its chief shortcomings is that the real architectural monuments that come most readily to mind are in the city of Rome, whereas the 'recycling' of materials from ancient texts took place mostly in Bologna, Oxford and Paris. These were the locations of the most important universities of thirteenth-century Europe – complex institutions without precedent in the ancient world, which were the heirs to the cathedral schools of the late eleventh and twelfth centuries.

It was of course these 'schools' – in the widest sense – that give us the adjective 'scholastic', which remains the best single word to characterise the kind of intellectual culture that forms the context of Dante's thought. It reminds us, among other things, that the most important thinking was done by professional teachers, organised in a corporation, who sold instruction in a classroom to young men who had, as it were, apprenticed themselves in order to obtain a marketable skill.

This is not the moment to attempt even the briefest summary of the long evolution of the *scholae* over a period of at least 200 years; and all the generalisations that follow cry out for qualification. Clearly, there were huge variations in place and time and a great diversity in the practice of any two contemporary masters in the same faculty, or even in different works by the same man. But the ensuing paragraphs will have served their purpose if they help to make sense of a single lesson given by a great teacher in the University of Paris, who was active during Dante's lifetime. This will typify scholasticism in action – a re-investment of the capital of the past to make possible the production of something entirely new.

The 'consecrated temples'

Very few words can be spared here for those classical works which were studied in their entirety, but it must be borne in mind that in many cases a master's course would consist of nothing other than readings (*lectiones*, whence our word 'lectures') in which he would guide the student through every page of some complete text. Proficiency in a subject might be virtually equivalent to the detailed knowledge of a limited number of books from the past.

This is not to say that the master contributed nothing of his own. Admittedly, his divisions and paraphrases, or the information he supplied about topics or proper names, did not allow much room for manœuvre. Sometimes, though, his lectures might be tantamount to a commentary to the text. He might contribute a prologue and introduce substantial digressions, which would give him the chance to make connections with other authors or develop his independent thought. In the later period, he would concentrate on controversial passages, in which his interpretation differed from those of his predecessors. If the work under study was a poem or a book of the Bible, a large part of his energy would be dedicated to the exposition of the presumed allegorical meanings. In all these ways, his exegesis might be very different from that which would win approval from modern scholars; and a medieval *commentum* could and often did become a work in its own right. This was the book the student had to know in order to pass his examination.

It should also be said that dramatic advances could and did come about simply through the adoption of hitherto unstudied texts, either by the same author, or by a new author, no less venerable. This is what happened during the first half of the thirteenth century when the whole corpus of Aristotle's writings became available in translation for the first time. The university authorities might proscribe the teaching of these works in the Faculty of Arts (as they did periodically from 1215 onwards), but there was no stemming the tide. By the 1260s a student of philosophy in Paris had to acquire an extensive knowledge of the man who became known antonomastically as 'the Philosopher'. A change in the set texts meant that the subject was no longer the same. It was as though a whole group of classical temples had been excavated, restored, and 'consecrated for contemporary worship'.

Reclamation and sorting of materials

The disciplines that most narrowly concern us in this book are philosophy and theology, as these were practised in Paris in the third quarter of the thirteenth century. But there are certain features of the works produced in this period which cannot be understood without glancing back to the twelfth century and taking note of developments in the study of civil and canon law.

As we saw in Chapter 1, the committee of jurists employed by Justinian in the early sixth century had produced an introduction to the *jus civile* (the *Institutes*), which explained the main concepts, principles and guidelines with exemplary clarity. But this remained the only school-book one might recognise as such. The fifty books of the *Digest* were no more than a selection of statutes, edicts, decrees and rescripts from the past, organised by topic, and accompanied by the interpretations given by earlier great jurists. To open the work at any page is to be thrust *in medias res* – straight into the practice of the law; and this is an area where there must of necessity be a constant interaction between abstract reasoning and deference to precedent, and a constant struggle to apply both of these to contentious situations in unique circumstances. In essence, the lawyer or student of law was always faced with a particular case in which two parties had come before an arbiter or judge to settle a dispute, precisely because the correct answer was not obvious. In the real world, the task of the judge was to identify the issue, to look for guidance in the decisions of his revered predecessors, to apply the general principles of natural justice in the light of a 'long and deep practical experience of the law' (which is a rather long-winded translation of the root-meaning of 'jurisprudence'), and, finally, to deliver his verdict (*sententia*). In the classroom, the master was required to do something very similar. He too had to identify the point of law, pick his way through the authorities who had spoken *pro et contra*, and propose soundly argued solutions to hypothetical cases – with the result that his lesson might be rather like a mock trial.

The main centre for the study of Roman civil law was the University of Bologna, which, in the early twelfth century, also became the centre for the institutionalised study of the law of the church. The first major task in this cognate field had been to produce a work similar in kind to the *Digest*, that is, a vast collection of papal decrees and decisions, grouped by subject, and encouraging the same kind of exposition as in civil law. This work was known as the *Decretale*, and the man who played the decisive role in its compilation was Gratian (who died c. 1150).

Now, although it is extremely difficult to establish relative dates (and therefore the relative direction of influences), the biggest single development in the study of theology in the middle of the twelfth century came when the Bible and the many writings of the Fathers and Doctors of the Church were subjected to a similar process of 'harvesting' and 'threshing'. In other words, pronouncements of a doctrinal kind were isolated and gathered into compilations resembling the *Corpus juris civilis* and the *Decretale*.

The first of these compilations announced by its very title that the adversarial mode natural to the law (the appearance before a judge of a plaintiff and a defendant) was to be applied to the teaching of theology as well. This was the notorious *Sic et non* ('Yes and no') by Peter Abelard, who died in 1143. It presented excerpts from the Fathers of the Church in such a way as to call attention to real or apparent conflicts of opinion between the authorities. Twenty years later Peter Lombard (who died in 1160 or 1164) produced a similar if less controversial compilation, the *Sententiae*, which became the standard textbook for students of theology in the thirteenth century. A hundred years later, every great master in Paris had to produce his own commentary to the *Sententiae*. And with his habitual insight, Dante would honour Justinian, Gratian and Peter Lombard in his *Paradiso* for the role they had played in producing textbooks made up of authoritative excerpts, arranged by topic, which focussed attention on contentious issues, and encouraged teaching in the form of a disputation leading to a solution.

The 'mortar' and the 'medium'

In terms of our governing analogy, the 'monuments' left by the authors revered in the faculties of law and theology had been broken up into manageable building blocks, sorted, and made available for modern use. To understand how these blocks were bound together in new 'structures', we must consider the contribution made by logic.

The study of logic was also inherited from the ancient world (where it was associated with the names of Aristotle and Boethius) and it not only provided the 'mortar' to hold the fragments of the past in place but also became the 'medium' of all independent discourse. Everyone who went on to study philosophy or theology had received a rigorous training in its use. Together with grammar and rhetoric, logic was the 'core subject' of the 'foundation years'; and it was so fundamental to all advanced study that nothing can be described as typically scholastic if it does not conform to its rules.

Logic has long been banished from the school curriculum, and it can be so dry and technical that it is difficult to empathise with Dr Faustus when he exclaims 'Sweet Analytics, 'tis thou hast ravished me.' But in that line Christopher Marlowe succeeded in capturing the enthusiasm that inspired generation after generation of medieval students, including Dante; and we must therefore make some effort to understand attitudes and assumptions that have long since been discredited.[1]

There are perhaps three linked postulates concerning language and truth which underlie the medieval teaching of logic. (a) There is such a thing as a true proposition, understood as one in which there is a 'proper match between reality and the words' (*adaequatio rei et verbi*). (b) A proposition known to be true commands our assent simply because we are rational, truth-seeking animals. (c) It is possible to discover a truth that is not self-evident by due process of reasoning, that is, by drawing valid inferences from what is already known.

These three assumptions have to be spelled out because so many statements which claim to be true turn out to be false (or true only under certain conditions), and because the cause of the error lies not in the ignorance or malice of the speaker, but in the numerous shortcomings of all natural languages. Words are often vague or ambiguous, signifying different things to different hearers or in different contexts. A statement may be correct grammatically, but conceptually defective; or more often, it may be placed after another statement, but does not necessarily 'follow' from it: it is a logical *non sequitur*.

The student of logic had to be made aware of these defects and taught how to overcome them. He had to learn how to define his terms with precision and how to make those terms follow each other coherently, which, in the Middle Ages, meant to express them in one of the valid forms of the syllogism (although this was not the only form of logically structured discourse). Only when he had been taught to articulate his thought 'in an ordered way, easily, and without error' could he begin the higher study of law, theology or philosophy. Logic gave him the instruments to philosophise.[2]

To be damned or not to be damned: that is the question

The vital importance of that early training is grimly but amusingly illustrated in the fictional fate of Guido da Montefeltro, as recounted in *Inferno* XXVII. For most of his life Guido was renowned as a wily fox of a general, whose many victories were due less to his bravery than to his cunning. As his life drew to an end, however, in the 1290s, he repented of his ways and renounced the world to become a Franciscan. In Dante's account of the moments immediately after his death, Guido is sent to Hell for one final sin of deceit, which he committed only after having been himself deceived by a promise of absolution in advance, made to him by Pope Boniface VIII, who, as St Peter's successor, possessed the power of 'binding and loosing in heaven'. The irony is that Guido might have escaped damnation if he had studied the principal work of Pope John XXI, who preceded Boniface by only a few years. The name by which this earlier pope had been known in the University of Paris was Petrus Hispanus, Peter of Spain; and he was famous for what had already become the standard textbook for logic by the time Dante was a student, the *Summulae logicales*.

We shall return to Guido's life and actions in Chapter 10, but enough has been said to make sense of the climax of his story. At the moment of his death, an angel appeared to escort his soul to Heaven, but this angel was immediately challenged by a devil, 'one of the black cherubim', who had come expressly to haul Guido down to Hell. The motif of a contest between angels and devils over the ultimate fate of a soul is an ancient one, and it was a normal feature in pictorial representations of the Last Judgement. In this case, however, there was to be no physical struggle. The devil had 'armed himself with reasons' (like the bachelor of arts in Dante's later simile). He refused to be baulked. Pope Boniface's promise of absolution in advance for Guido's late and mortal sin was based on an egregious error, since it broke the basic law of logic, the law of non-contradiction. 'One cannot absolve a person who does not repent', says the devil with perfect logic, 'since one cannot simultaneously will a deed and repent of it, because of the contradiction that forbids it.'[3]

'ch'assolver non si può chi non si pente,
né pentere e volere insieme puossi
per la contradizion che nol consente.'
(*Inf.* XXVII, 118–20)

And the devil rubs salt in the wound as he carries off his victim, by saying: 'Perhaps you didn't think I was a logician!', 'forse / tu non pensavi ch'io loïco fossi!' (123).

The science of logic and the art of dialectic

It seems likely that Dante was one of those who upheld the Aristotelian contrast between the science of logic and the art of dialectic, a contrast which entails a clear distinction between demonstrative and dialectical arguments. In 'demonstrative' reasoning (which, strictly speaking, is possible only in subjects like geometry or theoretical physics), one 'demonstrates' a truth by proceeding from a firm principle to reach a conclusion that is equally firm. In 'dialectical' reasoning (which is appropriate to ethics and the law), the point of departure is no more than probable – for example, the opinion of an 'authority' – and the conclusion cannot lay claim to any greater degree of certainty.

Not all thirteenth-century masters made this distinction, however; and even if the two disciplines were differentiated in this way, both logic and dialectic gave training in the precise definition of terms and their arrangement in impeccable syllogisms. Both encouraged the building of comprehensive systems (modelled ultimately on the geometry of Euclid, as expounded in the successive theorems of his *Elements*). And these systems were constructed by advancing logically from a self-evident or given truth to a true inference, using each successive inference as the starting-point of a new link in the chain of argument.[4]

Dialectic came into its own when it was applied to the *Corpus juris civilis*, the *Decretale* and the *Sententiae*, and, later, to similar excerpts culled from ancient works dealing with moral philosophy. It enabled the medieval thinker to clamber onto the shoulders of the giants from the past and to see further than they could. The pronouncements of two or more authorities would be re-cast in one of the valid forms of the syllogism. Any apparent inconsistencies or contradictions remaining between them would, if possible, be eliminated by distinctions of meaning, showing that the same word had been used in different senses, or that one assertion had been made 'absolutely', the other only 'relatively', subject to specific qualifications. (This stage is analogous to a judge's summing up, in his own measured words, of the pleas of plaintiff and defendant.) Where the assertions were genuinely at odds with each other, it would be the master's task to analyse the problem for himself, still using the same strictly logical procedures, and to give his own judgement.

The description that has just been given requires only a few modifications to make it fit the standard vehicle of scholastic thought, the *quaestio*. And rather than supply those extra details, it will be better at this point to examine a concrete example of the genre, taken from a work begun shortly after Dante's birth, by a master whom he revered. This will exemplify a great scholastic mind at work on an ordinary day – applying reason to authority, making something new out of the old.

Scholasticism in action in the 1260s

The chosen example is an 'article' (*articulus*) from the *Summa Theologiae* by St Thomas Aquinas ('il buono frate Tommaso d'Aquino', as he is called in the *Convivio*), to whom Dante assigns a major speaking role in the *Paradiso*. (An *articulus*, literally a 'little limb', is simply the name used for a *quaestio* when it forms one of a group dealing with different aspects of one problem.)[5]

The work was composed between 1265–6 and 1272; and the first word in its title, *Summa*, indicates that it offers a systematic treatment of the subject in the form of linked *quaestiones*. It was never referred to by Dante, but it has the great advantage that it was written for beginners in theology and its methodology is strikingly consistent throughout.

The article is to be found near the opening of the second part, where Aquinas turns his attention to ethics. In the first *quaestio* (divided into eight articles), he goes straight to the heart of the matter by inquiring into the nature of perfect happiness, considered as the supreme good possible for mankind. He argues that, whatever such happiness may be, it is the final goal of all human activity. (We do not seek it so that we can travel abroad, listen to music, get married, win honours or power, but the other way round.) In the second *quaestio*, he examines the competing claims of various goals that are widely believed to make men happy, and in which happiness might therefore be said to consist, dedicating one article each to the objectives that most people, then as now, consciously pursue, such as wealth, honour, glory, power and pleasure.

It is a foregone conclusion that he will refuse to identify any of these with perfect happiness – the highest good, the state sought for its own sake and not as means to some other end. But this is precisely what makes this *quaestio* so suitable for our present purpose. We are concerned not so much with the result (the final score, so to speak), but with the rules of the game, its conventions, and the hazards for the uninitiated; and these can be best illustrated in one of the least demanding articles – the third – in which Aquinas investigates the claim that perfect happiness consists in *fama* and *gloria*.[6]

The 'hazards'

It will be convenient to deal first with the characteristic 'hazards'. As in virtually every article in every *quaestio*, some of the key-words in the Latin do not coincide in meaning with their descendants in the modern European languages, or do not have exact equivalents in words derived from other roots. For example, in the present case *fama* means 'reputation' rather than 'fame'; and *gloria* still retains the connotations of a 'radiance' emanating from a source of light. *Notitia* can mean an item of information, like Italian 'notizia'; but the etymology suggests 'something known' (*notum*), a small part of knowledge (*cognitio*).

The word to be translated as 'happiness' presents a special difficulty. Given that Thomas is a Christian theologian, it is hardly surprising that his term is *beatitudo*, or that he will locate perfect happiness (*beatitudo perfecta*) in the afterlife, where he will make it dependent on God and on our relationship to him. But it is important to remember that *beatitudo* did not have the exclusively religious connotations surrounding 'beatitude' or 'blessedness' in English, and that it may be qualified by adjectives such as *inchoata* or *imperfecta* to denote states which are happy, but only 'just beginning' or 'lacking in something'. What Aquinas is seeking to define at this point in the *Summa* is a state of which we can have at least a foretaste on earth and is therefore relevant to ethics.

The 'rules of the game': (a) the judge's summing up

Each and every article opens in exactly the same way with the enunciation of a thesis. This is always introduced with the phrase 'it seems that' (*videtur quod*), a formula which is significant because the thesis is never one that Aquinas himself will endorse. Several independent arguments (usually three) are then adduced in support, and these are always cast in syllogistic form. (In the translation, attention will be called to this by inserting the letters (a) and (b) before the major and minor premisses and (c) before the conclusion.)

The truth of the premisses is usually guaranteed by reference to an 'authority'; and one important reason for choosing this particular article is the range of the references it contains: the Old Testament (Psalms), the New Testament (St Mark's Gospel and St Paul's Letters), a Latin father (St Ambrose), a Greek Christian Neoplatonist (posing as Dionysius the Areopagite converted by St Paul), and the last classical philosopher, Boethius. In some cases, however, the premiss may be an axiom, or a truth which has been 'demonstrated' by valid syllogisms in a previous *quaestio*.

The third article of the second *quaestio* of the first half of the second part of the *Summa Theologiae* (1a–2ae, 2, 3) begins like this:

> It seems that human happiness consists in glory.
>
> 1. (a) Happiness seems to consist in whatever is bestowed on the saints for the tribulations they suffered in this world. (b) This is what glory is, for St Paul says that 'temporal sufferings are not worthy to be compared to the future glory that will be revealed in us'. (c) Therefore happiness consists in glory.
>
> 2. Further: (a) Goodness is self-propagating, as is clear from Dionysius in *The Names of God*. (b) If human goodness is to become common knowledge, it is propagated most effectively through glory, because, as St Ambrose says, glory is simply 'distinct knowledge accompanied by praise' (*clara notitia cum laude*). (c) Therefore human happiness consists in glory.
>
> 3. Further: (a) Happiness is the most lasting of all goods (*stabilissimum bonorum*). (b) Reputation or glory can lay claim to lastingness because it is through them that people achieve some kind of eternity. As Boethius puts it in the *Consolation of Philosophy*, 'you seem to secure immortality for yourselves when you take thought for your reputation in future times'. (c) Therefore happiness consists in reputation or glory.

The thesis is then negated in a very brief section invariably beginning with the phrase *Sed contra*, meaning 'but against this' or 'on the contrary'. This is normally based on an authority with whom Aquinas will declare himself in agreement. In our case, but not always, the counter-claim itself is formulated syllogistically:

> But against this: (a) Happiness is the true good of man. (b) But reputation or glory may be false. Boethius says, 'Many people have often gained a great name through the false opinions of the common herd. What could

be more shameful than that? Indeed, those who are falsely extolled ought to blush at their own praises.' (c) Therefore human happiness does not consist in reputation or glory.

'The rules of the game': (b) the judgement

It will be clear that, in these two opening sections, everything has followed tradition, even though Aquinas has himself devised the arguments which he is apparently summing up in the impersonal language of a judge. Ancient 'building blocks' are being 'mortared' together with ancient dialectic. In the next section, however, invariably introduced by the rubric *Respondeo*, 'I reply', Aquinas is free to develop his own thought. The tone may not change. There will still be the same care for precision, still the same deference to the past. But his discussion may become quite independent of his sources. In the present article, indeed, the main argument is quite taxing and best presented in paraphrase.

It turns on the recurrent distinction between God and man, in this case with respect to the nature of knowledge. Divine knowledge can be and is the cause of all things (God created all things in the universe in accordance with a foreknown plan, that is, in accordance with his wisdom). But human knowledge is caused by the things known (*res cognitae*) and cannot itself bring those things into existence. Ambrose was right in his definition. Glory is nothing other than a *notitia*, a piece of information, existing in other people's minds. As such it is part of human knowledge and cannot be the cause of the good in the person whose goodness has become known.

The rest of the response is more straightforward:

> Man's good depends, as on its cause, on the glory which comes from God, as we read in Psalm 90: 'I shall deliver him and glorify him, I shall fill him with length of days and show him my salvation'. It should be borne in mind, moreover, that human knowledge (*notitia*) is often erroneous, especially with regard to particular events which may or may not turn out the way they do (*in singularibus contingentibus*), as is the case with human actions. And therefore human glory is often delusory. But since God cannot be in error, his glory is always true. This is borne out by the second letter to the Corinthians, where St Paul says 'the person to be admired is the one valued by God'.

The final part of any article always consists of a critical re-examination of the arguments adduced for the opening thesis. The intention is to expose any defects in the reasoning while showing reverence for the source. This usually demands a closer scrutiny of one or more of the three terms which have been linked in the syllogism, distinguishing, for example, between broader and narrower significations, or showing that the term in the text cited in support of the minor premiss is used in a different sense in the major premiss. Once again the headings – *ad primum*, *ad secundum* etc. – are identical in every article in the *Summa Theologiae*:

> As to the first argument. St Paul was not talking about the glory that comes from men, but the glory that comes from God in the presence of his angels, having in mind the words of Mark's Gospel: 'The Son of Man shall proclaim him in the glory of the Father, in the presence of his angels.'
>
> As to the second. If anyone's goodness is widely known thanks to reputation or glory, then, assuming that the knowledge is true, it must have derived from that person's goodness and so presuppose his happiness, be it complete or embryonic. If, on the other hand, the knowledge is false, it does not square with reality, and so there is no goodness in the person with the famous reputation. In either case, therefore, it is obvious that reputation does not make a person happy.
>
> As to the third. Reputation has no stability. On the contrary, it is easily lost through a false rumour. And if it does endure, this is fortuitous (*per accidens*). Whereas true happiness possesses stability as an inalienable condition (*per se*) and for ever.

So the great work proceeds, calmly and inexorably. There are 114 *quaestiones* in the first half of the second part (*Prima secundae*). In most of these Aquinas continues to tackle broadly philosophical problems – the nature of voluntary actions; what makes an action good; the passions of the soul; habituation; the virtues of the intellect and of the will in general. Later, however, he moves into distinctively Christian territory for a full discussion of sin, the laws of men and God, and the role of grace. All this is a preparation for the *Secunda secundae* which contains no fewer than 189 *quaestiones* dealing with the virtues and vices in detail. In the second part as a whole there are 1541 articles, each self-contained, each like a well-shaped piece of building stone, resting on those which have already been mortared in place, and ready to receive the weight of those still to be laid in accordance with the architect's plan.

First soundings in the 'Convivio'

There are of course many variants in the structure of the *quaestio* in other thinkers of the period and in other works by Aquinas (especially in works written for his peers rather than his students); and Dante nowhere writes anything so inflexible in its structure as the article we have just read. Nevertheless, his mind was formed in the scholastic mould and whenever he philosophises or theologises, he will formulate each topic as a problem concerning which various opinions are possible, turn to his authorities, express their thoughts in logical form, sharpen his definitions, and move forward independently, under clearly defined heads, towards a solution. The techniques have become second nature. They are like the invariable ground-bass in a chaconne, over which the composer writes his apparently effortless variations.

Let us take some soundings in the *Convivio* to illustrate the consequences of his training. This is a popularising work deliberately written in the vernacular in order to make it accessible to people like Dante's younger self (he was about forty when he wrote it), men and women whose involvement in the active life had left them no leisure or opportunity to learn Latin and study. But it opens with what advertising men would call a 'hard sell':

> Sì come dice lo Filosofo nel principio de la Prima Filosofia, tutti li uomini naturalmente desiderano di sapere. La ragione di che puote essere ed è che ciascuna cosa, da providenza di prima natura impinta, è inclinabile a la sua propria perfezione; onde, acciò che la scienza è ultima perfezione de la nostra anima, ne la quale sta la nostra ultima felicitade, tutti naturalmente al suo desiderio semo subietti. (*Con.* I, i, 1).

> As the Philosopher says in the beginning of his First Philosophy, 'all human beings by their nature desire perfect understanding'. The reason might be, and indeed is, that: (a) Every thing is inclined by desire towards its own fulfilment, guided in this by the impulse of its essential nature. (b) Sure knowledge is the highest fulfilment of our human soul, and that in which our highest happiness consists. (c) Therefore we are all subject to the desire for certain knowledge.

Dante wants to establish his credentials and simultaneously to indicate the kind of effort that will be required of his readers. So he begins with an appeal to 'authority' (the highest in the land), citing his precise source, Aristotle's *Metaphysics*, before translating the opening words of that work very closely from the Latin ('omnes homines natura scire desiderant'). If we were concerned with the content rather than the form, we should have to examine no fewer than four key terms in this, the very first paragraph: 'natura', 'perfezione', 'felicitade' and 'scienza'. (Perhaps it ought to be noted that the Latin verb *scire* is the root of *scientia*, which must usually be translated as 'perfect understanding of the causes', or 'full and certain knowledge'.) For the moment, however, it is enough to observe that the confident universal affirmation 'tutti li uomini naturalmente desiderano di sapere' is the major premiss of the whole *Convivio*.

Auctoritas, however, must be backed by *ratio*. Dante sketches out the reasoning underlying his quotation, and in so doing instinctively feels his way towards a syllogism – as the translation tries to make clear by inserting the letters (a), (b) and (c). At the same time, he discreetly veils the syllogistic form; and the underlying logical structure does not prevent his language from being elevated and rhythmical, very much in the style of the poetic prose in his earlier *Vita nuova*.

The 'Convivio' as a commentary

The *Convivio* offers countless other examples, all slightly different, of this free combination of *ratio* and *auctoritas* finding expression in vigorous and often impassioned prose. But it is also relevant to this chapter because it takes the form of a commentary on three of Dante's own poems, and displays many features deriving from thirteenth-century commentaries on texts from the past.

The first book, which forms the prologue or *accessus* to the whole work, shows how easy it was for an author to introduce new material while apparently discussing an old text. Book I, for instance, is of the utmost interest for what it tells of Dante's exile, for his defence of the vernacular tongue, and for the sustaining image of a celestial 'banquet' of learning (in the course of which Dante will do no more than provide some 'bread' of his own baking to help his readers 'digest' a few of the 'morsels' that have fallen from the 'table' of the angels).[7]

Book II takes the form of a commentary to Dante's canzone 'Voi che 'ntendendo il terzo ciel movete', and it illustrates to perfection the free and deliberate use of digression in a typical medieval commentary. For example, the poem's opening appeal to the angels who move the heaven of Venus provides the opportunity for an exposition of the Ptolemaic spheres and of the nine angelic choirs. (A later cognate digression in Book III, describing the revolution of the sun, and the equal distribution of sunlight over the surface of the earth, has been described as one of the finest passages of scientific prose in Italian before Galileo.)[8]

Book II is even more remarkable, however, for its explanation of the principle that a text may contain 'higher meanings' ('sovrasensi') in addition to the literal one; and, as we noted earlier, allegorisation of the

Bible, and of poets like Ovid and Virgil, provided a convenient way of adapting old texts to a contemporary situation. Dante's poem dramatises his attraction to a 'noble lady' some time after the death of Beatrice, but the author insists that this was in no way an infidelity. In its allegorical sense, the poem tells how he fell in love with Wisdom, who is personified as a 'donna gentile' (as she had been in the sapiential books of the Bible, or – as Philosophy – in Boethius). It describes the beginning of his love-affair with the truth. Allegorically, too, the heavens of medieval cosmology represent the seven liberal arts (including dialectic and rhetoric), together with metaphysics, ethics and theology.[9]

Of all the many passages of allegorical explanation in the *Convivio*, the most relevant for our purposes comes in Book III, since it is so revealing about Dante's passion for the scholastic way of philosophising. This book forms a commentary to another canzone, 'Amor che ne la mente mi ragiona', composed in praise of his new 'mistress' ('the most noble and beautiful daughter of the Emperor of the universe', as he calls her in the prose). In the fourth stanza of the poem, Dante had said that 'things appear in her countenance / which show some of the pleasures of Paradise, / I mean, in her eyes and her sweet smile'. The exposition of the literal meaning of these lines had already called forth one of his best-known paragraphs, in which he says that the eyes are the 'windows of the soul' and a smile like the 'coruscation of the soul's delight'. But when Dante comes to the allegorical sense, he declares that these two heavenly pleasures refer respectively to the 'proofs' given by Philosophy and her 'persuasions'.[10]

> E qui si conviene sapere che li occhi de la Sapienza sono le sue demonstrazioni, con le quali si vede la veritade certissimamente; e lo suo riso sono le sue persuasioni, ne le quali si dimostra la luce interiore de la Sapienza sotto alcuno velamento; e in queste due cose si sente quel piacere altissimo di beatitudine lo quale è massimo bene in Paradiso. (*Con.* III, XV, 2)

> Here you must know that the eyes of Wisdom are her proofs, through which the truth can be seen with perfect certainty, whereas her smile is her persuasions, through which the inner light of Wisdom is revealed under a veil of some kind. In these two things one feels the highest pleasure, perfect happiness, which is our highest good in heaven.

A 'proof' means the demonstration, by strict logic, beyond all doubt, that a proposition which was not self-evident is universally and necessarily true. It is as 'cogent' as a theorem of Euclid (which ends with the letters QED, *quod erat demonstrandum*). It compels our assent. A 'persuasion' has two senses. It may refer to what can be achieved by the art of dialectic, as we saw earlier, which is all that may be expected in the field of ethics, politics and the law. But Wisdom may also be persuasive if she uses metaphor and simile (as Plato and Boethius did) or shows a truth under the veil of allegory (as in the Bible). The lover of Wisdom (a 'philosopher' is the 'philos' of 'Sophia') will be led on by the 'smiling mouth' of the lady in whom he has placed his love and trust, in the hope that one day he will see those truths as though they were not just 'demonstrated', but self-evident, directly intuited by the intellect without ratiocination. Together, eyes and smile, proofs and persuasions, are 'food' for the mind, a foretaste of the celestial 'banquet', the *sacrum convivium*, from which the book takes its title.

First soundings in the 'Monarchia'

The work which reveals Dante's delight in syllogising most clearly is Book III of the *Monarchia*, where he is not engaged in mere shadow-boxing but is demolishing the real arguments of real opponents, who assert that the Holy Roman Emperor derives his authority from the Pope (and not directly from God, as Dante thought he could prove). It is difficult to focus on his purely technical mastery because the content of most of the arguments is so distractingly unfamiliar, but three short extracts will give some idea of his complete confidence and command.

His grasp of the principles is made clear in the following passage:

> Since an error may occur either in the matter or in the form of an argument, it is possible to go wrong in two ways (*dupliciter peccare contingit*), that is, by making a false assumption or by not syllogising. Aristotle accused Parmenides and Melissus of both, saying that they 'assume falsehoods and are non-syllogisers (*non sillogizantes*)'. If the fault (*peccatum*) lies in the form, the conclusion has to be demolished . . . by showing that the syllogistic form has not been preserved. If the error lies in the matter, it is because an assumption has been made which is either totally false (*falsum simpliciter*) or false in a certain respect (*falsum secundum quid*). In the first case, the argument is to be refuted by denying the assumption, in the second by drawing a distinction. (*Mon.* III, iv, 4–5)

In the next two excerpts Dante is following the standard, quasi-algebraic procedure of substituting letters for the actual terms in order to focus attention on the nature of the 'sin' against logic. In the first, the fault lies in the form (*peccatur in forma*):

> The thought process is rather like this: A precedes B in C; D is to E as A is to B; therefore D precedes E in F. But F ['birth'] and C ['authority'] are different things. Hence, the predicate of the conclusion [F] and the final term in the major premiss [C] are not the same and there is a defect in the form. (*Mon.* III, v, 3)

In the second, even briefer excerpt, the flaw is one of content, since it is falsely assumed that an effect can exist before its cause:

> Let the church be A, the Empire B, the authority or power of the Empire C. If C was in B before A existed, it is impossible for A to be the cause of C's being in B, since it is impossible for an effect to come into being before its cause.

The opening of the 'Monarchia'

There is, however, more than a hint of absurdity in quoting the *Monarchia* to illustrate Dante's delight in the nuts and bolts of thirteenth-century logic, given that the whole book is such a shining example of the way in which he applies the broad principles of scholasticism to forge a work of great originality and intellectual passion, which is as remarkable for its rhetorical fire as its logical rigour.

These qualities are already abundantly evident in the prologue. Dante begins by asserting his love of the truth. Then he proclaims his gratitude for the work of the ancients (*labor antiquorum*) and announces his own desire to work on behalf of posterity (*posteris prolaborare*). To this end he intends to offer something for the common good, something which has not been attempted by his predecessors. He gives examples of the definitive treatment of three different kinds of subject by the *antiqui*, and in so doing he manages to compare himself implicitly to Euclid, Aristotle and Cicero, who used logic to prove theorems (*theorema demonstrare*), dialectic to indicate the nature of happiness (*felicitatem ostendere*) and rhetoric to defend old age (*senectutem defendere*). Then, with a prayer to God to help him in a task otherwise beyond his powers, Dante proceeds, as he should, by offering a general definition of his principal term, *monarchia*:[11]

> Temporal monarchy, then, which men call 'empire', is a single sovereign authority (*unicus principatus*) set over all others in time, that is to say, over all authorities which operate in those things and over those things which are measured by time.[12] (*Mon.* I, ii, 2)

After this preliminary definition, he pinpoints three controversial topics; and in the very act of identifying the issues and problems, he formulates three *quaestiones*, to each of which he will assign one whole book:

> There are three main points of inquiry which have given rise to perplexity on this subject (*tria dubitata quaeruntur*). First (*primo dubitatur et quaeritur*), is monarchy necessary to the well-being of the world? Second, did the Roman people take on the office of the monarch by right? And third, does the monarch's authority derive directly from God or from someone else, his minister or vicar? (*ibid.* 3)

In this first book, which is devoted to the first of the three *quaestiones*, Dante intends to offer strict logical proof (*demonstrare analytice*). So he continues with a passage that immediately makes one think of Euclid and his theorems:

> Since every truth which is not itself a first principle (*principium*) becomes evident through reference to the truth of some such principle, it is necessary in any inquiry to know the first principle to which one may refer in the course of deductive argument (*analytice*) in order to ascertain the truth of all the propositions that will be adopted as premisses later on. And since this present treatise is a kind of inquiry (*inquisitio*), before doing anything else, we must seek out the principle that will enable later assumptions to stand on firm ground (*in cuius virtute inferiora consistant*). (*ibid.* 4)

'*Dubitatur et quaeritur*'

Painful as it is to interrupt Dante just when he is getting into his stride, enough has been quoted to illustrate the style of the *Monarchia* and to establish that in Dante's view, rational inquiry must always be a slow and laborious process. The mountain of truth, we might say, is out there, waiting. It can be scaled, but the climber must carry an ice-axe and pitons and be prepared to rope himself to a more experienced guide. At times he will come to a sheer cliff where he will have to hack out a new foothold in the rock-face for every step, while trusting his weight to the one that was cut a moment before. Although the ascent is not always so steep, ratiocination always involves a movement from one point to another, a mental trek from stage to stage; and it always demands effort and a motive force, a *vis motiva*. It is this aspect of the human quest for true and certain knowledge that Dante will represent with so many profound insights in the *Comedy* (which is, in its literal sense, the story of a journey to God, but symbolically a journey towards perfect understanding and love).

One very important clue as to the nature of these insights lies in the pairing of the verbs *dubitare* and *quaerere* in the passage from the *Monarchia* just quoted ('tria dubitata quaeruntur'; 'primo dubitatur et quaeritur'). But to understand why this coupling is so significant, we must follow medieval practice and turn aside for a brief digression.

'Et est digressio'

Reasoning is only one of four phases in the process that leads from total ignorance at the moment of birth to complete understanding in the afterlife. This process begins in the activity of the senses. Dante insists that all human beings must learn from 'il sensato', meaning that all our concepts are abstracted from impressions received by the external organs, chief among them the images that enter the eye. Unlike reasoning, seeing does not occur step by step (*gradatim*). It happens instantaneously (*statim*) and is effortless because the necessary energy is supplied from without by natural light.[13]

Before reasoning can begin, moreover, there must be a limited immediate intuition of certain self-evident truths – 'first truths' as Dante calls them. Otherwise there would be no *principium*, no firm ground on which to stand before taking the first deductive step. Intuition resembles seeing (that was what the Latin verb *intueri/intuitum* meant); and, once again, direct intellection of a *principium* does not require time, effort or energy.[14]

For the Christian believer, the end of the process will come only in the total, simultaneous understanding of 'all substances, qualities and their relationships' as part of the vision of God. This is the kind of understanding which is granted to Dante the pilgrim in a flash of lightning at the end of the poem, and which is enjoyed by the angels and blessed for all eternity. 'Perfect seeing' – 'perfetto vedere' as Dante calls it – is also effortless, because it is energised by the light of glory given through God's grace.[15]

Throughout all four phases – seeing, intellection, ratiocination and perfect seeing – the soul is 'moved' by its inborn love of the truth, its concreated *amor veritatis*. But this explanation refers, in scholastic terminology, to the 'final' and 'formal' causes of that motion (truth is the goal of our intellect, our *finis*, and our human *forma* inclines us towards it). What we still need to discover is the 'efficient' cause of reasoning, the actual motive force that drives us to seek the truth by 'inquiring', to continue on the long 'quest' by asking 'questions' and to structure our thoughts in *quaestiones* (all the key-words derive from *quaerere/quaestum*).

In ordinary life, the *vis motiva* required for bodily locomotion comes from a passion of the soul. In the simplest case (frequently used as a paradigm for all the others) the perception of some object which is either good or bad for the subject arouses either desire or fear. These passions are anticipations of pleasure or pain and they stimulate the muscles to move the percipient either towards the good object or away from the bad. Such is the mechanism presumed to be common to all animals, including man.[16]

Wonder and perplexity as the motive forces of inquiry

We may now (in another medieval phrase) 'return' from the digression. The rational human soul is capable of two distinctive passions which impel the mind to a purely mental movement. The first of these is most closely linked with the act of seeing. When we apprehend a 'cosa nuova' – something 'new', but with the implication that the thing is strange and cannot be accounted for – an emotion is aroused which is variously called 'wonder', 'marvel' and 'awe', or, in Dante's Italian, 'maraviglia', 'stupore' and 'ammirazione'. This is valuable because it drives us to seek explanations for the 'new' phenomenon. Aristotle said, in a much-quoted dictum, that men 'began to philosophise out of marvel' (*propter admirari incoeperunt philosophari*).[17]

The second of these forces is activated by the process of reasoning itself. (It was not classified as a passion distinct from 'wonder', but Dante represents it as though it were). We experience it every time a new act of comprehension calls into question the ordered pattern of truths that constitutes our present understanding of the world around us, of ourselves, or of the revealed purposes of God. The substance of the new deduction or the new explanation seems to be in conflict with what we already know, or what we thought we knew. Dante's name for this feeling is 'dubbio' or 'dubitazione', which is often best rendered in English by such words as 'perplexity', 'dazedness', or 'puzzlement', because 'doubt' has come to suggest 'disbelief', and 'uncertainty' is not an emotion. Perplexity, in short, is the motive force that prompts us to formulate a new question as soon as we have understood the answer which terminated the previous quest. It acts by kindling desire for a further act of understanding in the hope that this will grant rest to the unquiet mind.

The new growth at the foot of the the tree of truth

Every reader of the *Comedy* knows that Dante devotes a vast amount of his energy and skill to representations of the act of vision, to the wonder it arouses, and the questions to which it leads. Seeing, marvelling and inquiring provide the impetus that carries the narrative forward.[18]

It is less often remarked, though, that the secondary emotion of perplexity ('dubbio') is also represented again and again, since it is felt by the protagonist almost every time he receives an answer to a question he has formulated in reponse to something he has just seen or heard. In other words, *dubitare* and *quaerere* are coupled not only in the *Monarchia* but on many occasions in the *Comedy*, because Dante has grasped that they arise from the fundamental mechanism of our minds.

Seen in this perspective, the rigid structure of the scholastic *quaestio* – always focussing on a problem, always presenting conflicting arguments, always aiming at a solution – is far from being a straitjacket that inhibits our freedom to think. It is simply a formalisation of the psychological processes natural to human beings, considered as 'rational animals'. Similarly, the organisation of *quaestiones* into a *Summa* reflects the continuing process of discovery that we owe to the 'struggle between the multiple perplexities that arise', as Dante puts it in the *Convivio* ('lite di dubitazioni che . . . multiplicatamente surgono'). And a work like the *Summa Theologiae* – in so far as we can hold it in our minds as a totality – is the nearest approximation we can have in our earthly existence to the kind of perfect understanding promised in Heaven, when we shall know the 'order' that 'all things have among themselves, which makes the universe similar to God'.[19]

The *Comedy* offers a surprisingly rich and nuanced account of this 'lite di dubitazioni', which is conveyed through a succession of metaphors, deriving from a wide variety of concrete situations. We learn that the emotion may have its origin in calm contemplation of the sky (since the Milky Way 'makes really wise men perplexed', 'fa dubbiar ben saggi'), or simply in some unexpected words or conduct of an acquaintance. The 'doubt' may be so strong that we feel 'ensnared' by it, 'pregnant' with it, or as if we were 'bursting within it'. It must be 'stripped off' or 'loosened and removed' (this is the original meaning of the verb 'solvere' commonly used in this context). If the uncertainty lies in the field of human conduct, it is good 'to seek counsel' from a trustworthy person, 'one who sees, feels and loves uprightly'. In theology, we should look for the answer in Holy Scripture, proceeding cautiously and with reverence. In all cases, we shall be looking for an explanation that is full and unambiguous, for this is the only way to reach the certainty we crave. Like marvel, the emotion of doubt is urgent and demands action. But, like marvel, it is not necessarily painful, provided it is accompanied by hope. Even the expectation of the true explanation of the hidden causes can give pleasure. Nevertheless, this explanation, when it is understood, will often 'thrust us' on to further perplexities (Dante uses verbs as strong as 'sospingere').[20]

The passages alluded to in the last paragraph come from many different places in the poem; but perplexity is given particular prominence in the opening cantos of the *Paradiso*, where the intellectual part of the journey begins in earnest. The fullest account of the emotion comes towards the end of Canto IV. Here the protagonist has posed two difficult questions, each arising from what he has seen and heard in the Heaven of the Moon; and we may pick up the narrative with the second of these questions.

Beatrice, who is acting as Dante's guide, had earlier insisted that none of the blessed can utter a falsehood, since all of them see the truth in its primal source – in God. But Piccarda Donati seems to have contradicted Beatrice ('ella par qui meco *contradire*') when she asserted that she had remained constant to her religious vow, whereas Beatrice made it clear that her vow had in fact been broken. Beatrice resolves Dante's confusion by drawing the classic distinction between the use of a word without restriction (*absolute* or *simpliciter*) and its use with some kind of qualification (*secundum quid*). Piccarda's assertion of her desire to continue serving God as a nun was made *absolute*, since her desire to serve remained unaltered when she was unwillingly forced into a marriage by her brothers. But Beatrice's point is that Piccarda had nevertheless agreed to the marriage, out of fear of the consequences if she refused. *Secundum quid*, she had willed the breaking of her vow. Hence, Beatrice continues, 'both of us are speaking the truth, because Piccarda means the absolute will, while I mean the other': 'Piccarda . . . de la voglia assoluta intende, e io / de l'altra; sì che ver diciamo insieme'.[21]

Dante recalls that he was radiantly grateful for the satisfaction of 'both his desires', his intellectual thirst having been 'set at peace by a sacred stream flowing from the fountainhead of all truth'. He then thanks his 'sweet guide' with an answering flood of word-plays and metaphors in a passage that demands to be quoted.

'O amanza del primo amante, o diva',
diss'io appresso, 'il cui parlar m'inonda
e scalda sì, che più e più m'avviva,
non è l'affezion mia tanto profonda,
che basti a render voi grazia per grazia;
ma quei che vede e puote a ciò risponda.'
(*Par.* IV, 118–23)

I replied: 'O best beloved of the First Lover, sacred lady, whose words flood over me, and warm me, quickening me to ever greater life, my power of feeling is not profound enough to match your grace with my gratitude, but may He reply, who both sees and has the power.'

Notwithstanding his gratitude, the protagonist has another question to put; and, in justifying his importunity, he is led to reflect on the nature of the intellect and the truth it desires. The following lines are teeming with essential ideas, densely expressed through metaphors (of feeding, pushing, climbing, and illumination), and through brief similes (of a wild beast in its lair, or a sucker springing up from the foot of a tree).[22]

The ultimate source of truth is God; and none but he, or the divinely inspired word, will ever satisfy the intellect's desire completely. But the intellect can and does move successively to a series of truths, finding a moment of peace, satisfaction and repose as it is united with each in turn. A new source of puzzlement will arise, however, like a shoot from a plant, out of the very effort of integrating the new component into the existing system of ideas. This puzzlement generates a new desire, which leads to the formulation of a new question. All this is nature's way of driving us ever upwards, from one hill to a higher one, until we reach the top of the mountain.

'Io veggio ben che già mai non si sazia
nostro intelletto, se 'l ver non lo illustra
di fuor dal qual nessun vero si spazia.
Posasi in esso, come fera in lustra,
tosto che giunto l'ha; e giugner puollo:
se non, ciascun disio sarebbe *frustra*.
Nasce per quello, a guisa di rampollo,
a piè del vero il dubbio; ed è natura
ch'al sommo pinge noi di collo in collo.' (*ibid.* 124–32)

'I see clearly that our intellect will never be satisfied unless it is illuminated by the Truth beyond which no wider truth can range. As soon as it

> has reached its mark, the intellect finds repose there, like a wild beast in its den – and it *can* reach the truth, because if it could not, every desire would be in vain. Through this, another doubt springs up like a sucker at the foot of the truth. And this is nature, driving us up to the summit from one peak to another.'

This – one might say, continuing in the same strain – is how Dante interprets and fills out the Aristotelian dictum that 'all men naturally desire to understand'. This is why the *Summa Theologiae* is composed of individual *quaestiones*. This is why the *Comedy* is the story of a 'quest' leading the protagonist and reader ever higher, stage by stage, to the final understanding that can be achieved only as a gift from God.

CHAPTER THREE

Division and numeration

We turn now to the twin principles which underlie the construction of systems in thirteenth-century thought, and which also play a decisive role in the 'architecture' of the *Comedy*. Division and numeration (as these principles will be called) are the metaphorical equivalents of the ogival arch and the system of proportions based on the ratio of $1:\sqrt{2}$ – both utterly non-classical elements – which made possible the erection of the great Gothic cathedrals. It was thanks to these principles that the scholastics were able to take the materials bequeathed by antiquity and build them into rigorous, comprehensive systems of a totally new kind which are reflected in the rigorous and comprehensive structure of Dante's poem.[1]

'Le fronde onde s'infronda tutto l'orto'

It will be convenient to begin by exploring the implications of two very different images used by Dante himself. Both involve the relationship of a tree to its leaves. In the first, the protagonist is explaining that he loves every part of God's creation for what it shows him of the Creator. What he actually says – with the hypnotic word-play and bold metaphor one finds so often in the *Paradiso* – is that he loves 'all the fronds that enfrond the whole garden of the eternal Gardener in proportion to the amount of goodness he extends to each of them':

> 'Le fronde onde s'infronda tutto l'orto
> de l'ortolano etterno am'io cotanto,
> quanto da lui a lor di bene è porto.' (*Par.* XXVI, 64–6)

The second image occurs in the following canto. Beatrice compares time to a tree turned upside down. Its 'roots' lie hidden in the outermost of the celestial spheres, the invisible *primum mobile* (which carries all the lower spheres daily round the earth), while its 'leafy fronds' are the stars (which make the diurnal motion visible), and the planets (whose proper motions are like the movements of so many hands indicating the months, years and great-years on the face of a universal clock).[2]

To understand the import of these images, one might think of a large tree that has been stripped of its canopy of leaves by an early and severe frost. In a single night the whole structure of the trunk and boughs has been unexpectedly laid bare. And it is unnerving to realise that each of the thousands of leaves now carpeting the ground used to have its own unique place on those spreading branches above, and, further, that it would have been possible to record its precise location in a relatively simple way. It would be enough to number the main boughs that spring from the trunk, the branches from each bough, the twigs from each branch, the stems from each twig, and then designate each of these with a letter of the alphabet (giving a base of 26 instead of 10). It might be necessary to invent further sub-categories of 'branchlets' or 'twiglets', but, in principle, one could write the address of any leaf on the tree using at most six or seven letters – something as simple as BDKDMC (meaning on the second bough, the fourth branch, the eleventh twig etc.).

Dante's two extended metaphors of 'fronds' on the tree are both images of the cosmos, as described and celebrated in the first canto of the *Paradiso*. God created a cosmos in which 'all things have order between themselves'. The order is a hierarchical one, in which everything is 'inclined to its proper place', some 'nearer to their source in God', some 'further away' ('più al principio lor e men vicine'). The name of this order is 'form'; and it is through form 'that the universe is made to resemble God':[3]

Le cose tutte quante
hanno ordine tra loro, e questo è forma
che l'universo a Dio fa simigliante. (*Par.* I, 106–8)

'The tree of the knowledge of good and evil'

The spreading branches of the tree – especially when visualised upside down, as in Dante's second image – should send the mind towards Aquinas's *Summa Theologiae* and the *articulus* presented in the previous chapter. That 'little limb', too, has its precise and simple address, conventionally written *S.T.*, 1a–2ae, 2, 3. If one wanted to pinpoint an individual 'leaf' – for example, the pregnant quotation from Dionysius ('bonum est diffusivum sui') – it would be enough to assign further letters and numbers (such that A stood for *videtur quod*, and 2 for the second thesis, etc.). If the reference were drawn as an inverted tree, it might look like the diagram below.

opus	S.T.
pars principalis	2a
divisio	1a
quaestio	2
articulus	3
pars	A
thesis	2

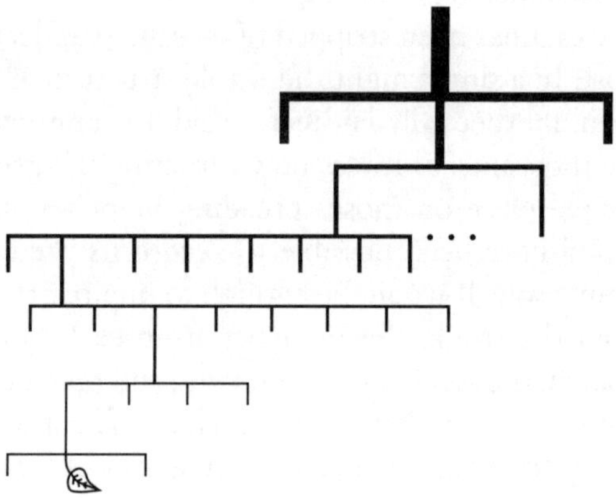

The general appearance of this hierarchical scheme will be familiar because of its recurrence in genealogies, chains of command and flow charts, or in representations of the evolution of species, telephone networks, or the world-wide web. But the diagram is not in any way anachronistic. Medieval manuscripts of works dealing with the vices and virtues were embellished by diagrams of a similar kind. These were usually plain and functional, but they may be beautifully drawn and coloured, as in the two examples reproduced as Figures 1 and 2 (pp. 54–5), which are taken from an English Psalter, executed for Robert of Lisle in the years when Dante was writing the *Purgatorio*. These works and the illustrations are called *The Tree of the Vices* and *The Tree of the Virtues* respectively (*Arbor vitiorum*, *Arbor virtutum*). They are medieval visualisations of the 'tree of the knowledge of good and evil' in the Garden of Eden.[4]

'Vostr'arte a Dio quasi è nepote'

With these images and associations in mind, we must now direct our attention to the attractions and the dangers inherent in the constant recourse to 'division' in all areas of scholastic thought. And before we come to moral philosophy, we must distinguish between various kinds of 'ramification' by thinking about the role played by division in physics and metaphysics. (Dante classified these two sciences as lying above the liberal arts, but below ethics, in the hierarchy of knowledge).[5]

The branchings of a tree are a physical reality and are essential to its operations. They are nature's way of exposing thousands of leaves to the light and the atmosphere, allowing the tree to 'breathe' and conveying photosynthesised energy back to all other parts of the organism. The branchings in any man-made system, such as a telephone network, are also physical realities, and also essential. It is thanks to them that by dialling a dozen digits a call can be routed to any subscriber in Italy from anywhere in the world. The artefact in this case resembles the natural thing and illustrates Aristotle's famous dictum that 'craft imitates nature' (*ars imitatur naturam*).

The branches in the diagram drawn out to represent the internal divisions and subdivisions of the *Summa* are rather different. They are hardly more than a conventional way of giving visual form to conceptual relationships. Nevertheless, the scheme drawn out above (or its shorthand equivalent, written *S.T.*,1a–2ae, 2, 3, A, 2) may claim higher status, so to speak, than a mere page and volume reference (which might vary from one edition to another), because it does represent the author's conscious plan and it does enable one to find the part while simultaneously grasping its relationship to the whole.

So far, so good. However, pursuit of the 'arboreal' analogy becomes both intoxicating and fraught with danger when it is extended, consciously or unconsciously, from the microcosm to the macrocosm, and from the physical to the purely conceptual plane. Dante's metaphors suggest that he saw parallels between the visible organisation of a tree – understood as a single, self-maintaining and self-reproducing system, comprising roots, trunk, branches, leaves and seeds – and the invisible organisation of what medieval thinkers called 'Universal Nature'. He supposed, that is, that there was a similar ramifying structure locating, uniting and vivifying all the interacting bodies and forces in the universe. As a Christian, he believed that God was the 'creator of all things seen and unseen' and that Universal Nature is governed by his Providence, so that all natural operations unfold in time according to his eternal purpose. In this perspective, all individual things in nature are conceived as copies of divine archetypes. Their relationship of mutual dependency within a hierarchical structure is based on the conceptual order of ideal forms existing in the mind of God. Their harmonious activity is the realisation of his plan. Nature, in short, as Virgil recalls in *Inferno* XI, citing Aristotle as his authority, 'takes its course from the divine intellect and its craft' ('natura lo suo corso prende / dal divino 'ntelletto e da sua arte'). It imitates God, and since craft imitates

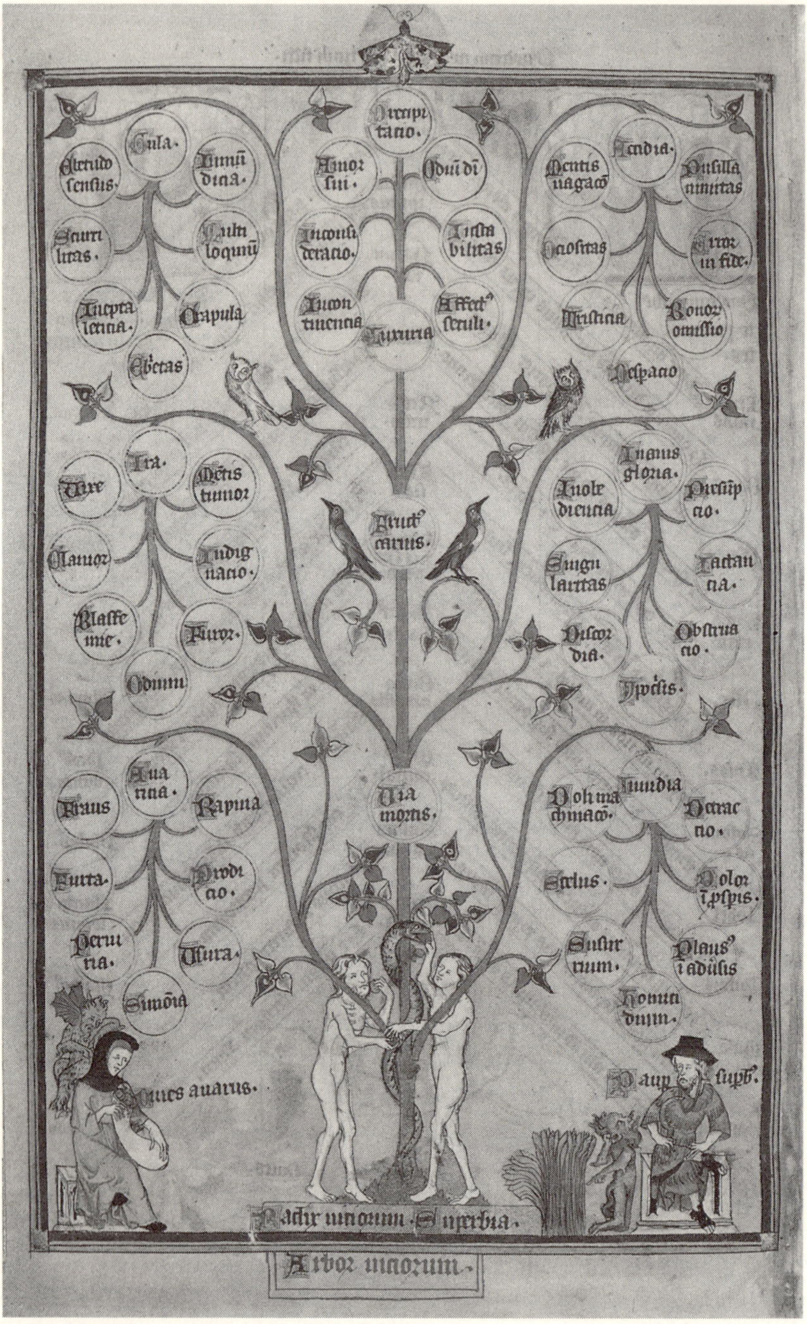

Figure 1 The Tree of the Vices

Figure 2 The Tree of the Virtues

nature, 'your human craft', says Virgil, 'is like a grandchild to God' ('sì che vostr'arte a Dio quasi è nepote').[6]

On this view, the pattern of division and subdivision, through which all things can be derived from a single source and united in a single ordered system, is the realisation of a plan in God's mind. The mental order preceded the physical and material one. If we are to understand the universe, we must elaborate a conceptual blueprint that will match the divine original. To put it more technically, the human mind will have achieved *scientia perfecta* when the concepts which have been abstracted from the images supplied by the senses, and the order in which the concepts have been arranged by the process of reasoning, coincide with the forms and order in the First Mind itself. Unless we divide and subdivide our concepts properly, we will never achieve the *adaequatio rei et verbi* that constitutes perfect knowledge. It is not contingent, but necessary, that the concepts should ramify.

Even in the field of physics (or 'natural philosophy', as it was more often called), this seductive paradigm helped to perpetuate many false deductions. But any attempt to elaborate a single ramifying hierarchy of ideas was doomed to failure in the domain of what came to be called metaphysics (Aristotle's own term was 'First Philosophy'), the discipline which deals with higher concepts such as goodness, being, truth, unity, causality, movement, or time. In the field of ethics, the risks were greater still, if only because the subject matter – consisting as it does of disputed facts, hidden motives and conflicting value-judgements – is so unstable and imprecise. Aristotle had warned (in a passage which Dante quoted several times), that one must not expect the same degree of certainty in the treatment of human affairs as one does in geometry. But his warning was regularly disregarded – not least by Dante himself in the moral maps he drew of Hell, Purgatory and Heaven. And in studying the role of division in the three canticas, one must remember that, in reality, as opposed to fiction or a pedagogical diagram, it is not possible to draw 'trees' of the virtues or vices, in which each concept, expressed by each abstract noun, has its unique proper place at the end of a particular twig on one particular bough.[7]

Exactitude, regularity and symbolism

Before we look at Dante's own conceptual schemes, we must examine the attractions and dangers of the concomitant principle of 'numeration', a term which, in what follows, denotes the restriction of each conceptual division within a given field to a few privileged, symbolically significant, numbers, notably 3, 4, 7,10 and 12.

When Julius Caesar opened his *Gallic War* with the crisp and much-imitated phrase 'Gaul as a whole is divided into three parts', his use of the numeral implied a claim to precision and exhaustiveness. Area-names other than those proposed by the author, the reader is made to feel, will prove to be synonyms for one of the three, or to lie outside Gaul, or to be contained within them. There can be no objections to this use of division. Its attractions are scarcely more than those of pithiness, factuality and memorability, and the dangers correspondingly small. But if there should be a preconceived bias in favour of certain numbers, whatever they may be, it is probable that a desire for regularity will triumph over love of the truth. And this probability will become a virtual certainty if the preferences are determined by a conviction that the numbers 'mean' something, in the sense that they point to things, beings or relationships beyond themselves.

Sometimes the presumed symbolic meaning amounts to little more than an association of ideas. Sometimes, more insidiously, the symbolism is derived from an arithmetical property of the number in question. For example, 6 is technically called a 'perfect' number, meaning that it is the sum of all its factors. From this fact it was easy to draw the inference (as medieval commentators did) that the Bible describes the instantaneous act of creation as the Work of Six Days in order to convey the perfection of the result.[8]

More beguiling still are the symbolic possibilities inherent in numerical ratios. Musical theory in the Middle Ages and the Renaissance was founded on the discovery, attributed to Pythagoras, that the relative pitches of two notes sounding at the consonant intervals of the octave, fifth or fourth can be expressed as 1:2, 2:3 and 3:4 respectively. From this it was irresistibly tempting to deduce that the consonances of human music were not arbitrary, but an expression of the perfect relationship of all forms in the mind of God. Even today, the most sceptical of minds can experience a certain awe on learning that the diagonals of a regular pentagon cut each other in a 'Golden Section', or that the ratio between the last two numbers in the Fibonacci sequence (1, 2, 3, 5, 8, 13, 21, 34, etc.) grows increasingly closer to the Golden Section, the longer the sequence extends (34:21 is closer to it than 21:13). Ratios like these seem to point to the existence of a mathematician God, who 'does not play dice', in Einstein's phrase, but 'disposed all things in measure, number and weight', just as the Bible said.[9]

'These three'

We have done no more than peer into the entrance of the numerological labyrinth, but our concern is not so much with the details of the presumed symbolism as with the numerically limited sets themselves. So the next task is to review some of the most widely diffused of these sets, limiting our attention to those which have a direct or indirect bearing on ethics. They will be presented, not in any logical sequence, but simply in accordance with the number of alternatives they propose. If the resultant juxtapositions are sometimes rather strange, this will serve to remind us once again of the heterogeneous nature of the materials that Dante and his teachers inherited from the past.

Ancient philosophers had analysed the activities of which human beings are capable and divided them into three: those we share with plants; those we share with animals; and those unique to our species. They assumed that these activities were controlled by three powers or faculties in our soul which they called vegetative, sensitive and rational. The vegetative power presides over the operations which are found in all forms of life, and these are neither more nor less than three: nourishment, growth and self-reproduction. The distinctively human or rational powers are also three, which Aristotelians called the speculative intellect, the practical intellect, and the will.[10]

In so far as human actions are directed towards external objects, they were grouped under the three heads of pursuit, flight and fruition. These were seen as the counterparts of the three 'simple' movements that were thought to characterise the elements, namely: rectilinear motion towards a central point; rectilinear motion away from it; and circular motion around it.[11]

Christians had a special predilection for sets of three because they worshipped a Three-Person God – Father, Son and Holy Spirit – whose attributes were Power, Wisdom and Love. The triune God was creator of all things and the cosmos bore his stamp. Even Hell (as we read in the inscription over the gate in *Inferno* III), was made by the 'divine power, supreme wisdom and primal love'. The twelfth-century writer Joachim of Fiore, whom Dante honoured with the teachers in the Heaven of the Sun, held that history was divided into three ages: the age of the Father and the Old Covenant; the age of the Son and the New; and the age of the Spirit, which was about to begin. Dante himself subscribed to the view that the normal span of human life was divided into Three Ages, from birth to twenty-five years, from twenty-five to forty-five, and from forty-five to seventy.[12]

The down-to-earth Roman jurists offered a three-part description of virtue: 'to live honourably, not to hurt other people, and to give everyone their due' ('honeste vivere, alterum non laedere, suum cuique tradere'). St Augustine and his twelfth-century followers at the Abbey of St Victor in Paris taught that we come to God in three successive steps: first, we discover and love things outside us (*extra nos*); then we look inwards (*intra nos*) to discover and love the image of our Maker; and this discovery leads us to look above us (*supra nos*) to know and love God directly. St Paul distinguished three Christian virtues par excellence – faith, hope and love – concluding: 'these three, and of them the greatest is love'.[13]

Sets of four

As regards the qualities required to live virtuously here on earth, the Stoics taught that they could be reduced to just four – courage, self-restraint, sound judgement of affairs, and fairness (*fortitudo, temperantia, prudentia, justitia*). These were the 'cardinal' – meaning 'pivotal' – virtues, around which the good life revolved. The *Corpus juris civilis* laid it down that the wrongs (*delicta*) for which a private individual could seek redress were also four: theft, robbery, loss or damage, and insult or injury (*furtum, rapina, damnum, injuria*).

Four is the number enshrined in the most influential attempt to classify the 'temperamental' or 'constitutional' causes which incline different people to different vices or virtues. Seemingly, it could not have been otherwise. Aristotle had shown that all the tangible properties found in natural bodies could be derived from four fundamental qualities: hot, cold, moist and dry. Since these comprise two pairs of contraries, there were only four ways in which they could combine (nothing can be simultaneously hot and cold, moist and dry). This is why there must be four elements from which all natural bodies are compounded. Fire, air, earth and water each exhibit one of the four possible combinations. This is also why there are four main fluids in the human body, which combine the four contrary qualities in the same way. Bile (*choler*), like fire, is hot and dry; blood (*sanguis*), like air, is hot and moist; phlegm (*phlegma*), like water, is moist and cold; whilst black-bile (*melancholia*), like earth, is cold and dry.[14]

The fortunate few who are born with these four fluids (*humores*) in the optimal proportion were thought to be 'well-tempered', with the implication that it was relatively easy for them to follow the dictates of reason and thus to practise the cardinal virtues. But the great majority, in whom one or other of the four 'humours' was predominant, would be 'choleric', or 'sanguine', or 'phlegmatic', or 'melancholic'; and they would find it more difficult to acquire certain virtues. For example, the dry heat of a 'choleric' individual disposes that person to anger and makes it hard for him or her to exercise self-restraint, but less difficult to show something resembling courage; while the converse is true of a 'phlegmatic' person, whose dominant humour is damp and cold. In this way, medical knowledge, natural philosophy, abstract reasoning, observation, and a weakness for metaphor (evident in the easy transference from 'hot' to 'hot-tempered') were bonded together by a love of numeration to produce a theory of human behaviour that challenged, or at least limited, the notion of human freedom and long outlasted the Middle Ages.[15]

Sets of seven and twelve

Seven had a special fascination both as a number in its own right and as the product of three plus four. Anyone who possessed the three theological virtues and the four cardinal virtues was perfect in every way. A medieval 'bachelor' who had mastered the three arts of language that make up the Trivium (*grammatica*, *dialectica*, *rhetorica*) and the four arts of number that make up the Quadrivium (*arithmetica*, *geometria*, *musica*, *astronomia*) had laid the foundation that would enable him to proceed to the advanced study of law, medicine and theology. The educationalists of the ancient world said that he possessed the skills that were worthy of a person who was 'free-born' (*liber*); and they contrasted these seven 'liberal' arts with the multiplicity of manual skills or crafts known as the 'mechanical' arts.

Seven was a number hallowed by God. The reason why there are seven days in the week is that, 'in the beginning', there were six days of creation followed by a day of rest. St John's vision of the last days of the world in the Book of Revelation pulsates with sets of seven (churches, candlesticks, stars, angels, trumpets) or animals with seven heads or seven eyes. There are seven gifts of the Holy Spirit (*sapientia*, *intellectus*, *consilium*, *fortitudo*, *scientia*, *pietas*, *timor Domini*). The church recognised seven sacraments. And all valid forms of prayer are variations on the seven petitions of the Lord's Prayer.[16]

Over a very long period of time, agreement had been reached that the most common flaws in the human soul could all be classified as species or sub-species of just seven principal defects of character, popularly known as the Seven Deadly Sins, but better described as the Seven Capital Vices.[17]

Seven was also the number associated with another all-pervasive explanation of the permanent differences between human beings which – like the theory of 'humours' – called into question the extent, or even the reality, of our freedom. It was widely assumed that our various temperaments are determined by the particular conjunction of heavenly bodies that were raining down their 'skyey influences' at the moment of our birth (or, in a rival theory, at the moment of our conception). Special importance was attributed to the influences of the seven planets (i. e. the seven 'wandering stars' that change position with respect to each other and with respect to the remaining 'fixed' stars). Their Latin names were (in order of their presumed distance from the earth): *Luna*, *Mercurius*, *Venus/Veneris*, *Sol*, *Martius*, *Jupiter/Jovis*, and *Saturnus*. And the nature of their presumed influence on human behaviour is reflected in the adjectives that still survive in modern English: 'lunatic', 'mercurial', 'venereal', 'martial', 'jovial', and 'saturnine'.[18]

Astrology provides the link to the most important of the sets of twelve. Christians had followed the Romans in dividing the year into twelve months, and were generally united in the belief that the twelve constellations close to the ecliptic (which form a backdrop to the annual path of the sun around the earth) exercise a strong influence on human character and behaviour, especially during the thirty days in which the sun is passing through the thirty degrees of arc to which these constellations give their name. During Dante's lifetime, in short, almost everyone attributed particular significance to the twelve Signs of the Zodiac.[19]

Curiously enough, of all the sets under review, this is the one that requires least introduction today. The four humours have been all but forgotten. Few people could state the relative positions of the planets at any given moment, or at the time of their birth. But an astonishingly large number know which 'sign' they were 'born under' and are willing at least to toy with the idea that its 'influence' may help or hinder the success of their actions. Just as Dante attributed his intelligence to Gemini, so modern Virgos feel themselves to be different from Leos, and Sagittarians know they are a group apart. To paraphrase Horace: 'You can throw superstition out with a pitchfork, but it will keep on running back.'[20]

Ten commandments and ten correlations

Our ten fingers were the original abacus. Ten is the basis of traditional arithmetic, and ten squared produces a 'century', which has become the standard unit for measuring long periods of time. It is therefore a little surprising that Europe had to wait until Napoleon before an attempt was made to impose a uniform decimal system for measuring distances, weights, areas and volumes, and that so few of the medieval sets should have been numerated in tens. What they lacked in frequency, however, they made up for in importance. Indeed, the 'exception that proves the rule' was the best known and most influential of all – the Ten Commandments.

Another very different set of ten was influential, paradoxically, because it encouraged dualism. It was known in the Middle Ages as the *Correlationes* or *Co-elementationes*, and it was the brainchild of the Pythagoreans, who taught that 'contraries are the principles of things'. The Pythagoreans – so we learn from Aristotle – were the first to take up mathematics. They came to the conclusion that 'the elements of number are the elements of all things'; and some of them said that there are 'ten principles, which they arrange in two columns of cognates':

limited	unlimited	*finitum*	*infinitum*
odd	even	*par*	*impar*
one	plurality	*unum*	*plura*
right	left	*dextrum*	*sinistrum*
male	female	*masculinum*	*femininum*
resting	moving	*quiescens*	*motum*
straight	curved	*rectum*	*curvum*
light	darkness	*lux*	*tenebrae*
good	bad	*bonum*	*malum*
square	oblong	*quadrangulare*	*longius altera parte*

Some of these pairs are 'mathematical' and have no obvious symbolical connotations (e.g. odd and even, one and many, square and oblong). But they occur in the same list as concrete terms which lend themselves to potentially emotive metaphors (light and dark, right and left, straight and curved/twisted). And all the 'limited' alternatives in the first column are presented as 'good' (*ex parte boni*, as Dante will say in referring to the *Correlationes*), while all the 'unlimited' in the second column – including 'female' – are 'bad', *ex parte mali*.

As Aristotle also noted, a contemporary of the Pythagoreans called Alcmaeon of Croton said 'something similar', but less precise. Alcmaeon observed 'that most human affairs go in pairs, meaning not definite contraries such as the Pythagoreans speak of, but any chance contraries, e.g. white and black, sweet and bitter, good and bad, great and small'. From this observation, it is only a short step to the dualisms of popular religion, because one could easily expand Alcmaeon's list of polar opposites to include God and the Devil, Heaven and Hell, Salvation and Damnation, or, more tendentiously, Soul and Body, or Spirit and Matter, because all these antithetical dualities have a strong appeal for the non-philosophical mind and all of them could be expressed, as Dante was to do, through imagery of 'light and darkness' or 'straight and twisted'.[21]

Division and numeration in the 'Comedy'

We are now ready to turn to the *Comedy* and consider the role played by division and numeration in the groundplan of Dante's poem. The literal subject of the whole work – as we learn in the letter to Can Grande, Lord of Verona – is 'the state of souls after death' ('totius operis *litteraliter* sumpti sic est subiectum, status animarum post mortem'). The allegorical subject is 'human beings in so far as they have deserved good or ill in the exercise of their freedom to choose, and receive just reward and punishment' ('totius operis *allegorice* sumpti subiectum est homo prout merendo et demerendo per arbitrii libertatem est justitiae premiandi et puniendi obnoxius').[22]

Whether or not Dante himself penned these words, they offer an admirable description of the poem, and there is no conflict between the two alleged levels of meaning, such as one often finds in medieval allegorisations of the classics or the Bible. The very place or zone in which Dante the protagonist encounters a given group of 'souls after their death' is itself the expression of a rigorous judgement on the relative value of their actions in life. The souls may be immersed eternally in a river of blood, confined for many years on a rocky terrace, or summoned to make a brief appearance in the body of a planet. But each of these different locations is situated on a distinct 'rung' of a single 'ladder' that climbs from the centre of the earth to the surface of the sea, continues beyond our atmosphere up the sides of an immense mountain, and rises through concentric spheres of aether to the outermost rim of the cosmos, beyond which lies the Empyrean, the abode of

God and the blessed. Any one location, and hence any one group of souls, must be either higher or lower than any other. Each distinct level in the universe, understood literally, corresponds to a distinct level in the allegorical universe. Physically 'higher' means morally 'better'. Or, to put the same truth in specifically religious terms, each group of souls is located at a different distance from God; and its 'human worth' is measured by its closeness to, or remoteness from, the 'first and ineffable Worth' ('lo primo ed ineffabile Valore'), which is one of the many divine names.[23]

Dante does not confine himself, however, to a single unified scale of values in which goodness 'shines out more in one part and less in another', depending on whether 'it is more less close to its divine source'. He divided and numerated his moral 'staircase' so that it consisted of three distinct and equal 'flights'; and he *sub*divided and numerated each flight so that it contained exactly ten 'steps'.[24]

The main division into three parts was virtually dictated by the *sensus litteralis* of the narrative, which embodies the teaching of the church that, after death, human souls must be in one of the three realms called Hell, Heaven and Purgatory. But tripartition did not of itself rule out a unified system. It would have been possible to graduate all three scales so that they reflected the *correlationes* between good and bad, virtue and vice, merit and demerit, or reward and punishment in the same way, even though Purgatory exists in time, while Heaven and Hell are eternal; even though the scale of values in Heaven is positive, running, so to speak, from +1 to +10, while the scale in Hell is negative, running from −1 to −10; and even though Hell punishes wrongful acts, while Purgatory rectifies wrongful tendencies. For example, if the greatest virtue (+10) is deemed to be charity, defined as love of God and love of one's neighbours through God, then the greatest vice (−10) might have been hatred of God and hatred of one's neighbours in contempt of God. If the next greatest virtue were loyalty, the next greatest vice would be treachery, and so on.[25]

As every reader of the *Comedy* will be aware, however, the *internal* divisions into sets of ten are anything but homogeneous from the conceptual point of view. Indeed, they illustrate to perfection what was bound to happen every time a powerful and original mind tried to synthesise and syncretise the heterogeneous materials of the past, despite the fact that the self-same principles of division and numeration were being applied in the same spirit of reverence and humility. Every thinker of any stature produced his own synthesis, his own ramifying hierarchy, delimited by number. Dante made the attempt three times in the *Comedy*, and the results are similar in kind and appearance, but profoundly different in emphasis. The three 'trees' of Inferno, Purgatorio and Paradiso have the same number of branches, but their 'fronds' are quite unlike each other.

Division and numeration in Paradise

Let us start with an analysis of the *Paradiso*. It was here that the *sensus litteralis* imposed the tightest constraints on the elaboration of a system of values. Dante had no choice but to take his fictional self on a journey through the nine celestial spheres ('heavens' with a small letter) beyond space and time into the Empyrean ('Heaven' with a capital letter). Unless Dante had been willing to defy his fellow intellectuals and the church, he was forced to accept or devise a corresponding moral scale, in which there would be ten major stages. This scale, moreover, had to recognise the distinction between 'Heaven' and 'the heavens'; and it had to respect the important difference between the seven planetary spheres and the two outermost spheres (the heaven of the fixed stars, and the *primum mobile*, whose operations and effects were considered to be more universal). In effect, then, he was more or less compelled by the *sensus litteralis* to introduce a further internal subdivision, which might be expressed as 7 + 2 + 1.[26]

Dante responded to this challenge with great resourcefulness. In the seven lower heavens, the protagonist converses with seven distinct groups of the blessed (*beati*), who descend from the Empyrean especially to greet him. In the eighth he sees all the blessed together. In the ninth he sees all the angels. But he perceives them only as 'effulgences', because his mortal eyes cannot penetrate the radiance they emit. Only at the very end of his journey, in the tenth heaven, is he allowed to see all the blessed and all the angels simultaneously in their true likenesses.[27]

Both the human souls and the angels are rewarded in proportion to their deserts. Their happiness is 'perfect', but it is not 'equal'. All angels are superior to all human beings, which is why they appear to the protagonist in the highest of the physical heavens, the *primum mobile*. They are perceived by him in the form of concentric, revolving circles of light; and the circles are represented as unequal not only in size, but in their brilliance and speed of revolution. These differences are emphasised in order to drive home the inequality of the nine choirs of angels, who are named in the order in which they had been ranked by the chief authority on the subject, Dionysius, in his *Caelestis hierarchia* ('hierarchy' being a compound of *hieros*, 'holy', and *archia*, 'order').[28]

In Dante's final vision of the blessed, in the Empyrean, they are portrayed as seated on thrones which rise in ranks one above the other, 'di grado in grado'. But the inequality of their worth and reward had been emphasised from the very beginning of the cantica; and it is kept in view throughout thanks to the principles governing the order in which the groups of *beati* appear in the seven lower heavens. Dante constructed his own 'terrestrial' hierarchy by combining and rearranging several distinct sets derived from the stockpile of the past, namely, the two 'lives', active and contemplative; the three theological virtues; the four cardinal virtues; and the seven planets as the presumed sources of our differing natural talents.[29]

From the philosophical point of view, the most striking feature of his hierarchy is the recognition it grants to the planets and stars. Although Dante is at pains to make it clear that the souls he meets in the planetary heavens do not reside there, he is no less concerned to stress that, in their earthly existence, they had been subject to the predominant influence of the planet in which they appear, and that this influence has persisted into eternity. The lovers appear in Venus, the warriors in Mars.[30]

The rewards that God bestows on the blessed are proportionately scaled to the *use* they made of their natural talents 'in the exercise of their freedom to choose', not to the natural talents themselves, which they received from the planets and stars at the time of their conception or birth. But Dante never forgets that human beings are unevenly endowed and that different people respond in different ways to the same recurrent situations. What is easy for one person may be difficult for another; and the influence of the planets may constitute either a help or a hindrance. This distinction leads to a further subdivision of the seven planets in a grouping of 4 + 3. The three lower planets (Moon, Mercury, Venus) all tend to impede the activities of the souls they influence; whereas the four upper planets (Sun, Mars, Jupiter, Saturn) all tend to assist them.[31]

We turn next to Dante's arrangement of the individual virtues in his *Paradiso*. At first sight, it is rather tame and conventional. At the top of the scale come the theological virtues. These are unambiguously associated with the eighth heaven, because this is the setting of the protagonist's 'examination' in faith, hope and charity, and because the souls of the *beati*, who come to witness the ceremony, must have possessed those virtues as a condition of their being in Heaven. Similarly, the four cardinal virtues of the Stoic tradition are linked with the four highest planets: prudence with the Sun, fortitude with Mars, justice with Jupiter, and temperance with Saturn.

This may seem straightforward enough. The rulers of the earth, who appear in Jupiter, were just. The crusaders, who appear in Mars, were courageous. The teachers who appear in the Sun are honoured for effective communication of the truth, rather than its discovery. It can thus be argued that they are honoured for the use they made of their practical, rather than their speculative intellects; and to that extent they could be called 'prudent'. Nevertheless, there are unresolved problems here of the kind that bedevil any attempt to synthesise inherited sets that are conceptually distinct. The schoolroom is hardly the place where prudence is much in demand. The monks who welcome the protagonist in the highest planet are certainly admired for their frugal style of life, but Saturn was not normally associated with self-control. It is also very eccentric indeed to rank temperance above justice. But the only way in which Dante might have preserved the correct *moral* order would have been to deny the accepted *physical* order of the heavens (Saturn is further from the earth and nearer to God than Jupiter).

In the case of the souls we meet in Saturn, moreover, it is probable that Dante was trying to introduce a further dualism, of a non-antithetical kind. He describes the monks as 'contemplanti uomini'; and his intention may have been to reassert that the 'contemplative life' ranks higher than all the various forms of the 'active life', represented by the teachers, crusaders and rulers who appear in the three planets immediately below.[32]

Division and numeration in Hell

The topographical and moral layout of Dante's Hell is explained with scholastic rigour and clarity in Canto XI of the *Inferno*, and we are therefore left in no doubt as to the criteria involved.

Dante imagined nine 'circles' cut into the walls of the conical pit of the Underworld; and he will occasionally refer to them by number, as in the famous opening line of Canto V, 'Così discesi dal cerchio primaio / giù nel secondo'. There is, however, a further 'zone', lying within the gate of Hell, though on the hither side of the river Acheron, which is often referred to by critics as the Vestibule. In this area – which brings the count up to ten – Dante was clearly inspired by the description in

Virgil's *Aeneid* of the souls who are denied a passage by Charon because their bodies have not been buried with the appropriate funeral rites. But he completely changes the ground of their exclusion from Hell, since we are told that the souls who are tormented here are those who willed neither good nor evil (they comprise the neutral angels, and humans who did nothing positive in their lives).[33]

Two of the circles are reserved for non-ethical shortcomings of a specifically Christian kind. The souls of the unbaptised – whether they were children or virtuous heathen – are confined, without torment, in Limbo, which lies at the rim of Upper Hell. The souls of heretics are roasted in the sixth circle, lying just inside the wall which constitutes the frontier of Lower Hell. No fewer than three of the ten zones, therefore, are peopled by souls who are eternally imprisoned for reasons that lie outside the scope of this book.[34]

The remaining seven circles are subjected to a major conceptual tripartition, being divided into sins of weakness ('incontinenza'), violence and fraud. The first group (which is divided into four sins, two of which are further subdivided) is based on the authority of Aristotle's *Ethics*, cited by name in *Inferno* XI. The distinction between the remaining groups, however – the sins of violence and sins of fraud – was made most explicitly by Cicero in his *De officiis*.[35]

It is in the treatment of the graver sins that the principles of division and numeration are allowed to run riot, so let us begin at the bottom and work upwards. The sins of fraud are distributed between the two lowest circles, depending on whether the person deceived was simply a fellow human being, or bound to the deceiver by a closer tie of trust ('fede speziale'). The closer bond admits four subdivisions, because the act of treachery may have been against family, city, guest or lord and benefactor. The less heinous forms of simple fraud are divided into ten distinct classes, and each of them is treated at the same length as one of the undivided sins of incontinence.

This yields no fewer than fourteen categories of fraud, and it would only be confusing to go into more detail at this stage. Nevertheless, attention must be drawn in passing to the heterogeneity of the ethical values which have been homogenised by means of the apparently rigorous classification.

The placing of treachery at the bottom of the pit of Hell may reasonably be interpreted as a tribute to a non-classical, non-biblical, but pan-medieval ethos, deriving in the last analysis from the feudal system (under which every personal relationship is both hierarchical and intimate: the vassal swears fealty to his lord, the lord to his overlord). Only one of the fourteen categories of fraud, simony, is distinctively religious (not, however, specifically Christian), whereas two of them – barratry and forgery – were obviously matters of particular concern in the Italian city-states. Theft (to be distinguished from robbery, which is a crime of violence) is almost the only kind of fraud to be actionable under Roman law; while seduction, flattery and hypocrisy would be more at home in a work of literary allegory, such as the *Roman de la rose*. 'Hotchpotch' might be too strong a term; but we must at least acknowledge that there are some very strange bedfellows here.[36]

Dante's analysis of violence ('malizia con forza') is an almost perfect example of the scholastic method, carried, some would say, to the point of self-parody. A first tripartition is made *ex parte obiecti*, that is, with respect to the sufferer. It has biblical authority, since Dante has deduced from the words of Jesus that the persons we can hurt are the same as those we are enjoined to love, namely our fellows, ourselves, and God. Each of the three forms of the sin is then subdivided by applying a distinction that runs all through Roman law. The victim may have suffered a hurt (*damnum*) either in himself (*in se*, *personalis*), or in his possessions (*in re*, *realis*).[37]

This distinction is perfectly straightforward in the case of the murderers, thugs and robbers who are punished together in a river of boiling blood. It becomes a trifle odd, however, when violence is directed against the self, because suicide is coupled with the deliberate squandering of property, and both sins are punished in the same dark wood. In the case of violence against God, the equivalences established by means of this distinction are little less than bizarre. In this case the 'personal' hurt refers to blasphemy. Hurting God in his 'possessions' is done through sins against Nature, which are subdivided into sodomy and usury. All three are punished in the same way, in the same place – by a rain of fire on the sterile sand.[38]

Division and numeration in Purgatory

Dante's Purgatory, too, is divided into ten zones, embodying yet another set of conceptual principles. Once again, though, there is a central block of seven circles, corresponding, formally at least, to the seven planetary heavens and the seven major circles of the Underworld (although in this case they are imagined as terraces running round a mountain island in the Southern Ocean). And it is in this major block that Dante excelled himself by creating a numerically controlled system which really does combine heterogeneous materials into a harmonious whole.

The circles are organised in accordance with the well-tried scheme of the Seven Capital Vices (presented in the definitive order established by St Gregory the Great in the sixth century, namely, pride, envy, anger, sloth, avarice, gluttony and lechery). On every terrace the penitent souls meditate on examples of divine punishment of their vice (drawn evenhandedly from classical literature and the Bible) and on three examples of the virtue to which they aspire (in each case, one example is classical, one from the Old Testament, and one from the life of the Virgin Mary). They sing an appropriate Latin hymn; and at the moment of their release from the circle, an angel pronounces the relevant Beatitude from Christ's Sermon on the Mount. There can be few more satisfying expressions in medieval art of the longing for order and synthesis which is so characteristic of the high Middle Ages.[39]

It could be argued, moreover, that it was the desire for numerically regulated symmetry of a more elementary kind that led Dante to his greatest feats of invention in this cantica. His account of Purgatory is far more detailed and subtle than anything to be found in earlier or contemporary theologians (who treat Purgatory as an annexe to Hell); and the fullness and freshness of his treatment has its origin in the tripartite structure of the whole *Comedy*. In other words, one reason why he gave so much attention to the realm of temporal correction, granting it equal importance with the realms of eternal punishment and reward, was that he wanted his poem to be divided into three canticas of equal length.

At a different level, Dante's desire to bring the number of zones in Purgatory up to ten (in a pattern of 7 + 2 + 1, as in the other canticas) led him to create two areas at the foot of his mountain (conventionally described as the Antepurgatory) which have no counterparts in orthodox theology. The lower slopes are the temporary abode of those who died excommunicate, or who delayed repentance until the hour of their death; and the encounters with these souls who escaped Hell by a hair's breadth convey some of Dante's most delicate insights into human worth. The remaining zone, the tenth, is placed at the top of the mountain. It is nothing other than the Garden of Eden, or Earthly Paradise, which Dante explicitly described as the symbol of the happiness possible in this life through the exercise of the moral and intellectual virtues – an incomplete happiness (*beatitudo imperfecta*, in Aquinas's phrase), which is nevertheless our final goal on earth. It is a foreshadowing of the Empyrean, the tenth of Dante's heavens, Paradise proper, which is where God will grant *beatitudo perfecta*, consisting in the eternal vision of himself.[40]

Multiplication (and addition!)

It would be wrong to leave the subject of division and numeration without a glance at their purely formal function in the *Comedy*, since it is literally true that they 'in-form' every single utterance in the poem, whatever its length or content may be. Every syllable takes its place like a leaf on a tree where all the successive divisions of the boughs and branches are controlled by just two numbers. Or – to express the same truth from the opposite point of view – the whole *Comedy* is constructed by taking the smallest unit of sound and multiplying it successively by just two factors, 3 and 11.

We may see how this is done by focussing on a brief passage, which is particularly appropriate thematically, since it reminds us that the three-part poem was written to glorify Three Persons in One God. The six lines quoted below describe how the souls of the blessed who appear in the Heaven of the Sun sing an antiphon to the Holy Trinity, repeating it three times. In the second line the numbers from one to three are repeated in inverse order, in order to imitate the two-way process of *exitus* and *reditus*, or 'breathing in and breathing out'. (The begetting of the Son and the procession of the Holy Spirit are matched by the answering flow of love back to the Father.) And the last line is central to the themes of this book, because to know the 'just reward' for a human life is to know its 'worth'.

> Quell'uno e due e tre che sempre vive
> e regna sempre in tre e 'n due e 'n uno,
> non circunscritto, e tutto circunscrive,
> tre volte era cantato da ciascuno
> di quelli spirti con tal melodia,
> ch'ad ogne merto saria giusto muno. (*Par.* XIV, 33–9)

The patterning of the sounds (not least, the alliteration linking 'merto' and 'muno'), together with the rhythmic movement of the verse, evoke the celestial beauty of the melody they describe; and yet the individual words may be translated almost literally, and almost in the same order, to make acceptable English prose:

> That One and Two and Three who always lives, and reigns in Three and in Two and in One, not circumscribed, and circumscribing all, was sung three times by each of those spirits with a melody such that it would be a just reward for every merit.

Let us leave style and content, though, and focus on the metre and on the metrical constants. The minimal unit – the 'atom', so to speak – is the syllable. The basic building block – the 'molecule' – is the line of verse, which always contains eleven metrically relevant syllables, as will be seen most clearly in the fifth line, where there are no elisions or other complications:

di-quel-li-spir-ti-con-tal-me-lo-di-a.

The hendecasyllables in their turn are grouped by syntax and rhythm into sets of three called terzinas. A terzina may be a complete sentence or even a complete paragraph (as is not uncommon in the poem); but it is always at least a distinct part of a longer sentence, and the end of a long sentence always coincides with the end of a terzina. Dante had come to think and feel in blocks of three. In addition, the rhyme-sounds establish the pattern ABA, BCB (continuing CDC, DED etc.), so that each terzina is simultaneously forged into a circle and joined to its neighbours like a link in a chain. Each rhyme-sound occurs three times (except at the two ends of the chain), and this is the main reason why the metre has come to be called 'terza rima'.

Every so often the concatenation is interrupted when a given terzina is followed by a single line, rhyming in the pattern YZY, Z; and the next terzina begins with two unrelated rhymes (ABA etc.). By this simple device the poem is divided into 'chapters' or 'songs' (the early commentators often use the word 'capitolo', as in the Bible, while Dante's own word is 'canto'). Taking this as the main unit of his narrative, Dante multiplies it by both his earlier multipliers (3 x 11) to create the next highest unit, which he called a 'cantica', consisting of thirty-three cantos. And since there are three canticas, the whole poem is the product of a final multiplication by three.

There are, however, two very important 'irregularities' or 'deviations', which are wholly typical of the medieval practice of constructing through repeated multiplication or division. The number of terzinas in a canto ranges from as few as 38 to as many as 53, with an average of 47; so it is clear that Dante did not tie himself hand and foot, but asserted his freedom to follow the dictates of the subject matter in the act of composition. And the first cantica has an extra canto, with the result that the total number is not 99 but 100.

It is tempting to object that the act of *addition* constitutes a kind of 'cheating'. But almost every reader of the poem ignores this equivalent of the troublesome 'comma of Didymus' (which makes it impossible to tune a piano by implementing the perfect ratios of Pythagorean theory). We rejoice that the three-part poem in tercets can also claim to be a century of cantos, ten times ten, the Pythagoreans' perfect number multiplied by itself. *Tout se tient*. Our critical faculties are lulled to sleep by proportion and symbolic number.[41]

PART TWO

Competing values

CHAPTER FOUR

Aristotelian values through Dante's eyes

Documenta philosophica et spiritualia

In the first part of this book we saw that Dante acknowledged a great many authorities in the field of moral philosophy, and that he was typical of his culture both in his desire to synthesise old insights and values in a new conceptual framework, and in the way he pursued that goal. In this second part we shall begin to focus on the content of his ethical thought, as opposed to his sources or procedures, but we shall still be concerned with broad issues, rather than with detailed analysis of Dante's ideas in relation to his art. (That will come in Parts 3 and 4.)

Our first task will be to simplify the complex testimony of his authors by polarising their approaches to 'human vices and human worth'. This will be done by sharpening the obvious distinction between philosophical and religious texts – between those which proceed 'per via naturale' and those which follow the 'via teologica', those which set out from what we might call the South Pole of observable phenomena, and those which start from the North Pole of revealed truth. The two 'hemispheres' will be contrasted in separate accounts of Aristotelian and Christian values in this chapter and the next. Chapter 6 will draw the threads together again by showing how Dante's thought lies on the 'equator' common to both hemispheres. It will concentrate on his first major contribution to ethics – the fourth book of the *Convivio* – and it will show how Dante took a value that was of central importance to laymen in thirteenth-century society and subjected it to an analysis that was both philosophical and theological to reach new conclusions concerning 'the "valore" through which a person is truly noble' ('dirò del valore / per lo qual veramente omo è gentile').[1]

There are of course many objections to distinguishing so sharply between the two approaches. The great scholastic thinkers of the thirteenth century habitually worked in both directions. It was as though they were driving a tunnel through a mountain range, operating from both sides simultaneously in the confidence that the two shafts would meet in the middle. And many people today incline to the view that all discourse about ethics originates in the human mind – including the pronouncements of a deity whom we have constructed 'in our image, after our likeness'.[2]

The provisional response, however, must be that we are trying to place Dante's thought in its context, and that the scholastics themselves, however sanguine they might have been of 'meeting in the centre', always distinguished rigorously between philosophy and theology. The two *scientiae* employed similar methods but had totally different *principia*. More important, Dante himself, even in a work as late as the third book of the *Monarchia*, asserted that there are two distinct 'goals' for mankind, two distinct happinesses (the one symbolised by the Earthly Paradise, the other by the Celestial). To the first of these we come 'through philosophical teachings' ('per *philosophica* documenta'). To the second we come 'through spiritual teachings that transcend human reason' ('documenta *spiritualia*, quae humanam rationem transcendunt').[3]

The Master of our reason and life

There is no doubt as to which of the *philosophica documenta* should be given pride of place in this chapter. At the time of writing the *Convivio*, Dante admired the man who was universally known as the Philosopher with a reverence that was little short of idolatry. Aristotle, he says, is 'most worthy of trust and obedience': he is the 'Master of our reason' and 'Master of our life'; he 'reduced moral philosophy to perfection'; his teaching is now almost 'universal opinion', so that wherever he has voiced his 'divina sentenza', all other opinions should be ignored.[4]

Dante's judgements are based on one work in particular, the *Nicomachean Ethics* (which in what follows will be referred to simply as the *Ethics* – *Ethica*, 'Etica' – which was how it was generally known in Dante's day). Occupying about 200 pages in a modern edition, it is written clearly but tersely in a style that has led some scholars to conclude that it consists of Aristotle's notes for a lecture course, or perhaps notes taken down from a course of his lectures. It was of course ransacked and 'put to the question' in the thirteenth century, so that its leading ideas are quoted out of context again and again; but it must be emphasised that this was one of the classical works that was studied in its entirety in Dante's day, and that Dante would have had access to full and faithful expositions by the Moorish philosopher known in the West as Averroes ('Averroè che il gran comento feo'), by Albert the Great, and by Aquinas, who caused the text to be retranslated from the original Greek.[5]

Aquinas's commentary, to which Dante refers explicitly, is a model of what a commentary should be, not the least of its virtues being that it constantly fills out and clarifies Aristotle's ethical thought by reference to his metaphysics, physics and psychology (indeed, it forms a splendid introduction to the whole corpus of his philosophy). This contextualisation is of vital importance because the great attraction of the *Ethics* lay in the fact that Aristotle analysed what is good and bad for human beings with the same calm objectivity and with the same criteria that he brought to the analysis of any other body or being in the natural world. It is these criteria that will be summarised in a general and informal way in the following survey, which will be conducted in the spirit of this well-known passage in the *Ethics*:[6]

> No doubt the proper procedure is to begin by making a rough sketch, and to fill it in afterwards. Also the warning given above must not be forgotten: we must not look for equal exactness in all departments of study, but only such as belongs to the subject matter of each, and in such a degree as is appropriate to the particular line of enquiry. (*Ethics*, I, vii, 16, translated by H. R. Rackham)

The engineer's approach: structure, species, function

Aristotle set out to answer the following questions (as accurately as the nature of the subject allows). What is good for human beings? What is the relationship between human goodness and happiness? How can we achieve that happiness?[7]

In modern parlance, one could say that his approach to all these questions is that of an engineer. He assumes that there should be a perfect match between the form or structure of a thing and its function or purpose; and most of his assumptions, categories and terms can be illustrated by looking at some simple artefacts, where the word 'form' may be replaced by the word 'shape'. So let us visualise two knives, a fork and a spoon taken from a set of utilitarian modern cutlery, where all the pieces are cast from stainless steel, without handles of horn or plastic. (The example is inspired by two passages in the *Convivio*, and the principles it exemplifies can be applied, with due qualifications, to all bodies, organic as well as inorganic, however complex they may be.)[8]

An engineer would perceive these items as 'tools' or 'instruments' for eating politely at table. All four are made of the same substance, and the two individual knives are identical in every respect save that of their particular molecules of steel. The knife, fork and spoon differ from each other by their shape (*forma*), and it is the shape that makes them what they are. In Aristotelian terminology – still perfectly familiar – the knife, fork and spoon belong by virtue of their form to three different species of the same genus (cutlery), while the two knives 'differ in number' but are identical in species: they are individuated only by their matter (*materia*).

Every shape that is significant in this context (every 'substantial form') must differ in some 'essential' way from every other related shape ('accidental' variations have no importance). This distinctive aspect – what makes a spoon different from a fork, or a fork from a knife – is called its *differentia*, and is the most important element in its definition. One must be able to state the genus ('cutlery', in our example, to avoid any confusion between a pitch-fork and a fork used at table). It may be necessary to indicate the material (e.g. stainless steel, as opposed to the plastics used in picnic cutlery). But the essential part of the definition is the *differentia*; and this resides in the shape or form which determines the species. *Species*, *forma* and *differentia* are inseparable concepts.

In the very simple example under consideration, the shapes can be seen and drawn, but one cannot *understand* the knife, fork or spoon unless one knows 'what they are for' – what is their distinctive purpose – and unless one grasps the relation between the shape and this purpose (between *forma* and *finis* in Aristotelian terminology). We have seen that items of cutlery may be described 'generically' as tools for eating in polite society; and all three tools have convenient handles to fit them for this common end. But the 'specific' purpose of the knife is to cut solid foods; while the fork is designed to transfer solids, and the spoon to carry liquids, from plate to mouth. That is why they have a blade, prongs and a bowl respectively.

It should be clear that the *differentia* or distinctive aspect of the form is the very one which enables the body to achieve its primary purpose. It is the shape of the knife that enables it to cut, or gives it 'the power' of cutting. The concept of *forma* is always inseparable from that of inherent, inalienable powers – *potentiae*. (In different contexts these may be called 'virtues', *virtutes*, or 'properties', *proprietates*, from *proprium*, meaning 'belonging to'.)[9]

It should be noticed, too, that in another sense of the word *potentia*, the powers of the knife, fork and spoon are only 'potentially' present when they are lying in the drawer or on the table. They have to be 'actualised' by being put into use (*usus*) by a human hand and brain. They are *in actu* (as opposed to existing *in potentia*) only when they are operative or 'in operation'. *Operatio* is a key term in Aristotelian ethics, which is concerned with what Dante repeatedly calls 'operazioni umane'; and it derives from *opus/operis* meaning 'task' or 'work').[10]

Value-judgements: level 1

A few moments' mental conjuring with a knife, fork and spoon has introduced three sets of terms and shown how they are related to each other: (a) *genus*, *species* (*differentia*), *individuum*; (b) *forma* (*differentia*), *potentia*, *virtus*; (c) *finis*, *usus*, *operatio*. These are in fact all we need in order to understand Aristotle's approach to the concept of 'value', or, rather, his way of defining good and bad, and their relative degrees.

When is a knife good, or when is one knife better than another? The answer is self-evident. A knife is good when its form confers the powers, both generic and specific, that enable it to achieve its purpose, which consists in the operation of cutting. It is good if it can do its job well. It is good, too, if it possesses nothing that is superfluous and no feature which might obstruct its primary purpose.

Other things being equal, the better a knife cuts, the better it is. Of course, even with such a simple artefact there may be other factors to take into account. Stainless steel does not rust, but does not hold its cutting edge as well as ordinary steel. A table knife will serve its generic purpose better if it pleases the eye and matches its companion-pieces in the same set. It is convenient to have a blade wide enough to spread fats. Nevertheless, these are secondary considerations. Items of cutlery are bad if they cannot perform their distinctive functions. And it is for this very precise reason that one can condemn the infuriating pieces of modern cutlery that inspired this section (joining forces imaginatively with the sword chosen by Dante in the *Convivio*). They look elegant, and the handles have handsome runes. But the knife will not cut; the fork will not spear; and the spoon is so flat that it will not carry liquids. They are bad because they are 'use-less', because they do not 'work'.

The biological engineer: from artefacts to living organisms

The criteria illustrated in this example were applied by Aristotle to the analysis of all bodies that exist in nature – minerals, plants, animals and mankind. And since human craft was thought to imitate the model of nature, the principles were generalised to cover the whole system – *Natura universalis*, or Nature personified. They found expression in two of the most common axioms in the whole of scholastic philosophy (and, indeed, scholastic theology, where, for 'Nature', one must read 'Providence' or 'God'). The first runs: 'Nature does nothing without a purpose', *natura nil facit otiose*; the second: 'Nature is never lacking in what is necessary', *natura non deficit in necessariis*. (These are significantly close to the ancient adage that lies at the heart of Aristotle's account of the moral virtues, 'not too little, not too much'.)[11]

We may pass now from artefacts to living bodies. Considered 'generically', a living body is one capable of causing change to itself. It uses itself. It always has distinct parts and each part is employed as a tool to carry out a distinct task, all of which are subordinated to the purpose of the whole body. The Greek word for 'tool' was *organon*, taken into Latin as *organum*, and into English as 'organ'. By definition, a living body has organs; it is 'organic'; it is 'tooled up' for its job – and that was the original meaning of 'organised'.[12]

A living body exists by virtue of its 'form' in just the same way as any inanimate body. But the notion of *forma* must now be extended from that of a visible shape to include what we would today call 'structure', something that may well be totally inaccessible to the senses. It is the *forma* or structure of steel (the way in which its constituent atoms are arranged and attached) which makes it exist as steel and confers its specific properties. It is the *forma* of a living body that enables it to use itself and cause change to itself. Any form that confers this power is known as an *anima* ('soul', in Greek, *psyche*), and bodies that can change themselves are called 'animate'.[13]

In principle, everything that has already been said about the interrelationship between *forma*, *finis*, *potentia*, *differentia* and *operatio* is valid for living bodies as well. And since Nature does nothing in vain and nothing to excess, we may expect that every plant and animal has all the powers and organs it needs to achieve its purpose and nothing it does not need (forms withhold powers as well as conferring them). This can easily be exemplified in plants. A typical garden plant has organic parts that can be distinguished by the naked eye – roots, stem, branches, leaves, and flowers which become seed-bearing fruit. If we ask the Aristotelian question, 'what are these distinct parts for, what is their *finis*?', we conclude they are there to keep the plant alive, to enable it to grow to maturity and then to reproduce itself. Aristotle said that all plants have these three basic *operationes* which he called *nutrimentum*, *augmentum* and *generatio*. For him, they are kinds of self-use, kinds of self-change.[14]

The time has come to take note of another sense of the word *potentia*. A tree exists as a seedling, grows to maturity and reproduces. At a certain point, it ceases to grow, ceases to be capable of reproduction, and finally ceases to be capable of any kind of self-change at all (at which point it is by definition no longer an animate body). While it was a seedling, it was still *in potentia*. In the process of growing it was already actualising its mature form, equipping itself with the organs it would need. But even when it was fully *in actu* – mature, with all its organs and powers – it did not make use of its power of reproduction during the winter. The power lay dormant: it was there only 'in potency'. So, strictly speaking, the tree is only fully 'in act' when it is currently exercising its final, distinctive power (what Dante called its *vis ultima*), that is, when it is producing the seeds that will give existence and life to other trees of the same species. Only then is it performing the *operatio* that no plant of another species can perform. This is its own function, its *operatio propria*, the reason for its existence.[15]

Value-judgements: level 2

We are now ready to consider the question of what is 'good' for a plant. Aristotle's answer is cumulative and in three parts. Its first good is simply existence (*esse*) as an individual, living plant of a given species. It can do nothing if it is not there and alive. Its second good is fullness or completeness of being, maturity, possession of all its properties and organs. Aristotelians called this its *perfectio*. Its third and highest good is the exercise of its distinctive power, its *operatio propria*, the function unique to its species, inherent in the *differentia* of its specific form. This is the activity of self-reproduction, otherwise called *generatio*.[16]

The three goods are not of equal value – the first is subordinate to the second, the second to the third – but *esse*, *perfectio* and *generatio* are all primary and intrinsic goods. In addition to these, a plant will have numerous secondary or external goods, which are good to the extent that they are means to the end of achieving one or more of the primary goods. For example, a plant needs sunlight, water and mineral nutrients.

It is crucial to note that all these secondary goods must be supplied at the right time, in the right way, and in the right quantity ('not too little and not too much'). And the 'rightness' of the quantity and the time varies according to the species. Some plants prefer acid soil, others alkaline; a willow likes its feet wet, a passion-flower can be killed even by modest watering. No body exists without a specified form. Any good whatsoever is always specific.

Having grasped this apparently objective definition of 'the good' (*bonum*), and learned to distinguish between primary goods and secondary goods, we can address the cognate question of what is 'bad' for a plant. What is the meaning in this case of the word *malum*?

A similar range of distinctions must be made. The first and greatest *malum* is 'non-being' – death. The second is imperfect being, stunted being, the lack of essential organs and powers. The third is inability to perform the *operatio propria* – the activity for the sake of which the whole plant exists. But there are also a number of external or secondary *mala*. There may be other bodies (animals or plants) that directly threaten the plant's existence, wholeness, or ability to reproduce. And to these we must add any condition or body which would deprive the plant of any of its external goods.[17]

Value-judgements: level 3

The whole point of this preamble is that 'good' or 'bad' for human beings can be defined along the same lines and with comparable objectivity. Whether we like it or not, we are animals. All animals perform the three activities of plant-life (*nutrimentum*, *augmentum*, *generatio*) together with three additional operations (called *apprehensio*, *appetitus*, *locomotio*) for which they are equipped with additional organs. Higher animals perceive objects outside themselves, experience emotions such as desire and fear (depending on whether the external objects are secondary goods or evils), and move themselves in space to pursue the objects of desire and to avoid the objects of fear. (Perception, it will be observed, is subordinate to emotion, and emotion to self-movement, which is the highest power.)[18]

These shared powers are generic and not distinctive of the human species. Their activities cannot therefore constitute the *operatio propria* in which our primary good consists. Our *differentia* resides in further powers collectively called 'mind' (Dante's words are 'mente' and 'animo'). These allow us to understand concepts such as 'good and bad' or 'ends and means', to weigh up possible actions in the light of these concepts, and to make conscious choices leading to action. The most precise terms for the mental powers are 'intellect' and 'will' (*intellectus* and *voluntas*), but the word 'reason' (*ratio*) was often used by the scholastics as a synonym for the intellect – sometimes for the deliberative power of the intellect acting in conjunction with the will, and sometimes for the mind in general.[19]

So at last we are in a position to understand the character of Aristotle's answers to the questions formulated earlier, namely: What is good for man? What is human happiness?

Defined by genus and species, man is a 'rational animal' (*animal rationale*), or at least an 'animal capable of reason' (*animal rationis capax*). Human beings exist in order to exercise their distinctive mental powers (their 'reason' in the widest sense). This is their *finis* and *operatio propria*. A life is not human unless it is lived at least in accordance with reason (*secundum rationem*). Happiness is the state produced by the present activity of our highest and differentiating power.[20]

We shall see shortly that these simple answers require important qualifications. Individuals differ widely in temperament and native talent. Man is a 'political animal', fitted by nature to live in a community. The relationship between our generic and specific powers (between instincts and reason) is complicated, to say the least. The two operations of the intellect, theoretical and practical, are radically different. Hence the good of one individual may be distinct from that of another, and the good of any individual may be distinct from that of the community. The good of the generic animal powers may be distinct from that of reason, the good of pure contemplation distinct from the good of conscious, voluntary action. But however complex the problems posed by these and similar factors may seem, they can all be analysed – and some of them resolved – by applying the basic principles that are valid for domestic tools and garden plants.[21]

Summaries by Dante and Aristotle

It will be worth pausing here to read some brief extracts from Dante and Aristotle which exemplify this objective, engineering, biological approach to the subject of human worth.

The first is a passage from the *Convivio*, in which it is important to note that two of the key-words in Dante's ethics, 'virtuoso' and 'ordinato', have a much wider range of meaning than their English descendants, 'virtuous' and 'ordered'. 'Virtuoso' denotes the full and proper use of a particular *potentia* or *virtus* which is inherent in the given substantial form. 'Ordinato' is used in a sense that oscillates between 'structured', 'intended', and 'ordained' (a term we normally reserve for the actions of the divinity); it seems to apply equally to both structure and purpose, *forma* and *finis*:

> Each thing is virtuous in its own nature which does that for which it is ordered. The better it does it, the more virtuous it is. So we say a man is virtuous who lives a contemplative or an active life for which he is ordered by nature. We say that a horse is virtuous if it runs strongly for a long time, for which it is ordered; we say that a sword is virtuous if it cuts hard things well, for which it is ordered.[22] (*Con.* I, v, 11)

The second is a slightly 'streamlined' version of a passage in Aristotle's *Ethics*, where the ideas paraphrased and exemplified above find their classic expression:

> Just as the eye, the hand, the foot and each of the various members of the body manifestly has a certain function of its own, so a human being also has a certain function over and above all the functions of his particular members. . . . If we declare that the function of man is the exercise of the soul's faculties and activities in association with rational principle (*secundum rationem*), it follows that the good of man is the active exercise of his soul's faculties in conformity with excellence or virtue, or, if there be several human excellences or virtues, in conformity with the best and most perfect among them. (*Ethics* I, vii, 10, 16, adapted from the translation by H. R. Rackham)

The next two passages are from the second and third books of the *Convivio*:

> Things must be named with reference to the highest and most perfect power in their form ('l'ultima nobilitade de la loro forma'), as for example, in the case of man, with reference to reason and not to the senses or anything less noble. Hence, when one says that a man 'lives', one ought to understand that he 'uses reason', which is his specific life and the actualisation of his noblest part ('atto de la sua più nobile parte'). So any one who abandons reason and uses only the sensitive part, lives not as a man but as a beast. . . . Human living is using reason ('vivere ne l'uomo è ragione usare'). (*Con.* II, vii, 3 and 11)

> Human perfection [lies in] the perfection of reason, from which, as from our supreme part ('principalissima parte'), our whole essence depends. All our other activities, such as sensation and nutrition, exist for the sake of reason alone, whereas this is for its own sake. (*Con.* III, xv, 15)

A 'circumscription' of Aristotle's Ethics

The passage from Aristotle just quoted is taken from his opening account of the views of ordinary men concerning the nature of human goodness and happiness, which occupies most of Book I. And this is a good point to offer a 'rough sketch' of what the rest of the *Ethics* contains.

In the final chapter of Book I Aristotle ceases to talk generically about the 'rational part' of man and distinguishes more exactly between the intellect and the will. He makes it clear that the only genuinely human activities are those which have their origin in, and are controlled by, these two linked powers: 'solo quelle sono nostre operazioni che subiacciono a la ragione e a la volontade', as Dante paraphrases him in the *Convivio*.[23]

In the next major part of the work he examines the functions of the intellect and the will in isolation from each other, using the same word – in Latin, *virtus/virtutis* – to denote the proper or best function of each. Books II–V are devoted to the virtues of the voluntary power, and Book VI to those of the cognitive power. The latter are known as 'intellectual virtues', while those of the will are properly called 'moral virtues'.

It is, of course, the *moral* virtues which have come to be considered as the 'virtues' par excellence. Ethics is not about ratiocination in general, but about rational choices that result in rational action. These proceed directly from the will, not from the intellect. Strictly speaking, therefore, ethics is limited to the study of operations which lie under the control of the will. This is a vital point which Dante will drive home and exemplify like this:

> Hurting and helping, running away from battle and standing firm, remaining chaste and fornicating, are completely subject to the will ('del tutto soggiacciono a la volontade'); and it is therefore from these operations that we are called good and bad, because they are specifically ours in every way ('elle sono proprie nostre del tutto'). Our [specifically human] activities extend to the limits of what the will can attain ('quanto la nostra volontade ottenere puote, tanto le nostre operazioni si stendono'). (*Con.* IV, ix, 7)

In the next book (VII), Aristotle investigates the inevitable conflicts between our instinctive appetites (which seek sensual pleasure) and our rational principle (which seeks the happiness of the whole human being); and he analyses the faults that arise when the sense-appetites prevail. Then he widens the discussion to consider another important element in the definition of mankind (*genus humanum*). Man is a gregarious animal (a 'compagnevole animale'). More precisely, he is an animal fitted to live in the kind of community which Aristotle called a *polis*, and Dante a *civitas* or 'città'. He is a 'political animal', an 'animale civile'. As a result, the virtuous cannot be happy as human beings unless they share their existence with friends who also live 'in accordance with reason' (the man who lives alone, says Aristotle, 'is either a beast or a God'). Books VIII and IX, therefore, are devoted to a detailed and subtle analysis of the 'good' called friendship and its relation to happiness.[24]

At this point, it is worth recalling parenthetically that the Latin word *amicitia* (like its Italian descendant, 'amicizia') still maintained its etymological link to the verb *amare* and the noun *amor*; and hence we must beware of contrasting love and friendship in the way we often do today. Dante fully accepted Aristotle's high valuation of loving friendship, although he probably regarded Cicero as his authority in this field, because it was to Cicero's dialogue *De amicitia* that he turned to find consolation for the death of Beatrice, and, looking for silver, as he put it, found gold.[25]

Value-judgements: level 4: the highest good of all

The final book of the *Ethics* reaffirms the earlier proposition that happiness must consist in the activity of the highest power – the human *differentia* – and it reaches a conclusion that is rather unexpected in a work of moral philosophy.

As we have seen, the intellect has two aspects, pure and applied. The applied or practical intellect (*intellectus practicus*) works in close alliance with the will and brings both experience and knowledge to bear on decisions that will lead to the best action in the here and now. The pure or theoretical intellect (*intellectus speculativus*) abstracts universal concepts from the particular data gathered by the senses and sets them in due order, seeking to understand what is necessary, unchanging, eternal. ('True knowledge bears on universals', *scientia est universalium*.) The difference between the two activities is so great that there are two distinct happinesses possible for human beings: the pursuit of truth and the pursuit of virtue. They are not of equal value. At the end of the *Ethics* Aristotle lays it down that the best and most human form of life is that which is dedicated to contemplation of the truth for its own sake.[26]

In the second half of this chapter – and for most of the rest of this book – we shall be concerned almost exclusively with the virtues of the will. But before we go on to examine the moral virtues, we must once again allow Dante to identify himself with Aristotle's position in his own words. In the *Convivio* he several times contrasts a life devoted to the quest for truth (and the loving enjoyment of the truth once understood) with the humdrum daily life of doing and making, exchanging services and objects for the satisfaction of our bodily and social needs. And he insists that the *vita activa* (as it came to be called) is good, but the *vita contemplativa* is better, or rather, 'ottima', best of all. At times he was troubled by this claim. (Was not the pursuit of *scientia* a recipe for unhappiness, given that our desire for full and sure knowledge can never be assuaged in this present life?) As a Christian, though, he could look forward to a *beatitudo perfecta* when God would grant the complete actualisation of his intellectual power, which would consist in contemplation of the whole truth, and nothing but the truth, for all eternity. The 'shade' of Aristotle is confined for eternity in Dante's Limbo; but his conclusion that human happiness lies in the exercise of our 'most noble part' is vindicated in Paradise.[27]

In the *Convivio*, however, Dante remains close to the text of the *Ethics* and to what is possible here on earth:

> Our highest perfection is to contemplate the truth ('la veritade speculare'), as the Philosopher says in the sixth book of the *Ethics*, when he says that truth is the good of the intellect. (*Con.* II, xiii, 6)

> That which is most delightful to us constitutes our happiness and bliss. . . . Our mind ('animo') has a dual use, practical and theoretical – where practical is as much as to say active ('operativo'). Both activities are highly delightful, although the theoretical is more so . . . Use of the practical intellect consists in our acting virtuously ('operare per noi virtuosamente'), that is, honourably, with prudence, self-control, courage and justice. Use of the theoretical intellect is not action, but contemplation of the works of God and nature. Our blessedness and supreme happiness consist in these uses. However, one of these uses gives a fuller bliss than the other, namely the theoretical, which is the use of our noblest part without admixture of any kind. (*Con.* IV, xxii, 10–11, 13, 18)

> The fact is we can have two happinesses in this life, corresponding to two different paths, the good and the best, which lead us to them. The first is the active life, the other the contemplative. One may arrive at good happiness through the active life, but the other leads to the best happiness and blessedness ('ottima felicitade e beatitudine'), as the Philosopher demonstrates in the tenth book of the *Ethics*.[28] (*Con.* IV, xvii, 9)

Virtues of the practical intellect

Before discussing the moral virtues, we must briefly consider the virtues of the practical intellect. In the sixth book of the *Ethics*, Aristotle distinguishes sharply between 'making' and 'doing' (*facere/factum* and *agere/actum*) and also between 'makeable' objects and 'doable' actions (*factibilia* and *agibilia*). Nevertheless, his treatment of 'practical wisdom' or the 'sound judgement of affairs' (these seem the best translations of *prudentia*) is illuminated by the parallels he draws with the 'craft' of a potter, painter or poet (the Latin word for 'craft' being *ars/artis*).[29]

'Right understanding' is required in making well and doing well; and the phrase *recta ratio* enters into the definition of both the virtues in question. Aquinas defines *ars* as the *recta ratio factibilium*, while *prudentia* is the *recta ratio agibilium*. Both virtues demand experience. Children may acquire mathematical knowledge very quickly, but the potter's art and the leader's statecraft take many years to perfect. In neither case, though, are theoretical understanding or experience sufficient in themselves. *Prudentia*, no less than *ars*, is a kind of skill, whose presence or absence is shown by success or failure in the here and now: the pots must hold water and the decisions lead to contentment.[30]

Prudentia, as Aristotle makes clear, is concerned with actions in a world of contingency, where circumstances vary and could always be other than they are. It presupposes an understanding of the true end or goal (*verus finis*) and rightness of desire for that goal. Without love for the good, it is no better than *astutia*, or becomes the vice of *malitia*. It is, however, concerned exclusively with determining the means to achieve the end (*ea quae sunt ad finem*). In this activity there are three phases: discovering and weighing up possible courses of action; making a judgement; and commending the most efficacious of them to the will (it is pertinent to think of the physician's 'art', which lies in considering the patient's symptoms, making the right diagnosis, and prescribing the correct remedy). *Prudentia* steers the chariot: it is the 'charioteer', *auriga*, of moral virtue, which cannot exist without it (good intentions are not enough). It may therefore be said to 'direct' or 'perfect' all the moral virtues.[31]

Human goodness as moral virtue

We certainly do turn for advice to people who have good judgement of affairs, and we accept their leadership. But we do not *love* them for their discernment; nor would we describe them simply as 'good' unless they put their own precepts into practice, and unless they do so consistently in the course of a whole life. 'One swallow does not make a summer', says Aristotle, and one or two good actions do not make a good man. Human goodness, in short, resides in the voluntary power, not the cognitive; and it denotes a permanent condition, a state of character.[32]

With that conclusion we have come to the first distinctive feature in Aristotle's analysis of the moral virtues. Each of the virtues is regarded as an actualisation of the will which 'disposes' it in such a way that the will is steadily 'inclined' to make the right kind of choice in all circumstances, even before the practical intellect has weighed up the pros and cons in a particular situation. The key-words in scholastic Latin are *dispositio* and *inclinatio*; and it is worth emphasising that both terms still retained their original connotations. The form which makes us human – the *anima rationalis* – has been structured or re-structured in such a way that the will 'bends' or 'leans' – Dante's word is 'piegarsi' – and permanently 'stretches out' in a certain direction.[33]

Such a steady inclination of the will may simply be the result of the individual's temperament (then attributed to the balance of the four humours determined by the influence of the stars), in which case it is a *dispositio naturalis*. It may, however, be the product of 'nurture', rather than 'nature' – the result of upbringing and custom – in which case, once it has become settled and 'difficult to remove', it is called a *habitus*. A *dispositio naturalis* or a *habitus* may, of course, be either good or bad, depending on the direction of the inclination it imparts. That is the whole difference between a virtue and a vice.[34]

To sum up so far, then: a *virtus moralis* may be provisionally described as a *habitus* which inclines the agent to make the right kind of choice. But what is the 'right kind of choice', what is a 'buona elezione'? Aristotle answers – and this is the second main feature of his account – that a good choice, in general terms, is one that aims at something which is good for the subject (it is 'conformable' with the *forma* which gives being and life to that individual person) in the right degree or measure, 'not too little and not too much'. When the two parts of Aristotle's answer are put together, one has – in Dante's approving words – the 'whole definition of moral virtue, as it is defined by the Philosopher in the second book of the *Ethics*. For one can say of all of the virtues in general that they are "a habit of choice [a settled disposition to choose] residing in the mean". These are the qualities that make men blessed, that is happy, in their activity.'

> . . . ponendo tutta la diffinizione de la morale virtù, secondo che nel secondo de l'*Etica* è per lo Filosofo diffinito. . . . Generalmente si può dicere di tutte, che siano abito elettivo consistente nel mezzo. E queste sono quelle che fanno l'uomo beato, o vero felice, ne la loro operazione.[35] (*Con.* IV, xvii, 1)

The eleven virtues and the twenty-two collateral vices

From virtue considered in isolation, we must now pass on to virtue considered in relation to vice – or rather to vices in the plural, 'li vizi umani' (what Dante will call the 'dispositions that Heaven does not want').[36]

If virtue always consists in a steady bent to choose the mean lying between two undesirable extremes, it follows that each individual virtue 'has two enemies', as Dante puts it very vividly, 'one on each flank, vices of too much and too little' ('ciascuna di queste vertudi ha due inimici collaterali, cioè vizii, uno in troppo e un altro in poco'). In Aristotle's analysis, therefore, a vice is not a settled disposition in the will to choose what is bad (nothing in the whole universe 'inclines' to what is bad for it in absolute terms) but a settled disposition to pursue certain good things excessively or not to pursue them enough.[37]

Let us see how Aristotle applies this model to the individual vices, beginning with four opposing pairs that affect the well-being of the individual considered in isolation. We need to preserve our body from harm, to keep it alive with food, to preserve the species through procreation, and to overcome obstacles placed between us and these goods. We also need material possessions (shelter, clothes etc.) which Aristotle regards as additional 'tools' for living well.[38]

When threatened by danger, however, we may be either reckless of our safety or, at the other extreme, too easily deterred by the prospect of being wounded or killed. With regard to the pleasures that accompany eating, drinking and making love, we may become either over-indulgent, or so puritanical that we are 'under-indulgent'. If we are frustrated by obstacles, we may get blindly furious with those who stand in our way, or we may shrug our shoulders and give up too easily. We may be irresponsibly prodigal in the management of our possessions, or we may be so preoccupied with them that we think of nothing but increasing them or hoarding what we already have.

We therefore need four virtues which aim at the mean between these extremes. Dante characterises them like this (following Aristotle very closely):

> Courage ('fortezza') is a spur and a rein to moderate our rashness and fearfulness with regard to things that destroy life. Self-control ('temperanza') is a rule and rein for greediness and excessive abstinence with regard to things that preserve life. Generosity ('liberalitade') regulates our giving and receiving temporal things. Good temper ('mansuetudine') moderates our anger and excessive patience with regard to external ills.[39]

Humans, as we have seen, are 'companionable' or 'civic' animals, intended by nature to live together with others in order to live well. In our relations with other people, however, we may be so concerned to project a favourable image of ourselves that we become boastful, or we may be so given to self-denigration that we 'undersell' ourselves. In ordinary intercourse, we may try too hard to ingratiate ourselves and thereby become obsequious, but we may also try too little and become surly or boorish. When it comes to special occasions – such as weddings and wakes – we may fail to enter into the spirit of things and be kill-joys, or we may go too far and behave like louts. With regard to our reputation in the community as a whole, we may go too far in our quest for public recognition, or we may be culpably indifferent to what people think.

What we need, therefore, are four more dispositions of the will aiming between these extremes, four further good *habitus*, which Dante describes as follows:

> Frankness ('veritade') restrains us from overrating or disparaging ourselves when we speak. Charm ('affabilitade') makes us get along well with others. Liveliness ('eutrapelia') makes us moderate in our recreations, causing us to take part in them and enjoy them as we ought. Proper ambition ('amativa d'onore') regulates and orders our desires with regard to the honours of this world.[40]

Aristotle discusses three further virtues, bringing his total up to eleven. The first two are possible only for those born with exceptional talents, or those who acquire or inherit very large fortunes. These happy few must seek great honours and spend on a large scale. What might be excess when measured by the 'rule' appropriate for the normal virtues of ambition and liberality, would be a deficiency in them; but even they must not go too far. This is how Dante characterises the virtues required in these special cases:

> Munificence ('magnificenza') regulates expenditure on great enterprises, taking them on and bearing the burden within a definite limit.

> Magnanimity ('magnanimitade') regulates and obtains great honours and renown.[41]

There remains one virtue, justice, which Aristotle defines in two ways. In its normal sense, it is the most important of the virtues that regulate our behaviour to other members of the community. It consists in giving to 'each his due' (*suum cuique*, implying, once again, neither more nor less than what is due). In its extended sense, it means something more like 'righteousness' ('dirittura'). In other words, it is almost a synonym for moral virtue *tout court* (although righteousness also implies that all the separate appetites are duly ordered with respect to each other and to the whole person). Dante, in his summary of Aristotle's account, gives preference to this wider sense (which will be examined in Chapter 9 below).

> Justice ('giustizia') orders our appetites to make us love what is right and do it in all things ('ordina noi ad amare e operare dirittura in tutte cose'). (*Con.* IV, xvii, 6)

'*La buona consuetudine*'

We have now dealt with all the most important features in Aristotle's general approach to the definition of human vices and human worth, and we have seen that as late as 1307–8 (the probable date of *Convivio* IV), Dante was still acknowledging the authority of the man who had 'brought moral philosophy to perfection'. There is, however, one last aspect of Aristotle's treatment of moral virtue that demands attention even though it has nothing directly to do with the scale of ethical values (which is the main subject of this book). It concerns the way in which the eleven virtues may be acquired.

'Natural dispositions' vary from one individual to another; and Dante is faithful to his culture, as we saw in Chapter 3, in attributing the cause of this variety to the changing conjunctions of the stars and planets, which determine our temperament by modifying the balance of the four elements, or the four humours, in our 'complexion'. Some of these dispositions are morally neutral (conferring an inclination towards mathematics or languages, soldiering or administrating; and here it is only important to respect the 'foundations laid by nature' in the choice of a profession). Other natural dispositions make it relatively easy to behave virtuously. Others again make it difficult to be moderate and choose the mean. Dante refers to the last group as 'innate' or 'connatural' vices; and the person unlucky enough to possess such a temperament can be described as 'mal naturato'. His example is the standard one of a man whose *complexio* is dominated by yellow bile (*choler*), which disposes him to excessive anger ('certi vizii sono ne l'uomo, a li quali *naturalmente* elli è disposto, sì come certi per complessione collerica sono ad ira disposti').[42]

However, not all dispositions of the will are given by nature. Others, both good or bad, can be induced simply by custom ('consuetudine'). If these incline the subject towards one of the vicious extremes – Dante's example is of alcohol abuse ('sì come la intemperanza, e massimamente del vino') – they are called 'vizi consuetudinarii'. If they incline the subject to the mean, they are good, and are, indeed, synonymous with one of the eleven moral virtues described in the previous section. 'Virtue,' says Aquinas, 'is a proper disposition of the soul and, as such, may be compared to health and beauty, which are proper dispositions of the body.'[43]

Dante insists that customary vices may be overcome 'by *good* customs, through which a person becomes virtuous, experiencing no effort in choosing the mean, as the Philosopher says in the second book of the Ethics' ('questi vizii si fuggono e si vincono per buona consuetudine, e fassi l'uomo per essa virtuoso, sanza fatica aver ne la sua moderazione, sì come dice lo Filosofo nel secondo de l'Etica'). And this leads him on to an important distinction between the two kinds of vice. Customary vices can be totally dispersed by good custom ('per buona consuetudine del tutto vanno via'), whereas the innate vices never go away completely as far as the first 'movimento' or 'impeto di natura' is concerned. They do, however, become 'light' by good custom; and they do 'go away completely as far as their persistence is concerned' ('vannosene bene del tutto quanto a durazione'); so that even the first flush of anger which affects a virtuous but naturally choleric man will become weaker, and he will not remain excessively angry for long. This is possible, as Dante promptly reminds us, because 'custom is comparable to nature' ('la consuetudine 'n noi è equabile a la natura'). Dispositions that deserve the name of *habitus* are by definition 'difficult to remove' (*de difficili mobiles*); a *habitus* is in us like a 'second nature' (*habitus inest sicut natura quaedam*).[44]

This piece of folk-wisdom is central to Aristotelian ethics; and the Greek word *ethos*, which refers to a trait of character (as opposed to *pathos*, which denotes a transient emotion), has its Latin counterpart in the noun *mos/moris*, from which is derived the adjective *moralis*.

Aquinas reports that *mos* may signify either a 'certain natural, or almost natural, inclination to do certain things', or simply custom (*consuetudo*), 'since custom in a sense changes into nature (*vertitur in naturam*), and causes an inclination similar to a natural one'.[45]

So, what exactly does 'custom' entail? Aristotle's answer, as usual, is influenced by the parallels he draws between nature and craft, bodily health and moral health, making and doing. He is thinking of an animal like a horse, which can be tamed to obey the will of a human master and trained to perform tasks like drawing a plough or carrying a rider into battle, and which will come to perform these tasks with ease and pleasure. He is thinking of athletes, freely submitting themselves to the will of a trainer, who coaches them in the skill of throwing a discus, for example, until they can do it in the most efficient way, effortlessly, and without reflection. He is thinking of the potter, who takes pleasure in the technique (*technê* is the Greek equivalent of *ars*) which he learned from his master in a seven-year apprenticeship. Horse, athlete and potter have all come through 'buona consuetudine' to perform their tasks as naturally as a bee makes honey.[46]

If we now press the point and ask, 'but how exactly does the potter acquire the skill ("l'abito de l'arte") that has become second nature to him', the answer is no less obvious, but still needs to be stated on the authority of the 'Master of human life'. A *habitus* of any kind whatsoever – be it a mechanical skill or a moral virtue – is acquired by repeating the very actions to which it leads. One must perform the correct actions over and over again, imitating the model and obeying the precepts of a master who possesses the skill or virtue in question. One becomes a good potter by making pots; one becomes courageous by doing courageous things. 'Manners maketh man' (in the dictum beloved of our grandmothers). Good people are those who have good 'habits' (even in the weaker sense of the word in modern English), which they usually acquired because they were well brought up by good parents and teachers, who made them 'sit up properly' and 'respect their elders and betters'.[47]

'Nurturing' the will in Purgatory

One of Dante's most vigorous affirmations of human freedom (over and against the astrological determinism that was so great a temptation in his culture) comes in Canto XVI of *Purgatorio*, which deals with the terrace where the wrathful undergo their penance. Marco Lombardo is made to say that humans on earth 'attribute all causality to the heavens, as if everything moved of necessity with them. But if this were so, there would be no such thing as *liberum arbitrium*, and no justice in receiving joy for good deeds, and grief for bad.' This is clearly false. We possess the 'light' of reason to distinguish 'good from bad'. 'And even if it be granted,' Marco continues, 'that the heavens initiate some or all of your movements', you have 'free will that overcomes everything, if it is well nurtured ("se ben si notrica"), even if it does have to endure hardship in its first battles with the heavens'.[48]

> 'Voi che vivete ogne cagion recate
> pur suso al cielo, pur come se tutto
> movesse seco di necessitate.
> Se così fosse, in voi fora distrutto
> libero arbitrio, e non fora giustizia
> per ben letizia, e per male aver lutto.
> Lo cielo i vostri movimenti inizia;
> non dico tutti, ma, posto ch'i' 'l dica,
> lume v'è dato a bene e a malizia,
> e libero voler; che, se fatica
> ne le prime battaglie col ciel dura,
> poi vince tutto, se ben si notrica.' (*Purg*. XVI, 67–78)

The last two lines take us back to the example of choleric anger chosen by Dante in *Convivio* III to illustrate the concept of an 'innate vice' and the way in which such a vice may be overcome by 'good custom' (if not in its first 'impeto' or 'movimento', at least with regard to its duration). Taken together, the two passages offer a key to the rationale of Dante's Purgatory – 'la religione / de la montagna' – and they suggest that Aristotle is just as much a living presence on 'the mountain that delivers us from evil' ('lo monte che . . . dismala') as he will be in the Empyrean, where perfect happiness is shown to consist in the exercise of our intellectual faculty.[49]

In essence, Purgatory is represented as a 'Reformatory' in which the penitent souls are prepared for the vision of God by a process in which they 'overcome' their dominant vices by constantly repeating the kind of virtuous actions to which they had been 'disinclined' in their earthly existence because of the bad *dispositiones* they had been born with, or the bad *habitus* they had acquired. The process may take a very long time (in the case of Statius, more than a thousand years for one single vice!), but in the end the vices, be they 'consuetudinari' or 'innati', will 'go away completely' thanks to a regime where nothing happens 'without order'.[50]

When the soul has undergone its 're-formation' through 'good custom' on each of the seven circles for whatever period is necessary (Dante indicates that he himself will have to spend a very short time curing himself of the inclination to envy and a very long time purging his pride), its *voluntas* will have been restored to 'health' and 'beauty' since it will have the *debita dispositio*. It will be like a tree that can at last stand 'upright' without its supporting stake. It will 'incline' towards its good. It will feel itself 'free' (free to ascend to the Earthly Paradise for a brief ceremony and thence to the Celestial Paradise). All these Dantean metaphors (and many others besides) are derived from the cool Aristotelian analysis of moral virtue as a *recta habitudo animae*, a *dispositio ordinata in anima*, a *habitus* which 'makes activity well ordered'. And the essential point is that a *habitus* of this kind may be 'acquired' by willing submission and conscious effort.[51]

'Il piacere de la morale dottrina'

In the next chapter we shall touch on the *theological* virtues – which are not 'acquired', but 'infused' by God's grace – and it will become apparent that there is a great deal more to say about Dante's concept of purification. But the main themes of this chapter can be combined and summarised by making another connection between the *Convivio* and a phrase used by Marco Lombardo – 'lume v'è dato a bene e a malizia'.

Becoming good is not just a matter of obedience and patient training of the voluntary power. The cognitive power, too, has an essential role. By the 'light' of the intellect we can discern what is good and bad for us. The intellect sees that the mind is free from the heavens, and that we must lead a life in accordance with our highest power, if we are to be happy as human beings. It was through these insights (as we are told by Virgil in *Purgatorio* XVIII), that the ancient philosophers, unaided by revelation, were able to 'bequeath morality to the world'. If we want to become good, we should also study the principles of ethics.[52]

It is therefore appropriate to end with some eloquent words from the third book of the *Convivio*. Here Dante is interpreting the allegory of one of his own love poems. It is he who reveals that the 'noble lady' whom he is praising is none other than Philosophy. It is he who decodes his own metaphors, telling us what he meant when he said that his 'lady's beauty rains down sparks of fire that generate all good thoughts, and destroy the inborn vices ("l'innati vizii") that make men base'.[53]

'The beauty of philosophy,' he says, 'is morality', understood as the due 'order of the moral virtues'. Morality 'confers righteous desire ("appetito diritto"), and is generated by the pleasure of ethical teaching'. This righteous desire, Dante continues, 'can drive out even the natural vices, not to mention the others'. 'Thence is born that happiness, which Aristotle defines in the first book of the *Ethics*, saying that it is "activity in accordance with virtue in a life that is perfect".' 'By following philosophy, each one of us becomes good.'

> Dove è da sapere che la moralitade è bellezza de la Filosofia . . . e resulta da l'ordine de le vertudi morali, che fanno quella piacere sensibilmente. . . . Sua bieltà, cioè moralitade, piove fiammelle di foco, cioè appetito diritto, che s'ingenera nel piacere de la morale dottrina: lo quale appetito ne diparte eziandio da li vizii naturali, non che da li altri. E quinci nasce quella felicitate la quale diffinisce Aristotile nel primo de l'Etica, dicendo che è 'operazione secondo vertù in vita perfetta' . . . Per seguitare lei diviene ciascuno buono. (*Con.* III, XV, 12–13)

CHAPTER FIVE

Christian values through Dante's eyes[1]

'Quid boni faciam?'

Only once in the Gospel narratives does someone ask Jesus simply and directly 'what good shall I do?' (*quid boni faciam?*), and the episode demands to be re-read in full since it takes us straight to the heart of Christ's ethical teaching, which forms the core of this chapter.

Our version of the story – one of three – is taken from the Gospel of Matthew, and no apology is made for quoting it in the Latin of the Vulgate, for this was the Bible that Dante knew. As usual, the Vulgate follows the original Greek very closely indeed, almost word for word, and the result is not always idiomatic. But the occasional strangeness and lack of elegance seem to be a guarantee that Jerome's translation is faithful. One can see why even such a sophisticated reader as Dante treats the Latin Bible as the Word of God.[2]

The exchange takes place just before Jesus returns from Galilee and Jordan to keep the Passover in Jerusalem. He has twice foretold his coming Passion; he has appeared 'transfigured' on the mountain, conversing with Moses and Elijah; and Simon Peter has already recognised him as the promised Messiah.[3]

Matthew 19.16–26	*Literal translation of the Latin*
Et ecce unus accedens ait illi: Magister bone, quid boni faciam, ut habeam vitam aeternam?	And, look, someone approaching says to him: 'Good master, what good shall I do, that I may have eternal life?'
Qui dixit ei: Quid me interrogas de bono? Unus est bonus, Deus. Si autem vis ad vitam ingredi, serva mandata.	He said to him: 'Why do you ask me about the good? [Only] one is good – God. However, if you want to enter the life, keep the Commandments.'

Dicit illi: Quae? Jesus autem dixit: Non homicidium facies; non adulterabis; non facies furtum; non falsum testimonium dices; honora patrem tuum et matrem tuam, et diliges proximum tuum sicut teipsum. Dicit illi adolescens: Omnia haec custodivi a juventute mea, quid adhuc mihi deest?	He says to him: 'Which?' Jesus said: 'You shall not kill, you shall not commit adultery, you shall not steal, you shall not give false evidence; honour your father and mother, and love your neighbour as yourself.' The young man says to him: 'All these I have kept from my youth; what is still lacking in me?'
Ait illi Jesus: si vis perfectus esse, vade, vende quae habes, et da pauperibus, et habebis thesaurum in caelo; et veni, sequere me.	Jesus says to him: 'If you want to be perfect, go, sell what you have, and give to the poor, and you will have treasure in heaven; and come, follow me.'
Cum audisset autem adolescens verbum, abiit tristis; erat enim habens multas possessiones.	When the young man heard these words, he went away sadly; for he had many possessions.
Jesus autem dixit discipulis suis: Amen dico vobis, quia dives difficile intrabit in regnum caelorum. Et iterum dico vobis: Facilius est camelum per foramen acus transire, quam divitem intrare in regnum caelorum.	But Jesus said to his disciples: 'Truly, I tell you that it is hard for a rich man to enter the kingdom of the heavens. And I tell you again: it is easier for a camel to pass through the eye of a needle than for a rich man to enter the kingdom of the heavens.'
Auditis autem his, discipuli mirabantur valde, dicentes: Quis ergo poterit salvus esse?	On hearing these words, the disciples were greatly astonished, saying: 'Who then can be saved?'
Aspiciens autem Jesus, dixit illis: Apud homines hoc impossibile est; apud Deum omnia possibilia sunt.	Looking at them, Jesus said: 'With men, this is impossible; with God, all things are possible.'

The language and style are characteristically plain and simple. Syntactically, it is no more complicated than the kind of anecdote one overhears on a bus, with its short phrases in direct speech and the compulsive repetitions ('I said to him' and 'He says to me' and 'I tell you straight'). But there is considerable art. The scene is unobtrusively framed by the arrival and departure of the rich young man who puts the question; and each successive exchange between him and Jesus moves the dialogue on towards its climax. The startling conclusion is driven home by the no less startling simile of a camel passing through the eye of a needle. Anyone over the age of five can understand these words, and few people are likely to forget them.

Yet although the passage is like a 'river shallow enough for lambs to paddle in', it is 'deep enough for elephants to swim'. (This lovely two-part simile was used by Gregory the Great to describe the Psalms and by Boccaccio to describe the *Comedy*.) It touches on eternal life, the kingdom of Heaven, the contrast between earthly and heavenly treasure, the relation of Christ's teaching to the Mosaic Law, the desire not just for goodness but for perfection, the quest for 'salvation', the need to 'follow' Christ, the impotence of human agents and the omnipotence of God.[4]

'Iota unum aut unus apex non praeteribit a lege'

We may begin our survey of Christian values by considering Jesus' attitude to the moral teaching of the existing Jewish Law. His popular reputation had made him an object of suspicion to the religious establishment (the Scribes and Pharisees); and the young man's question – especially his use of the phrase 'good master' – was interpreted by some of the Fathers as one of many attempts to embroil Jesus with the authorities. But from the beginning of his mission, Jesus had insisted that he came not 'to replace the Law but to fulfil it' ('non veni solvere, sed *adimplere*'). With his usual vividness, he had declared that not even the 'smallest letter or superscript sign' would ever be omitted, and that the person who has both 'done and taught' the commandments 'shall be called great in the kingdom of Heaven'. In this episode, too, the young man is told that if he wants to 'do something good' (*facere aliquid boni*), he must observe the *mandata* (or *praecepta*, as they are called in Mark's version of the story).[5]

It is clear from his brief checklist ('non homicidium facies' etc.) that Jesus is thinking primarily of the Commandments which Moses received from God on Mount Sinai, written on tablets of stone. These are only ten in number, but are so comprehensive that Aquinas said of them 'all the moral injunctions of God's law are contained in those of the Decalogue' ('omnia praecepta moralia legis divinae continentur in praeceptis decalogi'); so it is to these we must now turn.[6]

Praecepta moralia

The text of the Commandments is given with only minor variants in two different books of the Old Testament (Exodus 20 and Deuteronomy 5).

The first four regulate the relationship of the chosen people to God, the remaining six govern the relationship of the individual to others (our parents, and those whom the Bible describes as people 'near to us', our *proximi* or 'neighbours').[7]

Let us start with the second group, which may be summarised as follows: honour your parents; do not kill, do not commit adultery, do not steal, do not tell lies in court; do not covet your neighbour's wife or anything belonging to your neighbour. It will be seen that five of the six are cast in negative form. The answer to the question *quid boni faciam?*, 'what good shall I do?', turns out to be *ne facies aliquid mali*, 'thou shalt not do anything bad'. The point is an important one. Aristotle had begun by defining the nature of goodness before going on to describe the vices as deviations from the norm. The Commandments, by contrast, seem to define 'human worth' in terms of 'human vices'. Moral 'health', we might say, means freedom from the moral 'diseases'. And the difference between the two attitudes is, in part at least, that between a guarded optimism concerning human nature and a deep-seated pessimism.[8]

Despite the difference of emphasis between the religious and the philosophical approaches, however, there is no disagreement at this basic level about what is good or bad. Aquinas comments that 'the moral precepts should always be observed by everyone because they are part of natural law' ('praecepta moralia servari debent semper ab omnibus quia sunt *de lege naturali*'). They are 'about the things that natural reason dictates' ('de iis, quae *naturalis ratio dictat*'). They may not include the most fundamental precept of natural justice ('do as you would be done by'), but they contain nothing abstruse or remotely controversial. They are primary and binding on everyone at all times.[9]

'Deus noster pepigit nobiscum foedus'

The first four Commandments – which concern man's relationship with God – require that the people of Israel shall not worship other gods or make any carved image, shall not take the name of the Lord in vain, and shall remember to keep the Sabbath day holy. Considered in themselves, they may seem to lie beyond our brief, but the words that frame the commands prove to be of the utmost importance. As Moses reminds his hearers in Deuteronomy 5, 'our God made a pact with us' ('Deus noster pepigit nobiscum *foedus*'), 'speaking to us face to face' ('facie ad faciem locutus est nobis'). The Israelites are his people; he is their God. He is jealous (*aemulator*) of rivals. Wrongdoing becomes tantamount to hating him. He promises to 'be merciful to those who love him and keep his commands' ('*diligentibus* me et custodientibus praecepta mea'), but to punish 'those who have hated him' ('qui *oderunt* me'). All the commandments are to be interpreted within the context of a covenant (*pactum*) implying a personal, 'I–thou' relationship ('*Ego* sum Dominus, Deus *tuus*').[10]

It is also important that this pact between God and the Israelites presupposes a highly specific vision of time and human history, in which all significant events can be dated generation by generation from the beginning of the world. The positive command to keep the Sabbath holy is a reminder that God is the Creator of the universe and of mankind (God himself rested from his labours on the seventh day); and the three negative injunctions are framed by explicit reminders that it was God who led the Israelites out of 'the house of slavery' in Egypt. God will keep his promises (as will be narrated in the remaining books of the Bible). There could hardly be a greater contrast with the timeless or cyclical approach found in polytheistic religions, or in a philosopher like Aristotle.

'Love God, obey his voice and cleave to him'

During the years in the wilderness, Moses went on to enunciate a total of 613 *praecepta*, which further regulate relationships between individuals and the crucial relationship between Israel and God. Not for nothing does Dante refer to him in the *Comedy* as 'Moisè *legista*'! But the principles do not change. All the commands form part of the same *pactum*, and all of them are backed by promises of divine reward or retribution. Just before he died, Moses said that the people must choose between 'life and death', between the 'good' and a 'blessing' (*bonum, benedictio*), or the 'bad' and a 'curse' (*malum, maledictio*). He urged them: 'Choose life, that you may live and love the Lord your God, and obey his voice, and cleave to him, for he is your life' ('Elige ergo vitam, ut et tu vivas . . . et diligas Dominum Deum tuum, atque obedias voci eius et illi adhaereas; ipse est enim vita tua').[11]

Adam and Eve were punished by expulsion from Eden because they disobeyed the command not to eat of 'the tree of the knowledge of good and evil'. That knowledge (in Latin, *scientia boni et mali*) was subsequently revealed by God himself, especially in the Commandments he gave to Moses on Mount Sinai. But to do good (*facere aliquid boni*) still means to obey God. 'God alone is good' ('unus est bonus, Deus'). He is 'all goodness', 'omne bonum'.

This last phrase was used by God himself when he answered Moses' request to be allowed to see his 'glory': 'ego ostendam omne *bonum* tibi', 'I shall show you all good.' This in turn is the phrase that Dante will translate in *Paradiso* as 'Io ti farò vedere ogne *valore*.'[12]

'God is Love'

When the young man asked which commandments he should observe, Jesus reminded him of the first five in the group of six concerning our relationship with others, but he replaced the last one (forbidding us to covet anything belonging to anyone else) with another, in positive form, taken from the Book of Leviticus: 'You shall love your neighbour as yourself', 'diliges proximum tuum sicut teipsum'. A little later in Matthew's narrative, in answer to a similar question, he goes one step further. He says in effect that the whole of the second group can be summarised in the command 'Love your neighbour', just as the first group can be reduced to 'Love God'. The Decalogue has been pared down to two positive commands, both requiring us to love (*diligere*).

Matthew 22.35–40	*Literal translation of the Latin*
Et interrogavit eum unus ex eis legis doctor, tentans eum: Magister, quod est mandatum magnum in lege?	And one of [the Pharisees], an expert in the law, asked him a question, testing him: 'Master, which is the great commandment in the Law?'
Ait illi Jesus: Diliges Dominum Deum tuum ex toto corde tuo, et in tota anima tua, et in tota mente tua. Hoc est maximum, et primum mandatum.	Jesus says to him: 'You shall love the Lord your God with your whole heart, in your whole soul, and with your whole mind. That is the greatest and first commandment.
Secundum autem simile est huic: Diliges proximum tuum, sicut teipsum. In his duobus mandatis universa lex pendet, et prophetae.	The second is like it. You shall love your neighbour as yourself. On these two commandments hangs the whole of the law – and the prophets.'

This central lesson is universalised (without reference to the context of Mosaic Law) in the first letter attributed to St John the Evangelist. There we are told that the power to love each other comes from God; that love allows us to know God, and without it we cannot know him;

and, finally, that God *is* Love (just as he is *omne bonum*). Once again, these words demand to be re-read in the Latin that Dante knew, where the verb 'to love' is still *diligere*, but the noun becomes *charitas* (in significant word-play with the opening vocative, *charissimi*).[13]

First Letter of John 4.7–8	*Literal translation of the Latin*
Charissimi, diligamus nos invicem: quia charitas ex Deo est. Et omnis qui diligit, ex Deo natus est, et cognoscit Deum.	Dearly beloved, let us love each other; for love is from God. And everyone who loves, is born of God, and knows God.
Qui non diligit, non novit Deum: quoniam Deus charitas est.	The person who does not love, does not know God; because God is love.

'Be perfect, as your Father in Heaven is perfect'

Loving of this kind is not just a state of the heart or a matter of aspiration. (Jesus is always scathing about those who do not practise what they preach.) It demands the perfection that Jesus had earlier described in the Sermon on the Mount, to which we now turn.[14]

The Mosaic law that Jesus came to 'fulfil' laid down practical procedures for reconciling litigants; and it enjoined, but only where appropriate, forgiveness for injuries and the remission of debts. For graver offences it upheld the principle of retaliation – the so-called *lex talionis*, which demands 'an eye for an eye, a tooth for a tooth'. Jesus rejects this. In the Sermon on the Mount, he examines the chief commandments of the second group in turn. He insists that we should refrain not just from killing, but from being angry with our brother and calling him a 'fool'. To see and lust after a woman is already to be guilty of 'adultery in the heart'. With regard to the *lex talionis*, not only should we *not* demand an 'eye for an eye', we should not even resist attack. 'If anyone should strike your right cheek, offer him the other; if anyone sues you for a tunic, give him a cloak; if anyone forces you to walk a mile, go with him another two.' In short: 'Love your *enemies*'; because 'if you love those who love you, what merit will you have?' ('si enim diligitis eos qui vos diligunt, quam mercedem habebitis?'). 'Don't even non-Jews do that?' ('nonne et ethnici hoc faciunt?').[15]

Familiarity may have blunted the impact of these revolutionary demands because so many of Jesus' phrases have become proverbial. But the final rhetorical question should remind us that there was nothing remotely comparable in ancient polytheism, classical philosophy or Roman law. Perfect love and total forgiveness were the new and central values of what was to become a new and universal religion.

The form and content of a Hebrew beatitude

In the opening words of the Sermon on the Mount Jesus had already given eight overlapping answers to the other major question in moral philosophy: 'Who may be called truly happy (*beatus*)?' And the concept of happiness they propose is no less challenging than the notion of goodness we have been examining until now.

In the Old Testament, *beatus* occurs most frequently in the poetic books, that is, in the Psalms and the Wisdom literature. Typically, it occurs at the head of an exclamation embodying a universal statement. *Beatus vir qui* or *beatus qui* (literally, 'Supremely happy is he who') is equivalent to something like 'Supreme happiness consists in'. Hence 'beatus vir qui timet Deum' might be paraphrased as 'Perfect happiness comes from fearing God.' Usually, but by no means always, the context implies that God himself is the giver of that happiness, which is why the adjective is usually translated into English as 'blessed'. But, as we have seen earlier (p. 34), there was no absolute distinction between the words *beatus* and *felix* (they are used, for example, as synonyms in parallel clauses in Ecclesiasticus). And a divine 'blessing' (*benedictio*) may well be of a material kind. (In his last days, Job was 'blessed' with a huge increase in his flocks, and with ten children, his daughters being the 'most beautiful women on the whole earth'.)[16]

In texts from the Old Testament, blessedness will typically be ascribed to those who 'walk in the ways of the Lord and meditate upon the Law'; to those who 'love wisdom'; or those who are generous to the poor. At a more humble level, however, true happiness may come from finding a friend or having a virtuous wife.[17]

What is true happiness?

Such, then, were the patterns of poetical form and ethical content in a Hebrew 'beatitude', which must have been present in the minds of the 'many crowds' who at this time were following Jesus 'from Galilee and Decapolis, and from Jerusalem, and from Judaea, and from across the Jordan', because his fame as a healer and teacher 'had gone out through all Syria'.[18]

Jesus had begun his mission by teaching 'in their synagogues'; but at this point his hearers had become so numerous that he 'went up a mountain'. There he 'opened his mouth', uttering no fewer than eight consecutive beatitudes which have lost none of their power to move and astonish. (At the close of his discourse Matthew reports that 'the crowds were amazed at his teaching', because he 'taught them not like one of their scribes, or the Pharisees, but as one having authority': 'erat enim docens eos sicut potestatem habens'.)[19]

Who are the truly happy? Before we let Jesus reply in his own words, it will be helpful to indicate the claimants who are implicitly rejected; and it will be helpful also to follow Dante's example and examine the Beatitudes out of their canonical order.[20]

The *beati*, Jesus implies, are not those who seek sensual pleasures or unworthy advantages, nor those who submit to injustice for the sake of a quiet life. (These claims are hardly controversial, but they exclude the majority of mankind.) They are not those who proudly assert their own rights, seek restoration or retaliation when the law allows, and are willing to go to war. (It could certainly be argued that this group includes Aristotle's *magnanimi*, *justi* and *fortes*.) They are not those who would seem to have every occasion to rejoice, because they enjoy honour in the community and the kind of blessings that were heaped on Job at the end of his life. (Here the assertions become deliberately paradoxical.)[21]

No, the truly happy – to take them in the same order – are those with a pure heart (*mundo corde*), those who hunger and thirst for what is right (*qui esuriunt et sitiunt justitiam*), those who are humble and mild (*pauperes spiritu*; *mites*), those who are forgiving (*misericordes*), and those who make peace, not war (*pacifici*). Finally, the truly blessed are those who mourn and those who suffer persecution (*qui lugent*; *qui persecutionem patiuntur*). It is precisely the people in this last category whom Jesus tells to 'rejoice and exult' (*gaudete et exsultate*)![22]

'Merces in caelis'

The assertions seem somewhat less paradoxical when they are read in conjunction with the second phrase in each Beatitude, which is always introduced by the word *quoniam* ('because'), and – in all except the first – has its verb in the future tense. The merciful *will* find mercy. Those who grieve *will* be consoled. In other words, they can be called happy now, because they are filled with joyful anticipation of a state they can take only on trust.[23]

The promises made by God to the patriarchs were of flocks and lands – and of descendants to enjoy these if they themselves should not live to see the day. This is surely how the Jews in the wilderness would have understood the words 'for they shall possess the earth' ('quoniam ipsi possidebunt terram'). But in five of the eight beatitudes it is made clear that the future happiness will come only in another place. What they are being offered is 'abundant reward in *Heaven*' (*merces copiosa in caelis*). The 'kingdom of the heavens' is to be theirs. It is there that they will become 'sons of God' or 'see God' (the expressions are virtually synonymous). It is there they will enjoy the 'eternal life' (*vita aeterna*) sought by the rich young man, which in turn is the same as the 'treasure in heaven' (*thesaurus in caelo*) that would be his, if he were to sell his many possessions, give to the poor, and follow Jesus.[24]

The meaning of the Beatitudes is of course inseparable from the rhythms and repetitions of the poetic form, which can be seen (if not heard) in the Vulgate version of the first seven:

> Beati pauperes spiritu:
>   quoniam ipsorum est regnum caelorum.
> Beati mites:
>   quoniam ipsi possidebunt terram.
> Beati qui lugent:
>   quoniam ipsi consolabuntur.
> Beati qui esuriunt et sitiunt justitiam:
>   quoniam ipsi saturabuntur.
> Beati misericordes:
>   quoniam ipsi misericordiam consequentur.
> Beati mundo corde:
>   quoniam ipsi Deum videbunt.
> Beati pacifici:
>   quoniam filii Dei vocabuntur.[25]

It is difficult not to labour the obvious at this point or to be drawn away from the subject of 'human worth', but a few words must be added concerning the afterlife – if only because 'the state of souls after death' is the literal subject of Dante's *Comedy*.

Jesus himself offers no more than a few generic metaphors and parables to characterise what have come to be called Heaven and Hell, although he does refer to a place of torment by fire, Gehenna, in which there will be 'weeping and gnashing of teeth', as well as to a glorious land above the sky, where invited guests will sit down to feast with the Father. He frequently looks forward to the not too distant day when the

Son of Man will come 'to judge the living and the dead', a day when 'the first shall be last and the last shall be first' – an inversion of expectations, which, at one level, may be interpreted as his way of asserting the radical difference between this-worldly and other-worldly values. By sharpening the contrast between the judgement of men and the judgement of God, or between earthly and heavenly measures and rewards, Jesus was giving an opening (if no more) for the pessimism of those of his followers who would later deny the possibility of attaining any kind of happiness in this life. And he was also giving an opening – in the very much longer term – to those who would reject his notion of goodness because it seems to depend on a promise of 'pie in the sky when you die'.[26]

'Peccatores'; 'parvuli'; 'patiens usque ad mortem'

There are three further general points to make about the *doctrina* which caused such astonishment to those who heard the Sermon on the Mount.

First, Jesus' message appealed to the 'great crowds' because he deliberately addressed himself to the poor and the have-nots, to those with lowly occupations (his first disciples were fishermen), to the social outcasts (he was reproached for associating with prostitutes and tax-collectors), and to communities of non-Jews (such as the inhabitants of Samaria). His words were aimed not at the self-satisfied, but at those who had certainly not 'kept all the Commandments from their youth', who had never even dreamed of becoming 'perfect', and who regarded themselves as sinners (*peccatores*). He was celebrating virtues that are relevant to the forgotten two-thirds of the human race who are rarely mentioned in the moral philosophy of the *ethnici* or *gentiles* – women and children! (Immediately before the episode with the young man, Jesus had insisted that his disciples should allow children to be brought to him, repeating the promise he made to the *pauperes spiritu*: 'theirs is the kingdom of Heaven'.) The values he proclaimed were genuinely universal – 'catholic' in the original Greek sense of the word.[27]

Second, Jesus is promising blessedness to a group he is calling into existence, the people who will 'follow him' (as he invited the rich young man to do), becoming, in Dante's phrase, 'messaggi de l'etterno regno', 'messengers of the eternal kingdom'. They will have to endure slander, persecution and death in order to bear witness to his teaching and promise of salvation (*mártyros* is the Greek word for 'witness'). In a sense it was the paradoxical definition of happiness – the acceptance of suffering on earth to ensure joy in Heaven – that made it possible for the new faith to spread as it did.[28]

Third, Jesus did later suggest that suffering itself may sometimes be a good rather than an evil. One has to be prepared to 'take up the cross' in order to follow him. And suffering may develop capacities for unselfish goodness that would otherwise remain unrealised. Metaphorically, it may be like the fire which liberates a precious metal from the dross with which it is compounded in nature. Jesus taught his followers to pray that they might 'not be brought to the test' ('ne nos inducas in tentationem'). He himself asked that 'the cup might be taken' from him. But it was only by accepting a cruel death as the sacrificial 'Lamb of God' that he could 'take away the sins of the world'.[29]

'Locutus est multa in parabolis'; 'fac similiter'[30]

We have taken note of the marked contrast in style and impact between the crisp epigrams, uttered in the cut and thrust of debate, and the rhythmic incantations of the Beatitudes. But Jesus was also master of a third and very different literary genre, which has become inseparable in the popular mind from the content of his thought. This comprises the many little allegories and fables called *parabolae*, in which a complex message is conveyed indirectly through a few stark details in a narrative, or through concrete imagery taken largely from work in the fields or festivities in the townships.[31]

The parables cover a wide range of themes, and since they are by definition open-ended and multivalent, it will not be possible to do them anything like justice here. But they are much too important to be ignored altogether; and there is one distinctive element in Jesus' teaching which finds expression in the parables above all. This is the need to transform good feelings or intentions into 'good works', *opera bona* (and it may be remembered that, for Dante, ethics is a practical science, *ad opus*, dealing with '*operazioni* umane').[32]

A good tree is known by the goodness of its fruit. A fruitless tree, having been given a second chance, should be cut down and burned. Jesus' followers must not hide their light under a bushel, but let it shine so that men may see their good works ('sic luceat lux vestra coram hominibus, ut videant vestra *opera bona*').[33]

Prudence is required to direct one's actions to a good end. This may involve the calculation of risks before a battle, the choice of a suitable building site, the purchase of stores in advance, and the need for vigilance at all times. Great emphasis is laid on doing one's duty: the labourer must earn his wage in the vineyard, a judge must find time to administer justice even if the supplicant is only a poor widow. A good and faithful servant will not defraud his master, but seek to make a profit on his behalf. However, Jesus is also thinking of service well beyond the call of duty. A good shepherd is one who is willing to lay down his life to protect his flock.[34]

Help must be given to those in need, and not just to the poor, the hungry and the sick, but to those who may excite repugnance for various reasons – the blind, the deformed, the imprisoned, foreigners. Conventional values are continually challenged in this area. A beggar, whose wounds were licked by the dogs, may be received in the kingdom of Heaven, while the rich man, who gave banquets every day, may be consigned to Hell. The widow's mite is worth more, morally speaking, than the rich man's sovereign, because she has given all she had.[35]

Many of these themes come together in two of the best known of all the parables. The first, too long to quote, is that of the Prodigal Son, where the father angers the dutiful elder son by killing the fatted calf to celebrate the return of the wastrel who has repented and seeks forgiveness. The second is that of the Good Samaritan. It can lay claim to be the most effective piece of moral teaching ever put into words; and it demands to be read again here, by way of summary, in the unfamiliar Latin which was so familiar to Dante.

It is told at the point in Luke's narrative where Jesus has reasserted the Great Commandment ('diliges Deum . . . et proximum tuum'). His questioner goes on to ask: 'Quis est meus proximus?', 'Who precisely is my "neighbour", whom I must love?' And Jesus launches straight into his example, before replying, Jewish fashion, with his own question.[36]

Our emotions are immediately engaged on behalf of the nameless victim by the gratuitous violence of the robbers (expressed in the strong words *despoliare*, *plagae* and *semivivus*). We are then appalled by the indifference of two members of the religious establishment who refuse to turn aside or stop (in the Latin version, their coldheartedness is conveyed very simply by the verbs *praeterire* and *pertransire*, 'to go past' and 'to go through'). But even without this preliminary contrast, and even if we do not immediately understand the unfriendly relationship between Jews and Samaritans, we are moved by the hero's instant compassion ('videns eum, misericordia motus est'), and are stirred by the extra solicitude implied in his use of oil and wine, or in his final offer to reimburse the innkeeper for whatever he may spend in addition to the payment left in advance. This Samaritan *loved.* He loved an unknown person from a *rival* community. Above all, his love led to appropriate *action* ('*fecit* misericordiam). And the message to us is: '*Act* in the same way', '*fac* similiter'.

Luke 10.29–37	*Literal translation of the Latin*
Homo quidam descendebat ab Jerusalem in Jericho, et incidit in latrones, qui etiam despoliaverunt eum: et plagis impositis abierunt semivivo relicto.	'A certain man was going down from Jerusalem to Jericho, and he came upon thieves, who [not only robbed him, but] also stripped him, and having delivered blows, went off, leaving him [only] half-alive.
Accidit autem ut sacerdos quidam descenderet eadem via: et viso illo praeterivit.	It happened that a certain priest came down by the same road; and having seen him, went straight past.
Similiter et levita, cum esset secus locum, et videret eum, pertransiit.	Similarly, a Levite, when he was beside the place and saw him, went through.
Samaritanus autem videns eum, misericordia motus est. Et appropians alligavit vulnera eius, infundens oleum et vinum: et imponens illum in jumentum suum, duxit in stabulum, et curam eius egit.	A Samaritan, however, on seeing him, was moved by pity. And going up, he bound his wounds, pouring in oil and wine; and placing him on his mule, he led him to an inn and took care of him.
Et altera die protulit duos denarios, et dedit stabulario, et ait: Curam illius habe: et quodcumque supererogaveris, ego cum rediero reddam tibi.	And on the next day, he took out two coins and gave them to the inn-keeper, and said: "Take care of him; and whatever you may further spend, when I return, I shall repay you."
Quis horum trium videtur tibi proximus fuisse illi, qui incidit in latrones?	Which of these three seems to you to have been "neighbour" to the man who fell among the thieves?'
At ille dixit: qui fecit misericordiam in illum.	And he said: 'The one who took pity on him.'
Et ait illi Jesus: Vade, et tu fac similiter.	And Jesus said to him: 'Go, and you too, do likewise.'

'Quemadmodum ego feci vobis, ita et vos faciatis'

Up to this point we have concentrated exclusively on Jesus' words or sayings (*dicta*); but the person whose mission and death are described in the Gospels is someone who lived up to his own precepts, and his actions (*facta*) are, if anything, more persuasive than his words. We are certainly invited to imitate the example of the Samaritan in the literary example (*fac similiter*); but we are also invited to imitate the real Jesus. That is what 'following' Jesus really means.

Jesus not infrequently resorts to verbal violence, as in the diatribes (another literary genre inherited from tradition), in which his particular target is the hypocrisy of the Pharisees, whose deeds do not match their words. In other respects, though, he is unfailingly gentle. He loves his *proximi* even when – or above all when – they are unlovely and unlovable. He is full of compassion (*misericors*); and he is mild in manner (*mitis*), even when abused and beaten. He 'hungers for what is right' (as shown in his reverence for the spirit of the Law), and he is a 'peace-maker' (as in the episode of the woman taken in adultery). He is obedient to the will of God, suffering persecution patiently, accepting death on the Cross ('patiens usque ad mortem, mortem autem crucis'). He asks forgiveness even for the soldiers who crucified him, because 'they know not what they do'.[37]

These are the aspects of his life that Dante had in mind in the following passage from the *Monarchia*, which sums up everything that has been said so far:

> The substantial form of the church is quite simply the life of Christ, comprising both his words and his actions ('forma Ecclesiae . . . est vita Christi, tam in dictis quam in factis comprehensa'). His life is the model and pattern for the church on earth, particularly for its 'shepherds' [the priesthood], and, above all, for the supreme 'shepherd' [the pope], whose duty it is to 'guard the lambs and the sheep'. Hence Christ himself, in the gospel of John, when bequeathing the form of his life, said, 'I have given you a model, so that you should act as I have done to you' ('*Exemplum* dedi vobis, ut quemadmodum ego feci vobis, ita *et vos faciatis*'). And addressing himself especially to Peter, after he had entrusted him with the office of 'shepherd', as we read in the same gospel, he said: 'Peter, follow me.'[38] (*Mon.* III, xv, 3–4)

Christianity in Medieval Europe

We have now reviewed the central Christian values as they first found expression in the evangelists' record of Jesus' sayings and doings. In the remaining third of this chapter we must examine the so-called 'theological' virtues – Faith, Hope and Charity – as they were understood in Dante's time. To make sense of these, we shall have to touch on major subjects such as original sin, redemption, and grace (not to mention the doctrine of the Trinity), which lie well outside the scope of this book, but which do much to determine the Christian understanding of human vices and human worth.

On all these topics, as we saw in Chapter 1, Dante's *documenta spiritualia* were not limited to the Gospels, but included the writings of St Paul, the Doctors of the Church and the scholastic theologians. A few words therefore need to be said concerning the situation in which the Christian message was received thirteen hundred years after the birth of Christ, a situation that was radically different from anything to be found in the largely secular Western world today, and no less radically different from that in the Eastern provinces of the Roman Empire in the first century AD.

Christianity was no longer a minority cult, whose adherents were persecuted because they were considered subversive. Western Europe had a single, universal church headed by the Pope, who was acknowledged as the vicar of Christ on earth, and who exercised enormous political influence. The church had jurisdiction over everyone in holy orders and had its own elaborate corpus of canon law. It enjoyed huge revenues. It was physically present in every local community in the form of a consecrated building capable of holding all the members of a parish. This building was the workplace of a priest, who administered the sacraments that nourished and regulated the Christian life. Communal worship took place in regular services with an elaborate liturgy, varying from week to week, but unchanging from year to year. Readings from the Bible constantly reproposed the original moral teaching; and sermons in the vernacular showed how it should be applied in the daily life of the community. No other form of religious practice was officially tolerated by any of the political communities in Western Europe. In many respects, the church was so firmly established that it had come to resemble the synagogue in Jesus' culture. Well-off Christians were often far more like the Scribes and Pharisees than the 'many crowds' who had followed the 'son of the carpenter in Nazareth'.

Over the centuries, the core teaching had been been expanded by reference to countless other texts in the Old and New Testaments, and adapted to the infinite variety of circumstances in societies quite unlike those addressed by Moses and Jesus. It had been enriched by cross-fertilisation with the pagan philosophers. Learned saints (such as Augustine and Gregory) had acquired the status of 'authorities'. The ethic had been 'put to the question', 'divided and numerated', and taken up into syntheses of the kind we sampled in Aquinas's *Summa Theologiae*. In short, Jesus' *dicta* and *facta* might well have been smothered and lost to view by the year 1300 (the fictional date of Dante's *Comedy*), were it not for the fact that reformers periodically challenged the worldliness of the established church and the sheer complexity of theology or canon law, by returning to the values enshrined in the parable of the Good Samaritan, in the Sermon on the Mount, or in the answers given to the 'rich young man', with which we began.

Jesus as the 'Son of God', the 'Word made flesh'

The most recent example in Dante's society of this kind of challenge had been the astonishing career of Francis of Assisi in the first half of the thirteenth century. He too had been a rich young man. He too wanted to be 'perfect', to be 'saved', and to enjoy 'eternal life' in the 'kingdom of Heaven'. But he did not 'walk sadly away'. He renounced his father's 'many possessions' and imitated Jesus' *exemplum*. And his own followers (the 'Frati minori') continued his mission by bringing the message of the Gospels to men of good will in the rapidly expanding cities of central and northern Italy – not least in Dante's Florence.

Francis, then, was living proof that it was still possible to 'sell all one has and follow Jesus'. But his life of self-abnegation, coupled with the fact of his influence over the citizens of a mercantile, self-governing commune like Florence, do nevertheless raise some fundamental questions. Why should perfection be impossible for a virtuous man who has obeyed the Commandments? Why is it so hard for a rich man to enter the kingdom of Heaven? Why do we need to be 'saved'? And from what? These are the issues that must be addressed – however cursorily – before we can understand the 'theological' virtues.

At this point it is important to reflect that most of the words and deeds of Jesus presented in this chapter could, in principle, have been attributed to any of the Jewish prophets who were his predecessors. They too claimed to have a mission from God. They too used rhetoric and poetry to soften the hearts of the people of Israel, and to persuade them to return to the Lord and obey his commandments. They too suffered persecution for their preaching. But in many passages in the Gospels Jesus makes far greater claims on his own behalf. He is the Son of God (still a blasphemous assertion for Jews and Moslems). He has been sent to do the will, not just of God, but of his Father. He personally has the power to 'forgive sins' (a blasphemy for the Pharisees and High Priests). In the near future he will come in glory to 'judge the living and the dead', determining who shall be admitted to 'eternal life' on the 'right hand of the Father', and who shall be 'cast into outer darkness'. 'No one comes to the Father', he says, 'save through me'.[39]

'Cur Deus homo?' The nature of Adam's 'peccatum originale'

Jesus's claim to be the Son of God posed a new and totally different question, namely '*Why* did God become a man?', *Cur Deus homo?* This succinct formulation is the title of a work written at the beginning of the twelfth century by Saint Anselm. He was the man who defined theology so memorably as 'Faith seeking understanding'; and it is *his* solution to the problem that will be sketched out in what follows, since it was not only accepted by the scholastics of the thirteenth century, but expounded with characteristic verve and density by Dante in *Paradiso* VII.

To understand the kind of answer given by Anselm and Dante, one has to be aware of the interaction between three distinct patterns of thought deriving from three different areas – religion, justice and history.

The first – deep in the background – is the atavistic belief, common to many religions, that a god who has been angered by human wrongdoing may be appeased by appropriate sacrifices offered in expiation, and, especially, by the sacrifice, on behalf of a whole community, of a single human being, whose blood will wash away the stain of the crime.

The second – very much in the foreground – forms part of a sophisticated concept of justice, understood as a set of ordered relationships. If Gaius injures Titius in some way, he has disturbed the proper relationship between him and his neighbour; and, far more important, he has disturbed the proper relationship between himself and society (whose customs and laws forbid him to act as he did). Order can be restored, but only if Gaius makes 'satisfaction' (a crucial technical term). To do this, he must compensate Titius (in the simplest case by paying him 'damages' for the 'damage' he caused). But he must also suffer a penalty imposed by society (which, again in the simplest case, might be the payment of a monetary fine). Once satisfaction has been made, justice has been done and order restored.[40]

The third pattern of thought derives from the Jewish way of conceiving history as the narrative of a special relationship between the people of Israel and the Lord their God. It was a troubled relationship, as we have seen, which consisted of a series of insurrections and reconciliations that could be traced right back to the creation of the universe, when Adam promptly disobeyed God's only command by 'eating of the tree of the knowledge of good and evil'. In the later Christian interpretation of that 'first disobedience', Adam had not only offended God, but had injured *himself* to such an extent that he was no longer capable of making 'satisfaction'. In terms of the simple monetary metaphor, he no longer had the 'wherewithal' to pay either the penalty or the damages. And, far worse, he had transmitted that plight to his descendants. Human worth had been permanently devalued. Of all the many assumptions that differentiate the religious and philosophical approaches to morality in the Middle Ages, there is none more important than the Christian doctrine of 'original sin', *peccatum originale*.[41]

The nature of that self-injury was expressed and interpreted through a range of traditional images. In spatial terms, it was a fall from the heights of Heaven to earth (or to the pit below); or it was a self-distancing from God, a turning aside from the true way, a permanent exile from the native land. In terms related to the body, the injury was like a wasting illness, like being blinded, or like amputation of the limbs. If the soul was imaged as a kingdom, however, original sin became an act of rebellion, in which the throne was usurped by a tyrant (in the person of the animal instincts). Mankind now existed in a condition of permanent 'slavery'.

In this condition of bondage to original sin, the 'slaves' could never earn the means to purchase their lost freedom. If they were to be set free, someone else would have to 'buy them back out' of their bondage – to 'redeem' them. (The root of the English word is *redimere/redemptum*, from *emere/emptum* 'to buy'.) But who could assume the role of 'Redeemer'? The only person able to pay the infinite penalty (incurred by an offence against an infinite being) was God himself. And he was the stern judge whose task it was to ensure that satisfaction be made.

This was the impasse that remained unsolved – in the chronology accepted by Dante – for 5198 years.[42]

'Why God willed this means for our redemption'[43]

Christians, of course, know that the Redeemer was to be Jesus, considered as the Son of God. The question as formulated by Anselm could therefore be recast to read: 'Why did God choose the Incarnation of his Son for our Redemption?' Dante's answer to the question in this form is entrusted to Beatrice; and her long speech is so detailed and so clear that it will be enough to offer a prose translation of her words. (Apart from a few cuts and some minor expansions, the following version is extremely close.)

> Adam damned himself and all his descendants by refusing to accept a curb on his desires. Mankind lay infirm for many centuries until the Word of God was pleased to descend into Mary's womb, where he united human nature to himself in his own person by a single act of eternal love (*Par.* VII, 25–33).
>
> Adam was created in God's image, endowed with the gifts of immortality and freedom. Sin made him unfree and unlike God (64–78). To lose those gifts was to fall from the perfection or full dignity of his nature ('sua nobiltà', 'sua dignità'), to which he could never return, if he did not replenish, by means of just penalties, what guilt had emptied away ('se non si riempie, dove colpa vòta . . . con giuste pene'). The whole of human nature sinned in its first ancestor (79–85).
>
> Human nature could be recovered only by going through one of two fords ('guadi'). Either God in his courtesy would grant a pardon ('avesse dimesso'); or man by his own powers would make satisfaction for his presumption ('avesse *sodisfatto* a sua follia') (85–93). But man, in his limits, could never make satisfaction ('non potea mai *sodisfar*') and hence was precluded from so doing (l'uom fue / da poter *sodisfar* per sé dischiuso') (97–102).
>
> God had to use his own ways to restore man to fullness of life ('riparar l'omo a sua intera vita') – either by mercy, or by justice, or both together (103–5). In his goodness, he decided to proceed by all his ways ('per tutte le sue vie') to raise man up again (109–11).
>
> In giving himself, in order to enable man to raise himself, God was more generous than if he had simply granted a pardon ('s'elli avesse sol da sé dimesso'). Every other possibility would have been inadequate, if the Son of God had not humbled himself to take on flesh ('se 'l Figliuol di Dio / non fosse umiliato ad incarnarsi') (115–20). This was the mode God wanted for our Redemption (57–8).

The Holy Spirit and the role of grace

By suffering death on the Cross, Jesus paid the just penalty, on behalf of all mankind, which Adam and his descendants had been unable to pay. One man had 'corrupted' human nature (by metaphorically casting it down, infecting and maiming it, enslaving it to the instincts); and one man had 'regenerated' it (by metaphorically raising it, healing and restoring its powers, setting it free). The gates of the kingdom of Heaven, which had remained closed since the Fall, had at long last been opened to admit the souls of the virtuous. The *justorum animae* could now become 'children of God', and 'see God', and enjoy 'eternal life', just as Jesus had promised in the Beatitudes. More than this: by humbling himself to take on human flesh, and then rising from the dead, Jesus had in effect reconsecrated the body and had given a pledge (as Dante duly reminds his readers at the end of *Paradiso* VII) that on the Day of Judgement, the whole human person – body and soul – will rise from the dead.[44]

Nevertheless, each newborn human infant still inherits the consequences of Adam's original sin; and his or her individual nature must still be 'set to rights' again. ('Setting to rights' is offered as a reasonably faithful modern equivalent of what Paul and the theologians call 'justification'). The stain of original sin must first be washed away by baptism. Then the child must endure 'a curb on its will for its own good' (as Adam refused to do) until the years of discretion are reached. But even if it is baptised and brought up by good Christian parents in the most favourable conditions, its fallen nature leaves it powerless to 'follow Christ' by its own free will, and unable to model its conduct on 'the model and pattern he bequeathed'. Each one of us still needs further 'help' of a kind that only God himself can give. That help is forthcoming and is called 'divine grace'.

The virtues 'infused' by grace

The simple word 'help' (*auxilium*) is the one used by Aquinas as he approaches this complex and highly controversial topic. And its simplicity sets the tone for the following very schematic introduction, which does no more than summarise a few points from Paul's Letter to the Romans and the relevant articles in the *Summa Theologiae*, by way of a preface to Dante's own pronouncements.[45]

The word 'grace' itself is important. In Latin, *gratia* implies something that is given 'freely' (*gratis*) or granted 'as a favour' (*per gratiam*).

Men and women are free to decline God's offer of assistance, but they can never demand it or deserve it as a right.

Broadly speaking, it is correct to say that grace is 'given by God', but it is more precise to speak, as Paul does, of 'the Holy Spirit being given to us'. The receiving of grace (or the indwelling of the Holy Spirit) was often characterised with the aid of three related clusters of images. It is like being permeated by a subtle breath or vapour (*spiritus* is from the same root as *in-spir-are*). It is like a dark recess being illuminated. It is like an empty vessel being filled with the water of life, 'poured in' by the Holy Spirit. (The verbs *fundere/fusum* and *diffundere* are used, in the Vulgate, by Jesus and Paul respectively; and we shall shortly meet the technical terms 'infusion' and 'infused', deriving from *infundere*, 'to pour in, to fill'.)[46]

The principal effects of the presence of grace in the soul are the three theological virtues of Faith, Hope and Love (*fides*, *spes*, *charitas*), which are our main concern. The order in which they are always named is significant, not least because each is seen to grow out of its predecessor. It is belief (*fides*) that there is a 'kingdom of Heaven', together with trust (*fides*) that Jesus has the will and the power 'to save', which give rise to the hope (*spes*) that makes it possible to endure tribulations in the long struggle to obtain 'eternal life'. In turn, it is the hoped-for loving union with God in the hereafter that may engender here on earth the perfect, selfless love (*charitas*) for God and for our neighbour that Paul celebrates so eloquently in his first Letter to the Corinthians. But we must beware of dwelling too much on psychological plausibility. Although it is not difficult for a non-believer to empathise with what Paul and so many others have written concerning the three virtues, there is a fundamental difference between the trust one may place in a human beloved, or a human leader, and Faith as understood by the theologians. Christian Faith is a gift from God, granted *per gratiam*, entirely at his discretion. Without this gift, one cannot believe what is necessary for salvation. If God elects *not* to make the gift, one cannot be saved.[47]

Clarifications from Aquinas

Aquinas had the double task of reinterpreting Paul's teaching in the language of thirteenth-century philosophy and clarifying the link between the theological virtues and our actions or works (*operationes* or *opera*) in the here and now.

Virtues are defined by Aquinas as relatively stable dispositions of the rational soul which enable it to perform efficiently its tasks of understanding, doing and making. Faith is akin to the intellectual virtue of intuition (*intelligentia*), since it enables the mind to grasp revealed truths as surely as if they were self-evident. Charity and Hope, by contrast, are moral virtues. The first is a perfection of the *vis concupiscibilis* in the will (that is, of the virtues that incline us to seek the good as such). The second is a perfection of the *vis irascibilis* (which includes virtues like courage and good anger that incline us to pursue goods considered as difficult to obtain). There, however, the likenesses end. The Aristotelian virtues can be 'acquired' by training (they are *acquisitae*). But Faith, Hope and Charity are 'infused' (*infusae*) – they are 'poured into' the soul by the grace of God. One cannot believe, hope or love, in these special senses, unless God fills the soul with his spirit. Moreover, acquired virtues are by definition 'difficult to remove', whereas God can take away the infused virtues in an instant, whenever we sin against Charity.[48]

It may be tempting to think (and Dante himself was so tempted) that the theological virtues are relevant only to salvation and beatitude in the kingdom of Heaven, while the moral virtues are sufficient to gain the happiness possible here on earth. But orthodox Catholic teaching is different.[49]

The best way to grasp Aquinas's own position is to explore his extension of the 'water imagery' so often used to describe the receiving of grace, taking as our cue a phrase used by Paul: 'charitas Dei *diffusa* in cordibus', 'the love of God diffused in our hearts'. The verb *diffundere/diffusum* suggests that Charity permeates the mind. Not only does it fill the mind completely, but it 'overflows' into every part of the soul, including the sensitive powers (that is, the faculties that we share with the higher animals). Aquinas is fond of the verb *redundare*; and the 'overflowing' of the divine gift of Charity becomes, for him, a precondition for the acquisition of the moral virtues recognised by pagan philosophers. In his analysis of human nature after the Fall, the unaided passions will always be inclined to disobey reason, thanks to Adam's original sin of disobedience. Without grace, the fallen will does not aim steadily at God as the supreme good; and we do not love other goods in their due relationship to God (*in ordine ad Deum*). Without Charity, it is impossible to acquire the moral virtues to perfection.[50]

For Aquinas, there are also other 'infused' virtues, other powers 'added' to human nature by grace (*principia superaddita*). But all of them have their 'root' in Charity and are 'interconnected in Charity'. To forfeit Charity (by committing a mortal sin) is to lose them all. On this view, human worth itself comes as a gift from God; and no human act has 'worth' in the theological sense of the word – no act has 'merit' – unless it proceeds from a soul in a state of grace.[51]

Aquinas's model of the relationship between the infused and the acquired virtues explains both how human actions may have 'merit', and why our 'good works' (*opera bona*) may be of unequal worth and therefore receive an unequal reward (*munus*) in the kingdom of Heaven. 'Everywhere in Heaven is Paradise' (as we are told by Piccarda in one of the opening discourses in the third cantica). But the blessed are not equal in their happiness, if only because there must be a 'giusto muno' for 'ogne merto' – a 'just reward' for 'every desert' – implying a graduated system of rewards that will be expressed in the rank-order of the celestial hierarchy.[52]

'Dì, buon Cristiano, fatti manifesto'

The protagonist has to undergo a lengthy examination concerning each of the theological virtues – answering questions put to him by the apostles Peter, James and John in three separate cantos (*Paradiso* XXIV–XXVI) – before he is allowed to proceed to the highest heaven, the *regnum caelorum* par excellence. Each of these successive scenes is rich in imagery and dramatic invention and cries out for close attention to the poetry; but here we must limit our inquiry to the main conceptual emphases in Dante's presentation of Faith, Hope and Charity.

It is significant, first, that Peter should begin by inviting Dante to 'reveal himself' not just as a good 'man', but as a good 'Christian', defined as someone who possesses all three virtues, 'someone who loves, hopes and believes well'. (The inversion of the received order is for rhetorical effect; later Dante will make it clear that faith is indeed the 'dear jewel, on which all virtues are founded'.)[53]

There are no surprises in the answers given to Peter in the course of the first examination. Faith 'seals the truth of the Gospels in the mind'. Only through 'true faith' does one come to the 'kingdom'. The definition of Faith in the Letter to the Hebrews (then attributed to Paul) is duly quoted and correctly paraphrased: 'Fede è sustanza di cose sperate'; it is 'that on which deep hope is founded'. Dante completes the quotation by stating that Faith is 'an argument concerning things invisible' ('argomento de le non parventi'), something, that is, which enables the intellect to hold fast to truths that can be neither intuited nor proved, and to use these truths as points of departure for 'syllogistic deductions'.[54]

So far the protagonist has considered Faith as the infused virtue enabling belief (*fides qua creditur*). Now he passes to the content of his faith (*fides quae creditur*). But he limits his declaration to the opening words of the Apostolic Creed, which deal with God as Creator of the universe. It is only in the course of a later examination that he finds the right moment to affirm his belief in the blessedness of the righteous ('the souls whom God has made his friends') and his belief in Heaven as our 'native land'.[55]

The examination in Hope is much briefer. Once again Dante translates an authoritative definition of the virtue, this time taken from the *Sententiae* of Peter Lombard. 'Hope is a certain expectation of future glory, produced by divine grace and preceding merit.' He goes on to specify, as he should, that he 'hopes' for that which every 'believer' does, and that this causes him to 'love' well. But the personal touch is not lacking. Beatrice is made to say that the protagonist is second to none in the Church Militant with regard to the strength of the hope that 'blossoms in his mind'. It is typical of Dante, too, that in his own little commentary on the subject of eternal 'glory', he should lay great stress on the resurrection of the body on the Day of Judgement.[56]

The most surprising answers come in reply to the apostle John on the subject of perfect Love or *charitas*. Dante was also second to none, one might say, in his power to represent pure and intense love for and between 'persons' – a word which can be used both of human beings and God. (One thinks of passages describing his feelings for Beatrice in the poems and prose of the *Vita nuova*; or of almost every exchange between himself and the souls he meets in Purgatory; or of the radiant lines spoken by Piccarda on the subject of 'carità' in *Paradiso* III.) But this is not the mode he chooses here. Nor does he dwell on the self-sacrificing love shown by Jesus on the Cross ('greater love has no man than this, that he lay down his life for his friends'). Indeed, the Crucifixion is mentioned almost in passing ('the death he endured that I might live').[57]

At this climactic moment in the third examination, Dante's concerns are quite different. He wants to bring out the relationship between love and goodness, to stress that God alone is good without qualification, and that 'God is Love'. These are the points made with such simplicity by Jesus (in his reply to the rich young man: 'Unus est bonus, Deus'), and by the apostle John himself in the letter quoted earlier ('Deus est charitas'). But the stark brevity of the biblical passages could hardly be further removed from the closely argued, but passionately philomythical, lines in which Dante evokes, first, the movement of all love towards a good of some kind, and then the movement of our highest love towards the Highest Good.

'ché 'l bene, in quanto ben, come s'intende,
così accende amore, e tanto maggio
quanto più di bontate in sé comprende.
Dunque a l'essenza ov'è tanto avvantaggio,
che ciascun ben che fuor di lei si trova
altro non è ch'un lume di suo raggio,
più che in altra convien che si mova
la mente, amando, di ciascun che cerne
il vero in che si fonda questa prova.' (*Par.* XXVI, 28–36)

'For the good, simply by being good, kindles love as soon as it is apprehended; and the greater the goodness it contains, the greater the love [it kindles]. Therefore, the mind of anyone who perceives the truth on which this proof is founded, must move, in loving, towards that Essence where there is such superabundance that every good existing outside it is no more than a light from its ray.'

In the lines immediately preceding and following this passage Dante declares that his sources are 'the authority ("autorità") that descends from heaven', and, more specifically, the voice of God himself, the 'true author ("verace autore") who spoke to Moses'. But he is not content to confine himself to the Word of God, whether spoken by the Father, the Son, or the apostles John and Paul. Even at this point in the action of the poem, he insists that his convictions also rest on 'filosofici argomenti', and specifically, on Aristotle, the man 'who showed me the primal love of all the sempiternal beings'. True to the spirit of his age, Dante tackles the notions of goodness, happiness and worth both as a philosopher and as a theologian. He wants to work simultaneously 'from the bottom up' and 'from the top down', and to exploit all the resources of poetry.[58]

CHAPTER SIX

A courtly value in Dante's hands

'Dirò del valore / per lo qual veramente omo è gentile'

Dante's first essays in the field of ethics are all related in some way to the understanding of a single word, one which does not occur in Aristotle or in the Bible, but was of great importance in his own society and central to the code of values enshrined in the poetry of courtly love. The word is 'gentilezza'. Three times he tried to pin its meaning down: first in a sonnet written between 1285 and 1290; then in a canzone written at some time between 1295 and 1300; and finally in a long prose commentary to that canzone, written between 1305 and 1310, which forms the fourth book of the *Convivio*.[1]

In this chapter we shall be concerned chiefly with the second of these attempts, the canzone beginning 'Le dolci rime d'amor'. In the opening stanza, Dante announces his intention of abandoning for a time the 'sweet poems of love', in which he had celebrated his conversion to Philosophy, and of 'laying aside the melodious style in which he had treated of love', in order to 'speak with harsh and subtle rhymes of the quality ("valore") through which a person is truly noble ("gentile")':

> diporrò giù lo mio soave stile,
> ch'i' ho tenuto nel trattar d'amore;
> e dirò del valore
> per lo qual veramente omo è *gentile*,
> con rima aspra e sottile. (*Rime* LXXXII, 10–14)

'Valore' and 'gentilezza'

Before we see how the thirty-year-old Dante would delimit the meanings of the two words 'valore' and 'gentile', we must explore something of their semantic richness in the poems he wrote in his twenties.

'Valore' derives from the Latin verb *valere*, meaning 'to be strong', and its most common meaning in Dante's early poetry is probably 'strength'. It could, however, be synonymous with 'potenza' or 'virtù', where these words denote a natural property conferring a power of action, as, for example, in the medicinal properties of a plant or the influences attributed to the planets and stars. (In his prose commentary to the passage just quoted, Dante will paraphrase the word as 'quasi *potenza di natura* o bontade da quella data'.) When used in praise of a man or woman in the lyric of courtly love, it meant something like 'the virtues that arouse love in a noble heart' (an interpretation borne out by its not infrequent pairing with 'cortesia' and its constant linking, through rhyme, to 'amore'). In the *Comedy*, it does occasionally have the meaning of goodness in general (we have seen that Dante uses the phrase 'ogne valore' to translate 'omne *bonum*'), or of moral goodness in particular (as it must do in the line from *Inferno* XXVI which provides the title of this book, where it is contrasted with 'li vizi umani'). It is also important to appreciate that 'valore' is several times used simply as a name of God, in contexts where one might want to render it as Power, or Wisdom, or Goodness (the separate attributes of the Three Persons in the Trinity), or all these simultaneously. Hence, when Dante says he will 'speak of the "valore" through which a person is truly "gentile"', even the apparently neutral noun is polysemous and comes surrounded with a cluster of associations.[2]

There can be no doubt that if one had to choose a single rendering into modern English of the key-word 'gentile', it would have to be 'noble'. Dante himself endorses this view by using 'nobile' as a synonym in his prose commentary. But 'nobile' was a relatively formal, learned word, which Dante defined as meaning 'perfect in its kind' (one may therefore talk about a 'noble horse', or refer to gold as a 'noble metal'). 'Gentile', by contrast, could only be used of human beings; and in the courtly poetry of France and Italy it had long since acquired a broad range of positive meanings which Dante would both extend and intensify in the poems he wrote in praise of Beatrice.

In ordinary usage, 'gentile' referred to the dominant class in the later centuries of feudalism, that is, to the lifestyle and values of a social elite. Many of the connotations of the adjective were quite close to those of its English derivatives 'gentleman', 'gentry', or 'of gentle birth' – in the senses which these expressions retained until recently – and it is possible to build up an informal Identikit of a 'gentle man', which will fit the Italian 'omo gentile' of the thirteenth century and be strongly reminiscent of the English 'gentleman' in the late nineteenth century (as portrayed in the novels of the period).

A 'gentle man' does not work with his hands, does not engage in trade and does not follow the professions of medicine or the law. He is at the furthest remove from the condition of a serf or villein (a peasant cultivator, unable to leave the manor of his lord). He enjoys an independent income in the form of rents from agricultural land or real estate inherited from his forebears (the resonant word 'forebears' – 'maggiori' – suggests that they had been 'gentle' from time immemorial). Typically, he regards himself as a member of what we would now call the officer class, one who fights on horseback (he is a 'cavaliere' or, in Latin, *eques/equitis*). He values courage, loyalty and skill at arms; and he seeks to excel at paramilitary sports such as hunting or jousting. His attitude to book-learning or piety is probably a mixture of superficial respect and underlying contempt. He takes intense pride in his family and will resent any slight to its honour from a member of another noble family. But he joins with all other 'gentle men' in defining himself through opposition to those who work for a living and who fight on foot: they are base-born, ignoble, vile ('vili', 'villani'), in extreme cases hardly different from the brute beasts. Whatever else the 'gentle man' may be, he feels himself to be superior.

All this would be of little interest, perhaps, if the 'gentry' of Southern France in the later eleventh century had not begun to develop a distinctive, high culture, based on the 'court' of a local lord, in a period of relative peace and prosperity when social life could become increasingly 'refined' (the words 'fino' and 'cortese' – in their local Occitanic forms – were to be crucial to the participants). 'Gentle men' were consciously striving for the good and the beautiful, aiming to differentiate themselves from the 'vile villeins' in every aspect of their life and customs: in dress, accoutrements, buildings, food and drink, pastimes, and perhaps above all in the pleasures of social intercourse. They developed an ambience where women would set the tone, and where association between the sexes would not be subordinated to the pursuit of sensual gratification or procreation, but might be purified and pursued as an end in itself. The qualities admired in an 'omo gentile' became those which would win him the favour of a 'donna gentile' through his devoted love-service.[3]

'Gentilezza' in the Italian courtly lyric

We know of these aspirations because social life at these courts was enhanced by the singing of songs and the telling of stories that have been preserved. The lyrics and romances of the nascent vernacular literatures in France, Germany, Spain and Italy held up a magic mirror to real life, creating an imaginary world in which the adjectives 'cortese' and 'gentile' gradually ceased to denote a place and a caste and came to mean 'courteous' and 'noble-minded'.

It is impossible here to trace out the long evolution of the courtly code of conduct and values over a period of 150 years (this is Dante's estimate of the time separating him from the earliest vernacular love poems). But we can at least read one relevant list of the attributes desirable in an 'omo gentile', as these had crystallised in the early 1280s. The following lines are taken from a pretentious exchange of sonnets between the very young Dante Alighieri and his namesake Dante da Maiano.[4]

> Savere e cortesia, ingegno ed arte,
> nobilitate, bellezza e riccore,
> fortezza e umiltate e largo core,
> prodezza ed eccellenza, giunte e sparte,
> este grazie e vertuti in onne parte
> con lo piacer di lor vincono Amore:
> una più ch'altra ha più valore
> inverso lui, ma ciascuna n'ha parte. (*Rime* XLVII, 1–8).

Knowledge and courtesy; natural wit and acquired skill; nobility, beauty, wealth; strength and gentleness and generosity; valour and high distinction – these gifts and virtues, combined or separate, in all cases win Love over with their attraction: one may have more power with him than another, but each has a share in it.

The social and economic conditions of the Italian cities in Dante's lifetime were very different from those in the Languedoc, where the new literature had originated, or in Northern France where it was flourishing by the late twelfth century (the Arthurian verse-romances of Chrétien de Troyes were written between 1170 and 1190). And the troubadours, trouvères and 'dicitori per rima' (Dante's phrase) were not usually people of the highest social rank (although there were some royal poets). It was therefore almost inevitable that, when they came to reflect on their own values and to define the essence of 'gentilezza', they would seek to play down the importance of inherited wealth and political power and lay the emphasis on 'grazie e vertuti', such as those listed by the young Dante. They and all their readers who entered imaginatively into the collective dream of a never-never land, with its capital at

Camelot, felt themselves to be no less 'gentili' than the landed classes or the social upper tier. For them, the only thing that mattered was to be born with a 'gentle heart' (the same phrase is used in all the vernaculars). They regarded themselves, as 'Nature's gentlemen', a moral elite; and they identified true nobility with virtue (*vera nobilitas virtus*).[5]

Two last qualifications and we shall be ready to study Dante's own first pronouncement on the subject of the 'cor gentile'.

First, although authors and readers asserted the need to distinguish between the mere accident of noble birth and the pure essence of nobility, they were deeply attracted to the particular manifestations of feudal aristocratic life which were so beguilingly described in the courtly romances; and they were envious of the status and lifestyle of the upper classes in their own day, whose literal claims to 'gentilezza' were backed by the law, by wealth and, if necessary, by the sword. In the *Comedy* Dante presents himself as a member of the lower fringes of the noble or magnate class in Florentine society, and on one occasion he teases himself charmingly for his ineradicable snobbery. In *Paradiso* xv he uses the honorific pronoun 'voi' to address his ancestor Cacciaguida (allegedly knighted by the Emperor Conrad while on Crusade); and he ironically apostrophises 'our paltry nobility of blood' ('O poca nostra nobiltà di sangue'), which could still make him feel vainglorious even in Heaven.[6]

Second, Dante's early years coincided with the last phase in the long struggle for political power within his own commune. This struggle was between the descendants of the feudal lords (who had dominated Tuscany in earlier times and who traditionally sought external alliances with the Ghibellines, the imperial party) and the rising merchant families (who had organised themselves in guilds and aligned themselves with the Guelphs). The moment of final victory for the merchants can be dated precisely in 1293 when the 'Ordinamenti di Giustizia' formally excluded from political office any member of a family deemed to be noble. In 1295 the 'Ordinamenti' were slightly relaxed to allow someone of noble birth to participate in the Councils and to be eligible for service as one of the Priors, but only on condition that he became a member of a guild. Dante joined the Guild of Apothecaries in the following year and in due course served as a Prior for a term of two months. The tragic irony was to be that, seven years later, early in 1302, his faction within the ruling Guelph party in Florence was defeated and he was driven into perpetual exile, living as a suppliant first at the outlying courts of some aristocratic families in Tuscany and then with the noble rulers of Verona and Ravenna.

'Love and the gentle heart are one thing'

The first of Dante's three essays on 'gentilezza' is no more than a sonnet and remains well within the traditions of courtly literature. It might be described as a postscript to the canzone 'Al cor gentil rempaira sempre Amore' ('Love always finds its way to the noble heart'), written a few years earlier by the Bolognese poet Guido Guinizzelli, whom Dante would later describe as his 'father, and the father of all those who ever wrote charming poems of love'.[7]

This famous canzone is devoted to the relationship between true love and true nobility, and Dante summarises its conclusions – while also sharpening them – in the first line of his sonnet, which opens with the simple statement that 'Love and the noble heart are one and the same thing.' He immediately cites Guinizzelli as his authority ('as the wise man lays it down in his composition'). Then he adds a simple example, strongly redolent of elementary lessons in logic, to show what he understands by this identity. 'Love and the noble heart can no more exist apart from each other than reason and the rational soul.'

> Amore e 'l cor gentil sono una cosa,
> sì come il saggio in suo dittare pone,
> e così esser l'un sanza l'altro osa
> com'alma razional sanza ragione.
> (*Rime* XVI, 1–4; = *VN* XX, 3)

Having reformulated Guinizzelli's thesis in this bold way, Dante has to explain why a young person possessing a 'gentle heart' will not experience love until adolescence at the earliest. This he does obliquely through a metaphor which is as precise as it is suggestive:

> Falli natura quand'è amorosa,
> Amore per sire e 'l cor per sua magione,
> dentro la qual dormendo si riposa
> tal volta poca e tal lunga stagione. (5–8)

> Nature creates them when she is disposed to love – Love as the lord and the heart as his mansion, wherein he lies asleep, sometimes a little and sometimes a long while.

The image of the 'sleeping Lord' reappears in the second half of the sonnet ('e tanto dura [il disio] . . . / che fa *svegliar* lo spirito d'Amore'). On its second appearance it is used to emphasise that the 'spirit of Love' is not 'awakened' immediately by desire for the lady's beauty, but only after a further lapse of time. And this two-part metaphor of sleeping and waking proves to be the main vehicle through which Dante adapts the ideas expounded and illustrated by Guinizzelli, making them peculiarly his own.[8]

In the brief prose commentary to the poem in the *Vita nuova*, which may have been written up to five years later, Dante decodes these metaphors, introducing the categories of *potentia* ('sleep') and *actus* ('wakefulness'). Love is present in the gentle heart from the beginning, but only as a potentiality that must later be activated ('dico di lui in quanto di *potenzia* si riduce in *atto*'). In the prose, too, potency and act are joined by another pair of philosophical concepts. The relationship between love and the gentle heart, it is now made clear, is that between *forma* and *materia* (which is to say that true love is the very essence of nobility – the 'what it is that gives being and life').[9]

Now, the two correlated pairs – potency and act, form and matter – are quintessentially Aristotelian; and so it might be argued that, even in the early 1290s, Dante was drawing directly on the Philosopher to refine and deepen the concepts of his poetic predecessors. But Dante's knowledge of philosophy was still fairly superficial even in the prose of the *Vita nuova* (let alone in the sonnet, which seems to have been written before 1290). Hence the most important points to notice are that Dante intuited very early in his career that 'gentilezza' will manifest itself in different ways at different times of life, and that his intuition was first conceived and expressed philomythically, through metaphor.

'La gentilissima'

The sonnet 'Amore e 'l cor gentil' coincided with a breakthrough in Dante's development as a love poet. In the poems that he went on to write – the sonnets and canzoni in the 'praise style' that he later called the 'sweet new style' – 'gentile' became the epithet par excellence to characterise the nature of Beatrice and her influence on all who saw her. As a result, the meaning and associations of the word 'gentile' were widened and intensified. And the best way to convey its new connotations will be to consider some of the other words and concepts with which it now keeps company.[10]

'Gentile' is found together with 'dolce' and 'soave' (these being the words that Dante uses to describe the style of these poems of disinterested praise). It is associated more closely than ever before with 'amore'; and the connotations of 'amore' move further and further away from sexual love and closer and closer to Christian *charitas*. The name Beatrice means 'she who makes blessed ("beato")'; and the qualities she possesses, or calls into being in others, are those celebrated in the Beatitudes. She is often described as 'umile' and she banishes pride, making those who gaze on her sigh for their faults and forget the offences done to them. Her greeting ('salute') confers bliss, or even salvation ('salute'). She is said to have 'come down from heaven to earth to show miracles'. Twice she is explicitly linked with divine 'grace'. Time and time again her 'gentilezza' is represented as an active power ('valore') through which she is able to transmit her own essence to others and thereby make them 'gentili' too. These are the qualities that shine out in the best known of all Dante's early sonnets, where the word 'gentile' takes pride of place and becomes inseparable in our minds from the 'dolcezza' and 'soavità' of the verbal music that is the hallmark of the 'stil novo':[11]

> Tanto *gentile* e tanto onesta pare
> la donna mia quand'ella altrui saluta
> ch'ogne lingua deven tremando muta,
> e li occhi no l'ardiscon di guardare.
> Ella si va sentendosi laudare,
> benignamente d'umiltà vestuta;
> e par che sia una cosa venuta
> da cielo in terra a miracol mostrare.
> (*Rime* XXII, 1–8 = *VN* XXVI, 5–6)

> So gentle and so full of dignity my lady appears when she greets anyone that all tongues tremble and fall silent and eyes dare not look at her. She goes on her way, hearing herself praised, graciously clothed with humility; and seems a creature come down from heaven to earth to make the miraculous known.

The Christianisation of Beatrice – and, through her, of the epithet 'gentile' – is carried much further in the prose of the *Vita nuova*, where she is regularly called 'la gentil*issima*'. So it comes as no surprise to find the words 'speranza' and 'caritade' in Dante's later evocation of the miraculous effects of her 'salvific' greeting:

> Dico che quando ella apparia da parte alcuna, per la speranza de la mirabile salute nullo nemico mi rimanea, anzi mi giugnea una fiamma di caritade, la quale mi facea perdonare a chiunque m'avesse offeso; e chi allora m'avesse domandato di cosa alcuna, la mia risponsione sarebbe stata solamente 'Amore', con viso vestito d'umilitade. (*VN* xi, 1)

> I say that whenever she appeared in any place, simply through the hope of her miraculous greeting, no one could remain an enemy to me, but rather there came to me a flame of charity, which made me pardon anyone who had offended me. Had anyone asked me a question about anything whatsoever, my answer would only have been 'Love', with my face clothed in humility.

Continuity and innovation in the canzone 'Le dolci rime'

We may now turn back to the canzone 'Le dolci rime d'amor', which was written some years after the prose of the *Vita nuova*. The opening lines, it will be remembered, speak of the 'sweet rhymes of love', and of the need to 'forsake them, and to set aside the "soave stile" he had used when treating of love'. In other words, Dante is both stressing the continuity of his development and marking a break with his past – in the event, a *second* break.

The first break had come at the point when he began to study philosophy in his quest for consolation after the death of Beatrice, only to find that it seemed an act of disloyalty to her memory. This feeling was documented at the time in the canzone 'Voi che 'ntendendo il terzo ciel movete' and described more fully later, in the second book of the *Convivio*. But of course the change of direction had been far from complete. The attractions of study were imaged as those of a new mistress, Lady Philosophy, who was first and foremost a 'donna *gentile*'; and the conflict of loyalties was worked out within the conventions of the earlier love poetry. When Dante finally yielded to his new love, he wrote a canzone in praise of philosophy, still in the 'sweet style', of which he was intensely proud. In this poem ('Amor che ne la mente mi ragiona'), his mistress is said to be a 'cosa *gentil*', indeed, the 'most noble' under the sun. Once again 'gentlewomen' are advised to go and seek her out ('qual donna *gentil* questo non crede, / vada con lei e miri li atti sui'). The 'flames of love which rain down from her beauty' are said to be animated by 'un spirito *gentile*'. 'Plus ça change, plus c'est la même chose.'[12]

The second break or change of direction – the one recorded in our poem – came when he found certain aspects of Aristotelian metaphysics too difficult and resolved to devote his energies to ethics for a time. (That is how he explained events in *Convivio* IV: in the poem, his change of direction was attributed to a certain coldness and disdain in his mistress.) Even here, however, he foresaw that his difficulties would be merely temporary; and, as we have seen, the subject he set himself to treat in 'harsh and subtle rhyme' was none other than 'gentilezza'.[13]

Despite the elements of continuity, this canzone does break new ground. Dante takes the familiar but nebulous 'valore' of the courtly tradition and puts it to the question (in the sense given to this expression in Chapter 2), by subjecting it to rigorous logical analysis and relating it to the apparently alien categories of Aristotelian moral philosophy and Christian theology.

Scholastic techniques in 'Le dolci rime'

The canzone echoes the structure and modes of a typical scholastic *quaestio* in many different ways; and it is only fitting that in the final lines Dante should give his poem a title – 'Contra li erranti' – which echoes the *Summa contra gentiles* of Aquinas.

The *quaestio* itself gets under way in the second stanza with the statement of an erroneous definition of 'gentilezza', duly attributed to an *auctoritas*. (This corresponds to the *videtur quod* section in the paradigm translated in Chapter 2.) The definition is challenged and then 'destroyed' by use of *ratio*, that is, by an exposition of its 'sins' against logic. It thus becomes 'manifest to healthy minds' that the arguments of the adversaries are 'void'. So, having 'refuted them as false', Dante 'turns away from them to say what he himself feels'. He begins the second part, in good scholastic fashion, by stating three questions to which he will provide an answer, namely, 'what nobility is; where it comes from; and what signs distinguish the noble person'.[14]

> Per che a 'ntelletti sani
> è manifesto i lor diri esser vani;
> e io così per falsi li riprovo,
> e da lor mi rimovo;
> e dicer voglio omai, sì com'io sento,
> che cosa è gentilezza, e da che vene,
> e dirò i segni che 'l gentile uom tene.
>
> (*Rime* LXXXII, 74–80)

Dante's clear articulation of the logical structure of his *quaestio* is reinforced by the symmetries of the metrical form. Three stanzas are allotted to the refutation of the 'errant' opinions (the *pars destruens*), and three to the statement of Dante's views (the *pars construens*). The internal divisions of the stanzas (whose twenty lines are grouped in the pattern 4 + 4 + 12) act like so many numbered rubrics (*ad primum*, *ad secundum* etc.).

The false definition with which Dante began claimed that 'gentilezza' consists in the 'long-standing possession of wealth together with pleasing manners' ('antica possession d'avere / con reggimenti belli'). Dante points out that it contains three distinct factors – riches, the passage of time, and behaviour – all of which will now be subjected to close scrutiny.

The last 'particula', the one concerning behaviour, is the only one to have any validity at all. But we are told that it is often ignored by those 'who call someone noble if he can say: "I am the grandson or son of such and such a great man ('valente')", even if he himself is a nonentity'. To such people Dante retorts – more rhetorically than logically – that a worthless descendant is doubly base ('vilissimo') since he failed to follow the path he had been shown by his ancestor.[15]

The component of time is introduced into the flawed definition by the adjective 'antica'. As Dante points out, this would imply that 'no base-born person can ever become noble in his lifetime' ('né voglion che vil uom gentil divegna'), and that 'no family descended from a base-born father can be accounted noble'. This implication is refuted with a *reductio ad absurdum* backed by an appeal to the authority of the Bible. On this line of argument, 'it would follow that all of us must be either noble or base' ('segue . . . / che siàm tutti gentili o ver villani'), or, alternatively, that 'mankind did not have one beginning' (that is, one common ancestor, Adam) – a conclusion, which as Christians, his adversaries cannot allow! (One is reminded of the proverbial rallying cry, used later during the English Peasants' Revolt: 'When Adam delved and Evë span / Who was then the gentleman?')[16]

It is clear, therefore, that Dante still felt he had to contend with those of his contemporaries who considered nobility as a matter of lineage ('che fan gentile *per ischiatta* altrui'). But his main target was the belief that riches, whether accumulated in ancient times or recently, can have any bearing on the matter. This is one of the topics he will expand with great passion in the later prose commentary, and to which we shall return in the next chapter. From the point of view of scholastic methodology, however, it is enough to note that his refutation is based on the much-used axiom that 'nothing can give something it does not possess' (*nihil dat quod non habet*). Hence, riches (variously called 'avere', 'ricchezza', 'le divizie') 'can neither give nobility, nor take it away, since they are base by nature':[17]

ché le divizie, sì come si crede,
non posson gentilezza dar né tòrre,
però che vili son da lor natura. (49–51)

'Gentilezza' in relation to Aristotle's account of moral virtue

There are many other examples in the canzone of Dante's competence in logic and dialectic, but the time has come to shift the emphasis away from the techniques used in the *pars destruens* to the content of the *pars construens*, where Dante is developing his own ideas.

He begins the second part of the *quaestio* by clarifying the relationship between nobility and the leading ideas in Aristotle's *Ethics*. Clearly, 'gentilezza' must be connected in some way with the eleven moral virtues described above, all of which, we are reminded, have something in common, since 'every virtue stems ultimately from one root' ('ogni vertù principalmente / vien da una radice'). And by virtue is meant that which 'makes a man happy in his actions' ('fa l'uom felice in sua operazione').[18]

Felicitas and *operatio propria* are fundamental concepts in Aristotelian ethics, so it comes as no surprise that Dante should now quote the exact words in Aristotle's definition of this 'root' of all virtue:

Questo è, secondo che l'Etica dice,
un abito eligente
lo qual dimora in mezzo solamente;
e tai parole pone. (85–8)

This is, as the *Ethics* states, 'a habit of choosing which keeps steadily to the mean', and those are the very words.

Dante now seeks agreement that both 'nobiltate' and 'vertute' 'denote a good in the person to whom they are attributed'. Then he argues that, since they both have the same effect ('èn d'uno effetto'), they must 'come together in one definition' ('in medesmo detto / convegnono ambedue'). One must therefore ask: is nobility simply the same thing as the 'root' of every virtue, that is, a disposition to choose the mean? Or does one concept embrace the other? And, if that be the case, which is the broader term?[19]

Dante's answer is that, of the two, nobility is the more comprehensive term. There can be no virtue where there is no nobility, but there can be nobility where there is no virtue. ('È gentilezza dovunqu'è vertute, / ma non vertute ov'ella.') In support of this claim he points out that some traits are regarded as noble which cannot be analysed as a 'habit of choosing the mean'. For example, shame or bashfulness is certainly something 'gentile' in women and children ('in donna e in età novella'), but it is only a transient emotion, and it is not to be admired in men of mature years. (Aristotle categorised shame as a 'laudable passion', rather than a moral virtue.)[20]

Dante therefore concludes that 'each of the virtues – or rather their genus – comes from nobility' in the same way that a plant comes from its seed. So, if 'virtue is what makes people happy in their actions', nobility may be described as the '*seed* of happiness', 'seme di felicità'. And in a moment we shall see that this phrase enters into Dante's own formal definition of 'gentilezza'.[21]

'Gentilezza' as a seed of happiness planted by God

Before we can answer the question 'che cosa è gentilezza?', however, we must discover whence it comes, 'da che vene?' To do this, we must abandon Aristotelian ethics in favour of Christian theology, 'la divina scienza', whose *principia* are truths revealed by God.

Dante was committed to the orthodox doctrine which has come to be called 'creationism'. This means he accepted as a matter of faith that God creates each individual human being *directly*, without any intermediary – '*sanza* mezzo'. He does this, however, by transforming an existing embryo, which has been conceived by natural means, which is growing naturally in the womb, and for whose existence God is responsible only *indirectly* – '*con* mezzo'.

God makes his intervention in the natural process only at a late stage in embryonic development, when the 'articulation of the brain' is complete. At this point he 'turns joyfully to the foetus, rejoicing in such a handiwork of Nature; and he breathes a new spirit, filled with power, which draws up into its own substance all that is active there and becomes a single soul [the *anima rationalis*] that lives and feels [as an animal does], and revolves upon itself [in self-knowledge, as only an intellectual being can do]':

e spira
spirito novo, di vertù repleto,
che ciò che trova attivo quivi, tira
in sua sustanzia, e fassi un'alma sola,
che vive e sente e sé in sé rigira. (*Purg*. xxv, 71–5)

These lines are taken, not from 'Le dolci rime', but from Dante's final account of the subject, in what is arguably the single most important doctrinal speech in the *Comedy*. But he had already elucidated the ideas at great length in *Convivio* IV, and stated its consequences for 'gentilezza' in the canzone itself.[22]

Children come into the world with differing and unequal gifts. There are several variables in 'Nature's great handiwork' (where the make-up of the foetus depends on the father's constitution and the condition of his seed, not to mention the ever-changing influences of the planets and stars). And God gives unequally in the subsequent moment of creation (as may be seen in the very different talents of twins, such as Esau and Jacob). Some children are born 'villani', simply because they have received less than others from Nature and God. But whenever the natural causes combine to produce a soul that 'sits *perfectly* in its body' and God freely decides to give 'grace without flaw' to this 'well-placed soul', then the newly created human being will be 'almost like a god'.[23]

With that we come at last to the promised definition of 'gentilezza', in which Dante specifies both 'what it is' and 'where it comes from'. It is difficult to imagine anything further in spirit from the evocation of 'la gentilissima' or from the sonnet 'Tanto gentile':

> ch'elli son quasi dèi
> quei c'han tal grazia fuor di tutti rei:
> ché solo Iddio a l'anima la dona
> che vede in sua persona
> perfettamente star: sì ch'ad alquanti
> che *seme di felicità* sia costa,
> *messo da Dio ne l'anima ben posta.* (114–20)

> Those who have this grace without any defects are almost gods; for it is God alone who gives it to a soul that he sees to be in perfect harmony with its body. Hence it is clear to some that *nobility is the seed of happiness, placed by God in a well-disposed soul.*

The 'marks' of nobility in the different Ages of Man

In the final stanza of the canzone Dante answers his third question, namely, 'what are the signs ("segni") that distinguish a noble person?' It is here that he is most original, as he develops his early insight that 'gentilezza' must assume different guises at different times of life.

Several quite heterogeneous concepts and images are combined in this stanza. The metaphor of the 'seed' of happiness points back to the Aristotelian categories of *potentia* and *actus*, which were introduced in the *Vita nuova*. (A tree exists only as a potentiality in the seed, and will not be fully actualised until it produces its fruit.) But the same metaphor is also linked to the teaching of Jesus, who insisted that the goodness of a tree may be judged only by its 'fruits', and that one should not 'hide one's light' but let it 'shine out in good works'. Dante is insisting that the gifts of Nature and God must be developed and made manifest. In a separate image (with a strongly Platonic flavour), he also suggests that the apparently pre-existent soul 'comes' from God and will eventually 'return' to its source: it is 'wedded' to the body, but finally '*re*-married' to God. All these separate components are combined in the opening lines of the final stanza:[24]

L'anima cui adorna esta bontate
non la si tiene ascosa,
ché dal principio ch'al corpo si sposa
la mostra infin la morte. (121–4)

The soul adorned by this goodness, does not keep it concealed; for from the beginning, when it weds the body, it shows that goodness forth until death.

The principal 'fruits' of this 'seed of happiness' – as Dante will explicitly say in the *Convivio* – are the Aristotelian moral virtues. Nevertheless, Dante is notably independent of the 'Master of human life'. He omits six of the eleven moral virtues in Aristotle's list (although he includes the related categories of shame and prudence). He mentions other distinguishing 'signs' such as bodily beauty. And, most important, he distributes the virtues among the different ages of human life. They are not all *in actu* simultaneously, in the way that they are presented in the *Ethics*.

Before he can list these 'fruits' or 'signs', moreover, Dante has to look beyond Aristotle in order to find a widely accepted division of human life into a suitable number of phases or ages. In the event, among several contenders, he commits himself to St Albert, who divided the normal span of our active life into three: 'Adolescenza', from birth to the age of twenty-five (the age of majority in Roman law); 'Gioventute', from twenty-five to forty-five; and 'Senettute' from forty-five to seventy (the Psalmist's threescore years and ten). A fourth age, 'Senio', is recognised for the happy few who survive, so to speak, into retirement.[25]

The 'harsh and subtle' style of the canzone becomes perceptibly more lyrical as the 'signs' are itemised and celebrated, age by age:[26]

Ubidente, soave e vergognosa
è *ne la prima etate*,
e sua persona aconcia di bieltate
con le sue parti accorte;
  in giovinezza, temperata e forte,
piena d'amore e di cortesi lode,
e solo in lealtà far si diletta; (125–31)

In her first age [the noble soul] is obedient, sweet and bashful, and provides the body with the beauty of well-matched parts. In the prime of life, she is self-controlled, brave, full of love, winning praises for courtesy, and takes delight only in observing the law.

è *ne la sua senetta*
prudente e giusta, e larghezza se n'ode,
e 'n se medesma gode
d'udire e ragionar de l'altrui prode;
poi *ne la quarta parte* de la vita
a Dio si rimarita,
contemplando la fine ch'ell'aspetta,
e benedice li tempi passati. (132–9)

In maturity [the noble soul] is prudent and just; she has a reputation for generosity, and rejoices to hear and speak good things of others. Then, in the fourth part of life, she returns to God as a bride, contemplating the end she awaits, and blesses the ages through which she has passed.

Dante's 'ars combinatoria'

The very last line of the stanza ('Vedete omai quanti son li 'ngannati!' – literally, 'See how many are the deceived') reminds us that the canzone is polemical, that contemporaries held different views, and that Dante's conclusions are his own. And yet there is nothing totally new in this list of the distinguishing marks of nobility. The novelty lies in the way they are divided, numerated, synthesised, and reordered by Dante's *ars combinatoria*.

Perhaps the best way to bring out Dante's indebtedness to the past, and, simultaneously his independence, will be to set out the 'segni che 'l gentile uom tene' in four columns, one for each of the Ages, and to pick out the Aristotelian terms in italics. (For convenience, the Italian names are taken from the prose commentary in *Convivio* IV, rather than from the canzone, with the exception of the final column, where no nouns are used in the prose.)

Table 1. *The Ages of Man*

Adolescenza	Gioventute	Senettute	Senio
obedienza	*temperanza*	*prudenza*	'ritorna a Dio'
soavitate	*fortezza*	*giustizia*	'benedice lo cammino'
vergogna	amore	*larghezza*	
adornezza	cortesia	*affabilitade*	
	lealtà		
Youth (1–25)	**Manhood (25–45)**	**Maturity (45–70)**	**Old Age (70+)**
obedience	*self-control*	*prudence*	'returning to God'
sweetness	*courage*	*justice*	'blessing the journey'
bashfulness	love	*generosity*	
beauty	courtesy	*charm*	
	respect for the law		

Of the eight *non*-Aristotelian 'signs' in the list as a whole, the first-named, 'obedienza', has no specific associations. The next four – 'soavitate', 'adornezza corporale' (meaning 'beauty'), 'amore' and 'cortesia' – are qualities at the centre of the courtly system of values; and it is significant that these are limited to the earlier part of life. Only two of the signs could be described as Christian (returning in thought to God, and blessing the past). Significantly, these appear only in the final phase of life, and they are presented in language that is reminiscent of Platonism (the soul prepares to return to its source) and of Hebrew poetry (the soul is the bride of God, as in the allegorical interpretations of the Song of Songs). 'Lealtà', which is explained in the *Convivio* as 'law-abidingness', belongs with the values of Roman law or the medieval commune. (In real life, it may be observed, the 'uomini gentili' in the Italian cities were notoriously disrespectful of the law.)

Aristotle, then, does not enjoy anything remotely resembling exclusive rights. And even if the remaining seven 'signs' (those italicised in the list above) are all important in the *Ethics*, it is enough to put four of the Italian names back into Latin (as *temperantia*, *fortitudo*, *prudentia* and *justitia*) to recognise that these are the cardinal virtues singled out by the Stoics and taken over into Christian morality by Ambrose. Six of Aristotle's moral virtues are apparently omitted altogether (munificence, magnanimity, proper ambition, good temper, frankness and liveliness);

and, as we have seen, bashfulness (or shame) is a laudable passion, while prudence is a virtue of the practical intellect.

On the other hand, there can be no doubt that Aristotle is the single most important source, as is made clear in Dante's careful analysis of the relationship between 'gentilezza' and 'vertute', which is treated as an 'abito eligente / lo qual dimora in mezzo solamente'. Three of the omissions are virtues of social intercourse, which might easily be subsumed in the phrase 'e 'n se medesma gode/ d'udire e ragionar de l'altrui prode'. *Magnificentia* is simply a higher form of generosity, possible only to those who have inherited 'gran ricchezza'; while the remaining virtue, *magnanimitas*, is the big brother, so to speak, of proper ambition ('amativa d'onore'). It could also be argued that Dante is indebted to Aristotle for his subtle use of the categories of *actus* and *potentia*, in that some of the later 'signs' can be interpreted as actualisations of earlier potentialities. Obedience foreshadows respect for the law, which prepares for justice; 'affabilitade' is a fulfilment of 'cortesia', which in turn grows out of 'soavitate'.[27]

Dante's third essay on 'gentilezza': the prose of 'Convivio' IV

At some time between 1305 and 1308 Dante returned to the themes of 'Le dolci rime' and re-elaborated his ideas at thirty times the length in a commentary to the canzone, which forms the fourth book of the *Convivio*. This is a splendid work, written by a man in his early forties at the height of his powers, and it should be essential reading for anyone who wants to dig deeper into the themes of the present book. It provides ample confirmation of Dante's reverence for authority, reason and order. It gives a much fuller account of Aristotelian, Christian and courtly ethics than has been possible here. And, in general, it stands as an antechamber to the poetry of the *Comedy*, which often proves to be a creative distillation of its superabundant material.

Being a commentary, the prose follows the sequence of ideas in the canzone and respects its proportions (after an introductory chapter, it dedicates fourteen chapters each to the *pars destruens* and the *pars construens*). Of course, the discussion is immeasurably fuller at almost every point; and, true to the models offered by earlier commentators, Dante allows himself some major digressions. In chapters iv–v, for example, he branches out from ethics to politics, describes the hierarchy of human societies from village to kingdom, and sketches the views he will elaborate later in the *Monarchia*. But there is no rethinking of the values expounded in the poem of a kind that need detain us in a chapter devoted exclusively to the larger issues.

The new authorities

The single most striking difference between the prose and the canzone is that Dante now has space to to quote at length from his *auctoritates*. One or more of the great names such as Aristotle, Cicero and Boethius, or Solomon, Jesus and Paul, appear on almost every page. It is in this book that Dante justifies scholastic practice by insisting on the need to revere our betters. Cicero is quoted with approval where he says that 'to fail through negligence to discover what others have said concerning the good ("mettere a negghienza di sapere quello che li altri sentono [de l'onesto]"), is the mark of a person who is not only arrogant but dissolute'. It is here too that Aristotle is singled out as the person most worthy of reverence in moral philosophy. And, from our point of view, the most important new material in *Convivio* IV relates to the *auctoritates* who are quoted to exemplify the 'signs' of nobility. The hallmarks of the noble soul are illustrated exclusively and systematically from the *poets* of ancient Rome – those of the First Age from Statius, of the Second from Virgil, of the Third from Ovid, and of the Fourth from Lucan.[28]

Earlier in his career, Dante had shown reverence for the same great names in a chapter of the *Vita nuova* devoted to poetics, in which he defended his use of the rhetorical figure of personification on the grounds that it had been freely used by the ancient 'poete', and that there was an analogy between them and the modern 'dicitori per rima'. Now, however, he treats the four poets as *auctores* in the field of ethics, as men who showed the truth about human 'operations' and their 'worth'. They are seen as his forerunners in the task he set himself in 'Le dolci rime'. Their symmetrically regulated appearance in four successive chapters signals a vital stage on the path that would lead Dante to write the *Comedy* (which is a long narrative poem, conceived as a contribution to ethics, and written in emulation of the *Aeneid*, the *Metamorphoses*, the *Thebaid* and the *De bello civili*). The moment of transition therefore deserves to be marked with a brief quotation that will also serve to illustrate the qualities of the prose.[29]

The Second Age ('gioventute') should be characterised above all by the virtues of self-control and courage. These are compared, respectively, to the 'reins' and 'spurs' which a skilled horseman must use in order to curb or spur on his mount (even when the horse is 'noble by nature'), so that it will not run after pleasures or take flight from danger. The poetic example is taken from Virgil:

> E così infrenato mostra Virgilio, lo maggiore nostro poeta, che fosse Enea, ne la parte de lo Eneida ove questa etade si figura.... E quanto raffrenare fu quello, quando, avendo ricevuto da Dido tanto di piacere ... e usando con essa tanto di dilettazione, elli si partio, per seguire onesta e laudabile via e fruttuosa, come nel quarto de l'Eneida scritto è! Quanto spronare fu quello, quando esso Enea sostenette solo con Sibilla a intrare ne lo Inferno a cercare de l'anima di suo padre Anchise, contra tanti pericoli, come nel sesto de la detta istoria si dimostra! (*Con.* IV, xxvi, 8–9)

> And Virgil, our greatest poet, portrayed Aeneas as well 'reined in' in that part of the *Aeneid* where this age is represented allegorically. What a 'reining in' that was, when, having taken so much delight from Dido and enjoyed such pleasure with her, he sailed away to follow a virtuous, praiseworthy course – and one that bore fruit! – as is recorded in the fourth book of the *Aeneid*. What a 'spurring on' that was, when Aeneas endured the descent into Hell, alone with the Sibyl, to seek the soul of Anchises his father, encountering such great dangers, as is shown in the sixth book.

Dante as 'poeta' and 'auctor' in the 'Comedy'

Dante's reverence for 'our greatest poet' (whom he would later call 'il mio maestro e 'l mio *autore*') led him to imitate the *Aeneid* at many different levels in the *Comedy*. There are brief quotations and similes, and adaptations of individual episodes. The first cantica is a sustained narrative of a terrifying journey through Hell. Dido provides the model for Francesca, and Anchises for Cacciaguida. Virgil himself will be assigned the duties of the Sibyl and become the second most important character in the poem. Dante the pilgrim takes on many of the attributes of Aeneas. And in this way the moral qualities he displays in the course of his adventures are those of the noble soul in its Second Age: 'temperanza', 'fortezza', 'amore', 'cortesia' and 'lealtà'.

In the *Comedy*, Dante will not only refer to himself as 'poeta' – something he had not dared to do in the 1290s – but contrive a meeting between himself and the classical poets Homer, Virgil, Horace, Ovid and Lucan, during which they will welcome him as the sixth member of their 'bella scola'. At the moment when he assumes the title of *poeta*, he also lays claim to the rank of an *auctor*. If one wanted to understand the final transformation of 'a courtly value in Dante's hands', one would have to leave behind the prose of *Convivio* IV and study the characterisation of the protagonist in Dante's own *narratio poetica*.[30]

PART THREE

Arch-vices and the supreme virtue

CHAPTER SEVEN

Covetousness

'Diseases are by thousands'

In the discussion of the three competing approaches to ethical values, and in the preceding account of the hallmarks of thirteenth-century thought, we were concerned predominantly with positive concepts such as goodness, happiness and virtue. We have been considering definitions of moral health rather than diagnoses of moral disease. But now the time has come to focus on the first element in the title of this book: 'li *vizi* umani'.

The treatment will be extremely selective if only for the practical reason given by Jonathan Swift:

> Health is but one thing, and has been always the same, whereas diseases are by thousands, besides new and daily additions. All the virtues that have been ever in mankind are to be counted upon a few fingers, but his follies and vices are innumerable, and time adds hourly to the heap.[1]

We shall have to spend a little time looking at the relevant terminology and introducing certain distinctions – for example, between sin and vice; between venial and mortal sin; between the Seven Capital Vices and their progeny. But once this has been done, we shall confine ourselves in this chapter and the next to Dante's poetic representation of the underlying causes of all wrongdoing, the two 'arch-vices', covetousness and pride, which are described in the Bible as 'the root of all ills' ('radix omnium malorum') and 'the beginning of all sin' ('initium omnis peccati').[2]

Vice as a 'habitus inordinatus', and sin as an 'actus inordinatus'

Let us begin by examining the key terms. Vice is in the same genus as virtue. Each can be defined as a *habitus operativus*, that is, a steady disposition of the will, whether natural or acquired, that inclines the agent to choose and to act in a certain way. And since vice is the opposite of virtue (*vitium virtuti contrariatur*), we can draw some inferences about its nature from our knowledge of how a Christian Aristotelian like Dante conceived virtue.[3]

If virtue is what 'makes people happy in their activity', vice is what makes them wretched. If virtue is like beauty or health, vice is like ugliness or illness. If virtue is defined as 'a right relationship of the soul' (*recta habitudo animae*), or a 'well-ordered arrangement (*ordinata dispositio*) of the powers of the soul with respect to each other and to things outside', then vice refers to a wrong relationship, an indisposition, a disorder. Virtue 'leads to well-ordered activity' (*operatio ordinata*), in the sense that each action is *secundum rationem* – in accordance with what is distinctively human in our nature, and subordinated to the true goal of our existence. By contrast, therefore, vice is what leads to irrational behaviour, violations of our nature, and insubordination. 'The acts that follow from vices, being against reason, are in discord with human nature' ('actus vitiorum, cum sint contra rationem, a natura humana discordant').[4]

All the elements in this brief circumscription of vice are fundamentally Aristotelian and they are all culled from Aquinas (who will be treated here as little more than a gifted lexicographer). The words that hardly ever fail to appear in Aquinas's dispassionate definitions of vice and sin are the adjectives *inordinatus* or *immoderatus*. What does the emotive word 'sin' signify to a scholastic theologian? Simply, 'a bad human act' ('peccatum nihil aliud est quam actus humanus malus'). What does a 'bad' act mean? Simply, one 'lacking due order' ('peccca-tum proprie nominat actum inordinatum').[5]

Right loving in Dante: 'il primo bene' and 'i secondi beni'

As Christians, however, both Aquinas and Dante push the Aristotelian analysis of the kind of 'order' required in virtue and virtuous action far beyond Aristotle. They accept a new definition of the ultimate purpose of human existence and the nature of the highest good. Our *finis ultimus* is conceived as spiritual union with an infinite being, who is identical with the God who first revealed himself to the Jews. The *summum bonum* is none other than this uncreated 'Creator of all things', who took on human flesh in Jesus, and subsequently poured his Holy Spirit into the minds and hearts of all who would receive him, in order to make it possible for them to achieve *beatitudo* or *vita aeterna*.[6]

Dante weaves the Aristotelian and Christian concepts together in the doctrinal discourses in the central cantos of the *Comedy*, particularly in *Purgatorio* XVII, where he presents all the Capital Vices as different kinds of misdirected love. God is referred to as the primal good ('primo bene'). Everyone is said to be 'confusedly' aware of such a good, as something 'in which the mind may be finally stilled' ('nel qual si queti l'animo'). He is 'all happiness', 'the root and fruit of all good'. It is he whom we are consciously or unconsciously striving to attain with 'the love of the mind' ('amor d'animo'). All the things he created are good. Many of them are necessary to us in our bodily existence. But they are secondary ('secondi beni'). They are not the 'true essence', they 'cannot make us happy' in themselves. They are to be 'used' as means, and not 'enjoyed' as the end.[7]

In this perspective, there are two aspects to the order required in the disposition of a virtuous soul. Love will not be 'the cause of *sinful* delight' (a) 'for as long as it is directed to God, the primal good', and (b) 'for as long as it exercises restraint with respect to secondary goods':

> Mentre ch'elli è nel primo ben diretto,
> e ne' secondi sé stesso misura,
> esser non può cagion di mal diletto. (*Purg.* XVII, 97–9)

It follows that the *dis*order in the soul (*inordinata dispositio animae*) which characterises every species of vice involves (a) a disregard of God and (b) a lack of measure in the pursuit of temporal goals.

Vice and sin; mortal and venial sins

The difference between a vice and a sin is simply that between a steady disposition of the will and a particular act ('vitium comparatur ad peccatum, sicut *habitus* ad *actum*'). And, as we have seen, a human act is bad when it proceeds from a disorder in the voluntary power that causes it. To quote Aquinas again: 'Every sin consists in the desire for some transient good, which is desired inordinately' ('omne autem peccatum consistit in appetitu alicuius commutabilis boni, quod *inordinate* appetitur').[8]

Our next task is to clarify the distinction between a mortal sin and a venial sin, and to discover the true meaning of the Seven Capital Vices. (It will become clear that their popular appellation – the Seven Deadly Sins – is wrong in everything but the number!)

One of Aquinas's favourite words for the soul's inclination towards a good is *conversio*; and it is important to note that the noun was still close in meaning to the verb *convertere/conversum* ('to turn towards something'), and still related through opposition to the noun *aversio* (from the verb *avertere/aversum*, 'to turn away from', or 'to turn one's back on something'). Hence Aquinas's dictum concerning the disorder to be found in every sinful act may also be expressed as follows: 'in omni peccato est *inordinata conversio* ad commutabile bonum' ('in every sin there is a disordered turning towards a transient good'). It must also be borne in mind that whereas a philosopher considers sin simply as an act 'contrary to reason', a theologian considers it as an 'offence against God' (*offensa contra Deum*).[9]

Now, says Aquinas, if the disordered turning towards a temporal good is done without deliberately turning one's back on God – *sine aversione a Deo* – there is an offence, but it is pardonable, and the penalty incurred is finite. Technically speaking the sin is 'venial' (from *venia*, 'pardon').

But 'when the soul is disordered by sin to the point of turning away from the final goal, namely God, then the sin is mortal', and it 'incurs the penalty of eternal punishment'. ('Quando anima *deordinatur* per peccatum usque ad *aversionem* ab ultimo fine, scilicet Deo . . . tunc est peccatum mortale', 'et consequitur reatus poenae aeternae'.) 'In any mortal sin,' Aquinas says elsewhere, 'the essence of the sin and its gravity lies in the fact that it turns away from God.' ('In quolibet peccato mortali principalis ratio mali et gravitas est ex hoc quod *avertit se a Deo*.')[10]

Since the distinction between the two kinds of sin is vital to the understanding of the first two canticas of the *Comedy*, it must be added that '*every* sin becomes pardonable through repentance' ('*omne* peccatum per poenitentiam fit veniale'). The only difference between the sinners in Hell and those in Purgatory is that the latter had felt remorse for the sins they committed, resolved not to sin again, and wanted to make 'satisfaction' for their sins and to be cleansed of the vice which had led them to turn their backs on God.[11]

The 'head-vices' and their 'progeny'

The vices of mankind, as Swift observed in the passage quoted above, are innumerable. Over the centuries, however, philosophers and theologians had laboured to classify them and to group them in families. And in the most influential of these classifications, the tendencies underlying the majority of vices were reduced to just seven: vainglory, envy, anger, sloth, avarice, greed, and lust (in Latin, *inanis gloria, invidia, ira, acedia, avaritia, gula, luxuria*).

It is these that are properly called *vitia capitalia*. The name tells us that they are the 'head'-vices (*capitale* comes from *caput/capitis*, 'head'). They deserve this title, says Aquinas, not only because they are the source (*principium*) from which many different species of vice arise, 'but also because each of them directs and, in a sense, leads the other vices' ('sed etiam est directivum et quodammodo ductivum aliorum'). What he means by this may be established by glancing at the examples he gives of their 'progeny'. The children of envy, for instance – *filiae invidiae* – include sorrow at other people's good fortune, exultation in their adversities, hatred and slander. The offspring of sloth include rancour, pusillanimity, apathy and despair; whilst among the daughters of avarice are numbered inhumanity, hardening of the heart, violence, perjury, fraud and treachery.[12]

The arch-vice of 'cupidigia'

The title of this chapter, however, alludes to something that can be described as even 'more fundamental than the Capital Vices', 'aliquid *principalius* capitalibus vitiis'. It is the deep-lying cause of every 'disordered turning towards a transient good' ('inordinata conversio ad commutabile bonum'), which is what St Paul is supposed to have had in mind when he spoke of the 'root of all ills' ('radix omnium malorum'). In a dense synthesis of Christian and Aristotelian elements, Aquinas defines it as 'an inclination ingrained in our fallen nature to seek transient goods immoderately' ('inclinatio naturae corruptae ad bona corruptibilia *inordinate* appetenda').[13]

Unfortunately, there is a problem with regard to the name of this 'root'. In English the old-fashioned word 'covetousness' is at once the most comprehensive and the least ambiguous (which is why it appears in the chapter title). But the word in ordinary modern usage is 'greed'; and one could certainly accept 'acquisitiveness' or 'graspingness'.

There are similar problems in medieval Latin. In Jerome's Bible, the crucial noun in the Greek (*philargyría*, meaning 'love of money') is translated as *cupiditas*. However, when the Pauline verse was quoted in isolation, *cupiditas* was sometimes replaced by *avaritia*. *Avaritia* was usually the narrower of the two terms, but there was no sharp dividing line between them. *Avaritia* is defined by Aquinas as 'a disordered desire for money, or for any goods that can be measured by money'; yet the word he uses for 'desire' in the definition is *cupiditas*. Conversely, in his discussion of *cupiditas*, Aquinas recognises that it can be used in three acceptations, of which the first two are synonymous with *avaritia* in the senses just recognised ('an inordinate appetite for riches, or for *any* temporal good'). When Dante in the *Comedy* makes his fellow Florentine Ciacco say that 'superbia, invidia e *avarizia*' are the three sparks that have kindled the fires of discord in their divided city, the context suggests that 'avarizia' means the 'arch-vice' of covetousness (what Dante will elsewhere call 'cupidigia'), rather than the Capital Vice of hoarding and stinginess.[14]

If the scholastics themselves recognised multiple and overlapping meanings in the two key terms, we must expect a far greater indeterminacy – and richness – in Dante's poetic treatment. It will soon become clear that he is drawing on many traditions with many different emphases. He combines the popular and the learned, the poets and the theologians. Here he draws on Horace, there on a troubadour. Now he aligns himself with Boethius, and now with the 'good friar, Thomas of Aquino'. The literary forms he adopts are no less varied. They include brief *exempla*, elaborate similes, extended metaphors, generalised invective, vividly dramatised encounters with historical people, symbolic punishments, conscious allegories, and re-creations of classical myth.

The following survey of Dante's representations of covetousness follows no predetermined order and makes no claim to completeness. It is selective and free-ranging in order to emphasise that Dante does not confine himself to a single system of ideas and does not accept any boundaries to his imagination. Our subject is a universal vice in the hands of a great poet.

Avarice in the canzone 'Doglia mi reca'

Let us begin with words and word-play. Dante uses many names for the objects of covetousness. He adopts the neutral term 'possessions' and abstract phrases such as the 'goods entrusted to Fortune' or 'present things'. Wealth is denoted by two different words, the colloquial 'ricchezze', and the learned 'dovizie'. Gold and silver ('oro e argento') are paired, as they are in the Bible, to signify not only the precious metals themselves but the money that can be exchanged for all objects of desire. And the simple verb 'avere' ('to have') may be used as a noun.

The last word is less bland than it might appear. With a typically medieval love for a fanciful etymology, Dante likes to think that the word 'avaro' ('miser' or 'miserly') is derived from 'avere'. It is as though the author of *Finnegans Wake* would have us believe that the English word 'avaricious' derives from 'have-riches' – the puns being subordinate to the point that a miser wants to *have* riches, rather than put them to good *use*.[15]

Dante's earliest pronouncement on the theme of *avaritia* comes in his canzone 'Doglia mi reca ne lo core ardire' (written c. 1304–5). The poem is dominated from start to finish by antitheses and surprising leaps of thought, all of which are reinforced by word-play (as in 'avaro' and 'avere') or by alliteration (as in the other italicised words in the following passage, where the patterning of sound hints at further etymological links between 'follower', 'lord' and 'slave'):[16]

> Chi è *servo* è come quello ch'è *seguace*
> ratto a *segnore*, e non sa dove vada,
> per dolorosa strada;
> come l'*avaro seguitando avere*,
> ch'a tutti *segnoreggia*. (*Rime* CVI, 64–8)

A slave [to vice] is like a servant following headlong after his master along a painful road without knowing where he is going, just like the miser pursuing wealth, which lords it over everyone.

Like its predecessor, 'Le dolci rime d'amor', this canzone is written 'con rima aspra e sottile'. Like the earlier poem, too, it could be said to treat a courtly virtue – in this case generosity ('larghezza') – with insights gained from the study of philosophy. But there the resemblances end. 'Doglia mi reca' dates from the early years of the exile, when the author was dependent on the largesse of aristocratic patrons in Tuscany, and was learning 'how hard a road it is to go up and down other people's stairs', and 'how salty is the taste of another man's bread'. The poem is born of pain and anger. It develops into a fierce attack on the vice opposed to generosity, *avaritia*, in the particular form of the miserliness of patrons, who cover their own 'vile mud' with fine clothes, but allow men like Dante 'to roam naked over mountain and marsh'. It reminds us that Dante's knowledge of avarice came not only from his reading of poets or philosophers, but also from the sufferings of exile.[17]

The taste of gold

The popular image of the miser is one of a miserable old man gloating over a hoard of gold coins that he can neither eat nor drink, will never exchange for beautiful things, and never put to joyful use by relieving the needs of others. All he desires is to keep possession of the yellow-brown metal itself. The sheer absurdity of such behaviour is made evident in the *Comedy* through two classical *exempla*, which are recited as a kind of litany by the souls of the penitent misers in Purgatory, who at nightfall meditate on various disasters caused by their vice. Among other names they repeat those of Midas (who could neither eat nor drink once Apollo had granted his wish that everything he touched should turn to gold) and of the oriental tyrant Crassus, whose thirst for gold was quenched when his captors poured the molten metal down his throat.[18]

It can scarcely be said that Dante brings the figure of Midas to life, but he does remind us of the derision aroused by his plight. 'Laughing' (in Latin, *ridere/risum)* may be an expression of joy; but when laughter is directed *at* someone (*deridere/derisum*), it is anything but joyful. Fear of derision is a powerful deterrent. And derision is precisely what Dante conveys in the brief snatch of direct speech used in the taunting of Crassus:

> '[Noi repetiam] la miseria de l'avaro Mida,
> che seguì a la sua dimanda gorda,
> per la qual sempre convien che si rida.
> . . .
> ultimamente ci si grida: "Crasso,
> dilci, che 'l sai: di che sapore è l'oro?"'
> (*Purg*. xx, 103, 106–8, 116–17)

'We repeat the wretchedness that followed the greedy request of Midas the miser, at which men must always laugh. Finally we call out to each other: "Crassus, tell us, you who know the answer: what is the taste of gold?"'

The sterility of money

The thirteenth century did not distinguish between the market value of a rare metal like silver or gold, and the value assigned to a coin considered as a token. Few people were able to conceive money in abstract terms as a way of measuring incommensurables on a single scale, which facilitates the exchange of goods and services, and enables a vendor to save the value of whatever he has sold until such time as he wants to buy goods or services of comparable value from a third party. To the medieval moralist, an accumulation of money was not capital, not a present potential for future exchange, but an inert heap of metal.[19]

This confusion helps to account for the widespread detestation of usury. The stereotype of the usurer was that of a person who had put together a 'pile' of money, just like the miser, but who neither hoarded it nor gave it away to win the friendship and gratitude of poets in need. Instead he preferred to lend it to some merchant-venturer or to a king who had an army to pay during a campaign. For this loan the usurer charged interest. Indeed, in the case of a merchant or a king, he charged a high rate of interest that matched the high risk of never seeing his money again.

There was of course nothing objectionable in making an interest-free loan to a friend, and nothing wrong in asking a modest return on a loan to a farmer that would enable him to buy seed or ewes. He would repay the loan out of his profit when he sold the crop or the lambs; and it was right for the lender to have his share of the natural increase in order to compensate for the use (*usus*) that had been made of his capital. All this was thought to be 'in accordance with nature', *secundum naturam*. But there seemed to be a difference in kind between loans at low interest on high security and loans at high interest on low security. The latter did not involve *usus*, but *usura*. Money was being made to breed money. This was 'against nature', *contra naturam*.[20]

Such was the pattern of thought that led Dante to classify usury as a form of violence against nature and to punish the sin in the same area of Hell as sodomy. The collocation seems extraordinary today; and the syllogistical reasoning by which it is justified (accompanied as usual by clear-cut divisions and symmetrical numeration) seems almost a parody of the typical procedures of scholastic thought illustrated in Part One. Yet it is difficult not to respond to Dante's philomythic imagination, when he 'makes manifest to our eyes' the terrifying 'revenge' exacted by God ('vendetta di Dio'), and the 'horrific art of his justice' ('di giustizia orribil arte').[21]

Human beings are 'known by their fruits'. They are required to be active – to do and to make (*agere et facere*). They must not expect inanimate gold to increase by itself. So the sterility of sins against nature is punished and symbolised by an eternal rain of fire ('etternale ardore') on a plain of infertile sand ('sabbione'), a rain all the more terrifying because 'the slow falling of the broad flakes of fire' is compared to that of 'snow in windless mountains', and because 'the sand itself catches fire, like tinder under the flint, to redouble the torment'.

> Sovra tutto 'l sabbion, d'un cader lento,
> piovean di foco dilatate falde,
> come di neve in alpe sanza vento.
> . . .
> tale scendeva l'etternale ardore;
> onde la rena s'accendea, com'esca
> sotto focile, a doppiar lo dolore. (*Inf.* XIV, 28–30, 37–9)

The 'wretched hands' of the violent against nature have become active at last, but only in a vain and never-ending 'dance' as they try to 'brush off the ever-fresh burning, now on this side, now on that':[22]

> Sanza riposo mai era la tresca
> de le misere mani, or quindi or quinci
> escotendo da sé l'arsura fresca. (40–2)

Philosophy and philomythy in proofs of the 'vileness' of riches

From the sterility of gold, we turn to the 'baseness' of all possessions. In 'Le dolci rime d'amor', Dante had asserted that riches cannot confer 'gentilezza', because they are 'ignoble by their nature' ('però che vili son da lor natura'); and in his later prose commentary he devotes no fewer than three chapters (*Convivio* IV, xi–xiii) to prove this inherent 'viltate'.[23]

With a typically scholastic distinction between 'absolute' and 'qualified' meanings, Dante establishes that riches, such as gold, pearls and fields, are 'noble and perfect' when considered in themselves, as parts of God's creation, but 'vili e imperfette' when considered as human possessions. Then he argues – with no less typical divisions and subdivisions – that riches must be imperfect because (a) they are often acquired undeservedly, violently or dishonestly, (b) their increase never brings the contentment they promise, and (c) their possession causes unhappiness by making the owner continually fearful for their loss, and envied and hated by his fellows. These claims are supported by quotations from a wide range of Dante's authorities, including poets ancient and modern, the Roman moralists, civil and canon law, not to mention Aristotle and both testaments of the Bible. There are also one or two vivid examples drawn from Dante's own observation, such as his account of the anxieties of merchants when accompanying their wares, or the chance discovery of an ancient treasure by the 'vilest peasant in Falterona'.[24]

The most original paragraphs come in the long discussion concerning the increase of riches. Dante strikes out boldly as a thinker in his distinction between the ignoble and inhuman desire for possessions and the noble and quintessentially human desire for understanding. He also sketches out in his own words the fundamental contrast between 'il primo bene' and 'i secondi beni', that is, between created goods, which can never satisfy human longings, and the Creator, in whom alone we shall find perfect peace and happiness. But this section of the *Convivio* is important above all because it is here that Dante the 'philomythes' takes over for a time from Dante the 'philosopher', the poet's imagination being fired in quick succession by religion, science, and personal observation.[25]

For the first time in his œuvre, he takes up and develops the ancient image of the 'journey' of human life ('il nuovo e mai non fatto *cammino* di nostra vita'). The soul is represented as being on a return journey to God and as being continually deceived in its belief that each new 'house' on the skyline must be the 'inn' of its final destination. This extended metaphor is followed by a learned simile, taken from the science of optics. The finite goods we pursue are said to be like the 'base' of a pyramid with its 'apex' in our eye: the further we proceed, or the further we can see, the bigger the base becomes; and so ad infinitum. The objects of our successive and ever expanding desires, meanwhile, are charmingly exemplified from thirteenth-century life. 'We see children first desire an apple, then, as they get older, a pet bird, then, a little later, fine clothes, then a horse, then a woman, then modest riches, then great riches, and then more.'[26]

> Onde vedemo li parvuli desiderare massimamente un pomo; e poi, più procedendo, desiderare uno augellino; e poi più oltre, desiderare bel vestimento; e poi lo cavallo, e poi una donna; e poi ricchezza non grande, e poi grande, e poi più. (*Con.* IV, xii, 16)

Personification and 'bestiarisation'

The gap between the *Convivio* and the *Comedy* may be illustrated by seeing how Dante represents the insatiability of the desire for greater wealth. In the prose work, Dante still feels himself under an obligation to quote his authorities; and he limits himself to a rather pallid personification of riches as 'traitresses' or 'temptresses'. His sentences are characteristic of medieval rhetorical prose in their balance, rhythms and antitheses, and, not least, in their wordiness (the following excerpt has been discreetly pruned):

Promettono le false traditrici sempre, in certo numero adunate, rendere lo raunatore pieno d'ogni appagamento; e con questa promissione conducono l'umana volontade in vizio d'avarizia. E per questo le chiama Boezio, in quello De Consolatione, pericolose, dicendo . . .

Promettono le false traditrici . . . di tòrre ogni sete e ogni mancanza . . . e poi che quivi sono adunate, in loco di . . . refrigerio danno e recano sete . . . E però dice Tullio in quello De Paradoxo, abominando le ricchezze . . . 'in nullo tempo si compie né si sazia la sete de la cupiditate'. (*Con.* IV, xii, 4–6)

These false traitors always promise that if they are amassed in a certain quantity, they will fill with every contentment the person who so amasses them; and by this promise they lead the human will into the vice of avarice. This is why Boethius, in his *Consolatio*, calls them dangerous, saying . . .

These false traitors promise to take away every thirst and every want; and then, when they are amassed, instead of refreshment, they bring thirst. This is why Cicero, in *De paradoxo*, inveighing against riches, says that . . . 'the thirst of covetousness is never satisfied or quenched'.

In the very first canto of the *Comedy*, personification gives way to what we might call 'bestiarisation', implying that Dante combines imagery from the Hebrew prophets with elements of contemporary heraldry to create an allegory of the kind found in medieval bestiaries. When the protagonist emerges from the 'selva oscura', he tries to climb a sunlit hill but is driven back by three beasts: first, a leopard, 'light and swift'; then, a lion rampant 'with head held high', and finally – decisively – by a female wolf ('una lupa'), whose chief attribute is emaciation ('magrezza').[27]

Whatever the first two beasts may represent allegorically, there can be no doubt that the wolf symbolises the arch-vice of covetousness and above all its insatiability. Skin and bone though she is, she seems 'crammed with all longings'. She is a 'beast without peace'. 'Her nature is so wicked and depraved that she can never satisfy her greedy appetite; after the meal she is hungrier than before':

> e ha natura sì malvagia e ria,
> che mai non empie la bramosa voglia,
> e dopo 'l pasto ha più fame che pria. (*Inf.* I, 97–9)

The effects of this ravening hunger are hinted at in the details of the allegorical narrative. It is fear of the wolf that makes the protagonist 'lose hope of the heights'. It is the wolf, not the leopard or the lion, who 'drives him back down to where the sun is silent'. The help he will implore from Virgil is, above all, help from her ('Aiutami da *lei*'). She is the arch-enemy of all men. Not only has she made 'many peoples live in wretchedness', but she will 'allow no one to pass, obstructing all comers until she kills them'.[28]

The allegory is pursued into the future in Virgil's prophetic words which bring the episode to an end. The wolf 'mates with many animals and will do so with many more' (perhaps an image of the way in which arch-vices and Capital Vices combine to beget many *filiae*). She will be overcome, however, by the Greyhound ('veltro'), who 'will not feed on lands or lucre, but on Wisdom, Love and Power' (the attributes of the Trinity), and who will 'drive her back to Hell, whence Envy first unleashed her'.[29]

The consequences of covetousness expressed through metaphor

In *Purgatorio*, Dante created another allegorical figure to express, not the 'driving' force of greed within us, but the 'pulling' force of the things outside. Before we glance at his representation of the Siren, however, we must see what may be learnt from the metaphors that cluster round this theme.

The *Paradiso* opens with an assertion that the 'radiance of the First Mover penetrates the whole universe, and shines out more in one part and less in another':

> La gloria di colui che tutto move
> per l'universo penetra e risplende,
> in una parte più, e meno altrove. (*Par.* I, 1–3)

Two contrasting ideas are yoked inseparably in this terzina. On the one hand, the different parts of creation are unequal in goodness, varying in the extent to which they absorb and reflect the light of their Creator. On the other, the whole of the material universe is *valde bonum* – 'very good', in the phrase from Genesis – and everything that attracts us in temporal things is some ray or reflection of the divine glory.[30]

All the manifold objects of our love are good in themselves, but their sheer number and magnitude can be dangerous. Human loving is good only if it is *ordinatus*. This is the theme on which Dante allows his metaphorical imagination to run riot in a later canto of the *Paradiso*. Covetousness (defined as the '*inordinatus* appetitus rerum temporalium') can 'swamp mortal men' like the sea, 'so that no one has the strength to lift his eyes above the waves'. Or – switching to a different kind of flood-water – the 'continuous rain' of secondary goods 'turns the early blossom on the human will into sour and withered fruits ("bozzacchioni"), rather than true plums':

> Oh cupidigia, che i mortali affonde
> sì sotto te, che nessuno ha podere
> di trarre li occhi fuor de le tue onde!
> Ben fiorisce ne li uomini il volere;
> ma la pioggia continüa converte
> in bozzacchioni le sosine vere. (*Par.* XXVII, 121–6)

In two of his high-flown Latin letters, Dante treats the subject with a further extended metaphor, in which the attractions of worldly things become the blandishments of a whore:

> Blind as you are, you are unaware of this all-mastering lust (*cupido*), blandishing you with its poisononous whisperings, coercing you with deceiving threats, and enslaving you to the law of sin. (*Epist.* VI, 22)

> Ah, do not let covetousness (*cupiditas*) seduce you with her wiles, deadening the vigilance of reason with an indefinable sweetness, as the Sirens do. (*Epist.* V, 13)

The unmasking of the Siren by divine grace

The metaphors in the Latin letters are more conventional than those of the 'waves' and the 'rain' in the *Paradiso*, but the allusion to the Sirens leads us on to Dante's most subtle personification of our disordered love for temporal things.

In classical myth the Sirens were mermaids, who sat on the shore of a rocky island and lured sailors to their doom by the irresistible sweetness of their singing. Ulysses, it is true, was able to hear their song and live to tell the tale; but to do so, he had to plug the ears of his crew with wax, and have himself lashed to the mast. For many centuries the Sirens had been used as a relatively inert symbol of all kinds of meretricious attraction; and if the last phrase in Dante's letter is in any way remarkable, it is only for the seductive euphony of its rhythms and sounds ('more Sirenum nescio qua dulcedine vigiliam rationis mortificans').[31]

In his own adaptation of the myth, Dante limits himself to one Siren, who makes her appearance during the protagonist's second dream in Purgatory. The precise moment is important because it comes just before the meetings with the souls who had surrendered themselves to covetousness, and – more importantly – just after Virgil has explained in philosophical language the difference between the Primal Good and secondary goods.[32]

At the beginning of the dream, the Siren appears in her true guise – squinting, bent and twisted, her hands amputated, her speech impeded. It is Dante's gaze that 'loosens her tongue, straightens her up, and gives colour to her pallid face, as Love would like to see it'. Only then does she sing her hypnotic song ('Io son dolce serena, / che i marinari in mezzo mar dismago'), in which she boasts – falsely – that she was successful in luring Ulysses from his journey, and that she 'rarely loses any habituee ("qual meco s'ausi"), because she satisfies his desires so completely'. Before she has finished her song, however, St Lucy appears at Dante's side, rips the Siren's garments open, and wakens the dreamer with the stench that rises from her midriff.[33]

Dante had a special reverence for St Lucy because she is the patron saint of sight. In the *Comedy* we first encountered her in *Inferno* II, where she was shown to have acted as an intermediary between the Virgin and Beatrice in the special process of grace through which Dante is to be delivered from evil. A careful reading of the dream shows it to be a complex statement about the roles of grace, reason and the imagination. It was Dante's imagination that made the hideous woman attractive in the first place by summoning up 'false images of the good' ('immagini di ben . . . false'). Reason – in the person of Virgil who failed to rout the primeval enchantress ('antica strega') – could only stand by impotently, unable to save the dreamer from his error. It required divine intervention, in the person of Lucy, to reveal the truth and set man free from the bonds of 'le presenti cose / col falso lor piacer[e]'.[34]

Symbolism in the mode of penance: the earthward gaze

The dream of the Siren made an enduring impression on the protagonist, who walked along with his eyes lowered, lost in thought, until he was reproached by Virgil for looking only at the ground ('che hai che pur inver' la terra guati?'). Virgil then revealed the meaning of the 'novella visione' and urged Dante to 'strike the ground with his heels, but to lift his eyes to the circling heavens above'. These 'great wheels' ('rote magne') are the immortal parts of God's creation, whose beauty we admire, but never dream of possessing. They are the parts intended to lead our thoughts directly to God, the 'eternal king' ('lo rege etterno'). It is in this sense that Virgil can refer to the spheres as a 'lure' ('logoro'), using the word in the original, technical sense of the term, that is, a bunch of feathers attached to a thong that a falconer would whirl around in order to summon his falcon back. Virgil's successive images embody some very rapid transitions of thought, but the protagonist has no difficulties in following him and responds to the reproof just as he should, by metaphorically imitating the falcon:[35]

> 'Bastiti, e batti a terra le calcagne;
> li occhi rivolgi al logoro che gira
> lo rege etterno con le rote magne.'
> Quale 'l falcon . . . / tal mi fec' io . . .
>
> (*Purg*. XIX, 61–4, 66)

The ideas adumbrated in the metaphor of the 'logoro', and in the simile to which it gave rise, are clarified immediately afterwards in another literary mode. Dante and Virgil arrive on the fifth circle of Purgatory. This is the circle of the avaricious, who lie on the ground, weeping, facing downwards. They sing a verse from a psalm, 'Adhaesit pavimento anima mea' (literally, 'My soul cleaved to the floor'), which is simultaneously a description of the nature of their vice and of the penance and purification they now endure.

The unnaturalness of their position is emphasised by two locutions that border on the grotesque, as the protagonist asks why they have 'their backs upwards' ('perché avete i dossi / al sù'), and one of the souls promises to tell him 'why heaven turns our backsides to itself' ('perché i nostri diretri / rivolga il cielo a sé'). The colloquial realism of these phrases also makes an effective contrast to the answer soon to be given by Dante's as yet unnamed interlocutor, which is as measured and dignified in its rhythms as it is precise in vocabulary and thought:[36]

> 'Quel ch'avarizia fa, qui si dichiara
> in purgazion de l'anime converse;
> e nulla pena il monte ha più amara.
> Sì come l'occhio nostro non s'aderse
> in alto, fisso a le cose terrene,
> così giustizia qui a terra il merse.
> Come avarizia spense a ciascun bene
> lo nostro amore, onde operare perdési,
> così giustizia qui stretti ne tene,
> ne' piedi e ne le man legati e presi.'
>
> (*Purg*. XIX, 115–24)

'What avarice does, is here made manifest in the purification of the souls who turned to God; and the mountain has no penalty more bitter. Just as our eyes refused to lift themselves on high, remaining fixed on earthly things, so Justice sank them here to the earth. Just as avarice extinguished our love for every good, nullifying all activity, so Justice holds us fast here, as captives, bound hand and foot.'

Selling 'the things of God' for gold and silver

The speaker here is a churchman who tells Dante that his soul had been 'completely avaricious', and therefore 'utterly wretched and cut off from God', until he was elected as 'the Roman Pastor' (taking the name of Hadrian V in 1276). Only then did he realise that 'his heart could not find rest in the fallacious life', and only then did he feel his 'love kindled for life in Heaven'. It was a late conversion, he stresses (he died still uncrowned a month later); and we are to understand that there was something almost miraculous in his change of heart. Dante is making the polemical point that it was far from certain that a man's thoughts would turn to God on becoming pope. In his view, no fewer than three of Hadrian's succcessors had viewed their elevation as an opportunity to abandon themselves completely to a particular sin deriving from covetousness, which was possible only for those in holy orders.[37]

This sin is called simony (after a sorcerer named Simon, who much admired the miracles worked by the Holy Spirit through the apostles Peter and John, and offered them money to acquire their spiritual power). It refers in the narrowest sense to the selling of ecclesiastical offices to the highest bidder, and in a wider sense to all misapplication of the revenues of the church. It is arguably the worst possible form of *cupiditas* or *avaritia*, since any priest ought to have his heart and mind 'directed to the Primal Good'. It is supremely damnable in the supreme pastor. Dante devised a special 'bolgia' in the eighth circle of his Hell for the eternal punishment of 'the followers of Simon Magus, who rapaciously prostitute the things of God for gold and silver'; and he devised one of his boldest dramatic scenes to expose the nature of the sin and to humiliate the papal sinners.[38]

The *mise en scène* depends on the particular mode of punishment, which, as usual, is highly symbolic. The simoniacs are half buried, head downwards, in holes in the rock. Flames play over their kicking legs in a parody of the tongues of fire, symbolising the Holy Spirit, that flickered over the heads of the apostles at the first Pentecost. When the protagonist walks across to the most agitated of these legs, the unsighted victim hails him in some amazement as 'Boniface' (mistaking him for the reigning pope at the time of Dante's journey, who is destined to occupy this same hole, but not just yet!). The sinner then reveals that he had been a member of the Orsini family in Rome and that he too had been pope (taking the name of Nicholas III). In a series of grim wordplays, he says that he was a 'true son of the bear ("orsa"), since I was so greedy for the advancement of my cubs, that I put wealth into my purse on earth, and myself into a purse here in Hell'. He goes on to foretell the damnation not only of Boniface VIII (who reigned from 1295 to 1303), but of the Frenchman Clement V (1305–14), both of whom are to be consigned to the same round hole in the rock.[39]

The protagonist remains close by the thrashing legs of Nicholas, and, undeterred by his 'reverence for the supreme keys', delivers him a scorching homily in the style of a popular preacher. The biblical phrase 'gold and silver', used in the definition of simony at the beginning of the canto, returns as a refrain to punctuate his diatribe against the simoniac popes.

> 'Deh or mi dì: quanto tesoro volle
> Nostro Segnore in prima da san Pietro
> ch'ei ponesse le chiavi in sua balìa?
> Certo non chiese se non "Viemmi retro".
> Né Pier né li altri tolsero a Matia
> *oro od argento*, quando fu sortito
> al loco che perdé l'anima ria.
> . . .
> Fatto v'avete dio d'*oro e d'argento*:
> e che altro è da voi a l'idolatre,
> se non ch'elli uno, e voi ne orate cento?'
>
> (*Inf.* XIX, 90–6, 112–14)

'How much treasure did our Lord demand from Peter before he entrusted the keys to him? Surely he asked nothing except "Follow me". Neither Peter nor the others took gold or silver from Matthias when he was chosen to replace the vile soul [Judas]. . . . You have made for yourselves a god of gold and silver; and what difference is there between you and the idolaters [who worshipped the Golden Calf], except that they prayed to one such god, and you to a hundred of them?'

'Sedare fluctus cupiditatis'

To understand the vehemence of this attack, we must turn away from Dante's ethics for a moment and glance at his political thought. In the last chapter of his *Monarchia* Dante declares that human beings have to be shown the way to happiness in this world and the next by 'philosophical and spiritual teachings'. But teaching alone is not enough. They must be 'held in check with bit and bridle like horses on their journey', because otherwise 'human covetousness would simply disregard those logical deductions' ('has conclusiones . . . *humana cupiditas* postergaret, nisi homines, tanquam equi . . . "in camo et freno" compescerentur in via'). It is for this reason that there must be two sets of laws – one secular and one sacred – and two men with absolute power in their own sphere to ensure that the laws are implemented justly. These 'guides' (as Dante calls them in *Purgatorio*) are 'the Supreme Pontiff, who should lead mankind to eternal life in accordance with revelation, and the Emperor, who should guide mankind to temporal happiness in accordance with the teachings of philosophy'. And the central tenet of Dante's political thought is that the two 'governances' must never be 'confounded'. The 'sword' and the pastoral 'crook' must never be in the same hand.[40]

Strictly speaking, it is the task of the Emperor to 'calm the waves of covetousness' (*sedare fluctus cupiditatis*) that threaten to 'drown' mankind before it can reach its earthly 'port'. But although the Roman Prince ought to be completely independent of the Roman Pontiff, Dante recognises that he is 'in some matters subject to him, since mortal happiness is in some sense subordinate to immortal happiness'. 'Caesar should show Peter the same reverence that a firstborn son shows his father', in order that, 'enlightened by the light of paternal grace, he may illuminate the world more effectively'.[41]

With these words in mind, we may return to the 'bolgia' of the simoniacs. Far from confining themselves to the spiritual sphere, Nicholas, Boniface and Clement (and others of their ilk) had seized the sword and constantly intervened in political struggles for temporal power. Far from aiding the Emperor in the task of holding *cupiditas* in check (by reminding mankind of its true treasure – the 'treasure in heaven' that Jesus promised to the young man), the three popes were themselves tainted by covetousness and guilty of the worst sin springing from that vice. In Dante's judgement, they destroyed all prospect of happiness in this life through their 'idolatry of gold and silver'. That is why they are treated with such violence and scorn.

'Cupiditas' and 'caritas'

Before leaving Dante's political thought, we ought to recall that he regarded covetousness as the worst enemy of happiness at every level of society. Possession of riches creates envy and hatred within the family, within the commune, and within a national kingdom like France. 'What else', Dante asks rhetorically in *Convivio* IV, can 'daily endanger and destroy cities, provinces and individual human beings, as much as someone suddenly amassing wealth?' 'What are canon law and civil law intended for other than to remedy the harm done by covetousness ("riparare a la cupiditate"), which grows by increase of riches?'[42]

This train of thought culminates in an eloquent and exemplary chapter in the first book of the *Monarchia*. Dante quotes Aristotle to the effect that covetousness is the vice 'diametrically opposed to justice'. In the same breath he contrasts *cupiditas* with *caritas* in this respect, drawing on the thought and rhythms of St Paul in 1 Corinthians 13. And for his own part he contributes a half-hidden image of the sword of justice being 'tarnished' by covetousness, but 'sharpened and burnished' by charity:

> Remota cupiditate omnino, nichil justitiae restat adversum . . . Praeterea, quemadmodum cupiditas habitualem justitiam quodam modo, quantumcunque pauca, obnubilat, sic caritas seu recta dilectio illam acuit atque dilucidat . . . Cupiditas namque, perseitate hominum spreta, quaerit alia; caritas vero, spretis aliis omnibus, quaerit Deum et hominem, et per consequens bonum hominis. (*Mon.* I, xi, 11, 13)

> When covetousness is totally cast out, nothing remains to oppose justice. Even a breath of covetousness in some way casts a dull cloud over justice, considered as a moral virtue in the will; but charity or right loving sharpens and brightens it. Covetousness, spurning the true nature of man, seeks other things; whereas charity, spurning all other things, seeks God and man, and in consequence seeks what is good for man.

Extravagance, evangelical poverty, and the Aristotelian mean

Cupiditas, it will be remembered, is 'something more fundamental than the Capital Vices'. It embraces not only avarice and simony, but a great many vices and sins relative to sensual pleasures, especially those of 'wine, women and song'. These, too, are bad to the extent that they are expressions of an 'inordinate love of temporal things'; and many of them were condemned by Dante, as by other contemporary moralists, in connection with the Capital Vices of lechery and gluttony.

This is not the place to examine Dante's treatment of these other vices (which between them occupy fully seven cantos in *Inferno* and

Purgatorio). Dante was not interested in *luxuria* in its ordinary manifestations. The punishments he devised for *gula* are illuminating, but need no commentary here, since they may be interpreted in the same spirit as those of the usurers and the avaricious. Even the protagonist's encounters with two individual 'golosi' – each of them a Florentine friend – do not reveal much about the nature of their vice, since the focus is shifted on to high living in Florence and its social consequences. In other words, Dante has relatively little to say about 'immoderate desire for pleasure in food and drink' (Aquinas's definition of *gula*), and he passes rapidly from an attack on private self-indulgence to condemnation of the public ostentation of wealth.[43]

Anthropologists have taught us to look in a more favourable light at extravagant expenditure on feasts and finery by analysing them under the head of 'conspicuous consumption', and seeing them as an inevitable feature of life in any hierarchical society where the distribution of wealth is glaringly unequal. But from Dante's point of view, they were a misuse of resources which might have been devoted to the common good, or to the relief of individuals in distress, rather than to the selfish gratification of bodily appetites.

Dante was particularly scathing about the self-indulgence of people in holy orders. Like so many other critics of the worldliness of the clergy, he contrasted the corporate wealth of the church, and the squandering of its revenues by certain prelates, with the total renunciation of property that Jesus enjoined on his disciples, and the relatively austere regimes followed by monastic communities who observed the Benedictine rule. As was noted in Chapter 5, the ideal of evangelical poverty had been reasserted by St Francis of Assisi; and it was still upheld in an extreme form by his more radical followers, the Spirituals (whose teaching was to be explicitly condemned as heretical by Pope John XXII in 1323, just two years after Dante's death). The Spirituals believed that the Franciscan order itself (as a legal entity, distinct from the individual friars who took the normal vows of chastity, obedience and poverty) should own nothing corporately and should not even lay up stores of provisions.

There can be little doubt that one part of Dante was extremely sympathetic to this ideal. In his panegyric of Francis in *Paradiso* XI, he gave great prominence to the mystic marriage between the saint and the 'widow' of Christ, whom no one had ventured to approach for 'eleven hundred years and more' – the marriage between 'Francesco e *Povertà*'. For Dante, the classical myth of the Golden Age was a dream-like recollection of Adam and Eve in the Garden of Eden before the Fall; and while he conceded that it takes hunger to make acorns appetising, and thirst to make stream-water taste like nectar, he could evoke the delights of plain and homely fare in a lovely phrase he used to describe the monastic diet: 'cibi di liquor d'ulivi'.[44]

On the other hand, Dante was by no means opposed to the institution of private property for the majority of mankind, and not at all inclined to deny the body's natural needs. He accepted the Aristotelian teaching that we shall not 'come to happiness' in this life, unless we possess sufficient worldly goods to enable us to live healthily, rear a family, make provision for times of famine, assist the destitute, and create leisure for the enjoyment of friendship and study. External goods are to be considered as 'tools' for 'living well'. It is just as foolish to renounce them altogether, as it is for a carpenter to give up his chisel and saw.

The key-word here is 'sufficient'. The analogy suggests that one needs to own just so many tools as are required to perform the job in hand – not too few, certainly, but not too many either. And with those simple words we have returned to the Aristotelian analysis of human goodness, in which each of the eleven moral virtues consists in a disposition to choose the mean between too little and too much, and in which, therefore, every virtue has two collateral vices, 'uno in troppo, e un altro in poco'.[45]

Avarice and prodigality as 'collateral vices'

One of the main reasons for reviewing Dante's authorities in Chapter 1 was to bring out the wide range of his sympathies. Although he asserted that 'where Aristotle had opened his mouth', his opinion should prevail, Dante did not follow the 'Master of human life' consistently – not even in such a fundamental aspect of his ethics as the doctrine of the mean. Hell is not organised according to a system of paired, collateral vices (which is understandable, given that it is a place for the punishment of misdeeds). Nor is Purgatory (which is somewhat surprising, given that the emphasis falls on the underlying *habitus* – the vice, not the sin). There is, however, one exception to this apparent neglect. Dante decided to follow Aristotle in the single case of avarice and prodigality, which are treated as the two vices opposed to *liberalitas* (which denotes the proper inclination of the will with respect to possessions). In both Hell and Purgatory, misers and spendthrifts are punished in the same zone in the same way.[46]

This decision is given great prominence in *Purgatorio* XXII. Virgil there expresses mild surprise that his fellow poet Statius should have 'given place in his bosom to avarice' and have been a 'miser in the other life'. But Statius smilingly answers: 'You must know that avarice was too far removed from me; and thousands of months have punished this lack of measure' ('questa dismisura'). A phrase in the *Aeneid* had persuaded him that 'hands could open their wings too wide in spending', and led him to repent in time. And he explains that where 'a fault is in direct opposition to some sin', it is 'purged together with its contrary'.[47]

The passage is as leisurely and gentle as the corresponding lines in *Inferno* VII are compressed and violent. In Hell the protagonist sees two groups of the damned moving in opposite directions round the fourth circle. As they come face to face, they clash together like knights jousting, or like waves in a tidal rip, and hurl a ritual insult at each other. Then they reverse direction and proceed until they reach the opposite point, where the same performance is repeated – and will be repeated for all eternity.

All the souls in the 'dark circle' are rolling great weights before them with their chests. But it emerges that those on the right are spendthrifts, while those on the left (many of whom have shaven heads to show they had been clerics) are the avaricious. This is why the questions they 'bay out' at each other in their 'shameful metre' are differentiated: 'Why do you hold on?'; 'Why do you fling away?'[48]

They are separated and yet united by their 'contraria colpa'. Both are shown to have been 'cross-eyed in the first life'; and they are alike in that 'they made no expenditure with due measure' ('nullo spendio con misura ferci'). The objects of their 'dismisura' were the same; and these objects are revealed as no more than inert 'pesi', a source of torment here in Hell, just as they had been on earth, whether they tried to keep them or get rid of them. In either case – whether through 'bad giving' or 'bad holding' – they have lost the 'beautiful world' of Heaven for the sake of lumps of matter.[49]

'I ben che son commessi a la fortuna'

Both groups of sinners in *Inferno* VII also lost their distinctive personalities through contact with material goods. They cannot be recognised as individuals, says Virgil, because 'the unknowing life that soiled them has made them dark to all knowledge'. They were and are insatiable. Even on the Day of Judgement the avaricious will arise with their 'fists still clenched'. 'All the gold that is or ever was under the moon,' Virgil concludes, 'could never give rest to one of these weary souls.' What Dante has just witnessed is the 'short-lived cheat of the goods entrusted to chance ('la corta buffa / d'i ben che son commessi a la *fortuna*').[50]

The next thirty lines of *Inferno* VII are given over to an excursus on 'Fortuna', in the course of which Dante completely transforms the familiar personification of good and bad luck (a goddess turning her wheel without regard to human intentions or deserts). In his hands Fortune becomes a half Neoplatonic, half Christian Intelligence, ordained by God, and placed on a par with the angelic movers of the heavenly spheres ('li splendor mondani'). A new perspective is opened on the movements of the 'empty goods' ('beni vani') of this world, as they are shown to be under the control of a 'general minister and leader', whose task it is to oversee their 'permutations', causing them to pass ceaselessly 'from one people and one race to another, beyond the power of human wit to prevent'.[51]

> Similemente a li splendor mondani
> ordinò general ministra e duce
> che permutasse a tempo li ben vani
> di gente in gente e d'uno in altro sangue,
> oltre la difension d'i senni umani. (*Inf.* VII, 77–81)

The sound of contempt

We have glanced at many different poetic modes in this survey of the arch-vice of *cupiditas*, ranging from a passing reference to Midas to dramatic encounters with two popes, from allegorical figures as unlike each other as the Wolf and the Siren to symbolic punishments as different as impaling and a rain of fire, from an extended metaphor of the waves of the sea to a prose simile of the journey of life. But the representation of the avaricious and prodigal in the fourth circle of Hell embodies two further qualities that are inseparable from its meaning and impact. The nature of the punishment – the incessant rolling of the weights, symbolising the permutation of the 'beni vani' – calls forth a new energy in the images, the power of which resides in the active verbs. And Dante's angry contempt for the sinners and their sin finds its correlative in the deliberate harshness of the rhymes.

Before he wrote the *Comedy*, Dante had made deliberate and sustained use of 'rime aspre' in some of his most original and powerful poems. He turned to them again in his representation of the gluttons in

Inferno VI. But there had been nothing earlier to match the sustained onslaught on our ears that begins in the first line of Canto VII. One simple statistic may serve to establish the point. Of the first twenty-four rhymes, no fewer than seventeen contain two harsh consonants within the final syllables. Each of these bizarre sounds occurs three times; and it would be enough to chant them aloud to realise that the effect is more like Arabic than Italian: *-eppe*, *-occia*, *-abbia*, *-acca*, *-iddi*, *-oppa*, *-urli*, *-etro*, *-unto*, *-ostra*, *-erci*, *-erchio*, *-ozzi*, *-ulcro*, *-uffa*, *-anche*, *-ocche*. Crassus had been forced to discover for himself the 'taste' of gold. Here it is almost as though Dante were forcing us hear the 'sound' of it – and wanting us to understand that it always 'rings false'.

Three terzinas will be enough to exemplify the new features and to bring the chapter to an end in a crescendo of dissonance (by no means limited to the rhyme sounds) and an accelerando of frenzied activity (by no means limited to the italicised verbs and gerunds):

Come fa l'onda là sovra Cariddi,
che *si frange* con quella in cui *s'intoppa*,
così convien che qui la gente *riddi*.
Qui vid' i' gente più ch'altrove troppa,
e d'una parte e d'altra, con grand' urli,
voltando pesi per forza di poppa.
Percotëansi 'ncontro; e poscia pur lì
si rivolgea ciascun, *voltando* a retro,
gridando: 'Perché tieni?' e 'Perché burli?'

(*Inf.* VII, 22–30)

Just as the waves above Charybdis break as they clash together, so here the people are forced to dance their round. Here I saw far more people than elsewhere, both on one side and the other, rolling weights by chest power, with great shouts. They would crash against each other; and then just there, each one would swing round, rolling the weight backwards, shouting: 'Why hold?', and 'Why fling away?'

CHAPTER EIGHT

Pride

The subject of this chapter is Dante's treatment of the 'arch-vice' of *superbia*, with particular reference to the Capital Vice called *vanagloria* (or *inanis gloria*) and to some of the progeny of that vice.

As the reappearance of these terms suggests, there will be numerous similarities with the previous chapter. We shall again take note of divergences within the Aristotelian, Christian and courtly value-systems that Dante was trying to reconcile. We shall find that the poet was aware of distinctions drawn by scholastic theologians, but often chose to set those distinctions aside. It will become apparent, too, that Dante is idiosyncratic in his attempt to define the vice in question, and that the 'children of pride' he chooses to portray are far from identical with those in a brief checklist offered by Aquinas.[1]

But pride is very different from covetousness and is treated by Dante in a very different way. There are no allegorical figures like the Wolf or the Siren. Instead, we meet a number of individuals who defend and reveal themselves in the course of dramatised encounters. Their behaviour contains much to admire as well as much to blame, and they evince precisely that mixture of good and bad qualities which Aristotle held to be appropriate for characters in a tragedy. Pride, moreover, is Dante's own vice, and the only one to which the protagonist confesses explicitly.[2]

As a result of these and other differences, it will be possible to respect Dante's own poetic method and to follow him for a time as he plunges directly into the complex issues involved. There is admittedly some risk in assuming – even provisionally – that Dante's concepts and values are sufficiently close to our own to permit such a procedure. But we may take heart from a significant overlap between medieval and modern usage. In contemporary English, virtually all forms of pride may be described by words beginning with the prefixes 'over-' and 'self-' (for example, 'overbearing', 'overconfident', 'overshooting the mark'; or 'self-important', 'self-seeking', 'self-willed'). In medieval Latin, the accepted etymology of the principal word for pride (*superbia*) also involved the preposition 'over' or 'above' (*super*); and Aquinas remarked that 'it amounts to the same thing whether pride or self-love is posited as the "beginning of all sin"' ('ad idem pertinet quod ponatur "initium omnis peccati" *superbia*, vel *amor proprius*').[3]

'L'imagini di tante umilitadi'

From the Gate of Purgatory, the protagonist and Virgil climb a narrow flight of steps (as narrow as the 'eye of a needle'), which is cut deep into the mountain and allows them to see nothing save the setting moon in the morning sky. They emerge on a bare ledge, projecting about sixteen feet from the blank wall of rock above them and curving away on both sides, evenly and featurelessly, as far as the eye can see.[4]

The two are 'uncertain of their way', not knowing in which direction to proceed, or what to expect. But before they make any move, the pilgrim notices that the marble of the rock face is adorned with sculptures in high relief. The artist (as we are later told) is God; and they are of supernaturally expressive power. They can stimulate the senses of hearing and smell, suggest movement, convey emotion in a gesture, and evoke a whole dialogue between the persons represented. In this silent, rocky place, 'lonelier than roads in a desert', the protagonist discovers with delight the essence of the virtue opposed to pride, as he contemplates three 'images of acts of great humility'.[5]

Two of the scenes show a Jewish king and a Roman Emperor respectively, both of whom dared to abase themselves in the eyes of their subjects. The settings evoked are necessarily public, the spectators numerous. King David dances, with his robes lifted, in front of the ox-cart carrying the Ark of the Covenant. The Emperor Trajan pauses at the head of a densely packed column of cavalry in order to satisfy a widow's plea for justice. In each case a solitary woman is represented to heighten the impact of the 'storia'. The suppliant 'vedovella' catches the Emperor's bridle, her 'attitude showing tears and grief' ('di lagrime atteggiata e di dolore'), and by her simple but insistent words she stirs his sense of justice and compassion and compels him to do his duty, no matter how supremely inconvenient the moment may be. David's proud wife sits at a window, contemplating her husband's demeaning conduct 'sadly and disdainfully'. It is through her eyes that we see him as '*less* than a king' ('meno che re'), whereas the message of the whole scene is that the 'humble Psalmist' was also '*more* than a king in this case': 'e più e men che re era in quel caso'.[6]

The first of the three scenes is as common in Christian art as the story of David's dancing is rare. A woman is present here too, but the implied setting is private, and she herself is the heroine. She is being greeted by an angel, the 'sweetness of whose attitude' is 'so truthful that he did not seem a silent image, and one could swear he was saying *Ave*'. He is Gabriel, who 'has come down to earth with the decree of peace that had been sought with lamentations for many years', the decree that 'opened Heaven after its long denial'. She is the Virgin Mary, portrayed in the very moment in which she learns that, alone of all her sex, she has 'turned the key of divine love' by accepting God's choice that she become the mother of his Son. Far from showing pride, her attitude conveys the words with which she accepted her calling: 'Behold the handmaid of the Lord.'

> L'angel che venne in terra col decreto
> de la molt'anni lagrimata pace,
> ch'aperse il ciel del suo lungo divieto,
> dinanzi a noi pareva sì verace
> quivi intagliato in un atto soave,
> che non sembiava imagine che tace.
> Giurato si saria ch'el dicesse '*Ave*!';
> perché iv' era imaginata quella
> ch'ad aprir l'alto amor volse la chiave;
> e avea in atto impressa esta favella
> '*Ecce ancilla Dei*' propriamente
> come figura in cera si suggella. (*Purg*. x, 34–45)

This is Dante at his most characteristic. Without any warning, and in a totally unexpected way, he has chosen to show us the 'right disposition of the will' before he presents or explains the many forms of disorder. He has put the 'valore' before the 'vizi'. And the beauty and strength of his writing here must be held in mind as a touchstone when one tries to evaluate the stirring and seductive boasts of the children of pride in the *Comedy*.

'Antico sangue' and 'opere leggiadre'

For the remainder of this canto in *Purgatorio*, and for the first half of the next, Dante continues in the same mode, although he moves from the remote past to the present, and from what he calls 'visible speech' to words that can be heard. He continues to use suspense, surprise, and various kinds of direct representation in order to establish the norm, the *recta habitudo animae*. And he approaches the vice itself through the testimony of contemporary sinners who might be described as 'convalescent'. (*Convalescentes* are people recovering their *valor*.)

Dante and Virgil are distracted from contemplation of the sculpted figures in the reliefs by the approach of the souls of the penitent proud who are moving slowly and painfully round the rocky ledge, bent double under the weight of huge stones. As they struggle forward, they recite the Lord's Prayer in unison. Each of the petitions in the prayer is slightly expanded in order to emphasise the weakness and sinfulness of all human beings and our common dependence on the Father of us all ('O padre *nostro*'). In this way the prayer becomes a meditation on the lessons of the Sermon on the Mount (in the course of which the prayer was first proposed as a model by Jesus). Thus the first words spoken by the proud are a rejection of the assumptions made by all proud people, whatever particular form their vice may take, in that even the least arrogant of them assume that they are superior in some respect to others, or that there is no one above them.[7]

When Virgil makes a request for directions, the soul who replies cannot look his interlocutors in the eye, because he is 'impeded by the stone that tames his proud neck' ('la cervice mia superba'). Quietly and simply, he invites the two poets to 'come with us to the right' ('a man destra . . . con noi venite'); and as they move off, the protagonist bows his head to assume the same position as the soul. Tiny narrative details such as these can easily pass unnoticed, but Dante does not waste words. In just two delicate touches he has stressed the fellowship and common purpose of all the souls in Purgatory, and shown that he himself will be involved in the process of purification.[8]

The soul now starts to explain who he had been (the past tense is significant). Before he has spoken another two words it becomes clear that he is a representative of Dante's own society, and that his pride had lain in his noble blood. Since we already know what Dante thought of those whose claims to power and privilege were based on membership of a clan ('per ischiatta') or on 'antica possession d'avere', we may allow him to continue without further introduction:[9]

> 'Io fui latino e nato d'un gran Tosco:
> Guiglielmo Aldobrandesco fu mio padre;
> non so se 'l nome suo già mai fu vosco.

> L'antico sangue e l'opere leggiadre
> d'i miei maggior mi fer sì arrogante,
> che non pensando a la comune madre,
> ogn' uomo ebbi in despetto tanto avante,
> ch'io ne mori'; come i Sanesi sanno,
> e sallo in Campagnatico ogne fante.
> Io sono Omberto; e non pur a me danno
> superbia fa, ché tutti miei consorti
> ha ella tratti seco nel malanno. (*Purg.* xi, 58–69)

> I was Italian, and born of a great Tuscan: Guiglielmo degli Aldobrandeschi was my father; I don't know if his name ever reached you. The ancient blood and chivalrous deeds of my forebears made me so arrogant, that, not thinking of our common mother, I held everyone in such contempt that I died for it: *how*, the Sienese know, as does every child in Campagnatico. I am Omberto; and pride has hurt not only me, for it has dragged all my kinsmen with it into disaster.

The speaker is still using the same vocabulary that people of his class adopted when vaunting their claims to superiority: 'gran Tosco', 'antico sangue', 'opere leggiadre', 'maggiori', 'consorti' are all vibrant with positive connotations. Similarly, the name of his father rings out as a seven-syllable line within the hendecasyllable. At the same time, he is contrasting the person he *used* to be – a man defined by his father and his blood – with the person he now *is* – Omberto, a soul who is 'cleansing the grime of the world' ('purgando la caligine del mondo') and striving to be made 'clean and light', so that he may 'go forth to the starry spheres'. His tone is simultaneously self-assertive and conciliatory. In modern parlance, he speaks as an 'insider', but one who has been 'turned'. Dante has penetrated the mind of a man who is gaining in humility but has not yet achieved it; and he has presented him, as a dramatist does, through his own self-revealing words.[10]

'A gran dispitto'

At this point we may leave the sequence of exposition in *Purgatorio* x–xi to recall Dante's meeting with a proud member of a great feudal family who remained obdurately impenitent. In the sixth circle of Hell a soul hails the protagonist peremptorily from within the blazing tomb of his eternal prison, virtually ordering him to 'come to a halt in this place'. He explains that Dante's accent had proclaimed him to be a Florentine, or, rather, a 'native of that noble land' ('di quella nobil patria natìo') to which the speaker himself 'has, perhaps, done too much harm'. Everything in his bearing, voice and choice of words proclaims the autocrat, the man who believes himself born to command, so much so that it seemed 'as if he held Hell in great contempt'.[11]

Virgil names him as Farinata (Farinata degli Uberti, a mid-thirteenth-century leader of the Florentine Ghibellines, who had been driven into exile together with all his clan in the year after Dante was born). Then he pushes the awe-struck protagonist to the foot of the tomb, from where he has to look up at the other's 'towering chest and forehead'. (The relative positions of the two Florentines will prove to be indicative of the social standing of their families; and it should be remembered that the English verb 'to despise' comes from *despicere/despectum* 'to look down'.) Anything we have yet failed to deduce about Farinata's nature is conveyed in three further details. He looks at Dante 'a little', and then, 'almost disdainfully', he asks him: 'Who were your forebears?' Then – after Dante has stammered out his answer – 'he raises his eyebrows a little':

> guardommi un poco, e poi, quasi sdegnoso,
> mi dimandò: 'Chi fuor li maggior tui?'
> . . .
> ond' ei levò le ciglia un poco in suso. (*Inf.* x, 41–2, 45)

Even without the stage-direction – 'quasi sdegnoso' – the curt question is insulting in its tone, because the speaker so clearly anticipates an unsatisfactory answer about Dante's family. His 'disdain' is already present in the challenge of that brief preliminary gaze, and asserts itself fully in the final lifting of the eyebrows – all the more contemptuous because it is only 'un poco'.[12]

There is still much more to be learned about Farinata, but we have read enough to pause and take note of the similarities and differences between him and Omberto degli Aldobrandeschi. Omberto, too, is fond of the first-person pronoun. He too uses the ennobling word 'maggiori'. His 'Io fui *nato* d'un gran *Tosco*' is not unrelated to Farinata's opening apostrophe ('O Tosco') and to his deduction that Dante was 'natio' of his own city. 'Nato', 'natio' and 'natura' ('son', 'native', and 'nature') are all from the same Latin root – *nasci/natum*, 'to be born' – in silent confirmation, as it were, of the aristocratic assumption that 'you are what you are born'. But Omberto has understood that his own death and the 'malanno' of his clan were due to his holding all men 'in despetto', whereas the unrepentant Farinata enacts his *despectus* of the protagonist by contemptuously 'looking down' on him and extends the same 'dispitto' to everyone and everything – including the whole of Hell.

Farinata will later disclose other more complex and appealing traits of character; and we shall return to him at the end of this chapter. But before we leave him, we must read the terzina that immediately follows the raising of the eyebrow.

> Poi disse: 'Fieramente furo avversi
> a me e a miei primi e a mia parte,
> sì che per due fiate li dispersi.' (46–8)

> Then he said: 'They were fiercely opposed to me, and to my ancestors and to my party, so that twice I drove them into exile.'

The conversation that began in the names of Tuscany and Florence has rapidly degenerated into one about Family and Faction. It is no longer about the common 'patria', but about which 'parte' the speakers belong to, and which is currently in power. The reiterated 'me' and 'my' tell us that Farinata's pride in his own powers is inseparable from pride in his progenitors and pride in the party he felt himself born to lead (it would have been unthinkable that one of the Uberti should support the Guelph cause).

'Superbia' as a 'spark of discord' in the 'divided city'

Dante knew from personal experience that the pride of ancient, noble families led to unending, violent feuds in the name of family 'honour' and was among the chief causes of the bitter internal divisions in Florence and in all the city-states of Tuscany and the North. The point is made most forcefully in the sixth canto of *Purgatorio*, in the course of an encounter which also contains many deliberate echoes of the one between Dante and Farinata.

This time the main actors are Virgil and a 'soul from Lombardy', who is sitting apart from his companions, 'sola soletta'. He is characterised by two adjectives that constantly designate the proud – 'altera e disdegnosa'. His hauteur and disdain are manifested in an unwelcoming silence and a chilling gaze. He is like 'a lion in repose'. When Virgil goes up to him to seek directions, he does not answer the question. Instead he asks the travellers about their 'country and life' (in principle, just as Farinata had done). But no sooner 'did the sweet leader begin with the word "Mantua"', than 'the self-absorbed soul rose to his feet saying, "O Mantuan, I am Sordello, from your city," and each embraced the other':[13]

e 'l dolce duca incominciava
'Mantua . . . ', e l'ombra, tutta in sé romita,
surse ver lui del loco ove pria stava,
dicendo: 'O Mantoano, io son Sordello,
de la tua terra'; e l'un l'altro abbracciava.
(*Purg.* VI, 71–5)

The contrast could hardly be greater between Farinata, boasting of his victory over Dante's family, and Sordello, the 'anima gentile' who 'received his fellow citizen joyfully, simply because of the sweet sound of his city'; and the political lesson is spelt out at great length in an impassioned outburst by Dante the poet, which occupies the whole of the second half of the canto. It is in this diatribe that the Montagues and Capulets ('Montecchi e Cappelletti') make their first appearance in European literature; and *Romeo and Juliet* will be equally rich in insights into the social consequences of pride in family and rank.[14]

'Aversio a Deo pertinet ad superbiam per se'

From the contingencies of thirteenth-century society we must turn to the universals of Christian theology and clarify the relation between *superbia* and the phrase *aversio a Deo* which was used by Aquinas in his definition of mortal sin.[15]

For the medieval Christian, *superbia* was the 'beginning of all sin'. This much-quoted dictum comes from the tenth chapter of Ecclesiasticus, in a section which begins with the simple statement that 'pride is hateful to God and men'. The conqueror should not be proud, the author implies, for it is God who 'transfers power from one people to another because of their iniquities'; ruler and subject alike are struck down by illness and death; our common inheritance is 'reptiles, beasts and worms'. The chapter then continues as follows (and it is particularly important to read the Latin version that Dante knew):[16]

Initium superbiae hominis apostatare a Deo;
quoniam ab eo qui fecit illum recessit cor eius,
quoniam initium omnis peccati est superbia. (Ecclesiasticus 10.14–15)

The beginning of man's pride was rebelling against God;
for his heart withdrew from Him who made him,
for the beginning of all sin is pride.

According to the Latin Bible, then, the beginning of all sin is pride, and the beginning of pride is 'apostasy'. *Apostatare* is a transliteration of the Greek *apostatein*. Its primary meaning was to 'stand away from', or 'to depart'; and it was therefore very close to the Latin verbs *recedere/recessum* (used in the same verse) and *avertere/aversum* (which we met in Chapter 7). But even in classical times *apostatein* had come to mean 'to revolt' or 'rebel against', and this stronger sense of the verb was carried over into the theological use of the nouns *apostasia* and *aversio*.[17]

It will be remembered that, for Aquinas, there is a 'turning away from God' in sins of every kind. In a venial sin the turning *away* is merely an involuntary consequence of the soul's turning *towards* a transient good ('*conversio* ad bonum commutabile'). In a mortal sin, by contrast, the turning away is deliberate; and it now becomes clear that the cause of this *aversio* is pride. Defiance is of its essence: '*Aversio a Deo* pertinet ad superbiam *per se*.' In other words, a sin of pride is to be understood as an act of rebellion against God; and the vice of pride is a permanent state of apostasy.[18]

The point is so important that it is worth reiterating and amplifying with phrases taken from different articles in the *Summa Theologiae*. 'Pride shows a turning away from God in this, that it refuses to submit to God and his rule' ('superbia habet aversionem a Deo ex hoc ipso quod non vult Deo et eius regulae subiici'). 'The actuality of pride is contempt of God' ('superbia . . . cuius actus est Dei contemptus'). 'Boethius says that "pride alone opposes God"' ('sola superbia se Deo opponit'). 'St Gregory says that pride is "the queen and mother of all vices"' ('regina et mater omnium vitiorum'). 'It is something more radical ('principalius') than the capital vices'.[19]

'Initium superbiae apostatare a Deo'

Pride was the *principium* of sin in a purely temporal sense as well. Within seconds of their creation – 'before one could count up to twenty', says Beatrice – 'part of the angels' had rebelled against God and been driven by the archangel Michael from the heights of heaven to 'disturb the lowest of the four elements'.

> 'Né giugneriesi, numerando, al venti
> sì tosto, come de li angeli parte
> turbò il suggetto d'i vostri alimenti.'
>
> (*Par.* XXIX, 49–51)

The leader of the rebels was Lucifer, who had been 'the highest of all created beings' ('la somma d'ogne creatura'), and is now the lowest. He 'raised his brows against his Maker'. He was the 'primo *superbo*'; his rebellion was a '*superbo* strupo'; he fell to the very centre of the earth; and the '*principio* del cader fu il maladetto / *superbir*' ('the cause of his fall was the accursèd act of pride').[20]

The intimate link between the verbs 'superbire' and *apostatare a Deo* is confirmed by the fact that those inmates of Hell who are specifically said to be guilty of *superbia*, were all guilty of offences aimed directly and explicitly at God. At the lowest level, the Pistoian thief Vanni Fucci made an obscene gesture, accompanied by a phrase that means 'Up yours, God!' 'Through all the dark circles of Hell,' says the narrator, 'I saw no spirit so proud against God, not even him who fell from the walls of Thebes':

> Per tutt' i cerchi de lo 'nferno scuri
> non vidi spirto *in Dio tanto superbo*,
> non quel che cadde a Tebe giù da' muri.
>
> (*Inf.* xxv, 13–15)

The epic tone of this terzina seems as disproportionate to Vanni's vulgar gesture as it is appropriate to the figure of Capaneus, who is the 'quel' referred to in the last line. Capaneus was 'one of the seven kings who besieged Thebes' and he was known to Dante through Statius' *Thebaid*. During the assault on the city, he defied Jupiter to do his worst and was promptly struck down by a thunderbolt for his blasphemy. He is the only named representative of the 'violent against God' in the seventh circle of Hell, where he compounds his sin by launching into another tirade in which he renews his defiance of Jupiter. As Virgil comments, he 'held God in disdain ("ebbe . . . Dio in disdegno") and seems to do so still'.[21]

Like Farinata, Capaneus has sometimes been admired because of his disdain for the torments of Hell, and because of his boast that he is the same in death as he had been in life ('qual io fui vivo, tal son morto'). But before one seeks evidence of transgressiveness in Dante's subconscious mind, one ought to re-read Cantos x–xi of *Purgatorio* and contrast the ranting of Capaneus with the words of Omberto and Trajan, or with the opening of the Lord's Prayer as recited by the penitent proud. One should also meditate on the answer made to Capaneus by Virgil, namely, that the greatest punishment of his pride is that his pride has not abated ('in ciò che non s'ammorza / la tua *superbia*, se' tu più punito').[22]

Syncretism of myths

The encounter with Vanni Fucci in *Inferno* XXV leads back to that with Capaneus in Canto XIV, whereas the encounter with Capaneus points forward (via a reference to the 'battle of Phlegra') to Dante's sighting of the giant Ephialtes in Canto XXXI. This 'proud being' ('questo superbo') had also 'wanted to make a trial of his strength with great Jupiter'. Now he is punished together with Briareus and the other Titans who 'put fear into the gods'. Together they attempted to storm the heavens by piling mountain on mountain in the valley of Phlegra, but they were all dashed to earth by thunderbolts from Jupiter, who 'still threatens them when he thunders from heaven'.[23]

In *Inferno* the 'orribili giganti' who rebelled against 'il sommo Giove' are chained, half-buried in the ice, around the rim of the lowest circle of Hell. They are in the company of Nimrod, the mighty hunter of the book of Genesis, whose pride led him to try and 'build a tower whose top would reach Heaven' ('cuius culmen pertingat ad caelum'); and they are not far from Lucifer, who is pinned fast in the very centre of that circle. In other words, Dante is here combining classical and Jewish myths in the same spirit and with the same intentions as he and his masters sought to combine and reconcile the ethical values and philosophical concepts that they inherited from the Graeco-Roman and Judaeo-Christian past.[24]

For Dante, the gods of the classical pantheon were 'dèi falsi e bugiardi'. Nevertheless, he was faithful to a long tradition in interpreting the stories he read about them either as veiled perceptions of the activity of God and the angels – fallen and unfallen – or as allegories containing moral truths. Jupiter ('Giove', 'il sommo Giove') had become an acceptable poetic appellation for the God who refused to name himself except as 'I am'. Any personage from pagan antiquity in the *Comedy* who defies the will of Jupiter and seeks to usurp his power is treated by Dante on the same footing as Jews or Christians who rebel against the supreme being whom Jesus invited us to call 'Our Father'. And it was this 'philomythical' syncretism that enabled Dante to draw so often and so creatively on pagan mythology.[25]

There are several allusions in the *Comedy* to classical myths concerning human beings who sought to be equal with the gods and were punished for their presumption: for example, Niobe (who boasted that she was more fortunate in her children than Latona), Semele (who wanted to see her lover Jupiter in his divine form), and Phaethon (who persuaded his father Apollo to let him drive the chariot of the sun). Dante reminds himself, as well as his readers, of Marsyas and Arachne who thought their artistic skills greater than those of Apollo and Minerva. And he makes several crucial references to the myths of the Argonauts and Icarus, who dared to cross the seas or take to the air.[26]

Some of these allusions take the form of extended similes. Others are scarcely more than the mention of a name. But the most important group is treated with the strictest formal symmetry in the examples of *superbia* which are carved on the ground of the first terrace in Purgatory to complement the examples of *humilitas* carved on the wall. Six of the examples are taken from the Old Testament (Lucifer and Nimrod, the Jewish kings Saul and Rehoboam, and the Assyrian monarchs Sennacherib and Holofernes). And six of them come from classical sources (the rebellious giants Briareus and Timbraeus, Alcmeon, Niobe, Arachne, and Cyrus, king of the Persians). There could hardly be a more explicit statement of intent.[27]

'Superbus dictus, quia super vult videri quam est'

From the point of view of the Christian church, the first and greatest sin attributable to pride was that of Adam and Eve in the Garden of Eden. But before we can understand Dante's way of interpreting the Fall, we must examine the common element in some of the everyday manifestations of pride and remind ourselves of the principles of medieval cosmology.

Perhaps the best guide to that common element lies in the accepted derivation of the noun *superbia* from the preposition *super*, meaning 'over' or 'above'. In Book x of his *Etymologiae*, Isidore said that 'a man is called proud because he wants to seem higher than he is' ('*super*bus dictus quia *super* vult videri quam est'). 'Whoever wants to rise a step above what he is, is proud' ('qui enim vult *super*gredi quod est, *super*bus est'). More than five hundred years later Aquinas was making the same point, although with greater precision, when he stated that '*superbia* takes its name from the fact that someone voluntarily aims above what he is' ('*superbia* nominatur ex hoc quod aliquis per voluntatem tendit *supra* id quod est').[28]

To understand the full richness of meaning that a medieval Christian thinker could conjure out of the vague spatial metaphor implied by the etymology, we must recall once again the indissoluble link between *forma* and *finis* in Aristotle's analysis of all things in nature, and the

Neoplatonist vision of the *Scala Naturae* or 'Golden Chain of Being' which dominated the medieval world view. (The *Scala Naturae* refers to the hierarchical ordering of all species, which allows the universe to become a unity through the subordination of its parts to each other and to the whole.)[29]

Every animal or plant was thought to be provided by nature with precisely those properties – neither more nor less – that enable it to achieve its distinct purpose. Any two distinct species of animals must occupy different rungs (*gradi*) on the ladder (*scala*). All animals rank higher than all plants. To 'aim above what one is' is tantamount to pursuing ends that can never be achieved because the necessary means are lacking. It as though a tree should unconsciously try to move itself to a more favourable site. Human beings who aim too high by conscious choice (*per voluntatem*) are dooming themselves to unfulfilment and therefore unhappiness. In the attempt they will probably cause disorder in the microcosm of society which, no less than the macrocosm, demands respect for 'degree'. ('Take but degree away, untune that string,' as Shakespeare's Ulysses reminds us, 'and hark what discord follows!')[30]

From this cluster of images and concepts, it is only a short step to the guiding principle of Aristotelian ethics and to Aquinas's definition of sin. To 'reach beyond one's grasp' is to shun the 'mean'. It is both the effect and cause of disorder. Any action which lacks due order or moderation is a sin ('peccatum proprie nominat actum *inordinatum*').[31]

Pride as the cause of Adam's Original Sin

It is only within this sort of context that one can grasp Dante's interpretation of the nature of the Original Sin. He did not dispute that the immediate cause of the Fall was eating 'of the fruit of the tree of the knowledge of good and evil' in defiance of God's explicit prohibition. He would have thought that Milton was right to begin his epic by promising to sing 'Of Man's first *disobedience*'. But the protagonist of the *Comedy* is not satisfied by this analysis. When he finally meets and converses with the 'first soul ever created by the First Power', he wants to discover 'the *specific* cause of God's great disdain' ('la *propria* cagion del gran disdegno').

Adam grasps the import of the question immediately and therefore begins his reply by confirming Dante's assumption that 'the tasting of the tree was not *per se* the cause of the long exile'. The true, underlying cause, he explains, was 'solely overshooting the mark' (that is, going beyond the limits set on our nature as finite, corporeal, created beings). It is in this very precise sense that *superbia* – seen metaphorically here as a 'tendere *ultra* id quod est' – was the beginning of all human sin.[32]

> 'Or, figliuol mio, non il gustar del legno
> fu per sé la cagion di tanto essilio,
> ma solamente il trapassar del segno.'
>
> (*Par.* XXVI, 115–17)

Typical definitions of some species of pride

In the course of the three encounters with Farinata, Sordello and Omberto we came across a good many words and phrases relating to pride and proud behaviour, chief among them being 'altero', 'arrogante', 'avere in despetto', 'disdegnoso', 'magnanimo' and 'superbo'. In the second half of *Purgatorio* XI, which is given over to Dante's meeting with the vainglorious illuminator Oderisi da Gubbio, there is a similar crop of terms from the same semantic field, such as 'disio de l'eccellenza', 'fama', 'gloria de la lingua', 'glorioso', 'mondan romore', 'nominanza', 'onore', 'presuntuoso', 'superbia' and 'vana gloria'.[33]

There is nothing surprising in finding terms like these in a context of this kind. Nor are they difficult to understand, because they are all transliterations of medieval Latin words that have found their way into most Western European languages with little variation of meaning. But vigilance is never more necessary than when the terminology appears familiar. And a short anthology of relevant definitions taken from Aquinas will reveal that many of the key-words are morally neutral unless they are qualified, and unless the qualification indicates a lack of moderation:

> A well-ordered self-love ('amor sui *ordinatus*') is proper and natural. A man loves himself in that he wants his own pre-eminence ('quod sui excellentiam vult'). Pride signifies a disordered love of one's own pre-eminence ('*inordinatus* appetitus propriae excellentiae').
>
> Presumption ('praesumptio') attempts some great work above its powers ('*supra* suam facultatem'). It seems to imply a certain lack of moderation in hope ('importare quandam *immoderantiam* spei').
>
> Ambition implies a disordered appetite for honour ('*inordinatus* appetitus honoris'); whereas honour considered in itself is a special kind of good and the reward for virtue ('praemium virtutis').
>
> Greatness of soul ('magnanimitas'), which establishes the norm of reason ('*modus* rationis') concerning great honours, is a virtue, because it

uses honours appropriately ('secundum quod oportet'). By contrast, smallness of soul ('pusillanimitas') is a sin because it refuses to aim at what is commensurate with its powers ('recusat in id tendere quod est suae potentiae *commensuratum*').

It is no sin that someone should want his good deeds to be approved by others ('ab aliis approbari'), and, in itself, the appetite for glory ('appetitus gloriae de se') does not denote anything vicious; but glory should be desired inasmuch as it is useful for something, not to take empty delight in men's praise ('non quod in hominum laude *inaniter* delectetur').[34]

Vainglory and desire for pre-eminence in the encounter with Oderisi

Even such a brief sample as this can throw light on Dante's treatment of the kind of pride he knew best from personal experience – the artist's pride in his art.

While the protagonist is walking alongside the souls of the penitent proud as they struggle round the first circle of Purgatory under the burden of their stones, he bends down low in order to catch the words of Omberto, and as a result he is recognised by one of the other souls. Dante greets him in wonder as Oderisi of Gubbio, whose skill had brought honour to his native city and 'honour to the art which is called illumination in Paris'.

> 'Oh!' diss'io lui, 'non se' tu Oderisi,
> l'onor d'Agobbio e l'onor di quell'arte
> ch'alluminar chiamata è in Parisi?' (*Purg*. XII, 79–81)

Oderisi gently corrects him, turning the compliment aside to another illuminator. But one can detect a lingering pride in the implied claim that some honour is still due, and hear a hint of regret that it is due only 'in part'. He is still in a state of moral 'convalescence' (just as Omberto had been); and it is easy to believe him when he admits that he would never have been so generous to a rival while he was alive.

> 'Frate', diss'elli, 'più ridon le carte
> che pennelleggia Franco Bolognese;
> l'onore è tutto or suo, e mio in parte.
> Ben non sare' io stato sì cortese
> mentre ch'io vissi . . .' (82–6)

'Brother', he said, 'the pages painted by Franco da Bologna smile more radiantly; all the honour is his now, and mine in part. In truth, I would not have been so courteous while I was alive . . .'

Up to this point the chief interest of the encounter may be thought to lie in the extraordinary circumstances of the meeting between old acquaintances, in the delicacy of Dante's insight into a twilight state of mind, or – for most readers – in the metaphor of the 'smiling' pages, and the technical language relating to the miniaturist's art. But the lines that follow are studded with no less technical terms taken from the art of ethics; and these suggest that every detail in the episode has been carefully chosen to reveal as much as possible about the nature of pride.

'. . . per lo gran *disio*
de l'eccellenza ove mio core *intese*.
Di tal *superbia* qui si paga il fio;
e ancor non sarei qui, se non fosse
che, *possendo peccar*, *mi volsi a Dio*.
Oh *vana gloria* de *l'umane posse*!' (86–91)

'[I would not have been so courteous while I was alive] because of the great desire for pre-eminence on which my heart was set. Here we pay the fine for pride such as this; and I would not be here yet, had it not been that, while I was still able to sin, I turned to God. O empty glory of human powers!'

Oderisi calls his sin 'superbia'. He defines it correctly as a great desire to be recognised as the best in his field. (In English, 'excellence' now means little more than 'high quality', but for Dante, as for Aquinas, 'eccellenza' meant 'pre-eminence'.) The verb 'intendere' is very close in meaning to *tendere* in Aquinas; and the phrase 'volgersi a Dio' is the vernacular equivalent of Aquinas's *conversio ad Deum*. The mention of God also introduces the vital contrast between divine omnipotence and the limitations of *potentiae humanae*.

The implications of Oderisi's use of 'vana gloria' are a little more difficult to tease out. On the one hand, this is the received name of the first of the Capital Vices. On the other, it must be remembered that, considered in itself, 'gloria' is a kind of honour ('onore' was used three times in the opening of the encounter); and, as we have just seen, it is proper to desire *honor* as a *speciale bonum* and a *praemium virtutis*. 'Glory' is 'empty' (*vana* or *inanis*) only if it is not deserved. 'Vainglory' is a vice in an artist only if his primary intention in the act of making is to achieve fame or to outdo his rivals.[35]

Those are the main elements in this passage when considered from the point of view of a moral philosopher. But in the lines that follow (with their well-known description of how Giotto drove Cimabue out of the 'field of painting') Dante's imagination is carried away by the simple idea that glory is empty, even when it is deserved, because it is no more than the 'puff of air' required to produce the words in which it consists. It cannot last. The 'shout' that once 'resounded' through 'all Tuscany' will soon become little more than a 'whisper' and then fade away altogether. Even if the 'wind' keeps blowing, it will continually shift to a new quarter, changing its name because it changes direction.[36]

> Non è il mondan romore altro ch'un fiato
> di vento, ch'or vien quinci e or vien quindi,
> e muta nome perché muta lato. (*Purg*. xi, 100–2)

'Resta, se dividendo bene stimo'

Even when his thought is studied in isolation from his poetry, Dante always proves to be his own man. And this independence of mind is particularly striking in the case of his brief definition of pride in a later canto, which takes the form of a characterisation of the typical proud man:

> È chi, per esser suo vicin soppresso,
> spera *eccellenza*, e sol per questo brama
> ch'el sia di sua grandezza in basso messo.
> (*Purg*. xvii, 115–17)

There is the person who hopes for pre-eminence by the downgrading of his fellow, and solely for this reason longs for him to be cast down from his greatness.

Considered in isolation, the characterisation is extremely odd – so odd in fact that, at first sight, it seems to fit envy better than pride. The word 'eccellenza' (in the sense of 'pre-eminence') links it to Oderisi's speech, but it is unclear whether Dante is thinking more of 'superbia' (the noun used by Oderisi in xi, 88), or of 'vana gloria' (the expression used only three lines later in xi, 91), since there is no mention either of an *aversio a Deo* or an 'empty delight in men's praise'.

When the lines are restored to their context, however, it becomes clear that their oddity – or originality – is the result of Dante's attempt to make his own personal synthesis of four pre-existing clusters of concepts. And the discourse in which it occurs is a perfect example of the strengths and weaknesses of the scholastic method in its rigorous use of formal logic and its constant recourse to division. Significantly, it is at the heart of this speech that we meet the revealing phrase: 'resta, se *dividendo* bene stimo' ('there remains, if my use of division is correct').[37]

The speaker is Virgil, who is seeking to synthesise the following elements: (a) the principle that all love is for some kind of good, and that all actions, good or bad, are motivated by love of some kind; (b) the distinction between secondary goods and the Primal Good; (c) the Aristotelian insight that vice consists in either an excess or a deficiency of love for a good; and (d) the Seven Capital Vices in the order in which they were listed by St Gregory.

The attempted synthesis seems to work quite well with respect to lust, gluttony and avarice (which can reasonably be classified as excessive love for secondary goods). It is defensible, too, with regard to sloth (understood, more controversially, as defective love for God). But it fails by a wide margin to do justice to anger, envy and pride.

In the case of the last three vices, Virgil is made to argue that it is possible to love what is bad (*malum*) in a qualified sense (*secundum quid*), since we can love harm to other people ('il mal del prossimo') if this is a condition of obtaining some good for ourselves. Hence, says Virgil, we find satisfaction in inflicting harm on someone else ('improntare il male altrui') when anger drives us to take revenge. When we envy people who possess 'power, favour, honour and fame', we are in effect desiring that they should lose these good things in order that we may possess them. And as we have just seen, in the terzina quoted above, pride may take the form of hoping that a rival may be 'soppresso' or 'messo in basso' if that is the only way of gaining pre-eminence. But although this aperçu may derive from Dante's knowledge of himself and other artists, it could hardly be described as an adequate account of either *superbia* or *inanis gloria*.[38]

'Quaestio de magnanimitate'

The proudest character in the *Comedy* is probably Ulysses, who will be the hero and the villain of the last chapter in this book. There we shall see just how difficult it is to separate the negative and positive elements in the character of a person with 'high self-esteem', and how impossible was the thirteenth-century dream of reconciling the different ethical insights and values celebrated by Dante's authors. But we can have a foretaste of these conclusions by returning to Farinata and considering the relevant meanings of the adjective 'magnanimo' as applied to him in the second half of Canto x of *Inferno*.

'Magnanimo' had many different connotations in the different traditions accessible to Dante; and it has been rightly said that the adjective is a 'verbal microcosm' which incorporates all the complexities in Dante's portrait of the Ghibelline leader. Ovid and Statius used *magnanimus* to describe the conduct of Phaethon and Capaneus, indicating that the word had been linked at a very early stage with the notion of defiance of the gods. Cicero and Seneca, on the other hand, gave it the sense of 'courageous', under the aspect of staunch resistance rather than audacious attack. For them, *magnitudo animi* meant much the same as the cardinal virtue *fortitudo*; and it was in homage to these disciples of the Stoics that Dante uses 'magnanimitade' as a synonym for 'fortezza' on the second appearance of the noun in the *Convivio*. Later Roman moralists presented magnanimity as a virtue of the ideal emperor, extending the term to cover *lenitas* and *liberalitas* (mildness and generosity). Among Dante's near contemporaries, however, the chroniclers and early commentators of the *Comedy* constantly associate the adjective 'magnanimo' with 'superbo' in contexts which suggest domineering, haughty behaviour of the kind lamented by Omberto.[39]

As was noted in Chapter 4, however, the term goes right back to Aristotle, for whom *magnanimitas* was one of the eleven moral virtues. His searching analysis of the virtue – and its collateral vices – was given a new lease of life in the thirteenth century when the *Ethics* was translated in full by Grosseteste, re-translated by Moerbeke, paraphrased and annotated in extensive commentaries, quoted in many *quaestiones* in the second part of the *Summa Theologiae*, and studied and revered by Dante. It is therefore to Aristotle's 'authoritative' account in *Ethics* IV, vii–viii that we must now turn. (All the quotations in the following sections are translated from the paraphrase and commentary by Aquinas, which Dante is known to have used.)[40]

'Magnanimitas' and 'gentilezza'

Magnanimitas is a calque translation of the Greek *megalopsychía*, the roots of which mean 'great' and 'soul'. As the etymology suggests, it is a virtue possible only to a few. In Aristotle's view, it 'cannot exist without the other virtues', which are 'made greater by it'. 'It is seemingly added to them like an ornament' ('videtur superaddi aliis tanquam *ornatus* earum').[41]

The great-souled man aims high. He limits himself to those actions that pertain to some great honour ('ad aliquem *magnum* honorem') or the doing of some great work ('vel ad aliquod *magnum opus* faciendum'). He does few things, but those few things are great ('est operativus paucorum, sed operatur *magna*'). His whole concern is with the good of the community and religion ('tota intentio est circa bona communia et divina').[42]

It is difficult to suppose that Dante himself did not aspire to a moral virtue described in such terms. And before we go on to read Aristotle's sketch of the behaviour of the man who possesses it, we ought to recall that Dante's understanding of *magnanimitas* must have been influenced by his beliefs about human embryology (as outlined in Chapter 6 above). For him 'greatness' of soul was not just a vague metaphor. It referred to the exceptional natural gifts transmitted to certain individuals at the moment of their conception, combined with the exceptional talents that were given directly by God at the moment of the creation of the rational soul. It was the actualisation of these joint powers that made such individuals 'almost godlike' ('quasi dei'). In other words, 'greatness of soul' is akin to 'gentilezza' as Dante defined it in 'Le dolci rime d'amor' and in *Convivio* IV – not 'antica possession d'avere', and not 'antico sangue', but the 'valore / per lo qual veramente omo è gentile'.[43]

Aristotle's portrait of the great-souled man in action

For our present purpose, however, the main interest lies in the details of Aristotle's portrait of the 'great-souled man'. The points of contact with Dante's presentation of Farinata are so numerous that it will be convenient to divide the material into short paragraphs and give each paragraph a letter for ease of reference.[44]

(a) The character of the great-souled man requires gravity of voice and slowness of speech and motion ('requirit *gravitatem* vocis et *tarditatem* locutionis et motus'). He is not easily amazed ('non est promptus ad admirandum').

(b) He does not lament if the necessities of life are lacking, nor will he entreat that they be provided ('*neque est plangitivus* si necessaria ad vitam humanam ei desint, *neque deprecativus* ut ei exhibeantur'). It is specially important that he should forget the ills he has received ('oblivisci malorum quae passus est'), because he despises them ('inquantum ea *despicit*').

(c) He is more concerned about the truth than men's opinion. He speaks the truth except when he says some things ironically in jest ('nisi forte aliqua *ironice* loquatur ex ludo').

(d) He is an open friend and an open enemy ('*manifestus* est amicus, et manifestus inimicus'). For if someone loves or hates secretly ('latenter'), it springs from fear of some kind; and fear is repugnant to the great-souled man.

(e) He should speak and act openly because he is contemptuous of others ('eo quod est *contemptivus* aliorum'), which is why he himself publicises his words and deeds ('et inde est quod ipse *propalat sua dicta et facta*'). However, he is not contemptuous in the sense that he despises others ('*despiciat* alios') to the extent of denying them proper respect ('quasi privans eos debita reverentia'), but in that he does not rate them more highly than he ought ('non appretiatur eos *ultra quam debeat*').

(f) He does not praise others much, nor speak ill of others, not even his enemies, unless it be to cast back some insult or injury he has received from them ('nisi propter *injuriam* sibi ab eis illatam *repellendam*').

(g) He should not be quick to associate with others ('non sit promptus ad *convivendum* cum aliis') unless they are friends.

'Farinata maganimo' in the first part of the episode

Many of the qualities singled out by Aristotle are clearly to be admired in any 'great man'. For example, Farinata's *gravitas*, which was so evident at the beginning of his encounter with Dante, is explicitly attributed to all the 'spiriti *magni*' in Limbo, who are described as 'people with slow, grave eyes, and looks of great authority, who spoke seldom with soft voices'.

> 'Genti v'eran con occhi tardi e gravi,
> di *grande autorità* ne' lor sembianti;
> parlavan rado, con voci soavi'. (*Inf.* IV, 112–14)

The same might be said of Farinata's open expression of enmity when he immediately said of Dante's forebears that 'fieramente furo avversi / a me'. Few characters in the *Comedy* could be less *plangitivus* than Farinata. And Aristotle would probably have approved of the 'dispitto' he showed towards Hell and, later, to the 'torment of his bed'.[45]

Other qualities shown by Farinata in the first half of the encounter might be interpreted as tending towards the unnamed 'collateral vice' consisting in excess. For example, the contempt he showed to the protagonist might certainly be said to 'deprive him of the respect' that

Dante deserved as a citizen of the same 'nobil patria'. And if Farinata despises his present torments, he cannot be said to have 'forgotten the ills he has suffered'. Indeed the whole of the second part of the meeting is dominated by the memory of his exile.[46]

'Farinata maganimo' in the second part of the episode

The first part of the meeting comes to an end as the protagonist himself begins to behave magnanimously by 'openly declaring' his own enmity, and ceasing to 'esteem Farinata more than he should'. He answers Farinata's boast that he had 'twice scattered' Dante's ancestors with the reply that 'if they were driven out, they returned from all sides, on the first occasion, and the second'. Then, warming to the fray, he uses irony in his counterthrust: 'But your followers did not master that skill' ('ma i vostri non appreser ben quell'arte').[47]

The verbal contest is interrupted by the sudden appearance of Farinata's fellow sufferer, Cavalcante de' Cavalcanti, whose every plangent word and hasty response proclaims him to be 'small-souled' (*pusillanimus*), that is, stamped by the other 'collateral vice' of too little dignity and resolution, exactly as described by Aristotle. It may be significant that the adjective 'magnanimo' appears in the line immediately following the description of Cavalcante's abrupt disappearance, as though to mark the contrast between the two souls.[48]

Farinata completely ignores the interruption by his fellow sufferer, as if to underline the fact that he is 'not fitted to associate with others' ('ad convivendum cum aliis'). Continuing with his first speech, he betrays no sign of emotion on hearing Dante's taunt. His total immobility is stressed by three successive verbs, all of them in the negative, but all in the past definite, as if each refusal to react were itself an action. 'He did not change expression, nor move his neck, nor bend his side':[49]

> Ma quell'altro maganimo . . .
> non mutò aspetto,
> né mosse collo, né piegò sua costa. (*Inf.* x, 73–5)

The irony of Dante's jibe about learning the 'skill' ('arte') of return does not escape Farinata, and he takes it up in order to 'cast back the insult he has received' by prophesying that Dante will soon learn for himself 'how much that "skill" can weigh'. From this point, however, the bitterness of exile is conceded on both sides, and the mood of the encounter undergoes a radical change. Farinata does now show his feelings. He acknowledges that the continuing sufferings of his family 'torment' him. There is deep pathos in the expression of his earnest request to know the reason for the Florentines' refusal to grant a pardon or amnesty. And more revealing still, he gives non-verbal signs of emotion when he 'sighs and inclines his head' on being reminded of the heavy Florentine casualties at the battle of Montaperti, at which he and his allies had been victorious forty years earlier. (This was the battle which led to the second 'scattering' of the Guelphs.)[50]

Nevertheless, Farinata has not ceased to be *magnanimus* in the Aristotelian sense of the word. It is he himself who 'broadcasts (*propalat*) his own deeds and words' when he seeks recognition for his one 'great work' – the *magnum opus*, for which Dante the author has in the event given him *magnus honor*. It was he, and he alone, he declares, who openly defended his native city when his allies wanted to raze its walls to the ground in the aftermath of the battle.[51]

'Farinata magnanimo?' 'Ai lettori l'ardua sentenza'

When Alessandro Manzoni heard of the death of Napoleon, he wrote a brief but remarkable ode, soon translated by Goethe, entitled *The Fifth of May*. Having surveyed the Emperor's rise and fall (Napoleon too was twice sent into exile), the poet asked himself 'Was it true glory?' and immediately declined any responsibility for an answer with a phrase that has become proverbial: 'Ai posteri / l'ardua sentenza' ('Let posterity pronounce the difficult verdict').[52]

The questions one might want to ask about Farinata would be such as the following. Did he show proper pride or false pride? Was he *superbus* or *magnanimus*? Did Dante the author have in mind the Christian vice or the Aristotelian (or the Stoic) moral virtue? Or what proportion of each? Or how much else besides? And the 'arduous verdict' does not rest with 'posterity', but with Dante's readers – who in the past have reacted differently to almost every aspect of the episode and will no doubt continue to do so for the foreseeable future.

There could hardly be a better example to illustrate both the subtlety of Dante's insights and the complexity of the issues raised by almost any form of pride. The bald paraphrase and the prose translations offered above were intended to give due weight to the negative or ambiguous elements in Farinata's character and conduct. But as one rereads the following lines in Dante's Italian, it is impossible not to think of the words spoken to Solomon by the Queen of Sheba – 'Behold, the half was not told me':

> 'E se tu mai nel dolce mondo regge,
> dimmi: perché quel popolo è sì empio
> incontr' a' miei in ciascuna sua legge?'
> Ond'io a lui: 'Lo strazio e 'l grande scempio
> che fece l'Arbia colorata in rosso,
> tal orazion fa far nel nostro tempio'.
> Poi ch'ebbe sospirando il capo mosso,
> 'A ciò non fu' io sol', disse, 'né certo
> sanza cagion con li altri sarei mosso.
> Ma fu' io solo, là dove sofferto
> fu per ciascun di tòrre via Fiorenza,
> colui che la difesi a viso aperto'. (*Inf.* x, 82–93)

'And as you hope to return to the sweet world, tell me: Why is that people so cruel towards my family in every law?' I answered: 'The anguish and great slaughter which dyed the Arbia red is what makes prayers like those to be recited in our temple.'

When he had sighed and let his head drop, he said: 'In that I was not alone. Nor, surely, without cause would I have acted with the others. But *there* I was alone, where everyone agreed to sweep Florence away – I was the only one who openly defended her.'

CHAPTER NINE

Justice

Justice as the brightest star in the moral firmament

The quotation at the heart of this chapter comes not from the Bible (like 'radix omnium malorum est cupiditas') but from Aristotle's *Ethics*. At the beginning of Book v, the Philosopher says that 'justice would seem to be the most illustrious of all the virtues' ('*praeclarissima* virtutum esse videtur justitia'), and he backs his comment with unattributed lines from two Greek tragedians, who had said that 'neither the Evening nor the Morning Star could arouse such wonder' ('et neque Hesperus neque Lucifer ita *admirabilis*', and that 'every virtue is present together in justice ('in justitia *simul omnis virtus* est').[1]

This much-quoted remark was clearly at the back of Dante's mind when he made his first extended reference to the virtue of justice in Book I of the *Convivio*. Having paraphrased Aristotle's ideas concerning the nature of virtue, he continues as follows:

> Avvegna che ciascuna vertù sia amabile ne l'uomo, quella è più amabile in esso che è più umana, e questa è la giustizia . . . Questa è tanto amabile, che, sì come dice lo Filosofo nel quinto de l'Etica, li suoi nimici l'amano, sì come sono ladroni e rubatori; e però vedemo che 'l suo contrario, cioè la ingiustizia, massimamente è odiata, sì come è tradimento, ingratitudine, falsitade, furto, rapina, inganno e loro simili. Li quali sono tanto inumani peccati . . . (*Con*. I, xii, 9–11).

> Although every virtue is lovable in man, the most lovable is that which is most human, and this is justice . . . This is so lovable, as Aristotle says in the fifth book of the *Ethics*, that it is loved even by its enemies, for example, thieves and robbers. And so we see that its contrary, injustice, is hated in the highest degree, as, for example, treachery, ingratitude, falseness, theft, larceny, deceit and similar things, which are such inhuman sins . . .

In the event, the paradox that even robbers love justice (because a pirate chief – *archipirata* – who failed to divide the booty 'justly' among his crew would soon be killed or abandoned) comes not from the *Ethics* but from Cicero's *De officiis*. But the lapse of memory on Dante's part helps to make this paragraph an excellent small-scale example of the confluence of distinct traditions that we find everywhere in his thought and art. Aristotle drew on the poets of his time; and Dante will later transform the abstract list of 'inhuman sins' into a vision of the lowest circles of Hell.[2]

Roman, Greek and Hebrew influences on the word 'giustizia'

It would of course be wrong to overstress the learned influences. Aristotle himself began his discussion of justice with a brief informal 'circumscription' that hardly takes us beyond the fundamental ideas of a *habitus* conferring an *inclinatio* to act (*operari*) in a certain way. 'We see that all men mean by justice that kind of state of character which makes men disposed to do what is just, and makes them act justly and wish for what is just.' The adjective 'giusto' must have been in continuous use in the vernaculars of central Italy for hundreds of years by Dante's time. It would have undergone changes in meaning because of changes in the circumstances of daily life, but these would have been hardly greater than the slight alterations of sound which occurred as it evolved from Vulgar Latin *justu(m)*. Ordinary people in Dante's society discovered the meanings of 'giusto' in exactly the same way that English-speaking children today learn the meanings of 'fair' (and children 'hate unfairness' from a very tender age).[3]

Nevertheless, it is not possible to establish what 'giustizia' meant in 1300 simply by seeking evidence of its use in the ordinary speech of Dante's day. In the cultural context of thirteenth-century Europe (where Latin had until recently been the only written language and was still the medium of law and all higher studies), vernacular words were being 'recharged' by exposure to their Latin originals. For an educated person, the connotations of 'giusto' and 'giustizia' were certainly modified by the renewed study of Roman law; and Dante was aware of a series of semantic relationships that were not evident to those who knew no Latin. A glance at a standard encyclopaedia such as Isidore's *Etymologiae* is revealing. For Isidore, *justum* derives from *jus/juris*, a noun meaning both 'right' and a 'system of written laws' (it is the genus, of which laws are the species). A man is called 'just' (*justus*) because he observes the laws (*jura*).

Something is *justum* because it is *de jure*, 'established by law'. A wrong or 'injury', *injuria*, is something which is definitely not *de jure*. When a 'judge' (*judex/judicis*) gives a 'judgement' (*judicium*), he is 'telling the people what is just and right' (*jus + dicere/dictum*). For Isidore, the abstract noun *justitia* is 'as it were, a conflation of *juris* and *status*' – a 'state of being right', or a 'condition in accordance with the laws'.[4]

Justus and its cognates had been part of the Latin language long before the full development of the Roman legal system (known to the Middle Ages, it will be remembered, through the *Corpus juris civilis*, prepared at the behest of the aptly named Justinian). Some of the earlier meanings (which modern dictionaries seek to capture with phrases like 'observant of custom', 'faithful to ancestral pieties') made *justus* the natural translation of Greek *dikaios* and Hebrew *tsedeq*, together with their respective derivatives. In the Latin Bible, in Latin translations of Aristotle, and in all the commentaries and independent works drawing on those sources, *justus* and *justitia* continued to carry overtones and nuances of meaning that reflect the values of the Greek city-states and of the nomadic tribes of the Near East, rather than those of the Roman Empire. It is helpful to remember that where the Vulgate has *justitia*, the King James Bible usually has 'righteousness'. And the key-words in such familiar quotations as 'The souls of the *righteous* are in the hands of God', or '*Righteousness* and peace have kissed each other', are in the Latin 'animae *justorum*' and '*justitia* et pax'.[5]

'Thirsting after justice' and 'preaching justice'[6]

In a phrase omitted from the opening quotation, Dante explained that justice is the 'most human' of all the moral virtues because it exists only in the will, that is, in the rational, uniquely human part of our nature ('è solamente ne la parte razionale o vero intellettuale, cioè ne la volontade'). Unlike the first ten Aristotelian virtues, it does not co-operate with the powers of the sensitive soul, and, specifically, it never acts in conjunction with the instinctive emotions. A courageous man may be strengthened in battle by the passions of *ira* and *audacia*; but the just man must always be dispassionate.[7]

Dante, however, would never write dispassionately about the virtue which is free from passion. He could not forget that he himself was the innocent victim of a gross injustice – the partisan sentence of a Florentine court early in 1302, which sent him into exile from the age of thirty-six until his death. Within three or four years of the catastrophe, he found sufficient peace of mind to conceive a 'Banquet of Wisdom' (the *Convivio*); but no sooner had he described the general plan of the work than he felt compelled to talk about his own misfortunes. So, having first excused himself for the breach of decorum, he launched into the following outburst:

> Ahi, piaciuto fosse al dispensatore de l'universo che la cagione de la mia scusa mai non fosse stata! ché né altri contra me avria fallato, né io *sofferto avria pena ingiustamente, pena, dico, d'essilio* e di povertate. (*Con.* I, iii, 3)

> Would it had pleased the Ruler of the universe that there had never been any cause for this apology; for then others would not have done me wrong, and I would not have suffered punishment unjustly – the punishment of exile and poverty.

In the same early years he composed one of his greatest lyric poems (the canzone 'Tre donne intorno al cor mi son venute'), in which he universalises his personal grief by imagining that Justice herself and two of her 'descendants' have been banished from the earth but have come to visit him in his exile. The three ladies 'assemble round his heart' and speak words of lament and consolation. In such company as this, Dante's exile is not a disgrace but an honour!

> E io, che ascolto nel parlar divino
> consolarsi e dolersi
> così alti dispersi,
> l'essilio che m'è dato, onor mi tegno.
>
> (*Rime* CIII, 73–6)

> And I who listen to such noble refugees taking comfort and telling their grief in divine speech, I count as an honour the exile imposed on me.

In 1315 he was offered a last chance to return to Florence, but the terms were so ignominious that he rejected them, expressing his feelings in a Latin letter which is no less eloquent and no less full of pain than the vernacular prose and poem:

> Is this the gracious summons by which Dante Alighieri is summoned back to his native land after suffering exile for nearly fifteen years? Is this what his innocence deserves, the innocence manifest to everyone? . . . Far be it from the man who proclaims justice that, having suffered injustices, he should pay money to those who inflicted that injustice as though they were his benefactors! ('Absit a *viro praedicante justitiam* ut perpessus injurias, injuriam inferentibus, velut benemerentibus, pecuniam suam solvat!') This is not the way to return to my native land. (*Epist.* XII, 5–8)

This is the voice and stance of the author of the *Comedy*. Dante will write as a 'vir *praedicans justitiam*'.

'Justitia est virtus ad alterum'; 'jus' and the 'bonum commune'

Like all the moral virtues in Aristotle's analysis, justice is a 'habitus electivus in medietate existens'; but unlike the others, the 'mean' to which it tends has nothing directly to do with the needs and desires of the self. 'Justitia est virtus ad *alterum*' – 'justice is a virtue directed towards others'. 'Justice' and 'just', that is, refer to the well-being of man considered as a social animal; and it would be hard to better Aristotle's definition of the root-meaning of the adjective: 'we call those things "just" which make or preserve happiness in a political unit' ('"justa" dicimus *factiva et conservativa felicitatis* politica communicatione'). It is therefore difficult to maintain a sharp distinction between ethics and politics in this area of Dante's thought. In fact, one cannot even define *justitia* as a moral virtue without first considering its wider implications.[8]

Justice is the 'brightest' virtue of the individual person, but the condition of justice is also the supreme good of the whole community. It is a good held in common (*bonum commune*). As Dante himself explains, humans cannot live well (*vivere secundum humanitatem*) and cannot achieve happiness (*felicitas*), except in the kind of social unit called a 'city' (in Greek *polis*, in Latin *civitas*). Individuals are unable to do or make 'enough' (*satis*, *sufficiens*) to 'satisfy' all their needs, and cannot therefore be self-'sufficient'. (In the following, otherwise very literal translation of a passage in the *Convivio*, the simple word 'enough' is deliberately repeated, although Dante himself is ringing the changes on 'satisfare', 'satisfacimento', 'sufficiente' and 'sufficienza'.)

> Human society is ordered towards a single goal, that is, the happy life ('vita felice'). No one can do enough to reach this by himself without the aid of another, since man needs many things of which one alone cannot supply enough. Hence the Philosopher says that man is by nature a companionable animal. And just as any one man requires the domestic companionship of the family, in order to get enough, so a household requires a village to provide enough; otherwise it would have to put up with many shortcomings which would be an obstacle to happiness ('impedimento di felicitade'). And since a village cannot provide enough for itself in all respects, there has to be a city to give it enough. (*Con.* IV, iv, 1–2).[9]

In this passage, Dante is keeping very close to the opening of Aristotle's *Politics*. In the *Monarchia* he will draw on Justinian's *Digest* to argue that the concepts of *jus* and *justum* are inseparable from the concept of what is good for the group (*societas*, *communitas* or *res publica*).[10]

> Whoever aims at the common good is aiming at the end of *jus*. '*Jus* is a relationship between one man and another based on proportion in property and personal rights.' If it is preserved, it preserves a human association, and if destroyed, destroys it. Since the goal of every association ('cuiuslibet *societatis*') is the common good of its members ('commune *sociorum* bonum'), the goal of *jus* must be the common good. It is impossible for something to be *jus*, if it does not aim at the common good. (*Mon.* II, v, 1 2)

'Suum cuique' and equity

Drawing on two separate traditions – Greek and Roman – Dante has emphasised that human beings will achieve happiness only if they live in a society large enough to be self-sufficient for a fully human life, only if they deal 'justly' with their fellows, and only if their society is regulated by *jus* or *justitia*. So we must now return to the simpler questions: 'What is the meaning of "justly"?', and 'What is the definition of *justitia*?'

The phrase that recurred in almost every thirteenth-century definition of justice was *suum cuique tradere*, or *suum cuique tribuere*, literally, 'to give to each his own'. For the jurist, the Aristotelian philosopher and the Christian theologian, 'dealing justly' meant 'giving others their due'; and 'to be dealt with justly' meant to 'receive one's due from others'.

The thing due may be pleasant or unpleasant. With regard to relationships between individuals, it is just to receive 'a fair day's pay for a fair day's work'; but it is also just to pay compensation for one's failure to fulfil a contract, for damaging property, or causing bodily harm (most of Roman law deals with private cases of this kind). With regard to relations between a *societas* and its *socii*, it is just for the community to reward public service with prizes, titles or other honours; and it is just for offences against the community to be punished with humiliations, fines, banishment or death.[11]

It is a central tenet in Dante's system of thought that human beings are not equally endowed and that their actions are not of equal worth. Hence to say that each person ought to receive a just wage or a just compensation, a just reward or a just punishment, does not mean that they ought to be treated equally. The principle of *suum cuique tribuere* demands not equality of treatment, but equity. It is not equitable that all lawbreakers should be punished in exactly the same way, regardless of what they did and whether they have offended before. It is not equitable that every public benefactor should be rewarded with the same honour or prize. Everyone ought to get neither less nor more than they have deserved. Equality is only equitable when the deserts are equal.[12]

It follows that the most important task of a judge – whether he be a father within the family, an arbitrator in a craft-guild, or a magistrate on the bench – is to weigh up the merits or demerits of a particular action and to make an evaluation by locating it on the appropriate degree of an appropriate scale. From the earliest centuries the iconographical attribute of Justice has been a pair of balances. Justice is seen to be done when the 'valore' of the judge's award is equal to the 'peso' of the action to be assessed.[13]

The single scale of merit and demerit conceived as distance from God

The Epistle to Can Grande states that the allegorical subject of the *Comedy* is 'man, insofar as he renders himself liable to the justice of reward and punishment by deserving good or ill in the exercise of his free will' ('subiectum est homo prout *merendo* et *demerendo* per arbitrii libertatem justitiae *premiandi* et *puniendi* obnoxius est'). And the single most striking feature of Dante's vision of divine justice in the afterlife is not the variety or fittingness of the *poenae*, but the simple fact that both punishments and rewards are graduated 'secondo più e meno'. The worth of each individual soul is expressed and made visible by its distance from God. Despite the fundamental difference between damnation and salvation, there is only one scale. The greatest 'retribution' lies in the remotest separation, the greatest 'tribute' in the closest union.[14]

In the *Inferno*, the verdict of 'Guilty' has in effect been pronounced before the souls of the damned are despatched to the Underworld. The moment of sentencing, however, is represented in one brief but unforgettable scene.

The task of assessment is delegated to Minos, who is demonised with respect to his classical original, but described as a 'connoisseur of sins'. Having heard the 'confession' and 'examined the guilt' of each of the souls who crowd into his presence, 'he sees which place in Hell is suitable for that soul'. And his sentence ('giudizio') – expressed by coiling his tail around himself the appropriate number of times – is limited to an indication of how many degrees ('gradi') the soul must descend in order to receive the 'final effect of what it has deserved'.[15]

> e quel conoscitor de le peccata
>   vede qual *loco* d'inferno è da essa;
> cignesi con la coda tante volte
> quantunque *gradi* vuol che giù sia messa. (*Inf.* v, 9–12)

In the *Paradiso*, by contrast, we are not shown the moment at which one of the *beati* is first assigned to his or her place in the Celestial Rose. But we are never allowed to forget that the blessed are unequal in their blessedness, just as the damned are unequal in their misery. Indeed, the first and last discourses on the theme of 'human worth' in this cantica take the form of *responsiones* to two separate *quaestiones*, in which Dante the protagonist expresses doubt concerning the equity of inequality, in order that Dante the author may assert its justice with greater force.[16]

The earlier of the two *quaestiones* arises from Dante's encounter with his Florentine neighbour, Piccarda Donati. Great stress has been laid both on Piccarda's radiant beatitude and on the relatively low position in Heaven to which she and her companions have been 'relegated' for failing to keep their vows. The protagonist formulates his 'dubbio' indirectly by putting the following question (which is the equivalent of the *Videtur quod* section in an article in the *Summa Theologiae*): 'You who are happy here, do you desire a higher place, in order to see [God] more, and to love and be loved by him the more?'[17]

> 'Ma dimmi: voi che siete qui felici,
> disiderate voi *più alto* loco
> per *più* vedere e per *più* farvi amici?' (*Par.* iii, 64–6)

Piccarda's *Respondeo* is one of the summits of Dante's art. She tacitly concedes that other souls are placed 'higher' than they are and enjoy a closer 'friendship' with God. But she begins by smiling gently at the absurdity of the idea that a soul could possibly desire anything more than what it receives from God; and she insists that the essence of beatitude consists in loving conformity to God's will. The souls 'rejoice in the *order* in which they have been formed by the Holy Spirit' ('letizian del suo *ordine* formati'): 'the way in which we are placed from rank to rank in this kingdom, is pleasing to the whole kingdom' ('come noi sem *di soglia in soglia* / per questo regno, a tutto il regno piace'). In just eighteen radiant lines, Piccarda convinces the protagonist that 'everywhere in Heaven is Paradise, even though God's grace does not rain down there in one way':[18]

> Chiaro mi fu allor come ogni dove
> in cielo è paradiso, *etsi* la grazia
> del sommo ben d'un modo non vi piove. (88–90)

In the next highest of the celestial spheres (the Heaven of Mercury), Justinian will add a codicil to her lesson, telling Dante that 'part of our joy lies in the commensuration of our rewards and deserts, because we see them as neither greater nor lesser than they should be'.

> 'Ma nel *commensurar* d'i nostri *gaggi*
> col *merto* è parte di nostra letizia,
> perché non li vedem *minor né maggi*.' (*Par.* VI, 118–20)

Inequality in the rewards of the innocent

In the speeches by Piccarda and Justinian, the relative positions of the souls in the celestial hierarchy are explicitly linked to the relative merits of their 'works' on earth (their *opera*, as the Bible would say, or their *operationes humanae*, as an Aristotelian would call them). Later in the cantica, however, Dante will stress that all merit comes from God, and that it is perfectly just for different souls to be given grace in unequal measure entirely as he should decide. This vital point is thrown into relief by an examination of two groups who never performed any 'operazioni umane' whatsoever. They are the angels, who are dealt with briefly in Canto XXIX, and the souls of innocent children, the inequality of whose blessedness is subjected to close scrutiny in Canto XXXII and demands our attention.[19]

Dante the pilgrim has passed beyond the physical heavens, and now, within the vast amphitheatre of the Rose, he is able to see all the *beati* seated on their thrones at different levels. We may resume the narrative at the moment when St Bernard explains that 'below the half-way mark ("dal *grado* in giù che fiede / a mezzo il tratto"), no one occupies a throne because of his or her own merits ("per nullo proprio merito si siede"), because all these spirits were released before they could make true choices'. They have been saved 'per *altrui* merito' – by the merits of others.[20]

St Bernard notices that Dante is in a state of perplexity even though he is silent ('or *dubbi* tu e *dubitando* sili'). It would seem – *videtur quod* – that either the innocent souls are seated higher and lower by pure chance, or there is no justice in the allocation of their thrones, given that they did nothing on earth to deserve such inequality of treatment. The 'subtle thoughts' of the protagonist have tied him in a 'strong bond', from which he can be 'released' only by the rigorous procedures of a scholastic *quaestio*.[21]

St Bernard opens his reply with a *Sed contra* to the effect that nothing in Heaven occurs by chance and everything is in accordance with justice. Then he begins his *Responsio*, which occupies six terzinas of extraordinary precision and metaphorical density:

> 'It is not without cause that these souls who hastened to their true life are more and less eminent than one another here ("intra sé qui *più e meno* eccellente"). The King, through whom this Kingdom rests in such love and delight that no will can dare to desire more ("nulla volontà è *di più* ausa"), creates all minds in his joyful sight and endows them variously with grace as he pleases ("a suo piacer di grazia dota / *diversamente*"). Here the facts are sufficient. And this is clearly indicated by Holy Scripture in those twins [Esau and Jacob], who quarrelled even in the womb.
>
> 'Hence it is entirely fitting that the light of grace should form a crown of varying intensity to match the varying "colour of their hair". [This bodily sign of the different spiritual gifts received by Esau and Jacob is used to indicate the different endowments of all souls.] It follows, then, that the souls are placed in different ranks ("locati son *per gradi differenti*"), without regard to what their conduct deserved ("sanza mercé di lor costume"), differing only in their first [God-given] keenness of vision.' (*Par.* xxxii, 58–75)

In the following lines, St Bernard goes on to explain the different conditions required for the salvation of the innocent during the three eras of the History of Salvation (that is, before the Mosaic Law; under the Law; and after the Atonement). But we may interrupt him at this point and return to the beginning of his speech in order to read the *Sed contra*. His words round off the present section, through their association of justice and 'fittingness' (in the homely image of the ring), and prepare for the next section through their linking of justice with law:[22]

> 'Dentro a l'ampiezza di questo reame
> casüal punto non puote aver sito,
> se non come tristizia o sete o fame:
> ché per etterna *legge* è stabilito
> quantunque vedi, sì che *giustamente*
> ci si risponde *da l'anello al dito*.' (*Par.* xxxii, 52–7)

'In the vastness of this kingdom there can be no place for chance, however small, just as there can be none for sorrow, thirst or hunger, because everything you see is ordained by eternal law, so that everything corresponds justly to everything else, like a ring on a finger.'

The Law as 'reason written down'

We must now return from Heaven to earth, and from the general principle of proportionality, which underlies all forms of justice, to what Aristotle called *justitia legalis*, that is to say, justice understood as the rule of law (*lex/legis*) here on earth.

Dante speaks of *lex* in the same breath and the same terms as he speaks of *jus*. Laws, too, are said to be necessary for the common good of the whole community and may be defined as the 'bond of society', because they 'should bind human beings together for their mutual advantage'. They are required for two main reasons, corresponding to the two aspects of lawmaking and law enforcement (*legis latio* and *legis executio*), which in turn reflect a fundamental distinction between the role of the intellect and the role of the will.[23]

Distinctively human actions are the result of rational deliberation about particular situations that are variable, complex and uncertain. The majority of people need help to reach the right decisions. They have to be told what '*right* reason' (*recta ratio*) would decide on their behalf. In one respect, a law does just that. Each law is addressed to a recurrent situation and provides a measuring rod or *regula* that makes it possible to know in advance the proper course of action in a particular set of circumstances. Of course, no law can provide for every conceivable conjunction of events (*de minimis non curat lex*); and lawyers and judges are needed to apply the paradigms to the individual case. Nor will there ever be certainties. There can never be a 'science' of the contingent, only an 'art'. But the whole body of the laws (*corpus juris*) constitutes just such an art. It is the best that can be done. It is reason written down ('la ragione scritta'), an 'art showing what is good and equitable' ('arte di bene e d'equitade').[24]

Laws are also needed for a very different reason. Most people suffer from weakness of will. (Medieval Christians believed that this was a *universal* consequence of Adam's Original Sin.) We follow the promptings of our sense appetites or we pursue the dictates of immediate self-interest rather than the good of the community. This is why the law does not simply 'show' us what equity requires in a given set of circumstances but 'commands' us to act in accordance with that knowledge. Commands are of no use unless they are obeyed and hence *legis latio* is of no avail without *legis executio*. All these ideas come together in the following brief paragraph from the *Convivio*:

> E con ciò sia cosa che in tutte queste volontarie operazioni sia equitade alcuna da conservare e iniquitade da fuggire (la quale equitade per due cagioni si può perdere, o per non sapere quale essa si sia o per non volere quella seguitare), trovata fu la ragione scritta, e per mostrarla e per comandarla. Onde dice Augustino: 'Se questa – cioè equitade – li uomini la conoscessero, e conosciuta servassero, la ragione scritta non sarebbe mestiere'; e però è scritto nel principio del Vecchio Digesto: 'La ragione scritta è arte di bene e d'equitade'. (*Con.* IV, ix, 8)

> Since in all voluntary operations some kind of equity must be preserved, and inequity must be avoided; and since equity may be lost for either of two reasons – not knowing what it is, and not wanting to pursue it – the written law was invented to show what equity is and to command it. So Augustine says, 'if men knew what equity was, and knowing it, preserved it, there would be no need for the written law ("la ragione scritta")'. And at the beginning of the Old Digest it is written: 'Law ("la ragione scritta") is the art of what is good and equitable.'

In *Convivio* IV, Dante exclaims that he can never read or write something that bears on civic goverment without feeling compassion for his 'unhappy native land'. And his sense of the indissoluble links between 'civilisation' and 'ancient laws' is vividly illustrated in his mockery of Florence at the end of the long digression in *Purgatorio* VI concerning the political misfortunes of Italy. The Florentines, he says, have the word 'giustizia' on the tip of their tongues. They eagerly volunteer to take on public office. The city is so much in love with legislation that new laws are made every month: 'the subtle measures that you spin in October do not last until mid-November'. 'Athens and Sparta did next to nothing for the good life compared with you!'[25]

> Atene e Lacedemona, che fenno
> l'antiche leggi e furon sì civili,
> fecero al viver bene un picciol cenno
> verso di te, che fai tanto sottili
> provedimenti, ch'a mezzo novembre
> non giugne quel che tu d'ottobre fili.
>
> (*Purg.* VI, 139–44)

Natural law, 'jus gentium' and 'jus positivum'

Dante quotes with approval a remark by Aristotle to the effect that, under an 'upright' form of government (*in politia recta*), the 'good man and the good citizen are one and the same thing', whereas under a 'deviant' form (*in politia obliqua*), 'a good man is a bad citizen'. In other words, not all laws are just, and a just man may therefore be required by his conscience to disobey a law that is 'iniquitous' (etymologically speaking, 'iniquity' and 'inequity' are the same word). Typically, he will do this when he is convinced that the offending edict contradicts the principles of '*natural* law' or '*natural* justice', and a few words must be said about this concept.[26]

The principles of natural law turn out to be old acquaintances under a new name. In the Aristotelian perspective, an animal's instinctive responses and drives may be described metaphorically as the 'laws' of its nature, since they are unvarying imperatives intended to secure the individual animal's existence, well-being, self-reproduction, and distinctive activity. Human beings are a species of animal. If we are to survive as individuals, we must be free to move from place to place in order to find food and drink; if the species is to survive, adult humans must combine in stable partnerships of male and female to procreate, feed and bring up their young. These are necessities and form part of our 'natural law'. Like many animal species, too, human beings are by nature inclined to live in communities; and so the *lex naturalis* dictates that we should not hurt or offend other human beings with whom we have daily dealings. Finally, our *operatio propria* consists in the exercise of our distinctive mental powers; and it is equally a 'law' of our *human* nature that we should be free to seek the truth and live *secundum rationem*. In essence, then, 'natural law' consists of a few self-evident truths about our nature as animals fitted by nature to live in 'cities', and intended by nature to actualise the powers of our intellect, both practical and speculative. All just laws, in the ordinary sense of the word 'law', must respect the essence of man as an *animal politicum, rationis capax*.[27]

In the Roman tradition, it was held that there are two distinct levels of *jus* lying between the universal axioms of natural law at the one extreme, and the local decisions of a judge or arbitrator at the other. At the first level come the provisions found in virtually all legal systems, such as the institution of private property, the enforcement of binding promises, and the regulation of buying and selling. Collectively they were called 'rights of peoples', or the 'law of the nations', *jus gentium*. Aquinas describes them as being like immediate conclusions from the premisses offered by natural law.[28]

The second level takes in all those laws that vary from one state to another, either because they are tailored to suit the requirements of societies with different climates, terrains and sources of wealth, or simply because there is no one way of achieving the rational end desired. For example, a fishing village may have no need to regulate road traffic, but a law of this kind is essential in a large modern city, and one such regulation was already operative in Rome during the Jubilee Year of 1300. There is, however, no reason in nature to drive on the left rather the right of the road. This is a matter of convention, of custom codified. All that matters is that people who are in daily contact with each other agree to do certain things in the same way. Laws of this kind – regulating particular, contingent needs – were said to have been 'put in place', *posita*, rather than 'infallibly deduced' from the principles of natural law. Collectively they were known as *jus positivum*.[29]

Justice as a Trinity: lessons from the canzone 'Tre donne'

We are now in a position to return to the canzone 'Tre donne' and to discover the exact identity of the three ladies, in whose company Dante found his exile an 'honour'.

As we have seen, they too are outcasts ('dispersi'). Having come to the 'house of a friend', they conduct a conversation with 'Amore', Love, who is the lord of Dante's life and dwells within his heart. Their spokeswoman tells Love they have sought him out because of their 'common nature' or kinship. She is his mother's sister and her name is 'Drittura'.

> 'nostra natura qui a te ci manda:
> io, che son la più trista,
> son suora a la tua madre, e son Drittura.'
>
> (*Rime* CIII, 33–5)

'Drittura' (or 'dirittura') is a relatively straightforward term whose meaning and connotations match those of *justitia* in the Latin Bible. To understand why this first lady can be Love's maternal aunt, however, we have to turn to classical mythology, where Justice was identified with a 'star-maiden' called Astraea. She was a daughter of Jupiter and hence a sister to Venus, the mother of Cupid. Virgil supplies the important detail that Astraea was a virgin who dwelt on earth during the Golden

Age; and from Ovid we learn that she was the last of the gods to be banished at the beginning of the Age of Iron.[30]

In answer to Love's question, 'Drittura' explains in deliberately enigmatic language that the other two ladies are her daughter and grand-daughter respectively, and that both were the result of *virgin*-births, which took place at the source of the Nile. This geographical reference serves to establish that both births took place in the Garden of Eden, which, for Dante, was the symbol of human perfection and temporal happiness, as these had existed before the Fall and the banishment of Adam and Eve:

> 'sovra la vergin onda
> generai io costei che m'è da lato
> e che s'asciuga con la treccia bionda.
> Questo mio bel portato,
> mirando sé ne la chiara fontana,
> generò questa che m'è più lontana.' (45–54)

'By the virgin wave [of the Nile] I brought forth her who is at my side and who dries her tears with her yellow hair. She, my fair child, gazing at herself in the clear spring, brought forth her who is further from me.'

Since Astraea is a daughter of 'il sommo Giove', we know that 'Drittura' derives immediately from God. Whatever the daughter and grand-daughter of 'Drittura' may stand for allegorically, we are to infer that they belong to our uncorrupted human nature and that they too come from God – not directly from him, it is true, but nevertheless without the admixture of any extraneous principle. (They do not, for example, represent justice as combined with political power or aided by prudence and experience; and they are in no sense a *remedium* for original sin.) Hence the obvious interpretation of the allegory of the double virgin-birth is that Dante wanted to represent the way in which the contingent and variable laws of the *jus positivum* are deduced from the universal provisions of the *jus gentium*, which in turn are like immediate conclusions from the premisses of *lex naturalis*, which is a way of describing God's intention for all beings in the natural world.[31]

In his presentation of Justice as a triple emanation from the divine source, Dante is affirming that human justice is not a matter of opinion or personal preference. God himself has given us an absolute standard that enables us to recognise what is equitable for all members of a society, what will ensure the common good of that society, and what will create or preserve the order based on proportion, through which every part of the universe shows the imprint of its creator and fulfils his purpose. Just laws, however limited in their application, are in accordance with the divine plan. The greatest of the non-Christian thinkers had reached the same conclusion. Aristotle said that 'Law is a kind of order, and a good institution of laws is a good setting in order.' 'Law is intellect without appetite. To ask the intellect to rule, is to ask for God and the law. The rule of man introduces the beast.'[32]

Justice as a moral virtue: literal and metaphorical meanings

We may now return to justice considered as a state of character, or, in Dante's words, as a 'singular virtue' which allows the 'judgements and authority' of a just man to be 'a light and a law to others'.[33]

It will be obvious by now why Dante classified justice as a virtue of the Third Age – 'Senettute' – which he believed to begin at around forty-five. In *Convivio* IV, he explicitly concurs with the 'ancient philosophers' who 'saw that justice is perfected in this Age' and who therefore 'entrusted the government of cities to men in this Age, which is why the college of magistrates was called the "Senate"'. Like all the moral virtues it is acquired by training, and in Dante's view, the necessary habituation takes twenty-five years of obedience to parental authority ('obedienza' being a sign of 'gentilezza' in the First Age), followed by twenty years of respect for the laws ('lealtà fare' being a virtue of the Second Age). It cannot be exercised without the intellectual virtue of *prudentia* (the gift that Solomon requested 'when he was placed in governance of the people'), which demands 'good memory of things seen, good knowledge of present things, and good foresight (*providentia*) into future things', none of which is acquired in a day. Practical wisdom must also be backed by a thorough grounding in *juris prudentia*, that is, by a knowledge of the laws that make up the *jus gentium* and *jus positivum*.[34]

Dante stresses that all the virtues proper to the Third Age are altruistic. 'Man is a civic animal who must be useful not only to himself but to others' ('non pur a sé ma *altrui* essere utile'). 'The sweetness of our fruit must be of benefit to others' ('*altrui* profittabile'). The prudent man's 'good counsels lead himself and others to a good end in human affairs' ('conducono sé e *altri* a buono fine ne le umane cose e operazioni'). Nevertheless, Dante would still have agreed with Aristotle that justice is the only virtue which is *always* 'directed to others', and that it is impossible to act either justly or unjustly towards oneself.[35]

There are two apparent exceptions to this general rule which are examined in the final chapter of *Ethics* v. The first hinges on the paradox involved in the act of suicide, and it throws light on Dante's characterisation of the imperial chancellor Pier della Vigna in *Inferno* XIII. The second leads Aristotle to recognise a *metaphorical* sense of the word 'justice' which is of the greatest importance.[36]

Aristotle acknowledges that human beings are motivated by the passions of anger and desire as well as by rational deliberation and choice. Technically speaking, there is more than one internal cause of our actions (more than one *principium actionis*). The soul is divided. It is as though there were two separate people within each one of us, so that the *diversitas animae* resembles a *diversitas personarum*. Now, if these two *principia* are in unresolved conflict with each other, there will be a state of anarchy. If the lower powers predominate, there will be tyranny. But if the distinctively human rational power rules over the passions as a good king rules over his subjects – maintaining authority over them, and allowing them neither more nor less than 'their due' – then, metaphorically speaking, reason is acting 'justly towards itself', and a whole human person can be called 'just'. It is in this figurative sense of the word that 'all virtue is present in justice' or that justice is 'all virtue'.[37]

Aquinas took over Aristotle's insight and extended it one stage further. Writing as a theologian, he said that metaphorical justice of this kind 'implies a rightness of order (*rectitudo ordinis*) in the interior disposition of a man, such that his highest part is subject to God, and the lower powers of the soul to the highest'. In this way he arrived at a Christian definition of *justitia*, which describes the condition of Adam before the Fall and the condition of all human beings who have been 'justified' by grace. His formulation also accords with the use of *justitia* in the Bible, where (as was noted earlier) the word usually means 'uprightness' or 'righteousness' (*rectitudo*), that is, virtue without qualification. This is what Dante means by the locution 'giusto e pio'. And this is clearly the sense in which the adjective 'giusto' is used of Mardocheus, whom Dante describes as 'il giusto Mardoceo / che fu al dire e al far così intero' ('a man of such wholeness in word and deed').[38]

'Is anyone just?'

In his first conversation about politics in the *Inferno*, Dante asks his fellow Florentine Ciacco what will become of their divided city and 'if anyone there is just?' – 's'alcun v'è *giusto*?' It is instructive to ask a similar question about the *Comedy*. 'Is there a just man in the whole poem?' If there were such a person, we could draw inferences about the virtue of justice from a study of his *operationes*. If there is not, we would have a better understanding of human nature after the Fall.[39]

It may be assumed that such a man would be a magistrate, prince, king or emperor. In principle, it is true, anyone of mature years might lay claim to the adjective 'giusto' in the literal sense of the word. But his 'operare' would only be evidently 'profittabile *altrui*' if he were in a position of authority; and the greater his sphere of influence or jurisdiction, the greater the good he would be able do for his fellow human beings. It is therefore not surprising that the lowliest person to be called 'giusto' in the *Comedy* had been the right-hand man of a Count of Provence. Nor is it surprising that Dante's hero in this regard should be Solomon. Solomon fell short of his own ideals, but he was a sacred king who prayed to God for the gifts of *justitia* and *judicium*; and he was also the presumed author of the Book of Wisdom, which begins with the much-quoted exhortation 'Love justice, you who judge the earth.'[40]

In the event, hardly any of the rulers named in the *Comedy* are praised for their 'giusto operare', because Dante had discovered that very few of those who 'judge the earth' have any 'love for justice'. Corroboration and explanation of this fact will be found in the first book of his *Monarchia*. Several of the abstract arguments he there develops in order to show the necessity of a single world-ruler are based on the premise that no lesser ruler could establish just laws or put them into execution. In Dante's view, only a *monarcha* with universal jurisdiction would regard himself as the servant of all and act for the common good. No one else could be the final arbiter in disputes between states or have the power to enforce his judgements. No one else could be totally free from the vice that is most opposed to justice – *cupiditas*; and hence no one else could possess a will that was pure and untarnished.[41]

With the exception of Trajan and Justinian, however, the real historical Emperors are passed over in silence, or blamed for neglecting their God-given *officium*. For Dante, as a Christian believer, there was only one ruler with the necessary power and will. He was the 'Emperor who reigns *on high*' – God himself. Hence the only 'Person' in the whole poem who is 'just' in the fullest sense of the word is the 'giusto rege' who cannot err ('cui fallar non lece'), whose 'giustizia' is 'infallibile', and whose kingdom is referred to as the place 'dove si puote / ciò che si vuole'. That is why we have already studied some of God's *judicia* and why we shall return to others.[42]

Of course, if this book had been written in a different spirit, it would have been necessary to insist from the very beginning that the only judge whose decisions are binding on readers of the *Comedy* is 'cunning old Fury' himself – Dante the author. He pretends to write down what he saw and heard, but in reality he has taken upon himself the duty of dispensing justice to all the characters in his poem. His poetic imagination is sovereign. He could be compared to Semiramis, who 'made her pleasure lawful in her law' ('che libito fé licito in sua legge'). And if there is any foundation in the popular view that Dante used the *Comedy* to settle a few personal scores and to recompense his benefactors, then the answer to the question 's'alcun v'è giusto?' has to be: 'No, not even the author.'[43]

It would nevertheless be monstrously unfair to suggest that Dante's countless acts of judgement are attributable to caprice, revenge or gratitude. His fictions are not arbitary, and he carries out his self-imposed duties as *scriba Dei* with great responsibility. It is he himself who calls attention to the difficulties of his task. Time and time again Dante the protagonist is made to 'call into question' the justice of divine judgements which Dante the author feels bound to uphold, bowing to the authority of the Bible or the exegetical tradition of the Church. The causes of his perplexity are stated openly and without irreverence, for his is a 'faith seeking understanding', 'fides quaerens intellectum'. As Beatrice will be made to say: 'it is evidence of faith, not heretical perversity, that our justice should seem unjust to mortal eyes' ('parere ingiusta la nostra giustizia / ne li occhi d'i mortali, è argomento / di fede non d'eretica nequizia'). In short, if we want to deepen our understanding of the nature of the *praeclarissima virtus* by studying the *operationes* of a single just man who embodies that virtue, we cannot do better than choose Dante the author.[44]

Doubts concerning the nature of God's justice 'spring up at the foot of truth' throughout the *Comedy*. We have already examined two *quaestiones* that arose from the inequality of beatitude. In a fuller treatment of the subject we should have to study problems such as the following, all of which are raised by the protagonist at some stage of his journey. How can a judge be both rigorous and merciful? How can a single tear of remorse at the moment of death change the verdict on a whole life? How can a just judge change his mind in response to prayer? Why does God not intervene to restore justice on earth? Why is his vengeance often delayed? How could it have been just to crucify Jesus justly and then to punish the Jews for their part in the proceedings?[45]

Fortunately, all the problems are tackled with similar methodology and in accordance with the same principles; and these are fully exemplified in the longest sequence in the *Comedy* to be dedicated entirely to themes relating to justice. This sequence begins in the middle of *Paradiso* XVIII and will occupy us for the remainder of the chapter.

'Figure', 'segni', 'la benedetta image'

An increase in the brilliance of Beatrice's eyes and a change in background colour from red to white reveal to the protagonist that he has ascended from the planet of Mars into the planet of Jupiter. A multitude of the blessed have descended from the Empyrean to greet him there. As always in the higher heavens, their features are concealed by the intensity of their own radiance, so that they appear as so many 'lights', or 'torches' or 'fires'. Outdoing their predecessors in the lower heavens (who had arranged themselves in the form of circles and a cross), the souls perform a succession of complex movements, as though they were a perfect corps de ballet and opera chorus in one. Singing as they move, they rise like birds from a meadow, or like sparks struck from a log. They are briefly silent as they settle and pause to form a shape. Then, singing again, they rise, settle, and pause in silence under a new form.[46]

These 'lucent fires' will prove to be the 'souls of the righteous' ('*justorum* animae', in the narrow sense of the word). But they are not simply 'running to and fro like sparks among the stubble'. Against the silvery background of the planet, they trace out in kaleidoscopic succession thirty-five golden letters (or rather, 'five times seven vowels and consonants') to spell the opening words of the Book of Wisdom: 'Love justice (righteousness), you who judge the earth', 'DILIGITE JUSTITIAM, QUI JUDICATIS TERRAM.'[47]

The bright-shining M in which they finally come to rest is the initial letter of the Latin word *Monarcha*, the 'supreme prince', the only ruler who could possibly 'love justice' *in fulgore suae puritatis*. That phrase, it may be remembered, comes from the first book of Dante's *Monarchia*. And it is there that one will find an illuminating account of the perfect freedom exhibited by each of the souls in Jupiter and the perfect unity of their corporate movements. In chapter xii, it is proved that mankind is, or would be, 'most fully free' (*potissime liberum*) under the rule of the Monarch. In chapters xiv–xv, it is argued that our greatest good consists in the greatest possible unity. Such unity comes about when all human beings act freely and voluntarily in concord, moving 'all at once together by their wills to one goal'. Concord is defined as 'the uniform movement of many wills' ('est enim concordia *uniformis* motus *plurium* voluntatum'); and we are told that concord cannot exist 'unless there is one will to govern and direct all the others towards one end' ('nisi sit voluntas una, domina et regulatrix omnium aliarum in unum'). In other words, it can exist only under the rule of a Monarch. This is the subtext of the elaborate semaphore, and it is no less important than the biblical text itself.[48]

The literal and symbolic messages conveyed by these pyrotechnics are not yet complete. More souls descend and cluster at the top of the final letter – a capital 𝔐. The newcomers rise and settle again 'to represent the head and neck of an eagle'. Then the first group of souls moves in concord to transform the three vertical strokes of the Gothic letter into the eagle's body and wings.[49]

The eagle is the symbol of Roman imperial power. In Canto VI, it had been called the 'sacrosanto segno'; and the conquests of Rome under Julius Caesar and his successors were there described through an extended metaphor of the eagle's 'flight'. Later in this heaven the eagle will be described as the 'sign that made the Romans revered in the world'. Hence, if the first sequence of movements gave visible expression to the arguments of the *first* book of the *Monarchia* (which shows in the abstract why mankind needs the 'rule of one alone'), the second sequence – culminating in the image of the eagle – makes visible the historical argument of the *second* book, namely, that God intended the Roman Emperor to be that 'one ruler', whose *officium* it was to bring peace and justice to the whole world.[50]

'Ov'è la giustizia che 'l condanna?'

Dante continues to lay great stress on the concepts of *concordia* and *unitas* (which are possible only under a ruler 'who loves justice'), by insisting that the eagle spoke not only with one voice, but as a single corporate personality, using the first-person singular pronouns 'io' and 'mio', instead of 'noi' and 'nostro'. But now Dante abandons poetic symbols for a time and challenges the intellect with a rational doubt concerning the justice of God's judgements.[51]

This 'dubbio', it is made plain, had tormented him long and often. It concerns the exclusion from heaven of all good pagans, especially the souls of 'Aristotle, Plato and many others'. Above all, it concerns the fate of the poet who pronounced these melancholy words, and who was perturbed and fell silent once he had done so – Virgil, his beloved 'author' and 'master', who, in the poem, had become his 'guide', 'leader', and 'sweetest father', but who has nevertheless been left behind in Eden, and has returned to eternal exile in Limbo.[52]

Dante refers to his doubt as a 'questione', and his treatment of it is once again modelled on a scholastic *quaestio*. The paradigm is handled with considerable freedom. The *Videtur quod* is delayed until after the first part of the *Respondeo*, which is highly rhetorical in character. Some of the logical steps leading to the conclusion in the second part are expressed elliptically or omitted altogether. But nothing could be plainer or more direct than the way in which the 'dubbio' is finally stated on behalf of the protagonist by the corporate voice of the Eagle:

> 'ché tu dicevi: "Un uom nasce a la riva
> de l'Indo, e quivi non è chi ragioni
> di Cristo né chi legga né chi scriva;
> e tutti suoi voleri e atti buoni
> sono, quanto ragione umana vede,
> sanza peccato in vita o in sermoni.
> Muore non battezzato e sanza fede:
> ov'è questa giustizia che 'l condanna?
> ov'è la colpa sua, se ei non crede?"' (*Par.* XIX, 70–8)

'You used to say: "a man is born on the banks of the Indus, and there is no one there to speak to him of Christ, or to read and write about him; and, as far as human reason can see, all this man's desires and actions were good, without sin in his life or words. He dies unbaptised and without faith. Where is this justice that condemns him? Where is his fault, if he does not believe?"'

The same problem is raised in the second book of the *Monarchia*; but there it is formulated even more challengingly, since Dante says that this is one of the *judicia Dei* that 'human reason on its own cannot see as just' ('hoc humana ratio per se justum intueri non potest').[53]

'Cotanto è giusto quanto a lei consuona'

In replying to his own persistent doubt, Dante commits himself absolutely to his religious faith and publicly acknowledges the limitations of those very philosophers who 'bequeathed morality to the world', and whose damnation – or condemnation to Limbo – caused him so much pain. In *Monarchia* II, he does no more than affirm that, while *humana ratio* is unable to 'reach the judgement by its own resources ("ex propriis"), it can do so with the help of faith in those things that are said to us in Holy Scripture'. In *Paradiso* XIX, however, the Eagle begins with an extended and impassioned assertion of the absolute gulf set between the Mind of the infinite Creator and the finite intellect of his creature. Drawing on Old Testament imagery, and describing the processes of intellection in the more familiar terminology of vision, the Eagle speaks eloquently of our 'shortness of sight', which prevents us from seeing the bottom of the sea more than a few feet from the shore. Whatever 'light' there may be 'comes from the sky that is never clouded', the rest being 'darkness, or the shadow of the flesh, or its poison':[54]

> Lume non è, se non vien dal sereno
> che non si turba mai; anzi è tenèbra
> od ombra de la carne o suo veleno. (*Par.* XIX, 64–6)

In itself, this reminder of the 'infinito eccesso' of the divine Word does nothing to resolve the doubt about God's justice in the particular case. But the first part of a scholastic response is often no more than a clearing of the ground; and Dante the author is by no means content to rely on the simple rhetorical question that opens the second half of the Eagle's reply: 'Who do you think you are, who want to sit on the bench and give judgement about something that lies a thousand miles away, when your sight is as short as a span?'[55]

What the Eagle does is to put us in a state of readiness. Its powerful and emotive analogies are what Dante called the 'persuasions' of philosophy (cf. p. 41 above). By making us reflect on the limitations of human reason, it disposes us to give rational assent to certain revealed truths that exceed our capacities. This is one of the ways in which philosophy can come to the aid of faith ('onde la nostra fede è aiutata'). To accept that we are 'earthbound animals with gross minds' is a first step towards the admission that God's 'sempiternal' justice may lie beyond our grasp.[56]

In the very brief second part of the response, Dante switches from the 'persuasions' of philosophy to her 'demonstrations' or proofs. He makes the Eagle speak as a logician, or as a metaphysician inquiring into the concept of God, rather than as a Christian believer. It is a matter of definition, he implies, that a Supreme Being who is the

Supreme Good can never intend something – never 'will' something – that is not supremely good. It follows therefore that 'the Primal Will has never moved away from its own nature, which is the Supreme Good'.

This is no more than the *principium* needed for the solution of Dante's doubt (as it were, the 'principio ond'elli indige'). And if Dante were writing in prose, or speaking in his own voice, he might have felt obliged to spell out the two syllogisms that are still required to reach his desired conclusion:[57]

1 (a) A divine act of judgement (*judicium Dei*) is an expression of God's will; (b) but everything willed by God is good; (c) therefore every *judicium Dei* is good.
2 (a) A *judicium* is good when it is just; (b) God's *judicia* are all good; (c) therefore every *judicium Dei* is just – including the fate of 'the man on the banks of the Indus'.

Speaking with the voice of the Eagle, however, he condenses these stages into a single line: 'those things are just which are consonant with God's will'.

> 'La prima volontà, ch'è da sé buona,
> da sé, ch'è sommo ben, mai non si mosse.
> Cotanto è giusto quanto a lei consuona.' (86–8)

The principle here enunciated extends far beyond the particular case of the virtuous pagan. It is in fact the single most important truth that a Christian needs to know concerning the nature of justice. So we must allow Dante himself to fill out the logical gaps in the Eagle's presentation, and to demonstrate the universal import of the principle, by quoting from a chapter in *Monarchia* II where he is setting out to prove that 'the Roman people took on the office of Empire by right'. (The phrase *ipsum jus* is used to to mean 'right itself, or 'the essence of justice'; while *jus in rebus* means 'whatever is right or just in human affairs'.)

> The divine will is *ipsum jus*. It follows, therefore, that *jus in rebus* is nothing other than a likeness of God's will ('similitudo divinae voluntatis'); hence, whatever is not consonant with God's will cannot be *ipsum jus*. Therefore, to inquire whether something was done by right ('quaerere utrum *de jure* factum sit aliquid') is the same as asking – even though the words are different – whether it was done as God wills ('secundum quod Deus vult'). (*Mon.* II, ii, 4–6)

Rhipeus: a 'test case' and a 'landmark judgement'

Despite these 'persuasions' and 'demonstrations', Dante's disquiet clearly persisted, or he would never have given such prominence to this *quaestio* and – more important – he would never have created the figure of Virgil in the *Comedy*. His doubt lay close to one of the 'fault lines' where the earth tremors caused by the tensions between secular and sacred values are felt most keenly.

Confirmation of this comes immediately when the Eagle repeats the warnings given by Jesus that there will be many reversals of expectation on the Day of Judgement. Then in the following canto – after six terzinas prophesying disaster for six contemporary European rulers, and after a sublimely lyrical description of the Eagle's corporate speech and song – six of the most important among the 'living lights' are named in a way that makes it plain that their presence in Heaven, or at least their presence in this company, should cause us to marvel and should make us exclaim with the protagonist: 'Che cose son queste?'[58]

Each of the six souls is described in two terzinas, the second of which begins with the phrase 'ora conosce' – 'now he knows'. Two of them are Jewish sacred kings, two are Roman Emperors, one a twelfth-century king of Sicily, and the last, Rhipeus, is a character who appears only as a name – and only once – in the *Aeneid*. There is a great deal that ought to be said about both Emperors (for Trajan died a pagan, and, in Dante's view, Constantine brought disaster through his well-meaning Donation), but we must concentrate on the single figure of Rhipeus, who should cause not just marvel, but amazement.[59]

In Virgil's epic, he is named along with four others who died on the night of the Fall of Troy. The narrator is Aeneas himself and it is he who adds the unforgettable passing tribute that Rhipeus had been 'the most righteous of all the Trojans, and the one who most upheld what is just, although the gods deemed otherwise':

> cadit et Rhipeus, *justissimus* unus
> qui fuit in Teucris et servantissimus *aequi*,
> (dis aliter visum) . . . (*Aeneid* II, 426–8)

Dante's imagination was clearly stirred by the beauty and pathos of these lines. Here was a man like himself who had given all his love to justice, and yet his *praeclarissima virtus* had not been recognised by his own gods. The fate of Rhipeus clearly became a 'test case' for Dante, which he resolved by deciding that the one true God must have known better, and that Rhipeus had been chosen and saved.

In modern terms, the *judicium* could be described as a 'landmark judgement', providing countless opportunities for speculation about the fate of others (and tending to re-open the case of Virgil himself). Indeed, it might have constituted a 'dangerous precedent' if Dante the author had not remembered his theology. But he is as punctilious as the most experienced *juris peritus*. He makes it clear that Rhipeus' first impulse to love righteousness came from God. God gave him a personal revelation of the future redemption of mankind through Christ, and also gave him – through a special act of grace – the gift of Faith which enabled him to believe in 'Cristo venturo'. Together with Faith came the other 'infused' virtues of Hope and Charity. It was 'these three' (personified as 'tre donne') who acted as 'godparents' at his symbolic 'baptism', centuries before that sacrament was instituted. (By insisting on the infusion of the three theological virtues, Dante has also dealt with the objection that none of the 'works' performed by an unbeliever can earn 'merit', and that for this reason Rhipeus could not possibly have been *justissimus* and *servantissimus aequi*.) The case of Rhipeus proves to be quite unlike that of the hypothetical dweller on the banks of the Indus, who could meet none of the conditions for salvation. God acted *de jure*:

> 'Chi crederebbe giù nel mondo errante
> che Rifëo Troiano in questo tondo
> fosse la quinta de le luci sante?' (*Par.* XIX, 65–7)

'Who in the erring world below would believe that Trojan Rhipeus could be the fifth of the sacred lights in this curve [of the Eagle's eyebrow]?'

> 'L'altra, per grazia che da sì profonda
> fontana stilla, che mai creatura
> non pinse l'occhio infino a la prima onda,
> tutto suo amor là giù pose a drittura;
> per che, di grazia in grazia, Dio li aperse
> l'occhio a la nostra redenzion futura;
> ond' ei credette in quella, e non sofferse
> da indi il puzzo più del paganesmo;
> e riprendiene le genti perverse.
> Quelle tre donne li fur per battesmo
> che tu vedesti da la destra rota,
> dinanzi al battezzar più d'un millesmo.
> O predestinazion . . .' (118–30)

> 'The other soul [Rhipeus], through grace, that flows from so deep a spring that no created being ever thrust his gaze back to the primal source, gave all his love on earth to righteousness; so that, from one act of grace to another, God opened his eyes to our future Redemption; and so he believed in it, and would no longer endure the stench of paganism, and reproved the perversity of the gentiles. The three ladies whom you saw at the right wheel [of Beatrice's chariot] were there in place of baptism, more than a thousand years before baptism began. O predestination. . .'

It will be seen that the case of Rhipeus leads to a mention of the doctrine of Predestination, which remains a far greater 'stumbling block to the gentiles' than the fate of the virtuous pagans. But there is no need for us to go any further. The principles have been established. What God wills is good and just. Mortals must not presume to know more than the Bible reveals, and they must keep a tight rein on their acts of judgement ('mortali, tenetevi stretti / a giudicar'). Not even the blessed who see God – says the corporate voice of the Eagle – know all the chosen, and they rejoice in their lack ('ché noi che Dio vedemo, / non conosciamo ancor tutti li eletti; / ed ènne dolce così fatto scemo').[60]

The salvation of Rhipeus provides the perfect 'happy ending' for Part Three of this book. It is typical of Dante that the unexpected fate of one obscure individual can illuminate the 'human worth' of all mankind, and typical, too, that one cannot understand *justitia* as a human moral virtue in his work without understanding *justitia* as an expression of the will of God. It is typical, further, that the Lamb of Christian faith should lie down with the Lions of jurisprudence and scholastic logic; and typical, finally, that all this *concors discordia* should have its roots in a pagan poem that Dante knew by heart.[61]

PART FOUR

Amid such wisdom ('tra cotanto senno')

Preface to Part Four

Part Four takes the form of a detailed case-study, in which the approaches, categories and themes that were treated in isolation and illustrated with brief multiple examples in the first three parts will be combined and applied to the interpretation of a single extended episode in the *Comedy*. We shall see what can be learned about Dante's poetry and ethics from his representation of one character. Simultaneously we shall see how many aspects of this – or any other – episode can be illuminated from within the context of Dante's literary and philosophical culture.

There will be no new material and nothing of more than passing interest that is not derived from Dante's own writings or the authors he reverenced. Aristotle, Augustine, Boethius and Cicero will put in a brief appearance; Aquinas will again typify the spirit and methodology of the thirteenth century; but the principal witnesses will be the poets of the 'bella scola' – Horace, Ovid, Lucan and Virgil (with the shade of Homer ever present in the background). It will be remembered that when the protagonist met these great spirits in Limbo, he was, so to speak, admitted into their guild. He became 'sesto tra cotanto senno', literally, 'sixth amid such wisdom'. This is the phrase that provides the title of Part Four.[1]

The chosen episode concerns the very man who was consumed by 'the desire to gain experience of the world, and of human vices, and of human worth' – Ulysses – and we shall focus exclusively on his own worth and vices. It is unlikely that any reader of this book will be unacquainted with the second half of *Inferno* XXVI, and a certain familiarity with its structure and contents will be taken for granted. But since Chapter 10 will open with a lengthy preamble, and since each successive terzina or group of terzinas will be studied in the light of a short excerpt from one of Dante's *auctores*, the whole episode is presented below, accompanied by a facing translation, line by line, so that all readers may start on an equal footing.[2]

Inferno XXVI, 55–142

Rispuose a me: 'Là dentro si martira
Ulisse e Dïomede, e così insieme
a la vendetta vanno come a l'ira;

[Virgil] answered me: 'Within it are tormented
Ulysses and Diomedes, and thus they go together
to vengeance as [they went together] to their crime;

e dentro da la lor fiamma si geme
l'agguato del caval che fé la porta
onde uscì de' Romani il gentil seme.

and within their flame they lament
the trick of the horse that made the gate
by which the Romans' noble seed went forth;

Piangevisi entro l'arte per che, morta,
Deïdamìa ancor si duol d'Achille,
e del Palladio pena vi si porta.'

within it they bewail the craft through which
the dead Deidamia still mourns for Achilles;
and the penalty is paid there for the Palladium.'

'S'ei posson dentro da quelle faville
parlar,' diss' io, 'maestro, assai ten priego
e ripriego, che 'l priego vaglia mille,

'If they can speak within those flames,'
I said, 'I earnestly pray you, Master, and pray again,
and may each prayer count for a thousand,

che non mi facci de l'attender niego
fin che la fiamma cornuta qua vegna;
vedi che del disio ver' lei mi piego!'

that you will not deny me leave to wait
until the horned flame draws near:
see how I lean out towards it with desire!'

Ed elli a me: 'La tua preghiera è degna
di molta loda, e io però l'accetto;
ma fa che la tua lingua si sostegna.

And he said to me: 'Your prayer deserves
high praise, and so I accept it;
but place your tongue under restraint.

Lascia parlare a me, ch'i' ho concetto
ciò che tu vuoi; ch'ei sarebbero schivi,
perch' e' fuor greci, forse del tuo detto.'

Leave it to me to speak, for I have understood
what you desire; and, since they were Greeks,
they might perhaps despise your words.'

Poi che la fiamma fu venuta quivi
dove parve al mio duca tempo e loco,
in questa forma lui parlare audivi:

After the flame had come
where my leader judged it to be the time and place
I heard him speak in these words:

'O voi che siete due dentro ad un foco,
s'io meritai di voi mentre ch'io vissi,
s'io meritai di voi assai o poco

'O you who are two within one fire,
if I deserved anything of you while I lived,
if I deserved much or little

quando nel mondo li alti versi scrissi,
non vi movete; ma l'un di voi dica
dove, per lui, perduto a morir gissi.'

when in the world I wrote the lofty lines,
do not move on; but let one of you say
where, being lost, he went to die.'

Lo maggior corno de la fiamma antica
cominciò a crollarsi mormorando,
pur come quella cui vento affatica;

The greater horn of the ancient flame
began to shake and murmur,
like a flame when harassed by the wind.

indi la cima qua e là menando,
come fosse la lingua che parlasse,
gittò voce di fuori e disse: 'Quando

Then moving its tip to and fro,
as though the tongue itself were speaking,
it flung forth a voice that said: 'When

mi diparti' da Circe, che sottrasse
me più d'un anno là presso a Gaeta,
prima che sì Enëa la nomasse,

I parted from Circe, who had beguiled me
more than a year there near Gaeta,
before Aeneas had named it so,

né dolcezza di figlio, né la pieta
del vecchio padre, né 'l debito amore
lo qual dovea Penelopè far lieta,

neither the sweetness of a son, nor reverence
for an aged father, nor the love I owed
to Penelope, that should have brought her joy,

vincer potero dentro a me l'ardore
ch'i' ebbi a divenir del mondo esperto
e de li vizi umani e del valore;

could overcome in me the longing I had
to gain experience of the world
and of human vices and human worth;

ma misi me per l'alto mare aperto
sol con un legno e con quella compagna
picciola da la qual non fui diserto.

and I put out on the deep open sea
with just one ship and that small band
of comrades who had not deserted me.

L'un lito e l'altro vidi infin la Spagna,
fin nel Morrocco, e l'isola d'i Sardi,
e l'altre che quel mare intorno bagna.

I saw one shore and the other, as far as Spain,
as far as Morocco, and Sardinia, and the other
islands whose shores are bathed by that sea.

Io e ' compagni eravam vecchi e tardi
quando venimmo a quella foce stretta
dov' Ercule segnò li suoi riguardi

I and my comrades were old and weary
when we came to that narrow strait
where Hercules set up his landmarks

acciò che l'uom più oltre non si metta;
da la man destra mi lasciai Sibilia,
da l'altra già m'avea lasciata Setta.

so that no man should pass beyond.
On my right hand I left Seville,
on the other I had already left Ceuta.

"O frati," dissi, "che per cento milia
perigli siete giunti a l'occidente,
a questa tanto picciola vigilia

"O brothers," I said, "who through a hundred
thousand dangers have reached the West,
to this so brief vigil

d'i nostri sensi ch'è del rimanente
non vogliate negar l'esperïenza,
di retro al sol, del mondo sanza gente.

of the senses that remains to us
do not deny experience of the world
without people behind the sun.

Considerate la vostra semenza:
fatti non foste a viver come bruti,
ma per seguir virtute e canoscenza."

Consider your race and origin:
you were not born to live as animals,
but to pursue virtue and knowledge."

Li miei compagni fec' io sì aguti,
con questa orazion picciola, al cammino,
che a pena poscia li avrei ritenuti;

With this little speech I made my comrades
so eager for the voyage, that I could scarcely
have restrained them thereafter;

e volta nostra poppa nel mattino,
de' remi facemmo ali al folle volo,
sempre acquistando dal lato mancino.

and turning our stern to the morning
we made wings of our oars for the mad flight,
gaining always on the left.

Tutte le stelle già de l'altro polo
vedea la notte, e 'l nostro tanto basso,
che non surgëa fuor del marin suolo.

Already night was showing all the stars
of the other pole, and our pole so low
that it did not rise above the ocean floor.

Cinque volte racceso e tante casso
lo lume era di sotto da la luna,
poi che 'ntrati eravam ne l'alto passo,

Five times the light below the moon
had been rekindled, and as often quenched,
since we had entered on the great crossing,

quando n'apparve una montagna, bruna
per la distanza, e parvemi alta tanto
quanto veduta non avëa alcuna.

when a mountain appeared to us, dim
in the distance, and it seemed to me higher
than any I had ever seen.

Noi ci allegrammo, e tosto tornò in pianto;
ché de la nova terra un turbo nacque
e percosse del legno il primo canto.

We were filled with joy, but soon it turned to grief;
for out of the new-found land a whirlwind rose
and struck the forepart of the ship.

Tre volte il fé girar con tutte l'acque;
a la quarta levar la poppa in suso
e la prora ire in giù, com' altrui piacque,
infin che 'l mar fu sovra noi richiuso.'

Three times it whirled her round with all the waters;
at the fourth it lifted the stern,
plunging the prow below, as it pleased Another,
until the sea closed over us again.'

CHAPTER TEN

The worth and vices of Ulysses: a case-study

Ulysses the voyager and Dante the pilgrim

Dante called him 'Ulisse' (from the Latin Ulixes), and it is right to go on using the corresponding English form, Ulysses, rather than Odysseus, if only to re-emphasise that Dante knew no Greek and had no direct knowledge of Homer's *Odyssey*. His characterisation of Ulysses is based on what he had learnt from the poets and moralists of ancient Rome. It was they who taught him to distinguish between the qualities that Ulysses showed during the ten years of the siege of Troy (first narrated in Homer's *Iliad*) and the traits that became prominent during the equally long years of his wanderings on the voyage back to Ithaca (which form the subject of the *Odyssey*). It is one of the great strengths of Dante's portrait that he will not admit any dichotomy, but it was of course the second Ulysses – the intrepid voyager – who exercised such a fascination over him (as he has done over so many readers and writers for nearly three thousand years).[1]

During his wanderings – as we are told in the third line of the *Odyssey* – Ulysses 'saw the cities and customs of many men', because a combination of personal temperament and celestial wrath drove him from Asia Minor half way across the Mediterranean as far as the western coast of Italy. (In the Latin tradition the island of the sorceress Circe was located near the promontory of Gaeta, just north of Naples.) In Homer's epic, Ulysses then returned eastward to his native Ithaca. But in Dante's poem, his invincible desire 'a divenir del mondo esperto / e de li vizi umani e del valore' makes him continue his journey to the West, seeing 'Sardinia and all the other islands' that are 'bathed' by the inland sea, and exploring 'one shore and the other, as far as Spain and Morocco'. And in Dante's free reconstruction of events, he persuades his small, remaining crew to continue their westward voyage out over the boundless ocean, into the southern hemisphere, in pursuit this time of 'the world without people'.

The voyage ends in shipwreck within sight of a 'new-found land' (a 'terra nova') which proves to be the mountain of Purgatory. Ulysses dies, frustrated, without ever setting foot on the shore which Dante, as protagonist of the *Comedy*, will later reach by another, subterranean route. And the true nature of Ulysses' last adventure, and the causes of his failure, cannot be understood in isolation from the journey made by Dante and the reasons for his success. Both men were seeking 'knowledge of good and evil'. Dante the author intended their quests to complement and illuminate each other; and the study of Ulysses and his 'folle volo' must be punctuated with reflections on the 'fatale andare' of Dante the protagonist. This is why we must begin by thinking about the symbolic meanings of the later, longer journey – the one with the 'happy ending' that justifies the title of Dante's poem.[2]

Preamble A: some extended meanings of the 'journey'

If the *Comedy* were to be made into a film again, critics might want to classify it affectionately as a 'road-movie'. Its plot is the journey. Subsidiary characters appear only once. The mainspring of each new action is the need to keep moving. If, on the other hand, it had been rewritten in nineteenth-century Germany, it would have been described as a *Bildungsroman*, 'a novel in which the chief character, after a number of false starts and wrong choices, is led to follow the right path and develop into a mature and well-balanced man'. Its plot concerns education and the formation of character (*Bildung*). Every scene 'lays its hand to the principal intent'. But the concepts of *Bildungsroman* and road-movie do not exclude each other, because the journey is a universal symbol of many kinds of progress and many kinds of achievement. Dante was doing little more than breathing new life into a commonplace when he said in the first line of his poem that he was 'half way on the *journey* of our life', 'nel mezzo del *cammin* di nostra vita'.[3]

The symbolism of the journey is so familiar that there is no need to enter into its infinite ramifications, but it will be worth making a few general points about certain implications of the concept of a 'journey' in the Middle Ages which are not self-evident today.

Travel was arduous in the thirteenth century and the majority of people never went far from their native village or city. However, one kind of extended journey would have been familiar to everyone from hearsay at least, and was charged with religious meaning. This was the pilgrimage to some sacred shrine, undertaken in thanksgiving for a benefit received ('per grazia ricevuta'), or in hope of a cure or remission of sins. Some of the pilgrimages were to far-flung places (Rome, for example, Compostella in north-west Spain, or the Holy Land itself). The major pilgrim routes were well defined and divided into clear stages ('journey' comes from the French word 'journée', and originally meant the distance one could cover in a whole day). Groups of pilgrims would be accompanied by a guide. (There is no need to pursue the subject because the parallels with the literal story of the *Comedy* will be sufficiently obvious.)

It should also be remembered that even the humblest medieval parishioner was able to participate in the small-scale symbolic journeys that marked out special days in the liturgical year, for example accompanying the image of a saint as it was carried through the city-streets from its local church to the cathedral. Such journeys were undertaken for the good of the soul. They made the pilgrim a better person.

For medieval theologians, eternal life in Heaven was dwelling *in patria* – 'in the homeland' – whereas our earthly existence was like being 'on the journey there' – *in via*. When Dante spoke so poignantly in the *Convivio* of his wanderings 'as a beggar through all the parts where this language is spoken', he may well have been remembering that ever since our First Parents were exiled from the Garden of Eden, all human life has been no more than a wandering in the wilderness, and that damnation is tantamount to exile for eternity ('*etterno* essilio').[4]

Aristotle and his followers took movement from place to place (*motus localis*) as a model for the analysis of every kind of change and action. Ethical discourse is dominated by 'principles', 'means' and 'ends' because all actions, like all rectilinear motion, must have a beginning, a middle and an end (*principium*, *medium* and *finis*). Clearly, there are many different types of locomotion. But we only speak of a 'journey' when we are thinking of a movement towards some definite goal, undertaken for the sake of reaching that goal (*propter finem*) and usually involving many intermediate stages. Hence a journey was the natural paradigm for any complex 'human operation', which is to say, any action consciously planned and executed with some end in view.[5]

What we still call the 'means' to the 'end' are analogous to the roads, fords and bridges that lie between the *principium* and the *finis*. We select or reject the *diversa media* (Dante's phrase), depending on whether we believe they will lead towards the desired end or away from it. And this is the idea at the heart of Aristotle's teasing and much-quoted dictum that 'in moral philosophy, the beginnings are the ends' (*principia sunt fines*). In other words, the 'principles' we apply in deliberating about the choice of 'means' are simply the 'ends' which those means are intended to achieve.[6]

The image of the journey also throws light on the distinction, frequently made by Aquinas, between a 'good' and an 'arduous good'. (When *bonum* is used without qualification, it can refer to any of the species of good that are desired for any of the reasons explained in Part Two; but a *bonum arduum* denotes a good that can be obtained only with difficulty, effort or pain.) An arduous task – for example, mastering the theorems of Euclid – will have moments that are like descending into a deep pit, climbing a mountain, flying through the air, braving monsters, or passing through a wall of fire (as Ptolemy remarked, 'there is no royal road to geometry'). Desire for the intended good is not sufficient in itself to overcome the 'obstacles' in the 'path'. And if the *bonum arduum* is nothing less than salvation, the 'traveller' will have to rely on the infused virtues of Faith and Hope as well as on the acquired virtues of Fortitude and Temperance. (Again, it should not be necessary to labour the relevance of these ideas to the literal and allegorical senses of Dante's journey in the *Comedy*.)[7]

Preamble B: two 'figural' journeys

Apart from these generic motifs and associations there are references in the *Comedy* to certain journeys by named individuals which form an integral part of the poem's web of meaning. The Argonauts were the first heroes to dare to cross the seas. Daedalus and Icarus were the first to fly. Theseus, Orpheus and Aeneas went down to the Underworld. Elijah was carried to Heaven in a chariot of fire and St Paul was 'caught up' into Heaven. Jesus descended into Hell when he yielded up his spirit on Good Friday, rose from the dead on Easter Day, and six weeks later ascended into Heaven.[8]

The names are drawn from both classical and biblical sources, but the allusions vary greatly in kind from a mere mention to a quotation, a simile, a meeting with one of the actors involved, or references to the movements of the heavenly bodies (which indicate that Dante's own descent began on a Good Friday and that he returned to the upper world on Easter Day). And while all the allusions are pertinent in some way, none of them is so vital to our understanding of the *Comedy* as an awareness of two further journeys involving a leader and a whole people.

These have special status. For Dante, they were datable historical events which resulted in conquests that changed the history of the world in fulfilment of God's providential design.

The first is narrated in the second and sixth books of the Old Testament, which tell how Moses and the Israelites made their escape – *exitus*, Exodus – from serfdom in Egypt; how they made a miraculous crossing of the Red Sea into the wilderness of Sinai; and how they finally crossed dryfoot over the River Jordan to win possession of the 'land flowing with milk and honey' that had been promised by Jehovah to the descendants of Abraham – the 'Holy Land', ordained for the incarnation and crucifixion of the Son of God.

The second journey is the subject of Virgil's *Aeneid*, which is set in exactly the same years and the same locations as Homer's *Odyssey*. Virgil tells how Aeneas and his followers also left the city of Troy, sailed past Ithaca, made their way by sea to the mouth of the river Tiber and subdued the inhabitants of Latium – all this being necessary to 'found the Roman people' ('Romanam condere gentem') and to fulfil the promise made by Jupiter to Venus, the mother of Aeneas, that the Romans would rule without limits of space or time over the whole of mankind.[9]

The influence of the 'higher', 'hidden' meanings of the Exodus

The Exodus was important to Dante primarily for the allegorical or mystical meanings it was thought to convey. For centuries, the opening of Psalm 113, *In exitu Israel de Aegypto*, had been the principal schoolroom example used to illustrate the three additional levels of signification – 'sovrasensi' – carried by the biblical narrative. And it is no accident that in the fiction of the *Comedy*, this is the psalm sung by the souls of the penitent as they disembark on the shores of Purgatory after a miraculous voyage from the mouth of the Tiber along much the same course as that of Ulysses.[10]

The 'higher' meanings are explained in the Epistle to Can Grande as follows:

> In the allegorical sense, the going forth ('exitus') of the children of Israel in the time of Moses signifies our redemption brought about by Christ. In the moral sense, it signifies the turning of the soul ('conversio animae') from the grief and wretchedness of sin to a state of grace. And in the anagogical sense it signifies the going forth of the sanctified soul ('exitus animae sanctae') from the slavery of this corruptible world to the freedom of eternal glory. (*Epist.* XIII, 21)

In the first of the three 'sovrasensi', the unique historical event is a prefiguration of another unique event (the Crucifixion and Resurrection, which 'redeemed' all mankind by 'buying us out' of slavery to sin). In the second and third senses, the 'exitus filiorum Israel' is an image of two decisive movements in the moral journey of every human soul: the 'going forth' to glory, at the end; and the all-important 'turning away' from sin and acceptance of God's grace, at any point 'in the middle of the way'.

All three senses are relevant to our understanding of the *Comedy*, but it is the *sensus moralis* that does most to illuminate the journey of Dante the pilgrim, and, indirectly, the voyage of Ulysses. Dante's pilgrimage begins with a *conversio* in the Dark Wood. He travels *in statu gratiae* on his quest for the final freedom, until he too is granted a foretaste of the 'exitus . . . ad aeternae gloriae libertatem' in his momentary enjoyment of the countenance of God (this being a definition of the 'blessedness of eternal life' which is the second of the 'two ends that Providence intended us to attain'). Not so Ulysses.[11]

The higher senses of the voyage of Aeneas

From the point of view of the author of the *Inferno*, the most important episode in the voyage of Aeneas was the descent to the Underworld (*Inferi*); and, as every reader will be aware, Dante quarried and recycled a prodigious amount of material from Book VI of the *Aeneid*. But the whole of Aeneas' journey from Troy to Latium provided a model for Dante's pilgrimage, in so far as it was undertaken at the command of Jupiter, 'il sommo Giove'. It was a 'fatale andare'. Aeneas and Dante the protagonist proved themselves to be 'righteous' by submitting to the will of God and accepting their calling and their mission.[12]

As was noted above, the voyage of Aeneas took place at exactly the same time and in the same seas as that of Ulysses. (Virgil was no less thorough than his pupil in his quarrying of the *Odyssey*.) Aeneas was warned to avoid Scylla and Charybdis, but he rescued one of Ulysses' sailors from the shores of the Cyclops; and his descent to Hades began in the grove with the Golden Bough, not far from Gaeta. When Ovid came to tell the stories of both Aeneas and Ulysses in *Metamorphoses* XIV, he cross-referenced the contemporaneous voyages to excellent effect.[13]

The two Roman poets, however, accepted that Ulysses had been driven so far off his course by the vengeful wrath of Neptune, whereas in Dante's recasting of the material, Ulysses was unwilling to return home after he left Circe, so that the last 'folle volo' was begun in conscious defiance of the gods. In the *Comedy*, therefore, the three expeditionaries form a triangle of relationships in which 'pious' Aeneas is paired with Dante at the base, so to speak, and both are contrasted with 'impious' Ulysses at the apex.[14]

Preamble C: Dante's analysis of the sins of fraud

We are now ready to look at the opening section of Canto XXVI of *Inferno* and to remind ourselves of the physical setting and the dramatic context of Dante's encounter with Ulysses. But before we do so, we must return briefly to Virgil's description of the *moral* framework of Hell in Canto XI, and recall what we have been led to expect about the eighth circle.

Virgil's speech was greatly admired by Dante the protagonist. Not without a hint of condescension, he told his master: 'your reasoning proceeds with great clarity ("assai chiara / procede la tua ragione"), and makes clear distinctions within this pit and the people it contains' ('ed assai ben distingue / questo baràtro e 'l popol ch'e' possiede'). And indeed the speech is a splendid example of scholastic division and subdivision, used, as so often, in an attempt to synthesise elements from four disparate sources. (From the Old Testament comes the concept of sin as an 'offence' against God; from the New, the idea that sin is a repudiation of Charity. The distinction between *animal* and *animal rationale* derives from Aristotle; the distinction between violence and fraud from Cicero.)[15]

As we begin to read the canto of Ulysses, then, we are in possession of a good deal of relevant information. We are aware that Dante has descended into the first of two circles reserved for the fraudulent; and we know that the 'frodolenti' are placed lower down than the violent (in the seventh circle), because 'fraud is an evil peculiar to man and therefore more hateful to God'. Fraud, we have also been told, 'gnaws at every conscience'; but there is less harm in the kind which is practised on someone who has no reason to trust his deceiver, because in this lesser form it destroys 'only the bond of love established by nature'. In the act of treachery, by contrast, 'there is a disregard of that added love which creates a special trust'. (This is why treachery is punished in the ninth and lowest circle.)[16]

The main species of simple fraud were succinctly listed for our benefit in Canto XI, and by the time we reach Canto XXVI, we have mentally checked off the sinners who are damned for seduction, simony, witchcraft, barratry, hypocrisy and theft. However, the list did not prepare us in any way for the sinners whom we are about to meet; and all we may safely infer is that Ulysses was not guilty of betraying members of his family, his countrymen, his guests or his lord.[17]

The setting and the build-up: Dr Jekyll and Mr Hyde

So to the narrative. Dante and Virgil climb the stony bridge over the eighth 'bolgia' (a deep circular trench forming one of the subdivisions of this circle). There is not a sinner or devil to be seen. All they can make out in the bottom of the 'bolgia' is a procession of flames, flickering like so many fireflies. 'Every flame is stealing a sinner' from their sight, because, as Virgil explains, 'the spirits are inside the fires, and each is sheathed in what burns it'.

One of these flames stands out from all the others because it is 'divided at the top'. It is this 'horned flame' that rivets the attention of the protagonist, whose only question is: 'Who is inside that fire?' In the event, it is clear that he has already guessed the answer; and this intuitive telepathy is one of a number of several unprecedented clues to the special importance of the encounter.[18]

Even before the narrative resumed, Dante the poet had spoken of 'the grief I felt then, and the grief I now feel, as I turn my mind to what I saw'. And he continued, even more significantly: 'I rein in my mental powers ("ingegno") more than usual, lest they may gallop away unguided by virtue; so that, if some propitious star or better thing has been good to me, I may not deny myself their gift':

Allor mi dolsi, e ora mi ridoglio
quando drizzo la mente a ciò ch'io vidi
e più lo 'ngegno affreno ch'i' non soglio,
perché non corra che virtù nol guidi;
sì che, se stella bona o miglior cosa
m'ha dato 'l ben, ch'io stessi nol m'invidi.

(*Inf.* XXVI, 19–24)

A further indication of the dangerous attraction exerted by the still unnamed figure of Ulysses was given before the protagonist put his question about the 'horned flame'. This time there was risk of another 'Fall':

Io stava sovra 'l ponte a veder surto,
sì che s'io non avessi un ronchion preso,
caduto sarei giù sanz' esser urto. (43–5)

> I was standing on the bridge, craning to see, so that, if I had not seized hold of a rock, I would have fallen to the bottom without being pushed.

Once the identity of the souls within the flame has been confirmed, we are given another visual signal as the protagonist 'leans towards it with desire'. And when Dante begins to speak, he pleads to Virgil with an urgency that will not be paralleled until St Bernard intervenes on his behalf in the final prayer to the Virgin (where the triple repetition of 'priego', 'ripriego', and 'il priego' will return in indirect self-quotation).[19]

> 'S'ei posson dentro da quelle faville
> parlar', diss'io, 'maestro, assai ten priego
> e ripriego, che 'l priego vaglia mille,
> che non mi facci de l'attender niego
> fin che la fiamma cornuta qua vegna;
> vedi che del disio ver' lei mi piego!' (64–9)

> 'If they can speak within those flames', I said, 'Master, I entreat you earnestly, and entreat you again, and may each entreaty count for a thousand, that you will not refuse me leave to wait until the horned flame draws near; you see I am leaning out towards it with desire!'

In later cantos there are several explicit references to the encounter. There are also several passages that indirectly confirm the exceptional closeness of the links between the protagonist and Ulysses. (To give just one minor example: in *Purgatorio* XVIII, we shall be reminded that 'leaning towards' something is an expression of love: 'quel piegare è amor'. And it was a scholastic axiom that love is caused by similarity – *similitudo est causa amoris*.) For the moment, however, it is enough to register the intimations given in lines 20–4 and 45 that Ulysses may prove to be a menacing *alter ego*. We have been given clear hints that he is a Mr Hyde – an older, less biddable, unreconstructed counterpart to the ingenuous Dr Jekyll who bears the author's name.[20]

The 'negative' tradition: the debt to Virgil and Ovid

Although Dante's Ulysses is to some extent re created in the author's 'likeness and image', and although his final voyage is mostly Dante's own invention, his personality and deeds are rooted in the classical hero who went under such names or epithets as Ulixes, Ithacus, Neritii dux, or Laertiades. Our next task, therefore, is to take note of Dante's principal sources in Latin literature, beginning with those that deal with the part Ulysses played in the Trojan war.

In the *Aeneid* (especially in Book II) Ulysses is presented unfavourably. His name is linked with 'deceptions' (*doli*) at its very first mention. The epithets used of him are 'cruel', 'terrifying', 'devisor of crimes' (*saevus, dirus, scelerum inventor*). Nor is this simply a consequence of the fact that those who speak about him are biased witnesses (Laocoön and Aeneas), or lying on oath (Sinon), because even in Greek literature of the post-Homeric period, Ulysses was often portrayed negatively for acts of cruelty, cowardice and deceit. In Virgil's epic he is closely associated with the most famous stratagem of all time – the Wooden Horse (which Dante will refer to as 'the *ambush* of the horse'). And Sinon is allowed to devote no fewer than fourteen wilfully exaggerated lines to his sacrilegious theft of a statue of Minerva, the Palladium, which had ensured the security of Troy for as long as it stood safe within the citadel.[21]

Dante's single most important source, however, was not the *Aeneid*, but Ovid's *Metamorphoses*. Ulysses makes his first appearance there in Book XIII. Achilles is already dead. The Greek chieftains have assembled to decide who should receive the shield and armour that had been forged for Achilles by Vulcan. The contendants are Ajax and Ulysses. Ajax speaks first and devotes most of his energy to an attack on his rival. Citing chapter and verse, he alleges that Ulysses' parentage is suspect and that he resembles his putative father, Sisyphus, in his 'thefts and fraud' ('furtisque et *fraude*'). Ulysses, says Ajax, is one who urges crimes on others ('hortator *scelerum*'). He is a coward, who knows it is 'safer to fight with lying words' ('*fictis* contendere verbis'). 'Take Diomedes away and he is nothing' ('nihil est Diomede remoto').[22]

Ajax continues in this not ineffective vein for 120 hexameters (as long as a canto of the *Comedy*), ending with a typical challenge to single combat. But he is totally eclipsed by Ulysses in a speech more than twice as long and three times as clever. It demands close attention if only because it is studded with terms familiar to Dante and contains all the other facts we need to know about Ulysses' role in the Trojan campaign.

Having been forced onto the defensive, Ovid's Ulysses proudly defends first his mental powers, *ingenium*, and then his eloquence, *facundia* (using one phrase in particular that lodged in Dante's memory). His rival has brawn without brains ('vires sine *mente*'), excelling 'only in body, not in mind' (*animo*), whereas those who were 'strong in arm yielded to my counsels' ('manu fortes . . . *consiliis* cessere meis').[23]

The noble Laertes was his father, and he can claim additional nobility ('altera *nobilitas*') on his mother's side. But let the Greeks 'weigh the case on its deserts'. He is not concerned with the relative rank of his blood ('*sanguinis* ordo'), but with the honour due to manly virtue ('*virtutis* honor'). Naturally enough, he goes on to describe some of his many feats of courage in battle. It is true, he concedes, that he performed them in the company of Diomedes; but 'it is something to be the only one chosen from so many thousands of Greeks by Diomedes!'. In any case, greater weight should be given to the success of his eloquence in turning the tide on the two occasions when the Greeks, including Ajax, wanted to abandon the siege.[24]

Next, Ulysses faces up to the charges of simulation, theft and fraud. He positively glories in his principal acts of subterfuge on the grounds that they were necessary means to the end. Oracles had made it plain that Troy could never be conquered unless certain obstacles were removed. His was the only way. It was he who persuaded Agamemnon to sacrifice his daughter Iphigenia for the common good, and he who 'deceived' Clytemnestra into sending her to Aulis. Achilles was 'captured by Ulysses' intelligence' ('deprensus Ulixis *ingenio*'), when he was tricked into revealing his identity among Deidamia and her sisters on the island of Scyros, where his mother had hidden him in a vain effort to save him from his destiny. Above all, it was Ulysses who succeeded in stealing the Palladium, which had guaranteed the safety of the city. In effect, he boasts – with the untranslatable pithiness and elegance of which Ovid was such a master – 'It was on that very night that I gave birth to victory in Troy: I conquered Pergamon, when I made it conquerable' – literally, 'when I compelled it (*coegi*) to be able (*posse*) to be conquered (*vinci*)':[25]

> illa nocte mihi Troiae victoria parta est:
> Pergama tunc vici, cum vinci posse coegi.
> (*Metamorphoses* XIII, 348–9)

'Si può formare una cotale quistione'

Having listened to both harangues, the Greek leaders rewarded Ulysses by giving him Achilles' armour. Dante condemned him to eternal suffering. Why should the verdicts be so different?

One of the most perceptive early readers of the *Comedy* (a man who was familiar with the *Summa Theologiae* of Aquinas) identified the central issue and recast the arguments for and against in the form of a *quaestio*. Having summarised the content of *Inferno* XXVI, the author of the so-called *Ottimo commento* continues as follows:

> Since in this canto Dante presents the penalty inflicted on those who won wars by fraud and deceptions ('per frode e inganni'), one may formulate a *quaestio* ('si può formare una cotale quistione') and debate whether it is legitimate ('licito') to deceive the enemy.
>
> It would seem that every art may be used to win a just war ('licita guerra'). Therefore, it is legitimate to deceive the enemy.
>
> On the other hand, it may be argued that no deception tending to harm someone is legitimate ('In contrario s'argomenta che nullo inganno, il quale tende a danno d'alcuno, è licito'). Therefore, one may not legitimately deceive the enemy ('Dunque non si puote ingannare licitamente il nimico').[26]

In his own 'soluzione' to the 'quistione', the anonymous commentator argues that if a war is conducted in a just cause and has been openly declared ('licitamente impresa per denunziazione'), then every art may indeed be used. And he clearly inclines to the view that Dante was unjust in his poetic punishment ('ingiustamente poetizza Ulisse . . . in cotale pena').

But for Dante, fraud is always fraud, and always wrong. Ulysses is explicitly damned for the very acts of deception of which Ovid's Ulysses had been so proud. So, too, is his invariable accomplice, Diomedes. Within the single flame, the two Greeks are punished together for the crimes they committed together – and the indictment specifies the 'ambush of the horse', the luring of Achilles, and the theft of the Palladium.

> Rispuose a me: 'Là dentro si martira
> Ulisse e Dïomede, e così insieme
> a la vendetta vanno come a l'ira;
> e dentro da la lor fiamma si geme
> l'agguato del caval che fé la porta
> onde uscì de' Romani il gentil seme
> Piangevisi entro l'arte per che, morta,
> Deïdamìa ancor si duol d'Achille,
> e del Palladio pena vi si porta.' (*Inf.* XXVI, 55–63)

> [Virgil] answered me: 'Within it are tormented Ulysses and Diomedes; and thus they go together to vengeance, as together they went to their crime. And within their flame they lament the deceit of the horse that made the gate through which the noble seed of the Romans went forth. Within it they bewail the craft through which Deidamia, though dead, still mourns for Achilles; and the penalty is paid for the Palladium.'

The distinction between 'prudence' and 'astuteness'

Before we leave the events of the Trojan war, we must take note of an important distinction. Ovid's Ulysses boasts of his practical wisdom and of what he achieved by the advice he gave – his 'counsels' (*consilia*). Dante too insists on the link between the virtue of prudence and 'good counsels':[27]

> From prudence come the good counsels that lead oneself and others to a good end in human affairs ('da la prudenza vegnono li *buoni consigli*, li quali conducono sé e altri *a buono fine* ne le umane cose e operazioni').
>
> A prudent man does not wait for someone to ask him 'Give me advice', but exercising foresight on that man's behalf, advises him without request ('questo cotale prudente non attende chi li domandi "Consigliami", ma proveggendo per lui, sanza richesta colui consiglia'). In this he is like the rose that yields its perfume not only to those who seek it, but to anyone who passes near. (*Con.* IV, xxvii, 6–7)

But Dante makes it clear, on the authority of Aristotle, that good advice can come only from a good person:

> In the third age, one should therefore be prudent, that is, wise ('conviensi adunque essere prudente, cioè savio'). And as the Philosopher says, 'it is impossible to be wise without being good' ('sì come dice lo Filosofo . . . "impossibile è essere *savio* chi non è buono"').
>
> And so one should not call someone 'wise' who proceeds with subterfuges and deceptions: he should be called 'astute' ('e però non è da dire savio chi con *sottratti e con inganni* procede, ma è da chiamare *astuto*'). One should not call a person wise who knows how to do something evil well ('non è da dire savio quelli che ben sa una malvagia cosa fare'). For in doing it, he always hurts himself before others ('prima sé sempre che altrui offende'). (*ibid.* 5)

Everything that Dante writes in these paragraphs from the *Convivio* is consistent with his verdict on Ulysses in *Inferno*. Ulysses was not prudent but astute. The things he did well were evil; and in doing them, he hurt himself. This was why he would eventually 'lead himself and others to a *bad* end'.[28]

'Opere di volpe' and 'accorgimenti' in thirteenth-century warfare

Confirmation of this judgement comes in the following canto where Dante is accosted by another of the sinners who are 'stolen from sight by the flame that torments them'. He is Guido da Montefeltro, a Ghibelline leader from the Romagna, who became a highly successful professional soldier, and whose (fictional) death and damnation have already been discussed in Chapter 2 above.

Guido describes himself, in the first place, as a 'man of arms' ('uom d'arme'). Within a few lines, however, he concedes that his 'works were not leonine' (like those of Ajax) but 'foxy' (like those of Ulysses). And he goes on to speak with pride and pleasure of the craft ('arte') for which he was famous, and to vaunt his knowledge of 'all the stratagems and hidden ways':[29]

> 'l'opere mie
> non furon leonine, ma di volpe.
> Li accorgimenti e le coperte vie
> io seppi tutte, e sì menai lor arte,
> ch'al fine de la terra il suono uscie.' (*Inf.* XXVII, 74–8)

In the last years of his life, Guido tell us, he repented of what had been so pleasurable. He made confession and retired from human affairs to become a Franciscan. In the *Convivio*, Dante had expressed his admiration for Guido's timely repentance, but by the time he wrote the *Comedy* he had changed his mind. Guido is now presented as a shallow personality, whose reformation was only superficial. Hence, when Pope Boniface sought his counsel ('consiglio') in a campaign against some local dissidents, Guido felt some minor qualms about falling ('cader') into what he knew to be a sin ('quel peccato'), but he was 'thrust back into his early faults' ('ne le prime colpe'). He accepted the pope's promise of absolution in advance, and advised him that triumph would come through deception, specifically through 'long promise and short keeping' ('lunga promessa con l'attender corto'). This was a 'consiglio frodolente'; and it was for this unabsolved – because unrepented – mortal sin that the devil hauled him down to Hell.[30]

There are many other fascinating aspects to this long encounter, but enough has been said to make it clear that Guido is presented as a thirteenth-century counterpart to Ulysses. The remorse he felt was not for the profession of arms, which in itself is honourable, but for his constant recourse to guile, which he knew to be a 'colpa' and a 'peccato'. Deception – even in warfare – is not legitimate in Dante's eyes, whether in ancient or modern times. Neither Ulysses nor Guido showed true repentance for their 'craft' and 'craftiness'. Unrepented counsels of fraud lead to damnation.[31]

The 'positive' tradition: Horace on Ulysses' virtues

We must return now to the 'alternative' Ulysses – the voyager and the hero. As was noted earlier, Dante had no direct knowledge of the *Odyssey*; but he did know its programmatic opening lines from two well-known passages in Horace. The first of these comes in the *Ars poetica* (lines 136–52), where Homer is praised for his narrative technique in 'sweeping the reader straight into the middle of things (*in medias res*) as though they were already known'. (This is the technique that Dante's Ulysses will himself exemplify when he begins his narration in mid-journey and mid-verse):[32]

> 'Dic mihi, Musa, virum, captae post tempora Troiae
> qui mores hominum multorum vidit et urbes.'
> (*Ars poetica*, 141–2)

> 'Tell me, Muse, the hero, who in the time after Troy was taken, saw the customs of many men and their cities.'

The other passage comes in the opening of the second Epistle, where Horace says he has been reading Homer again for moral instruction, and advises his young correspondent to do the same. The 'writer of the Trojan war' will tell him 'better and more plainly than the philosophers Chrysippus and Crantor, what is handsome and what foul, what is expedient and what is not'. The *Iliad* will show him the madness of the leaders on both sides (Paris, for example, seems to be 'denying that anyone can force him to reign in safety and live happily'!). 'Within and without the walls of Troy, sinning is rife – with sedition, deceptions, crime, lust and anger.'

> Troiani belli scriptorem . . . / . . . relegi;
> qui quid sit *pulchrum*, quid turpe, quid *utile*, quid non,
> planius ac melius Chrysippo et Crantore dicit.
> . . .
> Quid Paris? ut *salvus* regnet vivatque *beatus*
> cogi posse negat . . .
> . . .
> seditione, dolis, scelere atque libidine et ira
> Iliacos intra muros *peccatur* et extra.
> (*Epist*. I, II, 1–4, 10–11, 15–16)

The *Odyssey*, on the other hand, teaches a positive lesson. Homer has 'set Ulysses before us as an instructive pattern of what *virtue and wisdom* can do' ('quid *virtus* et quid *sapientia* possit, / utile proposuit nobis exemplar Ulixen'). Ulysses possessed the moral virtue of courage. (The Homeric quotation is here extended to include the words: 'he endured many hardships . . . on the broad sea': 'multorum . . . urbes / et mores hominum inspexit, latumque per aequor / . . . *aspera multa / pertulit*'.) He gave proof of the other Stoic virtue of self-control when he resisted the 'voices of the Sirens and the goblets of Circe'. Hence, even before we inquire into the meaning of the phrase 'quid *sapientia* possit', we begin to see why Ulysses held such a fascination for Dante, why the protagonist would beg with such urgency to be allowed to wait 'until the horned flame arrived', and why he would risk falling into the pit as he 'leant out towards it with desire'.[33]

Virgil-the-character shares this exalted view of Ulysses' worth. He tells Dante that his 'entreaty deserves great praise'. He takes upon himself the task of talking, lest the high and mighty Greeks should feel offence. He knows by intuition that Dante will want to find out what happened to Ulysses in the end. So, having carefully chosen the right time and place, Virgil addresses the 'horned flame' with an incantatory *captatio benevolentiae* that has no parallel in the *Comedy*:[34]

> 'O voi che siete due dentro ad un foco,
> s'io meritai di voi mentre ch'io vissi,
> s'io meritai di voi assai o poco
> quando nel mondo li alti versi scrissi,
> non vi movete; ma l'un di voi dica
> dove, per lui, perduto a morir gissi.' (*Inf.* XXVI, 79–84)

'O you who are two within one fire, if I deserved anything of you while I lived, if I deserved anything great or small when, in the world above, I wrote those noble lines, do not move on; but let one of you say where, being lost, he went to die.'

Ulysses, with equal intuition, takes it for granted that his interlocutor knows the story of his wanderings as far as the island of Circe, but no further. And the reason for this assumption – outside the fiction of the *Comedy* – is that Dante's primary source was, once again, the *Metamorphoses*.

The voyage of Ulysses as far as the island of Circe

Having related how Ulysses was awarded the armour of Achilles, Ovid draws on the first three Books of the *Aeneid* to tell how Troy was captured and how Aeneas made his way slowly westwards to Sicily and the slopes of Etna. Then, after a long mythological digression, Ovid summarises the main events narrated in Books IV–VI of the *Aeneid*, and in so doing he follows Aeneas to Carthage and thence to the shore of Italy near Cumae, where he re-tells the story of the descent to Hades. In Virgil's poem, at this point, Aeneas sails a little further to the north-west and goes ashore to bury his old nurse Caieta, calling the local promontory by her name (it is still called Gaeta). Ovid too refers to this event – obliquely and lightheartedly, but in a way that charmed Dante – saying that Aeneas 'went to the shores that did not yet have his nurse's name' ('litora adit nondum nutricis habentia nomen').[35]

The contemporaneous wanderings of Ulysses have not been forgotten in this long narrative sequence. We were reminded of him periodically – for example, when the Trojans passed Ithaca, or came to the haunts of Polyphemus and Scylla. But now his vicissitudes are brought into the foreground, because one of his followers – Macareus by name – suddenly appears on the shore at Gaeta, where he recognises, among the Trojan crew, a former shipmate, who had been rescued by Aeneas after he was left behind by Ulysses in Polyphemus' cave.[36]

This man is given the chance to recall those grisly events. Then it is Macareus' turn to recall two further calamities related in the *Odyssey*. From the second of these, Ulysses escaped with only one ship – another detail that caught Dante's eye – and it was this vessel that brought him to the nearby island of Circe. Macareus then tells how he and his companions were turned into swine and restored to human form, and how Ulysses settled down as consort of the sorceress for the duration of a whole year ('*annua* . . . mora', 'per *annum*') – a fact that Dante will not overlook. Finally, after another long mythological digression, Macareus explains how he came to desert Ulysses and to make his appearance on the shore:[37]

> 'Resides et desuetudine tardi
> rursus inire fretum, rursus dare vela jubemur,
> ancipitesque vias et iter Titania vastum
> dixerat et saevi restare pericula ponti:
> pertimui, fateor, nactusque hoc litus adhaesi.'
> (*Metamorphoses* XIV, 436–40)

'Listless and slow as we were through lack of activity, we were ordered once again to hoist sail and to put out to sea once again. Circe had told the hazards of our route, the vast length of the journey, and the dangers of the cruel sea that remained. I grew afraid, I confess, and having gained this shore, I stayed behind.'

Dante's account of the voyage from Circe's island to the Straits

It is at this very point in the story (where Ovid too abandons Ulysses in order to follow Aeneas) that 'the greater tongue of the horned flame' begins his narrative in mid-verse. There are several quotations from Macareus' version of events. But the verbal resemblances only serve to heighten our awareness of the gulf between the *Metamorphoses* and the *Comedy*, or, rather, between the deckhand who jumped ship and the captain who had ordered him to put to sea. Here, at last, we hear the voice of a hero in the normal sense of that word: a man of action, laconic, self-possessed, willing to let the facts speak for themselves. So it is only right to allow this new and noble Ulysses to describe in his own words the story of the westward voyage as far as the narrow 'mouth' between Spain and Morocco. (The reasons he gives for choosing this course are omitted for the moment. Italicisations call attention to the verbal debts to Ovid.)

'Quando
mi diparti' da *Circe*, che sottrasse
me *più d'un anno* là presso a *Gaeta*,
prima che sì Enëa la nomasse,
. . .
. . . *misi me* per *l'alto mare aperto*
sol con un legno e con quella compagna
picciola da la qual *non fui diserto*.'

(*Inf.* xxvi, 90–3, 100–2)

'When I departed from Circe, who beguiled me for more than a year, there near Gaeta, before Aeneas named it so, . . . I put out on the deep open sea, with just one ship and that small band of comrades who had not deserted me.'

'L'un lito e l'altro vidi infin la Spagna,
fin nel Morrocco, e l'isola d'i Sardi,
e l'altre che quel mare intorno bagna.
Io e' compagni eravam vecchi e *tardi*
quando venimmo a quella foce stretta
. . .
da la man destra mi lasciai Sibilia,
da l'altra già m'avea lasciata Setta.' (103–11)

> 'I saw both shores as far as Spain, as far as Morocco, and the island of Sardinia, and the others that are bathed all around by that sea. I and my comrades were old and slow when we came to the narrow outlet. . . . On my right hand I left Seville; on the other I had already left Ceuta.'

The 'positive' tradition resumed: 'cupiditas scientiae'

According to Horace, Homer 'set Ulysses before us' not only 'as a pattern of what virtue can achieve', but also 'as a pattern of what *wisdom* can do'. And the quickest way of establishing what kind of reputation for *sapientia* Ulysses enjoyed in ancient times will be to read a passage from another of Dante's *auctores* – Marcus Tullius Cicero.

In the fifth book of his *De finibus bonorum et malorum*, Cicero makes the point that Ulysses' desire for knowledge was so well known that, even in the *Odyssey*, the Sirens tried to lure him with the promise that he would return home a 'wiser' or, at least, a 'more learned' man ('doctior'). Cicero went as far as to translate all six lines of the Sirens' song, to which he added the following significant commentary:

> Homer saw that his tale would not win approval if so great a hero ('tantus vir') were to be ensnared by trifling songs. The Sirens promise knowledge, which, to a man desirous of wisdom, is dearer than his native land ('pollicentur scientiam . . . sapientiae cupido patria cariorem'). We hold it to be a mark of the merely inquisitive ('curiosorum') that they desire to know all things of whatever kind they may be ('omnia scire, cuiuscumque modi sint'). But it is the mark of the greatest men ('summorum virorum') that they should be led to the desire for knowledge by the contemplation of the highest things ('duci . . . maiorum rerum contemplatione ad cupiditatem scientiae'). (*De finibus*, v, xviii, 49)

The adjective *curiosus* was ambivalent in classical Latin, and Cicero makes it plain that it is not a virtue to desire 'to know *all* things, *whatever* they may be'. But the fact remains that, for Cicero, it seems praiseworthy to hold *scientia* 'dearer than one's native land'. Ulysses' *cupiditas scientiae* is being held up for our admiration. It is among the qualities that make him one of the *summi viri*.[38]

In this perspective, it is not difficult to understand how Ulysses came to be perceived not just as a long-suffering voyager, but as an intrepid explorer – not someone who *happened* to *see* 'the customs and cities of many men', but someone who travelled *in order that* he might *know* them. For some Roman writers, he became the very embodiment of the distinctively human 'pursuit' of the truth for its own sake; and his journey became a symbol of the 'quest' for pure knowledge. And it is this Ulysses whom Dante brings to life with his usual concision in two of the seventeen terzinas he gives him to speak.

In the first of these terzinas, (where he is justifying his refusal to return home), Ulysses describes his own *cupiditas scientiae* as being so intense that it overcame all ties of family and (in Cicero's phrase) 'made knowledge dearer to him than his native land'. In the second (which forms the peroration of a speech-within-the-speech, in which he persuades his crew to continue the voyage), the pursuit of knowledge is celebrated in universal terms as the badge of our humanity:[39]

> ['né dolcezza di figlio, né la pieta
> del vecchio padre, né 'l debito amore,
> lo qual dovea Penelopè far lieta,]
> vincer potero dentro a me l'ardore
> ch'i' ebbi a divenir del mondo esperto
> e de li vizi umani e del valore.' (*Inf.* XXVI, 94–9)

['Neither the sweetness of a son, nor reverence for an aged father, nor the love I owed to Penelope, that should have made her happy] could overcome in me the longing I had to gain experience of the world, and of human vices, and of human worth.'

> '"Considerate la vostra semenza:
> fatti non foste a viver come bruti,
> ma per seguir virtute e canoscenza."' (118–20)

'"Consider your origins: you were not made to live as animals, but to pursue virtue and knowledge."'

'Melius et divinius genti et civitati'

Nothing could be more central to Dante's ethics than the proposition that human beings are created 'to pursue virtue and knowledge' and not 'to live as brute beasts'. Taken out of their context and considered unconditionally – *simpliciter* or *absolute* – these two lines convey a universal truth, something that 'oft was thought, but ne'er so well expressed'. But, as Shakespeare's Antonio remarked, 'The devil can cite Scripture for his purpose'; and there are many qualifications to be registered when the implied argument is studied *secundum quid* and restored to its immediate context in the canto and to its wider context in Dante's thought.[40]

In another well-known work by Ovid (the first of the *Heroides*, a series of imaginary epistles purporting to be written by the great lovers of antiquity), Penelope urges Ulysses to return, reminding him that he is not simply a great-souled individual, but a husband, son and father: others have claims upon him. It is her pleas that Ulysses condenses in lines 94–6 (quoted in square brackets above); and they should make us reflect that if Ulysses were 'righteous' or *justus* in the biblical sense of the word – if he were unconditionally 'giusto e pio' – he might not have continued to disregard the love he 'owed' to his wife, and the reverence ('pieta') due to his aged father. ('Pieta' is clearly used with an eye on *pietas*; and the Virgilian word reminds us that *pius* Aeneas behaved very differently to his father Anchises.)[41]

Similarly, if Ulysses had been 'just' without qualification in the Aristotelian sense of the word, he would have taken a different view of his wider social obligations, especially given the fact that he was the 'leader' or 'king' of his people. As we have repeatedly seen, Dante thought of man as a 'civic animal', fitted by nature to live in a state or *civitas*. Every individual is 'a part of the city' (*quaedam pars civitatis*); and the 'well-being or preservation of the whole (*salus totius*) is a greater good (*melius bonum*) than that of the part'. Hence, as Dante tells us in the *Monarchia* – in a paragraph where he uses *civitas* and *patria* as synonyms – 'a man must be willing to risk death for the sake of his native land ("homo debet exponere seipsum pro *patria*"); for, as Aristotle says in his *Ethics*, it is desirable to seek the good of one man alone ("amabile quidem . . . *uni soli*"), but it is better and more godlike to do so for a people and a city ("melius et divinius vero *genti et civitati*")'.[42]

Of course, there may be circumstances in which the pursuit of knowledge for the benefit of all humanity ranks as a greater good than the discharge of one's duty to family or society. 'Circumstances alter cases', as the lawyers say (and there are circumstances in which it is lawful to eat human flesh). But it would be naive to 'propose' the Ulysses re-created by Dante as 'a pattern of what virtue can achieve' without expressing serious reservations. One should not therefore be swayed too easily by the rhetoric of Cicero's phrase about 'knowledge being dearer than one's native land' ('scientiam . . . *patria* cariorem'). Nor – to anticipate a little – should one assent unquestioningly to the proposition that it is possible 'to seek virtue' or 'gain experience of human vices and worth' in a 'world without people' – 'nel mondo sanza gente'.

A time to labour and a time to rest

Before we leave the subject of Ulysses' moral worth, we ought to recall that, in Dante's view, the various virtues are perfected and put into practice at different times of life. Ulysses' undoubted courage and self-control are proper to the Second Age (from twenty-five to forty-five). Justice and practical wisdom, to which Ulysses laid claim (in Ovid's long declamation, at least), are among the 'signs of nobility' in the Third Age (from forty-five to seventy), which is when a virtuous man seeks to be 'profitable to others', giving 'good counsels that lead himself and others to a good end'. But innate nobility should manifest itself in other ways if the 'uomo gentile' survives beyond the normal span of life into the Fourth Age ('senio', as opposed to 'senettute').[43]

Before we discover what these last manifestations might be, we must pause for a moment to consider Ulysses' age. How old was he when Iphigenia was sacrificed at Aulis? How old at the Sack of Troy? How old was he when he left Circe, and how old when he reached the longitude of Spain and Morocco?

At the risk of absurdity, one may conjecture that Ulysses was at least on the threshhold of his Third Age at the beginning of the siege of Troy (since we know he was already an experienced politician and orator, as well as the father of a son). Ten years later, therefore, at the time of the 'ambush of the horse', he would have been in his early fifties; and by the time he left Circe, he would have been not less than sixty, and possibly as much as sixty-five. We are not given any indication of how long he spent in that voyage of discovery around the islands and along 'both shores' of the Western Mediterranean, but it seems reasonable to assume that it lasted several years. Ulysses says that, on reaching the Straits of Gibraltar, he and his companions were 'old and slow' – 'vecchi e tardi' – and the above calculation seems to confirm that this was literally true. It was no rhetorical exaggeration to say that nothing more remained than 'a brief vigil of the senses'. They had lived out their allotted three-score years and ten. They were about to enter their 'ultima etade'.

To find out how a noble soul ought to behave in its last age, we must turn to a remarkable chapter in the fourth book of the *Convivio*, where we shall find an extended image of seafaring, which could not be more pertinent, and a contrast between Ulysses and 'la nobile anima' which could scarcely be greater. In essence, Dante is saying that a noble soul should cease from all worldly activity (the key-word is once again 'operazioni'), and prepare to meet its Maker.

> In its last age the noble soul does two things: first, it returns to God, as to the haven from which it set out when it entered the sea of this life ('nel mare di questa vita'); and second, it blesses the journey ('cammino') it has made, because it was straight and good ('diritto e buono') and without bitterness of storm.
>
> As Cicero says in *De senectute*, natural death is a kind of haven and repose to us after a long voyage ('porto di lunga navigazione e riposo'). It is like this. Just as a good sailor, when he approaches port, lowers the sails and enters it calmly, so ought we to lower the sails of our worldly activities and return to God with all our understanding and heart ('così noi dovemo calare le vele de le nostre mondane operazioni e tornare a Dio con tutto nostro intendimento e cuore'), so that we may enter that port with all calmness and peace. (*Con.* IV, xxviii, 2–3)

Having quoted Aristotle to the effect that 'death in old age is without sadness', Dante transforms his image briefly into that of a journey overland towards the 'gate' of the soul's 'city' ('la porta de la sua cittade'):

> The noble soul . . . awaits the end of this life with great desire and seems to be coming out of the inn and returning to its own dwelling place, to be putting the journey behind and returning to the city ('uscir le pare de l'albergo e ritornare ne la propria mansione, uscir le pare di cammino e tornare in cittade'). (*ibid.* 7)

Then Dante switches back to the language of the sea in a passionate apostrophe which is addressed to those who refuse to prepare themselves in peaceful meditation for the inevitable hour. Here it is essential to read every word in the original Italian:

> O miseri e vili che con le *vele alte* correte a questo *porto*, e là ove dovereste riposare, per lo *impeto del vento rompete*, e *perdete* voi medesimi là dove tanto *camminato* avete! (*ibid.*)

> O wretched and ignoble men who rush towards this port with all sails set, and there, where you ought to find repose, are shattered by the force of the wind, destroying yourselves in the very place to which you have voyaged for so long!

The metaphorical 'impeto del vento' in this sentence will later become the real whirlwind that strikes the prow of Ulysses' ship and sends it to the bottom just after he has sighted land for the first time in five months; and the concrete, transitive use of the verb 'perdere' ('to destroy') will later acquire the symbolic meaning of 'to send to perdition'.[44]

If it should be doubted whether Dante really had the *Convivio* in mind at the time he composed Canto XXVI, it is enough to read the following sentence in the prose, and the next canto in the poem, because Ulysses' modern counterpart, Guido da Montefeltro, makes his appearance in each. At the time of writing *Convivio* IV Dante called Guido 'nobilissimo' precisely because 'he did not want to enter port under full sail' ('con le vele alte'), and renounced the world to become a Franciscan. In the *Inferno* Dante has altered his view of Guido's moral worth. But he adopts the same image, making Guido say that he repented 'when I saw I had come to that part of my age where everyone should lower the sails and coil the ropes' ('ove ciascun dovrebbe / calar le vele e raccoglier le sarte'). And, as we have seen, the whole point of the episode in *Inferno* XXVII is that Guido was 'sent to perdition' because he relapsed into his 'mondane operazioni', having been himself deceived by the pope's promise of absolution in advance.[45]

'A useless scurrying through many lands?'

Having looked at certain problems connected with Ulysses' moral virtue – or lack of it – we must raise some doubts concerning his wisdom, *sapientia*, taking this word to refer to the actualisation of the higher, speculative intellect, of that part of the mind which seeks and takes delight in the truth for its own sake. We may begin by thinking about the Mediterranean phase of his last voyage and concentrating on its literal meaning.

Ulysses' *cupiditas scientiae* led him to seek knowledge 'of the world', on the one hand, and of 'vices and worth', on the other. Reasonably enough, it would seem, he set out to familiarise himself with yet more 'cities' and yet more 'customs'. It should be noticed that the locution he himself uses is 'divenire esperto di', meaning, first, 'to gain experience of something' and then 'to become expert about something'. The choice of adjective is by no means casual nor dictated by rhyme. Neither is the later appearance of the corresponding noun 'esperienza' in line 116, where it is linked with the phrase 'la vigilia d'i nostri sensi' ('the wakefulness of our senses'). Both adjective and noun are used in perfect conformity with Aristotelian epistemology. Knowledge was thought to have its origin in sense experience; and it was axiomatic that there is 'nothing in the intellect that did not first exist in the senses' (*nihil in intellectu quod non fuerit prius in sensu*). Dante's poem is packed with concrete details and particular examples for this very reason. As Beatrice will explain: 'This is the way one must speak to the human mind, for it is only from sense-experience that the mind apprehends what it later makes worthy of the intellect':[46]

Così parlar conviensi al vostro ingegno,
però che solo da sensato apprende
ciò che fa poscia d'intelletto degno. (*Par.* IV, 40–2)

Nevertheless, there is a radical difference between sensation and intellection, between the 'apprehension' of particular phenomena and the 'comprehension' of universal categories, principles and relationships (*sensus est particularium, scientia vero universalium.*) The senses register the effects, the intellect grasps the causes. Collection of data will never furnish an explanation of the data. *Scientia* comes not from going and seeing, but from sitting down and thinking.

At the heart of Aristotle's moral philosophy is the simple doctrine of 'not too little and not too much'. One might therefore reproach Ulysses with the objection that he must have accumulated sufficient data about 'mores . . . et urbes' long before he 'took leave of Circe'. It would be absurd to labour the point, but there is one phrase in the following passage from Aquinas's commentary on the *Ethics* which seems to fit the case of Ulysses 'like a ring on the finger' and to make further comment unnecessary:[47]

> The Philosopher poses the question whether a person ought to acquire as many friends as possible. But, as the proverb has it: 'let me be called neither "much travelled" nor a "non-traveller"'. That is, may it not be said of me that I scurry about too much through various lands in vain ('quod *nimis* discurram per *diversas* terras *inutiliter*'), nor, on the other hand, that I never leave home on a journey.[48]

'*Quaestio de curiositate*': *(a) a theological critique*

If we now consider Ulysses' voyage simply as a *symbol* of the human pursuit of 'canoscenza', we shall find that even at this level of interpretation his implicit aims and methods are open to numerous objections. Some of the most important of these are sketched out in just one article from the *Summa Theologiae* of Aquinas, and they will provide more than enough material for our purposes.

Aquinas begins by recognising a distinction between knowledge of the truth and the appetite or 'zeal' (*studium*) leading to its acquisition. Considered in itself – he says – the first is good ('ipsa veritatis cognitio, per se loquendo, bona est'). But the second may be either 'upright' or 'perverted' ('sed ipse appetitus vel studium cognoscendae veritatis potest habere *rectitudinem* vel *perversitatem*'). The intellectual virtue which ought to regulate the appetite for knowledge and keep it 'upright' is called *studiositas*. Its opposing vice is *curiositas*; and the *quaestio* on which we shall be drawing is entitled 'De curiositate'.[49]

The desire for knowledge of the truth, we are told, is perverted in the case of 'those who apply themselves intensely ("illi qui student") in order to puff themselves up with pride ("ut exinde *superbiant*")'. In illustration of this kind of perversity, Aquinas quotes a brief but very characteristic passage from Augustine that reads like a critique of what Ulysses did, and of the spirit in which he acted:

> Unde Augustinus dicit . . . quod 'sunt qui *desertis virtutibus*, et nescientes quid sit Deus et quanta sit maiestas semper eodem modo manentis naturae, magnum aliquid se agere putant *si universam istam corporis molem quam mundum nuncupamus, curiosissime intensissimeque perquirant*. Unde etiam tanta *superbia* gignitur ut in ipso caelo, de quo saepe disputant, sibimet habitare videantur.' (*S.T.* 2a–2ae, 167,1)

> Augustine says that 'there are people who, having abandoned all virtue, and not knowing what God is, nor the infinite greatness of a nature that remains always the same, think they are doing something great if they search with the utmost care and intensity ('curiosissime intensissimeque') through that whole vast body which we call the world. This engenders such pride that they think themselves in Heaven (so often the subject of their disputations!).[50]

For Aquinas, as we saw in Chapter 7, the 'perversity' of any appetite consists in a lack of due order. His task is therefore to identify the various species of perverse curiosity that arise 'ex ipsa *inordinatione* appetitus et studii ad discendam veritatem'. The first species is closely related to that described in the passage just quoted and is illustrated by another brief quotation from Augustine. It comes into being when

> someone desires to know the truth about the parts of creation ('circa *creaturas*') without referring them to their due end, that is, to knowledge of God ('non referendo *ad debitum finem*, scilicet ad *cognitionem Dei*'). Hence Augustine says: 'one should not bring a vain and transient curiosity to the study of God's creatures ("non est *vana et peritura curiositas* exercenda"), but use them as a step towards the immortal things that remain forever' ('sed *gradus ad immortalia* et semper manentia faciendus').[51]

'Quaestio de curiositate': (b) a philosophical critique

In his diagnosis of the other species of *curiositas*, Aquinas is speaking not as a theologian, but simply as an Aristotelian. A person may be drawn away from necessary subjects, he tells us, in pursuit of something less useful ('per studium minus utile'). Or the disorder can arise if 'someone strives to know a truth that lies above his own powers' ('aliquis studet ad cognoscendam veritatem *supra proprii ingenii facultatem*').[52]

Dante alludes to both these kinds of *inordinatio* in the Heaven of the Sun. In each case, the treatment is relevant to the interpretation of Ulysses and his voyage; and in each case the fictional speaker is none other than Aquinas. ('Il buono frate Tommaso d'Aquino', as he was called in the *Convivio*, has now become 'la gloriosa vita di Tommaso'.)[53]

King Solomon is praised because he confined himself to the necessary. The wisdom he sought from God was only 'kingly prudence' ('regal prudenza'), that is, the practical wisdom needed to make him a 're sufficiente'. (This was the kind of knowledge Ulysses needed in his role as chieftain, as 'Ithacorum dux'.) Specifically, he did not seek the abstract knowledge required to understand logic, geometry, metaphysics or theology. In short – to return to the terminology of the passage from Cicero quoted earlier – *cupiditas scientiae* did not make Solomon desire 'to know all things, of whatever kind they might be ('omnia scire, cuiuscumque modi sint').[54]

In Dante's poem, Aquinas passes immediately from the case of Solomon to a discussion of the second kind of *inordinatio*, insisting all the time on the need to accept one's personal intellectual limitations. It is 'worse than useless to set out from the shore to fish for the truth without the necessary art', because one returns as a changed man and with no catch. One must proceed with 'leaden feet', avoiding the example of the 'lowest kind of fool, who affirms and denies without making due distinctions'. One should beware of 'current opinion', for it often 'takes a false turn, and then the intellect is tightly bound by the passions' ('più volte piega / l'oppinïon corrente in falsa parte, / e poi l'affetto l'intelletto lega').[55]

Thomas continues in this vein, constantly varying his metaphors and similes, and referring evenhandedly to the errors of Aristotle's predecessors and of Paul's successors, until he reaches his conclusion in a terzina that seems to contain a precise allusion to the fictional voyage of Ulysses:

'e legno vidi già dritto e veloce
correr lo mar per tutto suo cammino,
perire al fine a l'intrar de la foce.' (*Par.* XIII, 136–8).

'I have seen a ship sailing a straight and swift course over the sea for the whole of its voyage, only to sink at the last in the harbour's mouth.'

The relevance of this terzina to the allegorical sense of Ulysses' voyage is confirmed by the solemn introduction to an earlier canto (*Paradiso* II), where Dante is apparently warning the majority of his readers to proceed no further, and where he makes extensive use of seafaring imagery to illustrate the dangers that await those who are over-confident in their powers and over-ambitious in their studies. His ship is now crossing the bar, and he is setting his course over water that has never been sailed before, confident in the fair wind of divine inspiration, a divine pilot, and divine navigational aids. Only those few who have lifted their heads to eat the 'bread of the angels' in good time should venture to trust their vessel on the salty deep – provided they take care to follow closely in his wake before it vanishes. But all his other readers, who have been following his ship in tiny skiffs ('O voi che siete in piccioletta barca'), should now return to the shore and not put out on to the ocean, lest, in losing sight of him, they should become lost ('non vi mettete in pelago, ché forse, / perdendo me, rimarreste smarriti').[56]

The passage is too long to quote and analyse here in the detail it deserves, but despite the profusion of metaphors and the learned allusions and allegories, the essence of the message is clear. The *appetitus cognoscendae veritatis* is not always *bonus*. It will be *disordinatus*, and therefore *malus*, 'if someone strives to know a truth that lies above his own powers' ('studet . . . supra proprii ingenii facultatem').

Intellectual pride

The real Aquinas had reinforced this message with a quotation from the Book of Ecclesiasticus: 'Do not ask for things higher than yourself' ('altiora te'); do not inquire into things that are too strong for you ('fortiora te'); and do not be inquisitive ('curiosus') concerning the rest of God's works.' Dante quotes the same text with evident approval in *Convivio* III, where he fills it out with a phrase omitted by Aquinas ('Think those things that God commanded you'), and prefaces it with another quotation from the beginning of the same book: 'Who has fathomed the wisdom of God, which lies at the origin of all things?'[57]

> . . . secondo quelle parole de lo Ecclesiastico: 'La sapienza di Dio, precedente tutte le cose, chi cercava?', e quelle altre dove dice: 'Più alte cose di te non dimanderai e più forti cose di te non cercherai; ma quelle cose che Dio ti comandò, pensa, e in più sue opere non sie curioso', cioè sollicito. (*Con.* III, viii, 2)

Despite the presence of the adjective 'curioso', this more extended quotation from Ecclesiasticus is pointing far beyond the specific vice of *curiositas* to the arch-vice of *superbia*. We should be reminded immediately of the words spoken by Dante's Eagle of Justice, and the Eagle's eloquent contrast between the infinite, inscrutable depths of God's wisdom and the 'shortsightedness' of human reason. We should also be reminded of the biblical story of the Fall in the Book of Genesis. Adam disregarded 'what God commanded'. His disobedience led him to eat of the 'tree of the knowledge of good and evil'. Satan tempted him with the promise that on the day he and Eve should eat of the tree, 'your eyes shall be opened and you shall be as gods knowing good and evil' ('eritis *sicut dii*, scientes bonum et malum'). For the Christian believer, it is God alone who enjoys total knowledge. Any attempt by man to make himself the equal of God and to know all things ('omnia scire') is 'going beyond the limit' set on our nature. And it will be remembered that in Dante's view, the real cause of Adam's banishment from the Earthly Paradise was not eating of the tree, but 'il 'trapassar del segno'.[58]

All that is wanting to transform the voyage of Ulysses from an image of intellectual presumption into a sin of *superbia* in the fullest sense of the word is the element of conscious defiance of God – of rebellion, or apostasy. And this is precisely what we find as we return to the words of the ancient mariner himself.

The 'mad flight', to 'the left', 'beyond the marks'

We left Ulysses in the Strait between Spain and Morocco, and we must now re-read the last two terzinas quoted above (p. 248), focussing attention on the italicised lines, which were omitted earlier.

> 'Io e ' compagni eravam vecchi e tardi
> quando venimmo a quella foce stretta
> *dov' Ercule segnò li suoi riguardi*
> *acciò che l'uom più oltre non si metta;*
> da la man destra mi lasciai Sibilia,
> da l'altra già m'avea lasciata Setta.' (*Inf.* XXVI, 106–11)

> 'I and my comrades were old and weary when we came to the narrow outlet, *where Hercules set up his landmarks, so that no man should pass beyond.* On my right hand I left Seville; on the other I had already left Ceuta.'

Seville and Ceuta (the city in south-eastern Spain and the promontory on the Moroccan shore) are named, anachronistically, for the benefit of

Dante's contemporaries. (They appear on the most up-to-date and practical charts of the day, and are indeed the only 'red-letter' place names in this area in Pietro Vesconte's amazingly accurate map, based on thirteenth-century portolans, executed in the year of Dante's death, 1321.)[59]

The 'riguardi', by contrast, are part of mythological lore. They refer to two mountains lying to the north and south of the Strait (modern Calpe and Abila, respectively), which the mythographers called the Columns of Hercules, or Pillars of Hercules. In the traditional 'world maps' or *mappae mundi*, they are usually shown as a pair of classical columns close to, or actually in, the opening of the 'foce stretta'.

A *mappa mundi* was intended to teach history and theology as much as geography and is more like a pictogram than a map. It is instructive to glance at a typical example such as the well-known 'Hereford Map', which was produced (probably in Lincoln) during Dante's lifetime, c. 1280. Like all such representations, it is 'oriented' with east at the top of the map, so that the Mediterranean Sea runs vertically from the centre to the bottom. Italy and Spain lie to the viewer's left. The inland sea is indeed filled with a great many (rather impressionistically drawn) islands. And one's eyes are opened (like those of Adam and Eve) on realising that – as Dante would have visualised the route – Ulysses was sailing downwards. His voyage was a descent, a moving away from the figure of Christ at the top of the map, another 'Fall'.[60]

In the classical tradition – as Ulysses himself tells us – the 'riguardi' were put there by Hercules as a sign (the verb he uses is 'segnare') to mark the limits of the continents of Europe and Africa, and with the clear intention (the conjunction is 'a ciò che') of warning man to proceed no further (*ne plus ultra*, 'più oltre non...'). Ulysses is deliberately disobeying a divine prohibition. His conscious defiance is emphasised by the repetitions in the last two lines just quoted. And since we have seen (in Chapter 8) that Dante interpreted all the pagan myths concerning acts of rebellion against Jupiter as acts of *superbia* in the Christian sense of the word, there can be no doubt that he intended us to understand that Ulysses was an 'apostate', no less than Adam. Both men went beyond a 'segno'. Both were lured by the thirst for knowledge – specifically, the 'scientia *boni et mali*', that would make them 'like gods'. Both of them disobeyed.

The rhetoric of Ulysses' 'little oration'

Ulysses lingers on this decisive moment by recalling the speech he made to his crew at the time, a speech we must now read in its entirety (lines 118–20 were quoted and discussed above, p. 250), for it is here that the heroic Ulysses of the *Odyssey* becomes inseparable from the astute Ulysses of *Metamorphoses* XIII.

> '"O frati", dissi, "che per cento milia
> perigli siete giunti a l'occidente,
> a questa tanto picciola vigilia
> d'i nostri sensi ch'è del rimanente
> non vogliate negar l'esperïenza,
> di retro al sol, del mondo sanza gente."'
> (*Inf.* XXVI, 112–17)

'"Oh brothers", I said, "who through a hundred thousand dangers have reached the West, to this so brief remaining vigil of our senses do not deny experience of the world without people behind the sun"'.

The first six lines form a single period of epic sweep and nobility, a *captatio benevolentiae* of the utmost persuasive power. The opening vocative turns the crewmen into 'brothers', to whom Ulysses does not give orders, but appeals with the courtesy-formula of a double negative ('non vogliate negar'). The dangers they have survived together are hyperbolically exaggerated, while those to come are correspondingly underplayed by reference to the briefness of their duration. Prosaic place names like Spain and Morocco, Seville and Ceuta, are transformed into the 'Occident'. The unspecified goal is poetically transmuted to a place behind the 'setting sun' (which is what 'occident' means) in a new world, a 'world without people'.

Then comes the appeal to reason:

> '"Considerate la vostra semenza:
> fatti non foste a viver come bruti,
> ma per seguir virtute e canoscenza."' (118–20)

'"Consider your origins: you were not made to live like animals, but to follow virtue and knowledge."'

On close inspection, however, there is no argument. The three self-standing lines have the feel and rhythm of a syllogism, but although they contain one universal truth which might well have formed a major premiss, there is no minor premiss and no conclusion. And in so far as a practical syllogism could be constructed, the crew is being urged to 'do the wrong thing for the right reason'.

Just how self-conscious is Ulysses' use of rhetoric is proved by his own evaluation of the result:

'Li miei compagni fec'io sì aguti,
con questa orazion picciola, al cammino,
che a pena poscia li avrei ritenuti.' (121–3)

'With this little speech I made my comrades so eager for the voyage that I could scarcely have restrained them thereafter.'

This was indeed an 'oration', even if small in scale. Ulysses is still proud of his powers of persuasion. He set out to rouse his listeners' emotions in order to make them act in the way he desired. (All the ancient and medieval rhetoricians agreed that action, not instruction or pleasure, was the goal of political oratory.) He succeeded because he was a 'good speaker'. That much is not in doubt. But it is still very much open to question whether he acted as a 'good man'.

In interpreting the ethical probity, as opposed to the rhetorical effectiveness, of the speech, it must be borne in mind that – unlike many moralists – Dante was not prejudiced against the art of rhetoric as such. None of the figures of speech or figures of thought to which attention has just been called is 'good' or 'wicked' in itself, any more than a sword is 'wicked' because it pierces and cuts, or a well-feathered arrow is 'good' because it flies straight to its target. Everything depends on the use to which they are put. (All the stylistic devices used by Ulysses could be matched in speeches made by the blessed in *Paradiso*.) Nevertheless, oratorical skill confers a kind of power; and, for Dante, the worst calamity that can befall any society is when 'the instrument of the mind is joined to an evil will and to power, because in that case the people have no protection':

'ché dove l'argomento de la mente
s'aggiugne al mal volere e a la possa,
nessun riparo vi può far la gente'. (*Inf.* XXXI, 55–7)

When Dante the poet recognised that he would have to curb his 'ingegno' more than elsewhere in dealing with Ulysses, so that it 'would not run where virtue does not guide', he must have been thinking of his own power of persuasive speech quite as much as his thirst for knowledge or his propensity to go it alone.

'Vir bonus peritus dicendi'

The educationalists of classical Rome defined a virtuous citizen as 'a good man skilled in public speaking' ('vir bonus peritus dicendi'). If we want to find an example of a 'good speech' of encouragement, made by a 'good man', we need look no further than a famous passage in the first book of the *Aeneid*, which Dante the author clearly took as his model.

Aeneas and his men have managed to struggle ashore after surviving a storm that has sunk (or seemed to sink) some of their other ships. Aeneas is 'cast down with enormous cares', but he 'represses his grief and feigns hope in his face' ('spem vultu simulat') as he addresses his men in these terms:[61]

> 'O socii (neque enim ignari sumus ante malorum),
> o passi graviora, dabit deus his quoque finem.
> vos et Scyllaeam rabiem penitusque sonantis
> accestis scopulos, vos et Cyclopia saxa
> experti: revocate animos maestumque timorem
> mittite; forsan et haec olim meminisse iuvabit.'
> (*Aeneid* I, 198–203)

> 'Comrades, we are not unacquainted with troubles in the past. You have endured greater hardships. God will grant an end to these as well. You have gone close to the rage of Scylla, within her howling rocks; you have experienced the boulders of the Cyclops. Call back your courage and put away gloomy fear. One day, perhaps, it will be sweet to remember even these things.'

> 'per varios casus, per tot discrimina rerum
> tendimus in Latium, sedes ubi fata quietas
> ostendunt; illic fas regna resurgere Troiae.
> durate, et vosmet rebus servate secundis.' (204–7)

> 'Through so many adventures and adversities, we are bound for Latium, where the fates show us a settled home. There it is fated that the kingdom of Troy shall rise again. Be steadfast, and hold yourselves ready for better days.'

Aeneas, too, appeals to his men as equals (*socii*) and not as subordinates. He too recalls their joint tribulations. He too structures his appeal in balanced phrases. But there the resemblances end. He does not exaggerate the number of dangers they have survived. He develops simple but valid arguments, based on those shared experiences. As the past is to the present, so the present will be to the future. Those earlier afflictions were greater (*graviora*). Surely he and his *socii* may hope to survive these lesser trials. Just as they now recall those past dangers, so one day, perhaps, they will recall these. Troy was burnt, but Troy will rise from the ashes.[62]

Aeneas is seeking to arouse an emotion; but the emotion is hope. (If he makes any concession to 'simulation', it is simply to assume a hopeful expression.) Unlike Ulysses, he can urge the strongest possible grounds for his hope. Far from the Trojans defying the gods (as Ulysses was doing), Jupiter is on their side: 'God will grant an end to these misfortunes too.' They have come through everything so that they may reach a definite, named goal. (Once again, the contrast could not be greater than with the 'mondo sanza gente'). The fates ('fata') are promising tranquillity and prosperity in Latium. There it is destined ('illic *fas*') that Troy shall rise again. They have only to show fortitude and endure.

The whole of Aeneas' speech has a timeless dignity and equilibrium that make one think of the Psalms. One could not possibly suspect a 'mal volere'. There is not a hint of 'astuzia'. Aeneas is not only 'peritus dicendi', he is a 'vir bonus'. By making this speech he is fulfilling, not defying, the will of Providence.

The 'follia' of Ulysses, Adam and Dante

If there were any lingering doubts about Ulysses' transgression, and his awareness of doing wrong, they would be removed by his own description of the result of his speech:

'e volta nostra poppa nel mattino,
de' remi facemmo ali al folle volo,
sempre acquistando dal lato mancino.' (124–6)

'And turning our stern to the morning we made wings of our oars for the mad flight, gaining always on the left.'

Not only did they set their course away from the Pillars, but they were inclining steadily to the 'sinister', left-hand side ('dal lato mancino'). They turned their backs on the morning sun, the rising sun of hope. Their 'cammino' ('journey') became a metaphorical 'volo' ('flight'), which, with hindsight, is characterised as 'folle'.

A word must be said here about Dante's use of the adjective 'folle', and the noun 'follia', if only to warn against the purely phonetic similarity with the English word 'folly'. The meaning implied is closer to 'foolhardiness' or 'reckless presumption'. The adjective will be used again in the *Paradiso* to describe the same voyage, when Dante the protagonist is able to look down to earth from above the meridian of western Spain and to imagine the 'varco *folle* / d'Ulisse' traversing the ocean below. Earlier in the *Inferno*, it had twice been used in contexts involving *superbia* of the kind when a living man attempts to enter the realms of the dead against the divine will (Dante the protagonist was afraid that his journey would be 'folle'; the devils who blocked his path called it a 'folle strada'). The same adjective is applied to Arachne and her challenge to Minerva in the circle of the 'superbi'.[63]

More importantly, the noun 'follia' is used to describe Adam's sin and 'fall from nobility'. And in the first canto of *Purgatorio* – in an episode studded with verbal echoes of *Inferno* XXVI – 'follia' is the word used to describe the conduct that had led the protagonist into the 'dark wood' of sin and brought him 'so close to the final evening [of damnation] that very little time remained'. If Dante successfully arrived on the very beach where Ulysses failed to come ashore, it was because Virgil was 'sent to save him' ('*mandato* . . . per lui *campare*'), and because 'a helping power descended from on high' ('de l'*alto* scende *virtù* che m'*aiuta*'). His journey, like those of Aeneas and Moses, was a 'fatale andare'. It was sanctioned by God, the result of a special act of grace.[64]

The 'mode of redemption' and the place of 'justification'

We come now to the single most original and most important aspect of Dante's re-imagining of Ulysses' voyage. It remains totally hidden from Ulysses and the first-time reader, and a full discussion would be out of place here. But some of the information that is released obliquely and at long intervals later in the *Comedy* must be summarised before we can interpret the final part of the canto.

In the fiction of his poem, Dante modified the received cosmography to place a mountain island in the otherwise landless southern ocean, situating it precisely ninety degrees of longitude west of Seville. On the best estimates of the circumference of the globe available to Dante, the island would lie just over five thousand miles from the 'foce stretta'. Hence, it might well take about five months to cover that distance, assuming one was in a small ship, powered by oars, and with an aged crew. (In other words, Dante the author knew exactly where Ulysses was sailing to, when he set his course west by south, and he knew how long the voyage ought to last.)

Dante also modified received cosmogony to explain the material and efficient causes of that island. It was formed by the upsurge of rock from the centre of the earth when the cone of Hell was hollowed out in order to receive Lucifer and the rebel angels as they fell from Heaven.

In addition, Dante went beyond traditional beliefs about the location of the Earthly Paradise by placing it on the summit of this mountain. And he transformed the whole conception of Purgatory by removing it from an 'annexe' to the Underworld (as it had been vaguely imagined before him) and placing it on the slopes of the same mountain. Finally, he fixed the latitude of the island by locating it as far to the south of the Equator as Jerusalem is to the north, so that it lay at the antipodes to the Holy City and the place of Christ's Crucifixion.[65]

By combining geography and the *historia salvationis* in one complex act of imagination, Dante was writing several powerfully suggestive equations. The Earthly Paradise – where mankind would be created to make good the defection of Lucifer and the rebel angels – was brought into being by the Fall of those angels. A straight line through the centre of the universe connects the site of the Original Sin with the site predestined for its Atonement. The place where the descendants of Adam and Eve would be 'justified', and cleansed of the stain of their sin, was already in existence before the sin was committed. When the souls of the penitent are finally purified and liberated from bondage to sin, they simply climb a little higher up the mountain to reach the Earthly Paradise, whence they ascend to the Celestial Paradise, there to enjoy the *beatitudo vitae aeternae*, which 'consists in the vision and fruition of God'.[66]

Everything that is necessary to enable human beings to find fulfilment and happiness after the Fall was ordained by God from the very beginning. The mountain of Purgatory was in existence at the time of the Trojan War. But it was, so to speak, 'out of bounds', and any 'trespassers' would be 'prosecuted'.

The final phase of the voyage of Ulysses is no longer an image of the human quest for the truth, but an image of the quest for happiness (first the *beatitudo huius vitae*, then the *beatitudo vitae aeternae*). In interpreting Ulysses' venture – and its failure – we must bear in mind three facts. (a) Purgatory and the Earthly Paradise lie in the realms of the afterlife, and no living person may enter there (save in the exceptional circumstances imagined in the plot of the *Comedy* as a whole). (b) No one can be admitted to the Earthly Paradise and proceed to Heaven without God's help – his *auxilium* – that is, without the gift of grace and the infusion of Faith, Hope and Charity. (c) For just over 5000 years after the creation of the world, not one of the souls of the dead could be admitted to Paradise – not even those who believed in the coming of the Son of God and observed all the commandments, not even those who also 'sold all they had and gave to the poor'. All human beings had to wait until the time was ripe, until the 'fullness of time' (*plenitudo temporis*). God had forseen the 'mode of our redemption' from the beginning. The Virgin Mary – through whom the Son of God would 'become flesh' – had been the 'fixed term of eternal counsel' ('termine fisso d'etterno consiglio'). However, 'the gates of Heaven could not be opened after the long interdict' before she had given birth, or before her Son had 'made satisfaction'.[67]

As we saw in Chapter 9, the reasons for every part of this providential plan remain inscrutable, and some of the reasons seem unjust to the human mind. But as we also saw, Dante was willing to humble himself intellectually and to accept that every decision taken by God (every *consilium Dei*) must be 'giusto', because it is the expression of his will, and 'cotanto è giusto quanto a lei consuona'. He tried to accept – to take it on trust – that even the best and the greatest representatives of pagan culture were still confined in Limbo, still in eternal exile from God. *A fortiori*, he tried to accept that Ulysses – an unbeliever, whose virtues were offset by numerous vices, and who felt no remorse – might be not only excluded from the vision of God, but tormented by a tongue of flame for all eternity. Nevertheless, Dante did not find such acceptance easy, as was clear in his treatment of Virgil and Rhipeus, and as will be clear in the last act of his *Tragedy of Ulysses*, where the 'flawed' hero meets his fate.

'Whither away?' and 'Land, ahoy!'

In the fiction of the *Comedy*, Ulysses knows nothing directly about God, nothing about his purposes for man, and nothing about what may or may not lie 'behind the sun'. But like every human being Ulysses was born with a 'confused awareness that there does exist a supreme good in which the human mind may find complete repose' ('ciascun confusamente un bene apprende / nel qual si queti l'animo, e disira'). As Lady Philosophy says in Boethius' *Consolatio*:[68]

> You earthbound animals also dream of your origin ('vestrum . . . *principium* somniatis'), even though in an insubstantial image. You look forward to the true goal of happiness ('*verum*que illum *beatitudinis finem* . . . prospicitis') with a process of thought that is anything but lucid, but is nevertheless thought ('licet minime perspicaci, qualicumque tamen cogitatione'). A natural intention is leading you there, and to the true good ('eoque vos et ad verum bonum *naturalis ducit intentio*'), whereas manifold errors are leading you away from it. (*Consolatio*, III, pr. iii, 1)

There seems every reason to assume that the 'ardore' experienced by Ulysses was, in essence, identical with this *naturalis intentio*, identical with the innate desire for a Supreme Good that the mind apprehends only through a dim, Platonic recollection of its eternal *principium*. Ulysses, in short, was propelled by the same 'concreated thirst' that would provide the motive force for Dante's own unmetaphorical, 'oarless' flight up through the aether.[69]

We must keep in mind this positive interpretation of Ulysses' quest, as we read his account of the final months and the last day, in which there are many other positive features. The crew have indeed become his 'companions' and 'brothers' (his use of the word 'frati' was no mere rhetorical device), and Ulysses tells the rest of the story consistently in the first-person plural. Once again he gives proof of fortitude and greatness of soul. Once again the story is related with the plainness of a mariner and yet with infinite suggestiveness. The slow elapse of time is indicated by the phases of the moon; the gradual change in latitude by the rise of new constellations. A mountain looms on the horizon, inconceivably high; but the voice of the narrator becomes, if anything, more prosaic, as he compares it to his past experiences. Everything Ulysses says is in character; and everything that matters in a five-month voyage covering five thousand miles is condensed into just nine lines:

> 'Tutte le stelle già de l'altro polo
> vedea la notte, e 'l nostro tanto basso,
> che non surgëa fuor del marin suolo.
> Cinque volte racceso e tante casso
> lo lume era di sotto da la luna,
> poi che 'ntrati eravam ne l'alto passo,
> quando n'apparve una montagna, bruna
> per la distanza, e parvemi alta tanto
> quanto veduta non avëa alcuna.' (*Inf.* XXVI, 127–35)

'Already night was showing all the stars of the other pole, and our pole so low that it did not rise above the ocean floor. Five times the light below the moon had been rekindled, and as often extinguished, since we had entered on the great crossing, when a mountain appeared to us, dim in the distance, and it seemed to me higher than any I had ever seen.'

Two shipwrecks

Before reading the last seven lines of Ulysses' narrative, we must turn for the last time to the man whom Dante called 'my author' and 'our greatest poet' in order to read the description of a shipwreck in Book I of the *Aeneid*. A tempest has driven three of Aeneas's ships onto a reef and another three into the sands. Then:

> before Aeneas's very eyes, another ship, the one carrying faithful Orontes and his Lycians, is struck on the stern by a mighty sea from the height of its crest. The helmsman is swept headlong overboard. Three times the waters swirl the ship round where she lies, till a rapid eddy swallows her under. A few swimmers appear in the vast turbulence, and, on the waves, the weapons of heroes, timbers, and Trojan tapestries.
>
> unam [navem] quae Lycios fidumque vehebat Oronten,
> ipsius ante oculos ingens a vertice pontus
> in puppim ferit: excutitur pronusque magister
> volvitur in caput, ast illam ter fluctus ibidem
> torquet agens circum et rapidus vorat aequore vertex.
> apparent rari nantes in gurgite vasto,
> arma virum tabulaeque et Troia gaza per undas.
>
> (*Aeneid* I, 113–19)

Dante the poet uses this passage as his model and his foil. What he will take over is the rhythmic and syntactic energy, especially the impact of the great breaker striking on the poop, and the motif of the ship being spun round three times before vanishing beneath the waves. What he will *not* take over – but would like his readers to remember for the contrast they offer – are the magical details of the last two lines. In Virgil, things come floating up to the seething surface – isolated swimmers and the incongruous flotsam of armour and ornaments. In Dante they do not.

> 'Noi ci allegrammo, e tosto tornò in pianto;
> ché de la nova terra un turbo nacque
> e percosse del legno il primo canto.
> Tre volte il fé girar con tutte l'acque;
> a la quarta levar la poppa in suso
> e la prora ire in giù, com' altrui piacque,
> infin che 'l mar fu sovra noi richiuso.' (136–42)
>
> 'We were filled with joy, but soon it turned to lamentation. For out of the new-found land a whirlwind rose and struck the forepart of the ship. Three times it spun her round with all the waters; at the fourth, it lifted the stern and plunged the prow below, as was Another's will, until the sea closed over us again.'

There are, of course, further vital differences between the two shipwrecks. The agent of destruction in Dante is not just a fortuitous giant wave, but a whirlwind that was sent at the will of a nameless power in order to defend the island and repel the invader. It was the single efficient cause that made the ship spin round, rear up and sink. It is clear from the context (and from back references in the *Purgatorio*) that the unnamed power (referred to by the impersonal dative pronoun 'altrui') was none other than God. The sinking was the result of a 'consiglio divino'. It was a *judicium Dei*, a 'vendetta di Dio', a punishment for *superbia*. The whirlwind was the equivalent of Jupiter's thunderbolt that struck down Capaneus or Phaethon. It was definitive. Nothing returned to the surface, and no one survived. The last word – 'richiuso' – brings to a close the voyage, the life, the episode and the canto.[70]

Ulysses' vices and worth: a summing up

Unlike in certain other episodes, there is no cross-examination of the defendant, and no comment from Dante's guide. Readers are allowed to retire to the 'jury-room' at this point to consider their own verdict, or, rather, to prepare their personal *responsio* to the *quaestiones* that have been posed and the *dubitationes* that have been propounded. But it may be helpful to attempt a brief judicial summing-up, recalling some of the main issues raised by the testimony of the accused and by the evidence of the witnesses who were summoned for the prosecution or defence.

The location of the encounter establishes that Ulysses was condemned for using fraud, and specifically for giving bad or false counsel. He was 'astute' rather than 'prudent'. The criminal charges relate to his conduct during the Trojan war, but the style of his last speech to the crew shows that he had not changed. His counsels did not 'lead himself or others to a good end'. He could not possibly be described as *justus*. Even the quest for knowledge, which he alleged in extenuation of his neglect of family and civic duties, was *disordinatus* in many ways. It was not pursued 'with measure, at the right time, in the right place, or in the right way'. More important than all this, his last voyage was an act of 'follia', which was all of a piece with his earlier life. He was struck down by God as a 'superbo'. As a living man, as a pagan, as an impenitent who showed no signs of *charitas* or *humilitas*, as a monomaniac who went 'beyond the limits', both literally and figuratively, and who consciously defied a divine commandment, he was not one of 'the souls worthy to ascend to God' ('l'anime degne di salire a Dio'), and he could not be allowed to set foot in the kingdom appointed for them. Above all, he could not do so centuries before the time was ripe; nor could he have ever come there by his own unaided powers, for Jesus said that 'no one comes to the Father, save by me'.[71]

Sed contra, it is not hard to see why 'Homer set Ulysses before us as a pattern of what virtue and wisdom can achieve', nor why Dante should have been attracted to the classical hero as he was to no other sinner. In the *Comedy*, Ulysses is totally free of covetousness and possesses fortitude to the highest degree. His last voyage is a perfect example of a *bonum arduum*. He is 'magnanimo' in the fullest and most complex meaning of that term. In his own way, he sought the truth. Even in defeat, he was 'valiantly vanquished'. In Hell, he retains a dignity and a nobility of utterance that are absent in other *superbi* such as Capaneus or Vanni Fucci. We are left in no doubt that God had endowed him with 'gentilezza' (the quality underlying all the moral virtues, which Dante defined as the 'seed of happiness'). And on that final voyage, he was in fact being led by what Boethius called his *naturalis intentio* to seek the *verus beatitudinis finis* – 'the true goal of happiness' – for that is precisely what is symbolised by the Earthly Paradise at the top of the mountain, from which one proceeds to the Celestial Paradise.

As we saw at the beginning of this chapter, Dante felt himself exceptionally close to the figure of Ulysses whom he had read about and re-imagined – just how close will appear from the following translation of excerpts from Beatrice's accusation in the great confession scene in *Purgatorio* xxx:

> Not only thanks to the influence of the heavens ('per ovra de le rote magne') . . . but through a generous infusion of divine grace ('per larghezza di grazie divine') . . . this man had such *potentiae* in his First Age ('questi fu tal ne la sua vita nova virtualmente') that every virtuous trait of character ('ogne abito destro') would have made a marvellous showing in him. But the more native vigour there is in the soil, the wilder and more malignant it becomes when the seed is bad, and when it is left uncultivated.
>
> He turned his steps along the wrong path ('via non vera'), following false images of good ('imagini di ben seguendo false') that never keep their promise in full. He fell so far ('tanto giù cadde') that all means for his salvation ('tutti argomenti a la salute') were short, except showing him the souls of the damned ('le perdute genti'). (*Purg*. xxx, 110, 112, 115–20, 130–2; 136–8)

As Dante the poet was breathing life into his own creation, he must have been thinking: 'There but for the grace of God go I'. Dante the protagonist (alias Dr Jekyll) would be aided by grace to see the 'perdute genti' before he died and thus be rescued from their fate. Ulysses (alias Mr Hyde) perished as a 'lost soul' – 'perduto'.

There is perhaps one last rider to add before giving Ulysses his 'licence to depart' (as Virgil gave him in the opening lines of Canto XXVII). 'Vizi' and 'valore' may coexist in the same person, and people often have the vices of their virtues. It can never be possible to weigh the worth of a whole life and determine a precise place on a single moral scale, at a measurable distance from God. Moreover, the values competing for Dante's adherence had evolved in so many different centuries and cultures, and had been expressed in so many forms, by so many great and individual poets and thinkers ('cotanto senno'), that it was impossible to reconcile those values in a unitary vision of the truth. The assumptions and the aspirations of scholasticism were being challenged even in the second decade of the fourteenth century.

There can be no *conclusio* to a case-study of this kind, but one last *Videtur quod* may be offered in its place. It seems that the only kind of synthesis that is able to survive the death of particular concepts, axioms and religious beliefs is the synthesis achieved in great works of literature. To borrow words from a nineteenth-century sonnet, addressed to Dante: 'Jupiter dies, but the poet's hymn remains'.

Muor Giove, e l'inno del poeta resta.[72]

Explicit ultima pars trilogiae de fabulis fictis et sententiis Dantis Alagherii, quae vulgariter Dante Philomythes and Philosopher *nuncupatur. Manum de tabula!*

Die xxx novembris MCMXCIX.

Notes

Straightforward references are grouped in such a way that there is only one note for each paragraph. These references are listed in the order in which the relevant passages are quoted, paraphrased or alluded to in the text (hence a reference to the *Purgatorio* may well come before one to the *Inferno*).

With three main exceptions, quotations follow the orthography and punctuation of the editions used. The exceptions are: (a) no indication is given when a passage begins or ends in mid-sentence; (b) where the editor has preserved a medieval Latin *e* which corresponds to a classical Latin *ae*, the more familiar classical spelling has been substituted in all cases; (c) *j* is used for consonantal *i*.

Dante's Latin works are quoted as they appear in the second volume of the *Opere minori*, published by Ricciardi (Milan and Naples, 1979). Dante's works in the vernacular are quoted from the editions of: Giorgio Petrocchi for the *Comedy*; Domenico De Robertis for the *Vita nuova*; Michele Barbi for the *Rime*; and Cesare Vasoli for the *Convivio*. For Aquinas's *Summa Theologiae* the edition used is that of the Pontifical Institute of Medieval Studies in Ottawa (Ottawa, 1943). Other quotations from Aquinas are taken from the complete edition of his works published by Marietti.

The following abbreviations are used:

Works by Dante:

Con.	*Convivio*
Dve	*De vulgari eloquentia*
Epist.	*Epistolae*
Inf.	*Inferno*
Mon.	*Monarchia*
Par.	*Paradiso*
Purg.	*Purgatorio*
VN	*Vita nuova*

II Works by Aquinas:

In Ethic.	*Commentary to Aristotle's Ethics*
C.G.	*Summa contra Gentiles*
S.T.	*Summa Theologiae*

III The first two works in the trilogy:

Man in the Cosmos	Patrick Boyde, *Dante Philomythes and Philosopher: Man in the Cosmos*. Cambridge, 1981
Perception and Passion	idem, *Perception and Passion in Dante's 'Comedy'*. Cambridge, 1993.

IV Dante's lyric poetry:

Foster–Boyde	Kenelm Foster and Patrick Boyde (eds.), *Dante's Lyric Poetry*, 2 vols. Oxford, 1967.

Introduction: the role of context

1 The personal example is presented with the intention of sending readers in pursuit of something similar in their own experience (this is one of the lessons of the *Comedy*: cf. *Inf.* I, 2; XXI, 94–6; *Purg.* XXX, 22, etc. in the light of *Con.* I, ii, 12–14). To understand the phrase 'Malt is both square' one needs to be familiar with four things: (a) the material culture of life in England in the 1960s, specifically, that one could buy wholemeal bread in a loaf with a rounded top, and a sweet loaf made with currants and sticky *malt*, which was distinctively square in section; (b) the social context of a period when children ate bread and butter for their tea, usually *half a slice* at a time; (c) the characters of the interlocutors, in this case a father given to gentle teasing, and a younger son who was fussy about what he ate, so much so that he would insist on a half slice of wholemeal bread being either the rounded upper half or the rectangular lower half; (d) the question to which the enigmatic reply came as an answer. My son Dan (then aged three and a half) had indicated that he wanted a half slice of *malt* bread. I asked him 'Do you want it round or square?' To which he replied: 'Malt is *both* square', meaning, 'Father, I am aware that you are teasing me, but must point out that both the top and the bottom half of a slice of bread taken from a malt loaf that is rectangular in section, must of necessity be rectangular in section.'

2 References in order: L. P. Hartley, *The Go-Between*, Prologue; *Dve* I, ix, 6 ('instabilissimum'; cf. *Par.* XXVI, 124–38); *Dve* I, x, 9 (Dante is calculating 'primary, secondary and sub-secondary' species); ix, 7 ('vetustissimi Papienses'); i, 2–3 ('vulgare' and 'grammatica'; Dante, of course, refers to a 'nutrix', not a 'minder'); *Con.* I, vii, 15; II, xiv, 6–7 (translations).

3 'Homo sum; humani nil a me alienum puto', Terence, *Heauton Timorumenos*, 77.

4 Cf. *Man in the Cosmos*, Introduction, *passim*; *Perception and Passion*, Chapter 1 *passim*.

5 As the title indicates, this book is limited to a discussion of ethical values and the meaning of words like 'good' and 'bad', 'virtue' and 'vice'. Dante's conception of the nature of human freedom, and his treatment of the virtues of self-control (*temperantia*, controlling instinctive desire, and *fortitudo*, controlling instinctive fear) are dealt with in Parts 3 and 4 of *Perception and Passion*.

6 The analysis is formulated in the spirit of, but not according to the letter of, Aristotle, *Poetics*, xxi, 3–4, 1475b 7–30.

7 All the examples are taken from the two volumes cited in note 4.
8 References in order: *Par.* XXII, 151–3; XXVII, 79–87; I, 103–8; XXXIII, 85–93.

1 Dante's authors

The following works in the Bibliography are particularly relevant to the themes of this chapter: Armour (1986), Brugnoli (1991), Comparetti (1955), D'Onofrio (1975), Foster (1965), Gilson (1948, 1952, 1953), Hollander (1983), Jacoff and Schnapp ed. (1991), Knowles (1988), Leo (1951), de Libera (1994), Luscombe (1969, 1971), Marenbon (1998, ed), Ryan (1982, 1982), Southern (1991), Took (1991).

1 References in order: *Purg.* XXXII, 103 ('in pro'); *Inf.* XXVI, 90–142, esp. 97–9, 114–17; Genesis 2.17; *Epist.* XIII, 40–1. The words used to indicate a journey are 'viaggio' (*Inf.* I, 91; *Purg.* II, 92); 'cammino' (*Inf.* XXVI, 122; *Purg.* XIX, 22; *Par.* XXXI, 95; cf. *Par.* VIII, 106, 'il ciel che tu cammine'); and 'volo' (*Inf.* XXVI, 125; *Par.* XV, 54; XXV, 50). As these passages show, 'cammino' may be used of a sea-voyage or a journey through space, 'viaggio' is not limited to a 'journey by sea', and 'volo' is used metaphorically of Ulysses's last voyage. See Chapter 10, below, pp. 232–6, 257–65, 268.

2 *Inf.* XXVI, 98, 116–17. See Chapter 10 below *passim*.

3 The phrase in quotation marks and the other adjectives are taken from *The New Shorter Oxford Dictionary*, s.vv. Syncretism and System. The themes of this paragraph will be developed throughout Chapters 2 and 3 below.

4 In the *Convivio* (I, vii, 15) Dante remarked that Homer remained untranslated because poetry, considered as rhetoric enhanced by music – the art of relationships – cannot be translated from one language to another without losing all its sweetness. The first proposition is quoted in *Mon.* I, x, 6. (The *sententia* is not unrelated to the line from the *Odyssey* quoted with approval in *Mon.* I, v, 5. Dante probably did not realise this text was from Homer, because he quotes it from the last line of the last book of Aristotle's *Metaphysics*.) The phrase 'ella non parea figliuola d'uomo mortale, ma di deo' is quoted in praise of Beatrice in *VN* ii, 8, where it is said to be 'parola del poeta Omero'. Dante draws on it again in the fourth book of the *Convivio* (xx, 4), where it is central to his concept of 'gentilezza'. It also underlies his treatment of the saints in *Paradiso* (one thinks primarily of Francis and Dominic in Cantos XI–XIII). Dante certainly saw himself as a person with 'almost godlike' powers, which God intended him to use for the good of humanity (see in particular *Purg.* XXX, 109–17 and *Par.* XXII, 112–20). For a fuller discussion of Dante's knowledge of Homer, see Chapter 10 below, pp. 231, 240, 245–9.

5 Dante did not know exactly when these philosophers lived and died, but he knew their succession in time (cf. *Con.* IV, vi, 14); and giving their dates is an economical way of calling attention to the important differences between the fifth, fourth and third centuries BC. The only dialogue of Plato's that Dante could have read in (an incomplete) translation is the *Timaeus*, but the weight of the evidence is that his knowledge of Plato's ideas was entirely second- or third-hand. For Plato's excellence, see *Con.* II, iv, 4; his views on the stars, *Con.* II, xiii, 5; IV, xxii, 2; *Par.* IV, 22–4, 49–50; on the nature of vision, *Con.* III, ix, 10;

on Aristotle's dissent, *Ethics*, I, vi, 1, 1096a 14–17 (to which Dante alludes in *Con.* III, xiv, 8, and IV, viii, 15, and which he implicitly takes as his justification for abandoning Beatrice for the sake of Philosophy in *Con.* II, xv, 6). In the *Comedy*, this same text is at the heart of his dramatisation of the protagonist's feelings for Brunetto Latini (*Inf.* xv, 79–87), and, more importantly, of his feelings for Virgil whom he must leave behind for Beatrice; cf. in particular, *Purg.* III, 37–45; VII, 35–6; XVIII, 46–8; XXVII, 22–36, 52–4; XXX, 43–57.

6 For 'morality as beauty', see *Con.* III, xv, 12–14, and *Purg.* XXII, 82–7. For Democritus' neglect of his appearance, and for Plato's (and other philosophers') indifference to wealth and even life, see *Con.* III, xiv, 8–9. For the deduction that Democritus attributed the origin of the cosmos to chance, see *Inf.* IV, 136 (Dante could have learnt all he needed to know in this connection from Aquinas's commentary on Aristotle's *De anima* I, ii, 404a 1, *lect.* iii, §34).

7 For the pairing, see *Con.* IV, xxii, 4; for Epicurus' denial of personal immortality, *Inf.* x, 14–15; for his views on 'voluptade' as 'non-dolore', *Con.* IV, vi, 11–12; for Dante's violent reaction to the first, *Con.* II, viii, 8; for his firm correction of the second, *Purg.* XVIII, 34–9. Given the normal sense of the word 'epicurean' in his culture, Dante is remarkably detached and balanced in his account. For Zeno (cf. also *Inf.* IV, 138), for Cato of Utica, for the Stoic belief in immortality, and for virtue as the end of human life, see *Con.* IV, vi, 9–10; for Dante's admiration of 'quello glorioso Catone', see *Con.* IV, v, 16; vi, 9–10; xxvii, 3, and, most startlingly, xxviii, 19; *Mon.* II, v, 15, 17; *Purg.* I–II. For Dante's 'mens sibi conscia recti', and his 'Stoic' acceptance of unjust suffering, cf. *Inf.* xv, 91–9; XXVIII, 115–17; *Par.* XVII, 22–7, 106–20. For Dante's view of the 'co-operation' between the passions of the sensitive soul and the intellect and will, see *Perception and Passion*, Part IV *passim*, but esp. pp. 159–60, 270–4.

8 The Peripatetics, together with the Epicureans and the Stoics, are the three sects of the 'active life' (*Con.* III, xiv, 15), all of whom failed to identify 'la beatitudine' (*Con.* IV, xxii, 15). For Aristotle as the 'master of those who know', but as confined to Limbo, see *Inf.* IV, 130–44 and *Purg.* III, 37–44. The role of the theological virtues will be discussed in Chapter 5 below, pp. 120–5.

9 *Mon.* II, especially, vi, 9–10. The argument of this book had already been developed in *Con.* IV, iv–v.

10 *Con.* II, xii, 2–5.

11 *Inf.* IV, 141. Other references in order: *Con.* IV, v, 19 (defender of liberty); I, xi, 14 (as using vernacular); *Con.* IV, xii, 6–7 (riches); viii, 3 (arrogance); xxix, 7 (decadence, a spurious reference); *Mon.* II, v, 7, 16–17; ix, 3–4 (history); *Con.* IV, xxiv, 9; xxvii, 2, 12 (ages of man); *Mon.* I, i, 4 (old age); *Con.* IV, xxviii, 3, 6 (death); *Con.* II, viii, 9 (immortality). See also Chapter 9, p. 199, and Chapter 10, p. 249.

On the cultural analogies, see *Man in the Cosmos*, pp. 4–5, 18, 29, 33; on the impact of *De amicitia*, *Con.* II, xii, 3–5; on its influence even in the *Vita nuova*, D. De Robertis, *Il libro della Vita nuova* (Florence, 1961), pp. 21–3, 93–100. Cicero's *Somnium Scipionis* (a fragment of his lost *De republica*) was a major influence on *Par.* XXII, 133–50.

12 References in order: *Par.* x, 121–9; *Epist.* XIII, 39–41; *Con.* II, xii, 3–5.

13 With regard to the shape or structure of the *Consolatio Philosophiae*, it is important to bear in mind that it takes the form of a dialogue between a pupil and a

'school-mistress', that is, between Boethius himself and a personification of Philosophy (there are frequent anticipations of the exchanges between Dante the protagonist and Virgil in the *Comedy*); and that passages of densely argued prose alternate with poems in different metres, thus providing a model for the *Vita nuova* and the *Convivio*. For Boethius as having made manifest the 'mondo fallace', see *Par.* x, 125–6; for his attack on the vanity of fame, *Con.* I, xi, 8 and Chapter 2 below, p. 35; and on wealth, *Con.* IV, xii, 4, 7; xiii, 12–14. For his vision of God as the 'most beautiful' creator of a 'beautiful' universe, see *Con.* III, ii, 17; for the theme that mankind would be happy if only our loving were governed by the love that orders the rest of the cosmos, *Mon.* I, ix, 3; *Epist.* XIII, 89 (in relation to passages such as *Purg.* XIV, 145–51; *Par.* I, 103–35; XXXIII, 85–90).

14 *Par.* VI, 12. This and the following paragraph draw heavily on two works: Nicholas (1969, pp. 1–59), and Kolbert's translation of Justinian's *Digest* (1979, pp. 7–68), as well as the classic chapter, 'The Revival of Jurisprudence', in Haskins (1927). The first phase of the medieval re-discovery had been completed with the *Glossa ordinaria* of Accursius, who died in 1260. The second phase was to end with the commentaries of Bartolus (died 1357) and Baldus (died 1400). Among the poets with a legal background who were Dante's predecessors and contemporaries, one may note Giacomo da Lentini ('il Notaio'), Guido delle Colonne (*judex*), Brunetto Latini, and Cino da Pistoia, a famous jurist.

15 References in order: *Con.* III, xi, 10; IV, xxvii, 8 (hostility to lawyers); *Con.* IV, ix, 8; cf. I, x, 3; IV, xii, 9–10; xix, 4; xxiv, 2, 17; *Mon.* II, v, 1 (the law as 'Reason written down'); *Par.* x, 109–14; XIII, 47–8, 88–108 (Solomon); *Mon.* I, xiii, 7, and more generally, I, x–xiii *passim*; II, ii, v, etc.; *Purg.* XVI, 91–108 ('monarcha' as 'legis lator et executor'); *Par.* VI, 10–12, 22–7 (Justinian); *Inf.* V, 4–15 (Minos). The details which reflect the *Digest* most closely include the different treatment of *rapina* and *furtum* (cf. *Inf.* XI, 34–9, 59; XII, 137–8; XXIV, 138) and above all the persistent distinction between *persona* and *res* in the subdivision of the sins of violence in *Inf.* XI, 28–51 (cf. Chapter 3 below, p. 69).

16 *VN* xxv, 9; *Inf.* IV, 70–102. See also Chapter 10 below, pp. 245–6. Only one of Dante's few specific references to Horace (*Con.* IV, xii, 8) has any direct connection with ethics, and this is very generic; the author of the *Poetria* (as Dante called his best-known work) remained pre-eminently a master of the 'Art of Poetry'.

17 The single most important reference to Ovid by name is in *Inf.* xxv, 97–102, where Dante says he will go beyond him in the description of a metamorphosis. In the *Convivio* Ovid is given as the source for the myth of Orpheus (like Dante, a poet who tamed and civilised his hearers), which is quoted as the only example of 'poets' allegory', 'concealing truth under the mantle of a beautiful lie' (*Con.* II, i, 3). See also Chapter 10 below, pp. 240–1, 246–8.

18 References in order: *Inf.* xxv, 94–6 (metamorphosis); *Con.* IV, v, 16–17; (Cato in roll-call of heroes in 'divino processo' of Roman history); *Con.* IV, vi, 10; xxviii, 19 (embodiment of all virtues); *Epist.* XIII, 63, quoting *De bello civili*, IX, 580 (belief in one God); *Con.* IV, xxvii, 3; *Mon.* II, v, 15 (Cato born for *salus* of whole world); *ibid.* 17 (Cato's love of freedom). It is hardly too much to say that

Lucan's Cato is like a Redeemer without charity. For Dante's fictional Cato and his basis in Lucan, see *Purg.* I, 31–9, 70–90; II, 119–23. Dante not only admired but clearly identified strongly with this 'lover of freedom' and victim of civil strife, who 'preferred the cause of the vanquished'.

19 References in order: *Con.* IV, xxix, 4; *Purg.* XXII, 13–15 (Juvenal); *Purg.* XXII, 55–7 (theme of *Thebaid* as 'le crude armi / de la doppia trestizia di Giocasta': the twins killed each other as a result of their father's curse on them and the hatred between them was visible even on their joint funeral pyre, *Inf.* XXVI, 52–4); *Purg.* XXI, 82–4 (Roman and Christian time linked through Titus' destruction of Jerusalem; cf. *Par.* VI, 82–93; VII, 19–51).

20 References in order: *Purg.* XXII, 90–2 (Statius as 'chiuso cristian', 'tepidezza'); *Purg.* XXI, 124–6, 94–9 (Statius' poetic debt to Virgil); XXII, 31–54 (cured of prodigality); 64–81 (the Fourth Eclogue); XXI, 16–18, 31–3, 58–72, 130–6; XXII, 67–9, 100–5 (the different situations of the two poets). Cf. the Introduction above, pp. 4–8.

21 See Chapter 10 below, pp. 235–7, 263–4.

22 *Inf.* I, 85. Virgilian figures who reappear in the *Inferno* include Charon, Cerberus, the Harpies, Ulysses and Sinon. Francesca is modelled on Dido, Pier della Vigna on both Polydorus and Andromache, the disfigured Brunetto on Hector and Deiphobus; later, Cacciaguida will be modelled on Anchises. For Virgil's 'tragedìa' mentioned within a few lines of Dante's 'comedìa', see *Inf.* XX, 113; XXI, 2.

23 *Mon.* III, iv, 11; cf. *Par.* XXIV, 133–8.

24 *Mon.* III, xv, 3 (Christ as *forma*, *idea* and *exemplar*).

25 *Mon.* III, ix, 9, 17 (Peter); *Inf.* II, 13–33; cf. *Par.* I, 73–5 (Aeneas and Paul).

26 For the acknowledgements of debts to vernacular poets, see *Purg.* XXVI, 91–102, 112–26, 139–47. For his joint celebration of Francis and Dominic, see *Par.* XI, 28–117; XII, 34–111. Dante acknowledges his general debt to later teachers in his list of the twenty-four 'luminaries' who appear to him in the Heaven of the Sun. It will be helpful to list, in chronological order of their deaths, all those mentioned who lived after the time of Boethius: Isidore, d. 636; Bede, d. 735; Rabanus Maurus, d. 856; Anselm, d. 1109; Hugh of St Victor, d. 1141; Gratian (mid-twelfth century); Peter Lombard, d. 1160 or 1164; Richard of St Victor, d. 1173; Peter Comestor, d. 1179; Joachim, d. 1202; Bonaventure, d. 1274; Aquinas, d. 1274; Peter of Spain, d. 1277; Albert, d. 1280; Siger of Brabant, d. 1283.

27 *Purg.* XXVI, 82–93 (love-poets); John of Salisbury, *Metalogicon*, III, lv, 900 A (Bernard).

28 *Inf.* I, 72.

29 The fourth and last Doctor was born 200 years later and became Pope as Gregory the Great from 590 to 604.

30 *Con.* IV, v, 16; *Par.* XXIX, 37.

31 Ambrose may well be referred to in *Par.* X, 118–20. For 'Te lucis', see *Purg.* VIII, 13–14.

32 The phrase is quoted in *Con.* IV, v, 16.

33 Augustine is named in *Par.* XXXII, 35. His writings are said to be inspired ('helped by the Holy Spirit') in *Mon.* III, iii, 13. The first two works are cited by

name in *Mon.* III, iv, 7–8. With the exception of the reference in note 34, the other acknowledged quotations do not relate to substantial or to distinctively Augustinian ideas: *Con.* I, iv, 9; IV, ix, 8; xxviii, 9.

34 *Con.* I, ii, 14.

2 *Putting authors to the question*

The following works in the Bibliography are particularly relevant to the themes of this chapter: Angelilli (1970), Corti (1981), Haskins (1927), Jackson (1971), Kolbert (trans.) (1979), Makdisi (1974), Marenbon (1981), Minnis (1988), Nicholas (1969), Rashdall (1936), Southern (1995).

1 *The Tragical History of Dr Faustus*, line 34.

2 The phrase 'ordinate, faciliter et sine errore' is used by Aquinas in the preface to his commentary on Aristotle's *Posterior Analytics*, *lect.* 1, §1.

3 Cf. *Con.* III, xiii, 2; *Par.* VI, 20–1.

4 For the distinction between dialectic and logic, see Vasoli's note to *Con.* II, xiii, 12 (with rich bibliography).

5 *Con.* IV, xxx, 3. In the Heaven of the Sun, Aquinas is described as 'la gloriosa vita di Tommaso' (*Par.* XIV, 6), and he is given two long speeches: a panegyric of St Francis, and a further major discourse, discussed in Chapter 10 below, p. 257.

6 It is worth noting in passing that Dante did consider fame to be a good and recognised that he himself was avid for the glory he hoped to achieve through his poetic art. He causes one of his interlocutors in the poem to preach him a sermon on artistic vainglory and he makes his fictional self reply, 'you have lanced a great swelling': 'gran tumor m'appiani' (*Purg.* XI, 119); see Chapter 8 below, p. 174.

7 *Con.* I, i, 7–11.

8 Foster–Boyde, vol. ii, p. 176.

9 For further discussion of the 'sovrasensi', see Chapter 10 below, pp. 235–6.

10 *Con.* III, viii, 9–11.

11 *Mon.* I, i, 1–6; ii, 2.

12 This and the following passage are given in the excellent translation by Prue Shaw (with some variations in punctuation). My understanding of these matters owes much to an unpublished Harvard Ph.D thesis by Dr Elizabeth Mozzillo-Howell. The Latin words are quoted in dictionary form, rather than as inflected in the sentence.

13 *Par.* IV, 40–8. See also Chapter 10 below, p. 254. Cf. *Man in the Cosmos*, pp. 18, 38, 347; *Perception and Passion*, pp. 64, 91.

14 *Purg.* XVIII, 56 ('prime notizie'); *Par.* II, 45 ('ver primo'); cf. *Purg.* VI, 45 ('lume fia tra 'l ver e lo 'ntelletto').

15 Cf. *Par.* V, 5; XXXIII, 141.

16 Cf. *Perception and Passion*, Chapter 4, esp. pp. 50–5.

17 Cf. *Man in the Cosmos*, Chapter 1, esp. pp. 47–51.

18 Cf. *Perception and Passion*, Chapters 5–6.

19 *Con.* II, xv, 5; *Par.* I, 103–5.

20 References in order: *Par.* XIV, 99 (Milky Way); *Par.* VIII, 92 (words, conduct); *Purg.* XXII, 29; *Par.* XXIX, 64; *Purg.* IX, 64 (certainty); *Par.* I, 96 (snaring), *Purg.*

xvi, 53 (exploding); xviii, 42 (pregnant); *Par.* i, 94 (divesting); *Inf.* xi, 92 ('solvere'); *Par.* xvii, 104 (counsel); *Par.* xix, 82–4 (in theology); *Par.* xi, 22 (unambiguous); *Inf.* xi, 92–3 (pleasure in expectation); *Par.* iv, 8 ('sospingere').

21 *Par.* iii, 31–3; iv, 94–9, 112–14.

22 *Par.* iv, 127, 130–1.

3 Division and numeration

The following works in the Bibliography are particularly relevant to the themes of this chapter: Gorni (1990), Mazzoni (1985), Moore (1969), Nohrnberg (1996), Vazzana (1989, 1997).

1 For the proportional system, see L. R. Shelby, *Gothic Design Techniques. The Fifteenth-Century Design Booklets of Mathes Roriczer and Hanns Schmuttermayer*, Carbondale, 1977.

2 *Par.* xxvii, 118–20.

3 *Par.* i, 1–6, 103–20. The multiplicity of species and individuals takes on a unity of *parts* that reflects God's eternal unity of *substance*.

4 Katzenellenbogen (1989), pp. 63–8.

5 In the first instance, 'division' will be considered separately from 'numeration', using this term in a restricted sense to be defined below. For the hierarchy of knowledge, see *Con.* ii, xiv.

6 *Inf.* xi, 97–105.

7 *Man in the Cosmos*, Chapters 3–5 *passim*.

8 Six is the only perfect number below 10; there is only one perfect number (28) between 10 and 100, and only one (496) between 100 and 1000. See *Man in the Cosmos*, pp. 217–22.

9 In a 'Golden Section', the line AC is cut at B, such that the ratio of the length of the whole line, AC, to its longer portion, AB, is the same as the ratio of the longer portion, AB, to the shorter, BC. The curve expressed by the Fibonacci sequence controls a great many natural structures. For proportion in music, see the relevant articles in *Grove's Dictionary of Music and Musicians*, London, 1975–80.

10 *Perception and Passion*, pp. 34, 174–5, 187.

11 *Man in the Cosmos*, pp. 133–4.

12 *Inf.* iii, 4–6; *Par.* xii, 140–1. *Con.* iv, xxiv, 1–7. Those who lived beyond seventy entered into a fourth age called 'senio'. See Chapter 10 below, pp. 252–3.

13 1 Corinthians 13.13.

14 *Man in the Cosmos*, pp. 58–9.

15 *Perception and Passion*, p. 260.

16 Isaiah 11.2.

17 See Chapter 7 below, p. 153.

18 For 'skyey influences', see *Measure for Measure*, iii, i, 9. Informally, we still say that someone has a 'sunny' disposition. The seven metals of medieval alchemy – silver, quicksilver (mercury), copper, gold, iron, tin and lead – were thought to be generated or governed by the planets .

19 *Man in the Cosmos*, pp. 145–6, 156. See below, p. 67.

20 For Dante, see *Par.* xxii, 112–20. The Romans used only ten months until July and August were introduced and named in honour of the first Emperors, thus

turning the 'seventh' month, September, into the ninth. Alas for symmetry, there are thirteen 'lunar months'; calendar months have different lengths and are not divisible (with the exception of February) into weeks; the year is not divisible into whole days; and the number of days as usually computed is an odd number (365) not divisible by either seven or twelve.

21 *Mon.* I, xv, 2. Aristotle, *Metaphysics* I, v, 986a 1, 21–28, 986b 2 (translated by W. D. Ross). The Latin terms are those in the translation by William of Moerbeke.
22 *Epist.* XIII, 33–4.
23 *Par.* x, 3.
24 *Par.* I, 1–3, 111.
25 See Chapter 9 below, p. 204.
26 *Man in the Cosmos*, pp. 135–7.
27 In the lowest heaven, the effulgence emitted by the souls is not intense enough to prevent the protagonist from recognising Piccarda de' Donati (*Par.* III, 10–21, 46–51). Contrast *Par.* v, 106–8, 124–9; XXXI, 1–6.
28 *Par.* XXVIII, 121–39. Dante there underlines his change of mind with regard to the authority of Dionysius. Earlier (*Con.* II, v, 6) he had followed St Gregory the Great.
29 As early as Cantos III and IV, the inequality of the *beatitudo* enjoyed by the *beati* was dramatised (through the life-story of Piccarda), turned into a *quaestio*, and resolved. It continues to be a major theme right to the end of the poem: see Chapter 9 below, pp. 205–7.
30 *Par.* IV, 28–63. In a recent book, Richard Kay (1994) argues in favour of an extensive and comprehensive debt to medieval astrology in the *Paradiso*.
31 *Par.* VI, 115–20; VIII, 1–12; IX, 32–6, 118–19.
32 *Par.* XXII, 46–7. If Dante intended this connection, *vita contemplativa* takes on a meaning that would not have been easily recognised by the philosophers of antiquity. See Chapter 4 below, p. 89.
33 *Inf.* v, 1–2; III, 34–51; *Aen.* VI, 322–30, 367–71.
34 *Inf.* IV, 25–42; IX, 106–31.
35 *Inf.* XI, 22–90.
36 It seems increasingly likely that Dante himself was the author of the anonymous abridgement of the *Roman de la rose*, known as *Il Fiore*, in which a character called Falsembiante plays a very prominent role (see the collection of critical essays edited by Z. Baranski and P. Boyde, *The 'Fiore' in Context: Dante, France, Tuscany*, Notre-Dame, IN, 1997). The very lowest point of the scale in Dante's Hell is reserved for Brutus and Cassius, who betrayed Julius Caesar, and Judas Iscariot, who betrayed the Son of God (*Inf.* XXXIII, 61–7). The *historia salvationis* is linked to the story of the Roman Empire.
37 *Inf.* XI, 28–33, 34–66, 97–111.
38 *Inf.* XII–XVII. To enter into Dante's thought processes here, it must be remembered that the noun *natura* still retained its etymological link with the verb *nasci/natum*, 'to be born', and that both the offences described as *contra naturam* can be referred to the 'birth rate'. A deliberately sterile act of copulation will make any birth impossible. A disproportionate rate of interest on a loan could only be met, in nature, if animals and plants were to multiply at an impossibly high rate.

39 See Chapter 5 below, p. 109, and Chapter 8, pp. 176, 185.
40 *Mon.* III, xvi, 7. See Chapter 10 below, p. 266.
41 For the comma of Didymus, see *Grove's Dictionary of Music and Musicians*, svv. Didymus, Interval, Just Intonation, and Temperaments.

4 *Aristotelian values through Dante's eyes*

The following works in the Bibliography are particularly relevant to the themes of this chapter: Barnes (1982), Corti (1983), Gauthier (1958), Lloyd (1966, 1968), McInerny (1982, 1992, 1993), Minio-Paluello (1980), Westberg (1994).

1 *Rime* LXXXII, 12–13. The 'global' imagery in this paragraph is freely inspired by *Mon.* III, xvi.
2 Genesis 1.26.
3 For example, Aquinas wrote his *Summa contra gentiles* for non-believers who refused to accept the authority of the Bible. Much earlier, Boethius made no mention of any distinctively Christian concept in his *Consolation of Philosophy*, although he was almost certainly the author of a work on the Trinity. For the two happinesses, see *Mon.* III, xvi, 7–8 (the whole argument of *Man in the Cosmos*, esp. pp. 294–5, culminates in this passage of the *Monarchia*).
4 For a fuller discussion of the context, cf. *Perception and Passion*, pp. 5–8. For Dante's reverence for Aristotle as a moral philosopher, see *Con.* IV, vi, 5–8, 16; viii, 4–10; xvii, 1, 4; xxii, 4; xxiii, 8.
5 *Inf.* IV, 144.
6 For Dante's familiarity with the *Ethics*, cf. *Inf.* XI, 80. For Dante's knowledge of Aquinas's commentary on the *Ethics*, cf. *Con.* II, xiv, 14; IV, viii, 1. The 'rough sketch' is limited to what must be known in order to understand value-judgements, as distinct from the source of the distinctively human faculties of intellect and will, described in *Man in the Cosmos* (pp. 270–95), or from their operations and the nature of the freedom they confer, described in *Perception and Passion* (pp. 173–214), which also deals implicitly with the virtues of self-control by showing how Dante conceived and represented the interaction of reason and the passions (pp. 217–301).
7 Cf. *Ethics* I, iv–xii.
8 Cf. *Con.* I, v, 11, in the light of viii, 9; xi, 11, 17; IV, xiv, 11; xxvii, 5.
9 *Perception and Passion*, Chapter 2, *passim*.
10 *Ibid.* pp. 27–31.
11 For 'Natura universalis' and 'ars imitatur naturam', see Chapter 3, p. 53.
12 *Mon.* I, iii, 1–2; *Perception and Passion*, pp. 39, 45–6.
13 *Ibid.* Chapter 3, esp. pp. 32–3.
14 *Ibid.* p. 35.
15 For 'operatio propria', cf. *ibid.* p. 38. For 'vis ultima', see *Mon.* I, iii, 3–6.
16 *Perception and Passion*, pp. 40–3.
17 *Ibid.* p. 42.
18 *Ibid.* Chapter 4, *passim*.
19 The powers of the mind are described in *Perception and Passion*, Chapter 9, pp. 173–92.
20 Cf. *Ethics* I, vii, 16, quoted below, p. 86; *Mon.* I, iii.

21 The last three chapters of *Perception and Passion* are devoted to the analysis of the 'combined operations' of the 'sensitive' powers and the distinctively human, rational powers.

22 As Vasoli shows in his note *ad loc.*, Dante was clearly influenced by a passage in Aquinas's commentary to Aristotle's *Ethics:* 'Sed hoc pertinet ad rationem virtutis, quod *unusquisque habens virtutem secundum eam bene operatur*, sicut virtus equi est secundum quam bene currit . . . Cuiuslibet enim rei habentis *propriam operationem* illa est *bonum* suum, et hoc quod bene est ei consistit in eius operatione . . . Si igitur opus hominis consistit in quadam vita, prout scilicet homo operatur secundum rationem, sequitur quod *boni hominis sit bene operari secundum rationem*, et optimi hominis, scilicet felicis, optime hoc facere.' ('It pertains to the notion of virtue that any thing possessing a virtue is acting well when it acts in accordance with that virtue. For example, it is the virtue of a horse that enables it to run well. If any thing has an activity proper to itself, then that operation is its good. So if the function of man consists in a certain kind of life – one in which he acts in accordance with reason – it follows that the mark of a good man is acting well in accordance with reason, and it is the mark of the best man, the happy man, that he should do this in the best way.' *In Ethic.* I, lect. x, §§128, 119, 128).

23 *Con.* IV, ix, 4.

24 *Con.* IV, iv, 1–2. See the texts quoted below, pp. 93, 202–3.

25 *Con.* II, xii, 1–5.

26 Cf. *Perception and Passion*, pp. 177–84; *Ethics*, x, vii–viii, *passim*.

27 Cf. *Con.* III, xv, 8–10; IV, xiii, 6–9; *Inf.* IV, 130–2; *Purg.* III, 34–45; *Par.* XXXIII, 132–41.

28 Cf. further, *Con.* I, i, 1. See also Corti (1983).

29 *Ethics*, VI, iv–v.

30 Ibid. viii, 6.

31 *S.T.* 2a–2ae, 49, 1 ('circa operabilia contingentia'); *In Ethic.* VI, *lect.* x, §1272 (*astutia*); *S.T.* 2a–2ae, 47, 8; *In Ethic.* x, *lect.* xii, §§2111, 2014; 2 *Sent.* 41, 1, 1 ob. 3 (*auriga*).

32 *Ethics* I, vii, 16; II, i, 1. Cf. further: 'Subiectum vero habitus qui simpliciter dicitur virtus, non potest esse nisi voluntas, vel aliqua potentia secundum quod est mota a voluntate' (*S.T.* 1a–2ae, 56, 3).

33 'Oportet in voluntate, et in qualibet vi appetitiva, esse aliquid quo inclinetur in suum obiectum, cum nihil aliud sit actus appetitivae virtutis quam inclinatio quaedam. . . . Necesse est quod in voluntate, et in aliis viribus appetitivis, sint quaedam qualitates inclinantes, quae dicuntur habitus' (*S.T.* 1a–2ae, 50, 5). For 'piegare', see Chapter 10 below, p. 239.

34 'Sicut dicitur in VII *Eth.*, habitus similitudinem habet naturae, deficit tamen ab ipsa. Et ideo, cum natura rei nullo modo removeatur ab ipsa, habitus difficile removetur . . . Habitus est qualitas de difficili mobilis' (*S.T.* 1a–2ae, 53, 1; 50, 1).

35 The literal Latin translation of the crucial phrase runs 'habitus eligens in medietate consistens'. Dante had earlier rendered this, in his canzone, as 'un abito eligente / lo qual dimora in mezzo solamente' (*Rime* LXXXII, 86–7).

36 *Inf.* XI, 81.

37 *Con.* IV, xvii, 7.

38 *Politics*, I, iv.
39 *Con.* IV, xvii, 4–5. These are numbers 1–3 and 7 in Aristotle's list of eleven moral virtues. In the translation, Dante's relative clauses are turned into main clauses.
40 *Con.* IV, xvii, 5–6, numbers 9, 8, 10 and 6 in the list (see note 39).
41 *Con.* IV, xvii, 5, numbers 4 and 5 in the list (see note 39). Cf. further Chapter 8 below, pp. 191–7.
42 *Par.* VIII, 142–8; *Con.* III, viii, 17. See also Chapter 6 below, p. 139.
43 *Con.* III, viii, 17. 'Et ideo virtus, inquantum est conveniens dispositio animae, assimilatur sanitati et pulchritudini, quae sunt debitae dispositiones corporis' (*S.T.* 1a–2ae, 55, 2; cf. *ibid.*, 1a–2ae, 59, 2.
44 *Con.* III, viii, 17–18; *S.T.* 1a–2ae, 49, 2; 50, 1; 53, 1. In *Con.* III, viii, 19, Dante says that those who have had to overcome an innate vice deserve greater praise than those who have had no such obstacle.
45 *S.T.* 1a–2ae, 58, 1.
46 For the horse and its rider as an analogy of the way in which the mind should train our instinctive appetites by applying the 'bridle' to restrain their excesses or the 'spurs' to urge them on where they are deficient, see *Con.* III, viii, 17–18; IV, xxvi, 6; *Purg.* VI, 91–6; XVI, 88–99. For the bee and honey, see *Purg.* XVIII, 58–9. Dante's point is made by Aquinas in plain language like this: 'Vires sensitivae natae sunt obedire imperio rationis, et ideo in eis esse possunt aliqui habitus . . . Virtutes autem morales habitus quidam sunt, quibus vires appetitivae disponuntur ad prompte obediendum rationi.' ('The powers of our sensual nature are designed to obey the rule of reason and there can therefore be *habitus* in them too; the moral virtues are *habitus* by which the appetitive powers are disposed to obey reason promptly', *S.T.* 1a–2ae, 50, 3; 68, 3.)
47 Aquinas distils the essence of this paragraph in the phrase 'multiplicatis actibus, crescit habitus' (*S.T.* 1a–2ae, 52, 3).
48 'Nutrix/nutricis' is the root of the three words 'nursing', 'nourishing', and 'nurturing'. The opposition between 'nature' and 'nourriture' was already current in thirteenth-century French.
49 *Con.* III, viii, 17–18; *Purg.* XIII, 3; XXI, 41–2.
50 *Purg.* XXI, 41, 67–8.
51 'De ratione virtutis humanae est quod sit habitus operativus . . . Facit autem virtus operationem *ordinatam*' (*S.T.* 1a–2ae, 55, 2); *Con.* III, xv, 14 ('li costumi sono *beltà* dell'anima'); *Purg.* II, 75 ('ire a farsi *belle*'); *Purg.* XXVII, 140 ('libero, dritto e sano'); XXI, 64–6; XXIII, 72 (willing submission).
52 *Purg.* XVIII, 61–9.
53 'Sua bieltà piove fiammelle di foco, / animate d'un spirito gentile / ch'è creatore d'ogni pensier bono; / e rompon come trono / l'innati vizii che fanno altrui vile' (*Rime* LXXXI, 63–7).

5 Christian values through Dante's eyes

The following works in the Bibliography are particularly relevant to the themes of this chapter: Armour (1979), Barblan (ed.) (1988), Caird (1980), Chiavacci Leonardi (1984), Lampe (ed.) (1988), Panvini (1988), Petrocchi (1988), Russo (1984), Ryan (1980, 1995), Smalley (1983), Southern (1991).

1 The title is important and implies all the following points. (a) The chapter is written as a companion piece to the presentation of Aristotelian values in the preceding chapter. (b) Discussion is centred on ethical values and their actualisation in this life: it describes not the Christian *Credo*, but a Christian *Facio*. (c) The presentation is consistently favourable and is intended to show why Dante believed what he did. (d) No account is taken of recent biblical scholarship. (e) The Latin Gospels are treated as the faithful, unproblematic record of true events; but they are always seen through the 'lens' of the Apostles' Creed. (f) Expressions such as *vita aeterna*, *regnum caelorum* and *beatitudo* are interpreted in the way that Dante understood them and represented them in the *Comedy*.

2 My translation aims at a similar literalness at the cost of a similar strangeness (e.g. 'kingdom of the heavens').

3 Matthew will be given precedence over the other evangelists in what follows, because his Gospel is placed first in the New Testament, because it contains the classic version of the Beatitudes, and because it is most often quoted by Dante.

4 Boccaccio, *Vita di Dante*, xxii, 'Difesa della poesia' (*Il comento alla Divina Commedia*, ed. D. Guerri, Bari, 1918, i, p. 39).

5 Matthew 5.17–19. The polemical context receives greater stress in the alternative versions in Mark (10.17–31) and Luke (18.18–30), where, however, it is made clear that Jesus already knew and loved the young man with many possessions.

6 *S.T.* 1a–2ae, 100, 3 (the phrase quoted is adapted from the *videtur quod*). All the articles in this *quaestio* are relevant. Cf. further 2a–2ae, 56, 1.

7 This paragraph and its successors follow the Anglican and Orthodox tradition of dividing the unnumbered list as 4 + 6, rather than 3 + 7, as in the Catholic and Lutheran traditions; cf. *S.T.* 1a–2ae, 100, 4.

8 On the negative commandments, cf. *S.T.* 1a–2ae, 100, 7.

9 References in order: *S.T.* 1a–2ae, 98, 5; 100, 1; *De veritate*, 14, 11. 'Omnia ergo quaecumque vultis ut faciant vobis homines, et vos facite illis' (Matthew 7.12: this phrase is often quoted in the negative form 'quod tibi non vis fieri, alteri ne feceris').

10 Deuteronomy 5.2–4, 9–10; Jeremiah 24.7; 30. 22; cf. John 14.21.

11 *Inf.* IV, 57; Deuteronomy 30.15, 19–20. The precise number of precepts (613) is taken from the *New Jerome Biblical Commentary*. Most of these are elaborate prescriptions for rituals and sacrifice, of which the most important are the rites of penitence and purification which periodically restore the broken bond.

12 Genesis 2.17; Matthew 19.17; Exodus 33.19; *Par.* XXVI, 42.

13 Cf. further, Romans 13.8–10.

14 Matthew 5.48.

15 Matthew 5.38 ('eye for an eye'); 5.21–2, 28, 39–41, 44–7; cf. 18.22.

16 Psalm 111.1; Ecclesiasticus 14.1–2; Job 42.12–16 (cf. 21.23). The phrase 'Wisdom literature' refers to the Book of Proverbs, Ecclesiastes, Ecclesiasticus, and the Book of Wisdom. Despite the explanation given in Chapter 2, p. 34 above, Christian readers may be perplexed by the treatment of 'blessed' and 'happy' as near synonyms, since the first seems to mean something like 'approved by God', and the second can be used to describe one's feelings at a party. But a survey of Dante's usage will show that when he is referring to 'l'ultima felicità' – the highest or supreme happiness – the word is synonymous with

'beatitudine'. See *Purg.* VI, 48; XVII, 133–4; XXX, 75; *Par.* III, 64; VII, 3; XXV, 139; XXXII, 118; *Con.* I, i, 1; II, viii, 14; xiv, 18; III, xi, 14; IV, xxii, 9 and 11 ('nostra beatitudine e somma felicitade'). See also Chapter 6 below, p. 138.

17 Psalms 1.1–3; Proverbs 3.13; 14.21; Ecclesiasticus 25.12; 26.1.

18 Matthew 4.24–5.

19 Matthew 4.17, 23; 5.1–2; 7.28.

20 In the system of Purgatory (cf. Chapter 3 above, p. 70), Dante combines the Beatitudes and the Seven Capital Vices, each beatitude being associated with the virtue opposed to the given vice. He follows the order in which the seven vices were traditionally listed. See the article by Chiavacci Leonardi (1984).

21 For the Aristotelian virtues, cf. Chapter 4 above, pp. 92–4; and Chapters 8 and 9 below, pp. 192–4, and pp. 198–9, 213–14.

22 Matthew 5.3–12. The beatitudes are translated or paraphrased here as they were understood in Dante's time.

23 The present tense used in the first beatitude suggests that the 'poor in spirit' are already in Heaven, or rather, that the kingdom of Heaven is already in them. Christian readers are again referred to notes 1 and 16 above.

24 See p. 101 above.

25 Matthew 5.3–12.

26 Matthew 5.22; 18.9 (Gehenna); Luke 14.15–24 (feasting); Matthew 20.16 (first and last). The author of the song 'Pie in the Sky' was a militant trade unionist, who finished up in front of a firing squad for his subversive beliefs (cf. *Oxford Dictionary of Quotations*, 4th edn, p. 338).

27 Matthew 4.18–20; 19.13–15; 21.30–2; Luke 5.30–1; 7.34; 18.9–14.

28 *Purg.* XXII, 76–87; *Par.* X, 128; XV, 148; cf. XXIV, 106–11.

29 Matthew 16.24; 27.32; 6.13; 26.39. The phrase 'qui tollis peccata mundi' is repeated five times in the Ordinary of the Mass, three times preceded by 'Agnus Dei'.

30 Matthew 13.3; Luke 10.37.

31 The best introduction to the genre of the parable is the third of the five discourses in Matthew's Gospel (13.1–51), which is given over entirely to this form. Jesus 'spoke many things to the crowds in parables' and 'without parables he did not speak'. He there defends the use of parables, despite their apparent obscurity; he points to their pedigree in the prophets who were his models; and, not least, he gives his own detailed explanation of two of the parables – those of the Sower, and the Wheat and the Tares – which perhaps for this very reason have become among the best known.

32 References in order: *Epist.* XIII, 40 ('non ad speculandum, sed ad opus'); *Con.* IV, ix, 1–2, 4–7, 9; cf. xxviii, 3, 16; Luke 11.28; John 5.29; 8.51; 13.15; 14.12.

33 Matthew 7.15–20; 24.32–3; Luke 6.43–5; 13.6; John 15.1–8, 16 (tree); Matthew 5.13–16 (light).

34 References in order: Luke 14.28–31 (battle, building); Matthew 25.1–12; 24.45–51 (buying oil); Matthew 24.42–4 (vigilance); Luke 20.9–16; Matthew 20.1–16, 21, 33–41 (labourers); Luke 18.1–8 (judge and widow; cf. the story of Trajan and the widow, *Purg.* X, 73–93); Matthew 25.14–30; Luke 16.1–8 (faithful servant); Luke 19.12–27 (profit); Matthew 10.5–14 (disciples); John 10.1–6, 11–16 (good shepherd).

35 References in order: Matthew 22.1–10; Luke 14.15–24 (blind and lame); Luke 16.19–31 (Dives and Lazarus); Luke 21.1–4 (widow's mite); Matthew 19.27–30; Luke 14.7–11; 15.4–7 (inversion of expectation).
36 Luke 10.25–9.
37 John 8.3–11 (adulteress); Philippians 2.8; Luke 23.34.
38 John 13.15; 21.15–19; cf. 10.11–16.
39 Mark 2.10 (forgiving); Matthew 24.30; 2 Timothy 4.1 (living and dead); Matthew 8.12 (outer darkness); John 6.43–8, 57–8; 14.6.
40 *S.T.* 1a–2ae, 87, 4; 3a, 86, 4. Cf. *Purg.* VI, 39; XI, 71, 126; *Par.* IV, 136; V, 63.
41 For Dante's understanding of the original sin, see Chapters 8 and 10 below, pp. 187 and 259.
42 *Par.* XXVI, 118–23.
43 *Par.* VII, 56–7.
44 *Purg.* X, 34–6; *Par.* VII, 145–8.
45 *Contra Gentiles* III, 147, §3203. Aquinas devotes forty-four articles to grace in *S.T.* 1a–2ae, 109–14.
46 See Armour (1979) for a very clear account of the infused virtues.
47 1 Corinthians 13.1–13. In a passage that has generated whole libraries (Romans 11.6), Paul said that we are 'saved by faith, and not by actions: otherwise grace would not be grace' ('*ex fide . . . non ex operibus*, alioquin gratia iam non est gratia'); cf. Ephesians 2.1–9. See Chapter 9 below, pp. 218–24, for Dante's difficulties with this issue. He lays stress on God's mercy (cf. *Purg.* III, 120–3) in keeping with another well-known passage in Paul (1 Timothy 2.4), where the apostle insists that God our Saviour 'wants all men to be saved and come to the knowledge of the truth' ('vult omnes homines salvos fieri, et ad agnitionem veritatis venire').
48 *S.T.* 1a–2ae, 65, 3; 71, 4.
49 *Mon.* III, xvi, 7–8. Cf. Foster (1965), pp. 52–4.
50 Romans 5.5. For 'redundare', see *S.T.* 1a–2ae, 3, 3; 4, 5, 6; 38, 4, 5; 61, 4; 65, 1; 68, 5, 6.
51 *S.T.* 1a–2ae, 62, 3; 65, 3.
52 *Par.* III, 88–90; XIV, 33. See Chapter 3 above, p. 66, and Chapter 9 below, pp. 204–7.
53 References in order: *Par.* XXIV, 52, 40, 74, 90.
54 References in order: *Par.* XXIV, 143 ('sigilla'), 43 ('regno'), 63–6 ('sustanza'), 76–8 ('silogizzar'); Hebrews 11.1.
55 *Par.* XXV, 90–3.
56 References in order: *Par.* XXV, 67–9 (definitions); XXVI, 60 (every believer); XXV, 52–4 (second to none), 46 (blossoms), 91–6 (glorified body).
57 *VN* xi, xxi, xxvi; *Par.* III, 70–87; John 15.13 (cf. 3.16); *Par.* XXVI, 59.
58 *Par.* XXVI, 25–7, 41–5.

6 A courtly value in Dante's hands

The following works in the Bibliography are particularly relevant to the themes of this chapter: Brewer (1982), Coghill (1971), Corti (1959), Dispenza Crimi (1993), Dronke (1997), Kirkpatrick (1980, 1981), Valency (1958).

1 As their symmetry implies, the suggested dates are approximations with generous margins of error. But they are not controversial and are compatible with what Dante would have us believe about his development as a poet and thinker. It is no longer fashionable to speak of 'courtly love', and medievalists prefer the Occitan expression 'fin' amors', used by the troubadours themselves. But there is nothing tendentious in the use of the adjective 'courtly' in this chapter, and the etymological link with 'court' and 'courteous' is important.
2 *Con.* IV, ii, 11 ('potenza'); *Rime* XIII, 10; XX, 26; XXIV, 5; XXXV, 3 (power or strength); XC, 3; *Par.* X, 29 (of heavenly bodies); *Rime* XXX, 1–2; LXXXVI, 3 (courtly virtue; cf. *Inf.* XVI, 67, and *Purg.* XVI, 116); *Par.* XXVI, 42; *Inf.* XXVI, 99 (goodness and *moral* goodness); *Par.* IX, 105 (divine wisdom); XIII, 45 (divine power); *Purg.* XV, 72 (divine goodness); *Par.* I, 107; X, 3; XXXIII, 81 (God).
3 Cf. Valency (1958).
4 For the estimate of 'cento e cinquanta anni', see *VN* XXV, 4. The attribution of the sonnets, as between the two Dantes, is not certain, although most critics would give this poem to da Maiano (cf. Foster–Boyde, vol. ii, pp. 6–9). The two poets had been engaged in a *quaestio*, in which they used the verb 'quistioneggiare' and alleged the need to 'argomentare' and to 'show by authority' ('mostrare d'autorità'); cf. *Rime* XLI, 12; XLV, 9–10.
5 This is the motto of Trinity College, Cambridge.
6 *Par.* XVI, 1–18.
7 *Purg.* XXVI, 92, 97–101.
8 *Rime* XVI, 12–13. Dante twice insists on the passage of time required for love to grow to perfection: *Con.* I, xii, 3; xiii, 10.
9 *VN* xx, 6–7 (cf. xxi, 1).
10 For 'lo stilo de la loda', see *VN* xxvi, 4; for 'il dolce stil novo', see *Purg.* XXIV, 55–7. The 'breakthough' is first described poetically in *VN* xviii–xix, and is confirmed in *Purg.* XXIV, 49–62.
11 References are given to the text of the *Vita nuova* only: *VN* ii, 1; xl, 10 (Beatrice); xix, 10; xxi, 2–3; xxvi, 6 (humbling); xi, 1–3; xxi, 2; xxvi, 5–6 ('salute' and 'miracolo'); xix, 10; xxvi, 10 ('grazia'); xix, 9; xxi, 1–2; xxvi, 4 (communication of 'valore').
12 *Rime* LXXIX, 14–52; *Con.* II, ii, 1–5; *Rime* LXXXI, 19–22, 39–40, 63–7; cf. *Purg.* II, 106–14.
13 *Rime* LXXXII, 1–8; *Con.* IV, i, 8.
14 *Rime* LXXXII, 21–8 (the *videtur quod*); 29–73 (the 'riprovagione'); cf. *Con.* IV, vii, 5; xiv, 1; *Par.* III, 2–3 (where 'provando' refers to *Par.* II, 106–48, and 'riprovando' to *ibid.* 61–105).
15 *Rime* LXXXII, 27, 35–40.
16 *Ibid.* 61–73. Cf. Chaucer, *The Wife of Bath's Tale*, 253–310.
17 *Ibid.* 31–3; 49–60. The words for wealth occur in lines 23, 31, 49. See Chapter 7 below, pp. 158–9.
18 *Ibid.* 81–4. See Chapter 4 above, pp. 92–4.
19 *Ibid.* 88–95.
20 *Ibid.* 101–8. *Ethics* IV, ix; *Con.* IV, xix, 8–9.
21 *Ibid.* 109–11, 114–20.
22 For a full discussion, see Chapter 11 of *Man in the Cosmos*, which is devoted to

Statius' account of the generation and creation of the human soul and to the consequences of this doctrine.

23 For Esau and Jacob, see Chapter 9 below, p. 207. The expressions 'tal grazia' and 'quasi dei' must be treated with care. In this context 'grazia' cannot mean 'grace' in any of the theological senses of the word. 'Quasi dei' must be read in the light of *VN* ii, 8; *Con.* IV, xx, 4; *Dve* II, iv, 10. The phrase echoes the words used by Satan in tempting Adam and Eve to eat of the tree of the knowledge of good and evil ('eritis sicut dii, scientes bonum et malum', Genesis 2.16; 3.5). Some of the difficulties are explored in Boyde (1983).

24 See above, pp. 81–3 (potency), p. 111 (fruits).

25 *Con.* IV, xxiii, 13; xxiv, 1–8. There was a rich and heterogeneous tradition concerning the Ages of Man (see Burrow, 1988).

26 The text of lines 127 and 138 follows Franca Brambillo Ageno in reading 'aconcia' for the earlier 'adorna'; and 'ch'ell'aspetta' instead of 'che l'aspetta'.

27 For *magnanimitas*, see Chapter 8 below, pp. 192–4. Cf. *Con.* IV, xxiv, 8; xxvi, 3–4; xxvii, 3 (development to perfection).

28 *Con.* IV, viii, 3 (Cicero); xxiv–xxviii *passim.*

29 *VN* xxv, 9. The name of Statius, however, does not appear in the *Vita nuova*.

30 'Et est comedia genus quoddam *poeticae narrationis* ab omnibus aliis differens', *Epist.* XIII, 28.

7 *Covetousness*

The following works in the Bibliography are particularly relevant to the themes of this chapter: Armour (1994), Di Giammarino (1977), Havely (1996), Langholm (1984), Mann (1986).

1 Preface to *The Tale of a Tub*. Text (repunctuated and slightly cut) from *Gulliver's Travels and Selected Writings in Prose and Verse*, ed. John Hayward, London, 1944, p. 305.

2 1 Timothy 6.10; Ecclesiasticus 10.15.

3 Cf. Chapter 4, above, pp. 91–4. *S.T.* 1a–2ae, 55, 2 (*operativus*); 71, 2 (*contrariatur*); cf. 54, 3.

4 Chapter 6, p. 138 ('felice'); *S.T.* 1a–2ae, 59, 2 ('sanitas'); 55, 2 ('ordinata dispositio'); 71, 1 and 2 ('secundum quod convenit suae naturae'); 54, 3 ('discordant').

5 *S.T.* 1a–2ae, 71, 6 (*actus malus*); 71, 1 (*inordinatum*).

6 Cf. Chapter 5, above, pp. 120–3; the Apostolic Creed.

7 *Purg.* XVII, 91–105, 127–39. The contrast between the verbs *uti/usus* and *frui/fructus* is Augustinian.

8 *S.T.* 1a–2ae, 71 ('De vitiis et peccatis'); 72, 2.

9 *Ibid.* 84, 1 ('conversio'); 71, 6 ('offensa').

10 *S.T.* 1a–2ae, 72, 5; 3a, 86, 4 ('sine aversione'); 2a–2ae, 20, 3 ('avertit').

11 *Ibid.* 1a–2ae, 88, 2; 3a, 86, 1. Cf. *Purg.* III, 118–23; v, 51–7; 97–108. For 'satisfaction', cf. Chapter 5, above, p. 000.

12 *S.T.* 1a–2ae, 84, 3 ('directivum'); 2a–2ae, 132, 5 ('filiae inanis gloriae'); 36, 4 ('filiae invidiae'); 35, 4 ('filiae acediae'); 118, 8 ('filiae avaritiae'). In the *arbor vitiorum* reproduced as Figure 1, p. 54 above, the *filiae* become *folia*.

13 *S.T.* 1a–2ae, 84, 1. The term 'arch-vice' has been coined for the purposes of this book.
14 *S.T.* 1a, 63, 2; 2a–2ae, 118, 2; 1a–2ae, 84, 1. *Inf.* VI, 61–2, 74–5.
15 See the line quoted below: 'come l'*avaro* seguitando *avere*'. Aquinas, for his part, presented the Latin adjective *avarus* as being a fusion of *aeris* and *avidus*, 'avid for bronze', i.e. money (*S.T.* 2a–2ae, 118, 2).
16 For a detailed study of the style of this canzone, see Boyde (1971).
17 *Par.* XVII, 58–60; *Rime* CVI, 83–6, 101–5.
18 *Rime* CVI, 27–37 (joy in giving); *Purg.* XX, 103–17 (cf. 16–32).
19 It is easier to grasp these truths in a society that operates with paper money and credit cards; but it is worth remembering that Britain returned to the gold standard with disastrous results as recently as 1925; and that the value of the dollar is still partly dependent on the reburied ingots in the vaults of Fort Knox.
20 *S.T.* 2a–2ae, 78, 1–4.
21 *Inf.* XI, 40–51; XIV, 16–18.
22 The description quoted is from the beginning of the episode involving the sinners against nature, but the burning fire and sand are not forgotten when Dante seeks out the group of usurers on the edge of the seventh circle (*Inf.* XVII, 43–54), finding them to be, with one exception, members of noble families from his own city (55–73).
23 *Rime* LXXXII, 49–51.
24 *Con.* IV, xi, 4–11; xiii, 11. For the chance discovery of treasure, see *Consolatio philosophiae* v, pr. 1.
25 *Con.* IV, xiii, 1–9, amplifying *Rime* CVI, 69–73. Cf. *Man in the Cosmos*, p. vi ('philomythes').
26 *Con.* IV, xii, 13–17. Cf. *Perception and Passion*, p. 4.
27 *Inf.* I, 31–54.
28 *Inf.* I, 58, 88–90, 94–9; cf. VII, 8–9; *Purg.* XX, 10–12.
29 *Inf.* I, 100–5.
30 Genesis 1.9, 12, 18, 21, 24 ('bonum'); 31 ('cuncta *valde* bona').
31 *Epist.* v, 13. For Ulysses and the Sirens, see Chapter 10 below, p. 249.
32 *Purg.* XVII, 91–139. For the relationship between the conscious thoughts and the unconscious images, see *Perception and Passion*, pp. 128–9.
33 *Purg.* XIX, 7–33.
34 *Inf.* II, 97–108, 124–5; *Purg.* XIX, 28 (reproof), 58 ('strega'); XXX, 130–2 ('immagini false'); XXXI, 34–6 ('presenti cose'). Cf. *Con.* III, ix, 15–16 for Dante's description of how he almost ruined his eyesight through excessive study.
35 *Purg.* XIX, 52, 56, 61–7.
36 *Ibid.* 71–5, 94–8.
37 *Purg.* XIX, 103–14.
38 Acts 8.9–24. *S.T.* 2a–2ae, 100, 1–6. *Inf.* XIX, 1–6.
39 *Inf.* XIX, 22–30, 45–57, 69–87. For Clement, see also *Purg.* XX, 91–3; *Par.* XXVII, 58–9; XXX, 142–8. There are further attacks on papal 'avarizia' in *Par.* IX, 127–42; XXVII, 40–2, 52–60.
40 *Mon.* III, xvi, 8–11; cf. iii, 14; x, 14; *Purg.* XVI, 91–112. For the *documenta*, see Chapter 4 above, p. 78.
41 *Mon.* III, xvi, 11, 17–18.

42 *Con.* IV, xii, 9; *Inf.* VI, 61, 74; XVI, 73–5; *Purg.* XX, 43–93.
43 *Inf.* VI, 40–93; *Purg.* XXIII, 40–75, 97–111. For Dante's treatment of sexual desire, see *Perception and Passion*, Chapter 13, pp. 275–301.
44 *Par.* XI, 58–87, 121–32; *Purg.* XXII, 145–54; XXVIII, 139–44; *Par.* XXI, 115, in the light of 127–35.
45 See Chapter 4 above, p. 92.
46 Some scholars hold that the souls who lie below the surface of the Styx (*Inf.* VII, 115–26) are those of people who were deficient in anger, in which case they are being punished in the same zone as those whose anger was excessive; but the weight of the evidence suggests that they are those whose anger was sullen and long-lasting.
47 *Purg.* XXII, 19–24, 34–45, 49–54.
48 *Inf.* VII, 25–48.
49 *Ibid.* 40–2, 55, 58.
50 *Ibid.* 56–7, 61–6.
51 *Ibid.* 67–96.

8 Pride

The following works in the Bibliography are particularly relevant to the themes of this chapter: Chiavacci Leonardi (1979), Forti (1965, 1977), Russo (1966), Scott (1977).

1 For Aquinas, the *filiae inanis gloriae* include boastfulness, hypocrisy, obstinacy, discord, strife and disobedience (*jactantia*, *hypocrisis*, *pertinacia*, *discordia*, *contentio*, *inobedientia*), *S.T.* 2a–2ae, 132, 5. Dante singles out 'arroganza', 'disdegno', 'avere in dispetto', 'disio de l'eccellenza', 'folle ardire'.
2 *Poetics*, xiii, 2–3 (mixture). For further discussion of Dante's own pride, see Chapter 10 below, p. 271. Implicitly, he admits to *luxuria* through his behaviour in *Inf.* V, 109–20, 139–42, and *Purg.* XXVII, 10–27. In *Purg.* XIII, 133–8 Dante declares he will have to spend a long time purging his pride on the first terrace of Purgatory. Earlier, he had made it clear that his pride lay above all in his art (cf. *Purg.* XI, 92–120). For his *vanagloria*, see also *Par.* XVI, 1–15, where it becomes clear that he was vain about his family's presumed noble blood. (The enigmatic episode in *Inf.* XXIX, 19–36 shows that he was aware of a nobleman's 'obligation' to avenge a wrong done to his family – in this case a violent death.) He was passionately concerned with his reputation both in his own day (cf. *Con.* I, ii, 12–16; iii, 3–11), and with posterity (cf. *Inf.* XXIV, 46–51 and *Par.* XXV, 1–9). For his own awareness of his great natural gifts, cf. *Purg.* XXX, 109–17; *Par.* XXII, 112–17.
3 *S.T.* 1a–2ae, 84, 2. Elsewhere Aquinas uses *amor sui* as a synonym for *amor proprius*.
4 *Purg.* X, 7, 13–16, 22–7.
5 References in order: *Purg.* X, 98 ('imagini'); 94–6 (God as artist); 39, 59–63, 82–93 (senses); 19–21 (roads in a desert).
6 *Ibid.* 66 ('più e men che re'); 55–69 (David); 73–93 (Trajan).
7 For an analysis of the slow arrival of the souls, see *Perception and Passion*, pp. 113–18. For the Lord's Prayer, see Matthew 6.7–13.

8 *Purg.* XI, 37–42, 49–54, 73 (cf. XII, 1–3).
9 The speaker was a member of a famous – or infamous – feudal family in Tuscany which had not been assimilated into the nearest city-state (in his case, the republic of Siena).
10 *Purg.* XI, 30, 34–6.
11 *Inf.* IX, 118–23; X, 22–30, 36. The protagonist had specifically asked about the fate of Farinata in *Inf.* VI, 79.
12 *Ibid.* 30–45.
13 *Purg.* VI, 58–71 (cf. *Inf.* VI, 60–3, 70–5).
14 *Purg.* VI, 106.
15 See Chapter 7 above, p. 152.
16 Ecclesiasticus 10.7–13. The Vulgate version of Ecclesiasticus, like that of the King James Bible, was based on a translation into Greek. But recent translations reflect the Hebrew original (which had been lost for many centuries), and they render the key phrase very differently. The passage thus bears out the warning given by the grandson of the author who explains, in a prologue, how he translated the text into Greek and found great difficulties, because 'Hebrew words lose their power when translated into another tongue.'
17 According to Liddell and Scott, the noun *apostatês* used to signify 'a runaway slave, a deserter, rebel'.
18 *S.T.* 2a–2ae, 162, 7.
19 *Ibid.* 162, 6; 132, 4; 162, 8.
20 References in order: *Par.* XIX, 47; *Inf.* XXXIV, 34–5; *Par.* XIX, 46; *Inf.* VII, 11–12; *Par.* XXIX, 55–6 (cf. *Inf.* IX, 79, 91; XXVII, 113).
21 *Thebaid*, X, 897–939; *Inf.* XIV, 46–7, 52–60; 69–70.
22 *Ibid.* 51, 63–4.
23 *Ibid.* 58; XXXI, 43–5, 91–108.
24 Genesis 11.4; *Inf.* XXXI, 67–81 (cf. *Purg.* XII, 34–6); XXXIV, 28–33, 109–11. In the *vetus Latina* translation of the Bible used by Augustine, Nimrod was described as a 'gigans'.
25 *Inf.* I, 72; XXXI, 92; *Purg.* VI, 118; cf. Chapter 10 below, p. 260.
26 *Purg.* XII, 37–9 (Niobe); *Par.* XXI, 4–6 (Semele); *Inf.* XVII, 107; *Purg.* IV, 72; *Par.* XXXI, 125 (Phaethon); *Par.* I, 19–21 (Marsyas); *Purg.* XII, 43–5 (Arachne); *Par.* XXXIII, 94–6 (Jason; cf. *Inf.* XVIII, 86–7); *Inf.* XVII, 109–11; XXIX, 112–17; *Par.* VIII, 125–6 (Icarus).
27 *Purg.* XII, 25–63. Dante passes backwards and forwards from biblical to classical with each new example. Each named figure is presented in one terzina (although in two cases, two names occupy two terzinas). The twelve terzinas are grouped in fours by the use of anaphora (the repeated words are 'Vedea', 'O' and 'Mostrava'. The thirteenth climactic terzina is devoted to Troy and uses the same three anaphoric words at the head of each line, enabling us to *see* the acrostic – the initial letters spell out VOM, or UOM, meaning 'uomo', Man. Troy (or rather, Ilium) had already been given its traditional epithet 'superbo' in *Inf.* I, 75.
28 *Etymologiae* X, 248; *S.T.* 2a–2ae, 162, 1. In his note to *Purg.* XII, 70, the fourteenth-century commentator Buti derives the verb 'superbire' from 'super alios ire', 'treading over others'.

29 *Man in the Cosmos*, Chapter 5, esp. pp. 128–31.
30 *Troilus and Cressida*, I, iii, 109–10. Etymologically, 'degrees' on a 'scale' are the same as 'rungs' on a 'ladder'.
31 Cf. pp. 92 and 150 above.
32 *Par.* xxvi, 113–17. The full import of 'trapassar il segno' will become apparent in Chapter 10 below, pp. 260, 267. Ulysses ventured beyond the Pillars of Hercules, which were 'set as a mark' (the verb is 'segnare') 'so that man should not go beyond' ('a ciò che l'uom *più oltre* non si metta'), *Inf.* xxvi, 108–9.
33 The words in the alphabetical list appear in the following order in *Purg.* xi: 'onore' (80, 84); 'disio de l'eccellenza' (87); 'superbia' (88), 'vana gloria' (91); 'fama' (96), 'gloria de la lingua' (98), 'mondan romore' (100), 'nominanza' (115), 'presuntuoso' (122), 'glorioso' (133).
34 References in order: *S.T.* 1a–2ae, 77, 4; 84, 2 (self-love); 2a–2ae, 131, 2; 21, 1 (presumption); 131, 1; 129, 4 (honour); 133, 1, 2 (greatness and smallness of soul); 132, 2 (vainglory).
35 For another critique of *gloria*, see the article from the *Summa Theologiae* translated in Chapter 2 above, pp. 35–7.
36 *Purg.* xi, 94–102, 110–11 (115–17).
37 *Purg.* xvii, 112.
38 *Ibid.* xvii, 113–23.
39 This paragraph rests on a seminal article by John Scott, '*Inferno* x: Farinata as "Magnanimo"', *Romance Philology* 15.4 (1962), 395–411; translated and revised in Scott (1977), pp. 9–45. Dante follows Aristotle in his definition of 'magnanimitade' in *Con.* iv, xvii, 5, but uses it in the Stoic sense of the word in xxvi, 7.
40 Internal evidence shows that Dante also used the commentary to the *Ethics* by St Albert, but he does not acknowledge this debt as he does that to Aquinas in *Con.* ii, xiv, 14; iv, viii, 1.
41 *In Ethic.* iv, vii, *lect.* viii, §749. (The following notes will specify only the paragraphs in Aquinas, not the chapters in Aristotle or the *lectio* in Aquinas.)
42 *Ibid.* §771, 779 (cf. 760).
43 See Chapter 6 above, pp. 137–9.
44 The passages from Aquinas are translated from the following paragraphs in his commentary (*In Ethic.*): (a), 782, 778; (b), 780, 778, cf. 195; (c), 773, 775; (d), 772; (e), 774; (f), 779; (g), 776.
45 See paragraphs (a), (b), (c) and (e) in the passages translated above; *Inf.* x, 36, 46–7, 78. There are several other points of great interest and relevance to the interpretation of the encounter with Farinata in *Ethics* i, x: see *In Ethic.* §181–2.
46 Cf. (in order) paragraphs (e) and (b).
47 Cf. (in order) paragraphs (d), (e) and (c).
48 The rhythm of *Inf.* x, 73 ('ma quell'altro magnanimo') suggests that Cavalcante too is *magnanimus*; and we know from ix, 130 that 'simile qui con simile è sepolto'. In this case the adjective 'magnanimo' would be used primarily in its negative connotation ('stiff-necked, apostate'). But Cavalcante's words and actions are contrasted with Farinata's at every point, so that it seems more appropriate to understand line 73 with an internal pause: 'but the other, (being) great-souled . . .'.
48 Cf. (in order) paragraphs (g) and (b). The strange phrase 'sé continuando' (line

76) has a parallel in another passage in Aquinas's commentary: 'subdit autem *se continuans* ad sequentia, dicens . . .', §1265. Lines 74–5 must be read in the light of lines 35 and 88.

49 Cf. paragraph (f); *Inf.* x, 78, 82–8. The best commentary might be *In Ethic.* §195: 'Et sic refulget in eis bonum virtutis, inquantum scilicet aliquis faciliter sustinet multa et magna infortunia: non propter hoc quod non sentiat dolorem seu tristitiam, sicut Stoici posuerunt; sed quia tamquam virilis et magnanimus huiusmodi tristitiis eius ratio non succumbit' (cf. §182–3).

50 Cf. paragraph (e); *Inf.* x, 91–3.

51 'Il Cinque Maggio', 31–2.

52 1 Kings 10.3–7.

9 Justice

The following works in the Bibliography are particularly relevant to the themes of this chapter: Ambrosetti (1988), Bellomo (1979), Colish (1996), Geri (1977), Gilbert (1925), McInerny (1992), Picone (1989), Scott (1989), Westberg (1994).

1 *Ethics* v, i, 15, 1129b 28–30. Dante quotes the phrase about Hesperus and Lucifer verbatim in *Mon.* I, xi, 5, developing the astronomical image, as Nardi shows in his note *ad loc.* Aristotle was quoting lines from lost plays by Euripides and Theognides (as Nardi also reminds us) but in medieval translations the whole three-part quotation was attributed to Aristotle himself.

2 *De officiis*, II, xi, 40. The complicated question of the ultimate and proximate sources of Dante's misquotation are discussed in Vasoli's long note *ad loc.*

3 The Latin phrases are from the commentary by Aquinas, *In Ethic.* v, *lect.* 1, §888.

4 'Justus dictus quia jura custodit et secundum leges vivit' (*Etymologiae* x, 124). 'Jus generale nomen est, lex autem juris est species. Jus autem dictum quia justum est' (v, iii, 1). 'Judices dicti quasi jus dicentes populo, sive quod jure disceptent. Jure autem disputare est juste judicare. Non autem est judex, si non est in eo justitia' (IX, iv, 14). 'Vocatum autem judicium quasi jurisdictio, et justitia quasi juris status' (XVIII, xv, 2).

5 Wisdom 3.1; Psalm 85.10.

6 Cf. Matthew 5.6; *Purg.* XXII, 4–5; *Epist.* XII, 7.

7 *Con.* I, xii, 9; cf. *In Ethic.* v, *lect.* 1, §886. On the theme of 'combined operations' see *Perception and Passion*, Part 3, *passim*.

8 *Ethics*, v, i, 15, 18 ('ad alterum'). A further difference between *justitia* and the other ten virtues is that it does not lie between two collateral vices (cf. *In Ethic.* v, *lect.* 2, §993–4).

9 'Lo fondamento radicale de la imperiale maiestade, secondo lo vero, è la *necessità de la umana civilitade*, che a uno fine è ordinata, cioè a *vita felice*; a la quale nullo per sé è *sufficiente* a venire sanza l'aiutorio d'alcuno, con ciò sia cosa che l'uomo abbisogna di molte cose, a le quali uno solo *satisfare* non può. E però dice lo Filosofo che l'uomo naturalmente è compagnevole animale. E sì come un uomo a sua *sufficienza* richiede compagnia domestica di famiglia, così una casa a sua *sufficienza* richiede una vicinanza: altrimenti molti *difetti* sosterrebbe che sarebbero impedimento di felicitade. E però che una vicinanza a sé non può in tutto *satisfare*, conviene a *satisfacimento* di quella essere la cittade.'

10 *Politics* I, ii. For the reference to the *Digest*, see Nardi's note *ad loc*. Cf. further, *Mon.* I, iii, 2, 5–9; vi, 4.

11 This highly compressed account ignores Aristotle's distinction between *justitia legalis* and *justitia particularis*, and that between *justitia distributiva* (the allocation of honours etc.) and *justitia commutativa* (the restoration of equity when it has been destroyed through injury or injustice). The principle of equity underlies all the Aristotelian categories. Aquinas deals with *jus* and *justitia* in *S.T.* 2a–2ae, 57 and 58.

12 *In Ethic.* V, *lect.* iv, §933–7; cf. *Politics*, III, ix, 1280a 11; xii, 1282b 20–5; V, i–ii; VI, iii.

13 *Par.* V, 61–3; cf. XIII, 41–2.

14 *Epist.* XIII, 25.

15 The final phrase (a translation of 'meritorum effectus sive terminus') is Dante's own definition of *dignitas* – meaning something like 'the public recognition of worth'. It occurs in a passage of the *De vulgari eloquentia* (II, ii, 3), where it is made clear that there is a 'dignitas *mali*' as well as a 'dignitas *boni*', for example, when a liar is publicly humiliated or a thief put to death. The vernacular word 'mer(i)to' is used in the same way in *Purg.* XVIII, 60. In other words, there is a 'merto di *biasmo*' as well as a 'merto di *lode*'.

16 The discourses are placed as early as Canto III (lines 70–90), and as late as Canto XXXII (49–84).

17 Piccarda is 'beata' together with 'questi altri beati' (*Par.* III, 50–1); but her 'sorte' is 'giù cotanto' (55); and she and her companions have been 'qui rilegate per manco di voto' (30). The translation of 'per più farvi amici' reflects the comment on the relationship between *amor* and *amicitia* in Chapter 4 above, p. 88.

18 *Par.* III, 67, 54, 82–4.

19 For the inequality of the nine angelic choirs, see *Par.* XXVIII, 106–14, in the light of XIV, 37–60.

20 *Par.* XXXII, 40–5; *Inf.* IV, 49–50.

21 *Par.* XXXII, 49–51, 73.

22 *Ibid.* 76–84.

23 'Leges enim oportet homines *devincire* ad invicem propter communem utilitatem' (*Mon.* II, v, 3). The phrase 'vinculum societatis', quoted there, is from Seneca. Aquinas defines *lex* as 'quaedam *rationis ordinatio* ad *bonum commune*, ab eo qui curam communitatis habet, promulgata' (*S.T.* 1a–2ae, 90, 4). For the distinction between legislation and execution of the law, cf. *Mon.* I, xiii, 7.

24 'Est enim lex regula directiva vitae' (*Mon.* I, xiv, 5). The last phrase is Dante's translation of a famous definition by the early jurist Celsius: 'jus est ars boni et aequi'. It is quoted in the passage from *Con.* IV, ix, 8 below.

25 *Con.* IV, xxvii, 11. The invective begins in *Purg.* VI, 76; the attack on Florence comes in lines 127–51 (the word 'digression' is used in line 128).

26 *Mon.* I, xii, 10–11, referring to *Politics* III, vii.

27 A long section of the first half of the second part of the *Summa Theologiae* is devoted to law: 'diversitas legis' (1a–2ae, 91), 'effectus legis' (92), 'lex aeterna' (93), 'lex naturalis' (94), 'lex humana' (95) etc.

28 '*Jus* sive *justum* est aliquod opus *adaequatum alteri* secundum aliquem aequalitatis modum. Dupliciter autem potest alicui homini esse aliquid adaequatum.

Uno quidem modo *ex ipsa natura rei*, puta cum aliquis tantum dat, ut tantumdem recipiat. Et hoc vocatur *jus naturale*' (*S.T.* 2a–2ae, 57, 2).

'Dicendum quod *jus gentium* est quidem aliquo modo naturale homini, secundum quod est rationalis, inquantum derivatur a lege naturali *per modum conclusionis quae non est multum remota a principiis*. Unde de facili in huiusmodi homines consenserunt. Distinguitur tamen a lege naturali, maxime ab eo quod est omnibus animalibus commune' (*S.T.* 1a–2ae, 95, 4).

'Ad *jus gentium* pertinent ea quae *derivantur ex lege naturae sicut conclusiones ex principiis*, ut justae emptiones, venditiones et alia huiusmodi, sine quibus homines ad invicem convivere non possunt, quod est de lege naturae' (*ibid.*).

'Tertio modo inest homini inclinatio ad bonum *secundum naturam rationis, quae est sibi propria*: sicut homo habet naturalem inclinationem ad hoc quod *veritatem* cognoscat de *Deo*, et ad hoc quod *in societate* vivat. Et secundum hoc ad legem naturalem pertinent ea quae ad huiusmodi inclinationem spectant, utpote quod homo *ignorantiam vitet*, quod *alios non offendat* cum quibus debet conversari, et cetera huiusmodi quae ad hoc spectant' (1a–2ae, 94, 2).

29 *Inf.* XVIII, 25–33 (traffic control). 'Alio modo aliquid est adaequatum vel commensuratum alteri *ex condicto* sive *ex communi placito* . . . et hoc dicitur *jus positivum*' (*S.T.* 2a–2ae, 57, 2). 'Habent namque nationes, regna et civitates inter se proprietates, quas *legibus differentibus* regulari oportet: est enim lex regula directiva vitae. Aliter quippe regulari oportet Scithas . . . et aliter Garamantes' (*Mon.* I, xiv, 5–6). Dante speaks of 'minima judicia', 'leges municipales' (4), 'inferiora judicia' (9); and he refers to the role of the practical intellect in supplying minor premisses and reaching practical conclusions (7).

30 *Eclogues* IV, 6, quoted in *Mon.* I, xi, 1 (cf. *Purg.* XX, 70–2; *Epist.* VII, 6; XI, 15); *Metamorphoses* I, 149–50.

31 For 'il sommo Giove', see p. 184 above. The interpretation offered here goes back to Pietro Alighieri. For a fuller discussion, see Foster–Boyde, vol. ii, pp. 285–7.

32 'Justitia, de se et in propria natura considerata, est quaedam rectitudo sive regula obliquum hinc inde abiciens' (*Mon.* I, xi, 3). 'Lex enim . . . *ordo* quidam est, et bona legislatio, *bona* quaedam *ordinatio*' (Aristotle, *Politics*, VII, iv, 1326a 29, paraphrased by Aquinas, *In Polit.* VII, *lect.* 4, §1093). This is why Dante praises Justinian for having improved the 'legum institutio' by removing the 'superfluous and the vain' ('il *troppo e 'l vano*', *Par.* VI, 12). 'Qui quidem intellectum jubet principari, videtur jubere principari *Deum* et *leges*; qui autem hominem jubet, apponit et bestiam . . . Propter quod quidem *sine appetitu intellectus, lex*' (Aristotle, *Politics*, III, xvi, 1287a 28, trans. Moerbeke).

33 *Con.* IV, xxvii, 10.

34 *Ibid.* vi, 10–11 (cf. *Par.* XIII, 88–108). Dante says very little about justice at this point, since he intended to dedicate the last book of the *Convivio* to the virtue; cf. *Con.* I, xii, 12.

35 *Con.* IV, xxvii, 3–4, 6.

36 Piero claims to have been a 'just' man, but to have been 'unjust to himself' when he took his own life in prison: 'l'animo mio . . . / *ingiusto* fece me contra me *giusto*' (*Inf.* XIII, 70–2). This episode should be read in the light of *In Ethic.* §§557, 1093, 1797, 1815, 1855.

37 This paragraph is based on *Ethics* v, xi, and on the commentary by Aquinas (especially *In Ethic.* §1106–7).

38 *S.T.* 1a–2ae, 113, 1; *Par.* XIX, 13 ('giusto e pio'); *Purg.* XVII, 29–30 (cf. *Inf.* I, 73–4).

39 *Inf.* VI, 62. Cf. Genesis 18.23–32; Psalms 14.1–3; 53.1–3; Romans 3.10–11.

40 *Par.* VI, 127–42 (Romeo; cf. *ibid.* 113, 121–3); XIII, 88–108 (Solomon; cf. *ibid.* 37–48; X, 109–14).

41 *Mon.* I, x; xi, 1–7, 11–20; xii, 9–13; xiii, 6–8; xiv, 4–11.

42 *Mon.* I, ii, 3; III, x, 5 ('officium'); cf. *Purg.* VI, 91–105, 112–14; VII, 91–6; *Par.* XX, 65 ('rege'); *Inf.* XXIX, 56, 120 (infallibility); V, 23–4 ('dove si puote').

43 *Inf.* V, 56 (Semiramis). Fury is the dog in the 'tail-shaped' poem in Chapter 3 of *Alice in Wonderland*: '"I'll be judge, I'll be jury," said cunning old Fury, "I'll try the whole cause and condemn you to death."'

44 Anselm, *Proslogion*, I, 155; *Par.* IV, 67–9.

45 References in order: *Par.* VII, 25–33 (mercy; cf. Psalm 85.10); *Purg.* V, 97–108 ('una lagrimetta'); *Par.* XX, 94–111 (prayer; cf. *Purg.* IV, 133–5; VI, 28–42); *Purg.* VI, 118–26 (delay; cf. *Par.* XXII, 16–18); *Par.* VI, 88–93; VII, 40–51 (punishment of the Jews).

46 *Par.* XVIII, 52–81.

47 *Ibid.* 88–96; cf. Wisdom 1.1; 3.7.

48 *Mon.* I, xi, 6 ('fulgor'); xv, 5–6, 9–10.

49 *Par.* XVIII, 97–114.

50 *Par.* VI, 32 ('segno'; cf. *ibid.* 100; XIX, 102); *Par.* VI, 58–62, 70–2, 79–82, 95, 106–8 (extended metaphor of 'flight'); *Mon.* II, i, 2, 6; ii, 6–8; iii, 1 (*officium* and the will of God).

51 *Par.* XIX, 7–21.

52 References in order: *Par.* XIX, 25–7, 33 (torment of doubt); *Purg.* III, 43–5 (Aristotle; cf. 34–42); *Inf.* I, 85, 113; II, 140; *Purg.* XXX, 50 (epithets for Virgil); *Inf.* I, 121–9; IV, 37–45, 61–3; *Purg.* VII, 22–36; XXI, 16–33; XXVII, 22–45, 127–9, 139; XXX, 49–51 (Virgil's 'eternal exile')

53 *Mon.* II, vii, 5.

54 *Purg.* XVIII, 67–9 ('bequest'); *Mon.* II, vii, 7; *Par.* XIX, 40–66.

55 *Par.* XIX, 79–81.

56 *Rime* LXXXI, 53, in the light of Dante's commentary in *Con.* III, vii, 15–16 (cf. Foster–Boyde, vol. ii, p. 180); *Par.* XIX, 85.

57 *Par.* XXXIII, 135 ('principio').

58 *Par.* XIX, 115–32 (six prophecies); XX, 1–30 (the song); 37–72 (six 'vive luci'); 82 ('che cose?').

59 *Par.* XX, 52–4, 94–117 (Trajan; cf. *Purg.* X, 73–93); *Par.* XX, 55–60 (Constantine; cf. *Inf.* XIX, 115–17; *Purg.* XXXII, 124–9; *Mon.* II, xi, 18; xii, 8; III, x, 1–9, 14–17; xiii, 7).

60 *Par.* XX, 130–8.

61 *Inf.* XX, 113–14 (cf. Ovid, *Metamorphoses*, I, 25).

Preface to Part Four

1 *Inf.* IV, 102.

2 The translation here is based (in homage, affection, and continuing collaboration)

on an unpublished version by Kenelm Foster which he prepared for a *Lectura Dantis* in 1979.

10 The worth and vices of Ulysses: a case-study

The following works in the Bibliography are particularly relevant to the themes of this chapter: Armour (1993), Avalle (1975), Basile (1990), Boitani (1992, 1998), Bosco (1966), Boyde (1996), Burrow (1988), Chiavacci-Leonardi (1979), Corti (1989, 1993), Freccero (1986), Fubini (1966), Nardi (1949), Padoan (1977), Pertile (1979), Russo (1984), Scott (1977), Stanford (1954), Stull and Hollander (1997), Truscott (1973).

1 For Homer's Odysseus and his later fame see in particular the two studies by Piero Boitani (1992 and 1998).

2 For the 'happy ending' of a 'comedy', see *Epist.* XIII, 29, 31.

3 The definition of *Bildungsroman* is quoted from the entry in *The Oxford Companion to German Literature*, ed. Henry and Mary Garland (Oxford, 2nd edn, 1986). 'Quella orazione si può dir bene che vegna da la fabrica del rettorico, ne la quale ciascuna parte pone mano a lo principale intento' (*Con.* III, iv, 3).

4 *Con.* I, iii, 4; *Purg.* XXI, 18; cf. *VN* xl, 6–7.

5 Cf. *Perception and Passion*, pp. 30–1, 222, 321, n. 26.

6 *Mon.* III, xvi, 8. Aquinas tempers the paradox: 'Principium autem in operativis est ultimus finis' (*In Ethic.* I, *lect.* xii, §139).

7 Cf. *Perception and Passion*, pp. 253–4; *Epist.* XIII, 51.

8 References in order: *Par.* XXXIII, 94–6 (Argonauts; cf. II, 16–18); *Inf.* XVII, 109–11; XXIX, 116–17; *Par.* VIII, 125–6 (Daedalus and Icarus); *Inf.* IX, 54 (Theseus); IV, 140 (Orpheus); II, 13–15, 32 (Aeneas; cf. *Con.* IV, xxvi, 8–9); *Inf.* XXVI, 34–9 (Elijah); II, 28–33; *Par.* I, 73–5 (Paul). For the time references, see *Man in the Cosmos*, pp. 160–5.

9 Genesis 17.3–8; Exodus 6.2–10; Joshua 3.11–4.14; *Aeneid*, I, 1–7, 33, 276–82.

10 *Purg.* II, 37–51, 100–5. Dante expounds the allegorical senses of the same psalm in *Con.* II, i, 6–8.

11 *Mon.* III, xvi, 7–8; cf. *Purg.* I, 71; XXVII, 140.

12 *Aeneid* VI, 264–899; *Inf.* II, 13–27, 32; V, 22.

13 *Aeneid* III, 420–32 (Scylla); 569–691 (Polyphemus); VI, 42–155 (Sibyl and Golden Bough). For Ovid, see below, p. 247.

14 See Padoan (1977). In his prose works, Dante treated the *Aeneid* as though it were a historical source. But he was clearly familiar with the allegorical interpretations of the poem proposed by Fulgentius in the late fifth century and Bernard Sylvester in the twelfth; and while he avoided their manifest absurdities and distortions, he accepted that, in Books IV–VI, Aeneas was meant to embody the qualities that mark out a 'uomo gentile' in his Second Age (that is, from his twenty-fifth to his forty-fifth year). In particular – as we saw in Chapter 6, p. 145 – Aeneas possessed or developed the cardinal virtues of self-control and courage that enabled him to overcome the temptations of Dido and the terrors of Hell. Dante's characterisation of himself as the pilgrim – whom he presents as being in the middle of his Second Age – is strongly influenced by his understanding of Virgil's intentions with regard

to Aeneas 'ne la parte de lo Eneida ove questa etade si figura' (*Con.* IV, xxvi, 8).

15 *Inf.* XI, 67–9. Cf. Chapter 3 above, pp. 53–6, 64

16 *Ibid.* 25–6, 52–6, 61–6.

17 'Ipocresia, lusinghe e chi affattura, / falsità, ladroneccio e simonia, / ruffian, baratti e simile lordura' (*Inf.* XI, 58–60).

18 *Inf.* XXVI, 16–18, 25–33, 40–2, 47–54.

19 *Par.* XXXIII, 28–33.

20 *Purg.* I, 59 ('follia'); 130–3 (shore of Purgatory); II, 16–42, 100–5 (the angelic vessel); XVIII, 26 ('piegare'); *Par.* XXVII, 77–84 ('il varco / folle d'Ulisse').

21 *Aeneid* II, 44, 164, 261; III, 273 (in a passsage imitated from this last, Ulysses is called *fallax* by Ovid: *Met.* XIII, 712). In *Aeneid* III, 613, 691, the rescued sailor Achaemenides twice refers to Ulysses as *infelix* (a free rendering of a Homeric epithet). For the Wooden Horse, see *ibid.* II, 15–20, 32, 45–56, 150–2, 185–8, 234–8, 258–67; cf. *Inf.* XXVI, 59. For Sinon's account of the Palladium, see *Aeneid* II, 162–75.

22 Ajax's speech is given in *Metamorphoses* XIII, 5–122. References in order: lines 32, 45, 100 (cf. 68–9).

23 Ulysses' speech is given in *Metamorphoses* XIII, 128–381. References in order: lines 137, 360–6. Ovid's Ulysses begins his reply only after a pregnant pause, 'nor is charm (*gratia*) absent from his eloquent words' (125–7). Soon he will wipe away imaginary tears and bear his breast to reveal the wounds he received in battle (*ibid.* 127, 132–3, 264–5; cf. 381). But these are no more than an orator's habitual tricks of delivery. *Ingenium* (362) anticipates 'ingegno' in *Inf.* XXVI, 21 (quoted above). Ovid may also be the half-remembered source of the strange phrase '. . . 'l *ben*, ch'io stessi nol m'*invidi*', because Ovid makes Ulysses express the hope that his eloquence may be be free from envy – '*invidia* careat' – insisting that 'no one should seek to deny his own good gifts' – '*bona* nec sua quisque recuset' (*Met.* XIII, 139).

24 *Met.* XIII, 147, 150, 152–3; 173ff., 205ff.; 239–42; 224–37.

25 *Ibid.* 184 ('durae . . . sortes'), 336 ('responsa deum'), 339 ('prohibebant fata'); 373 ('obstantia fata'); 181ff. (Iphigenia); 162ff. and 304–5 (Achilles); 336–49, 373–4.

26 *L'ottimo commento della 'Divina Commedia'*, Pisa, 1837, pp. 439–40.

27 *Metamorphoses* XIII, 205, 361; cf. *Inf.* XXVII, 98.

28 The early fourteenth-century commentator Benvenuto da Imola says that the bolgia as a whole is devoted to 'astuzia', and that Dante speaks with two 'astuti'. Benvenuto calls Ulysses 'astutissimus'.

29 *Inf.* XXVII, 67.

30 *Ibid.* 82–3; 71, 100–4, 110–11, 115–16.

31 As in Canto XIX – cf. p. 166 above – Dante is using this episode to attack the pope who was still reigning in 1300, his personal enemy, Boniface VIII. He is also preparing the ground for the encounter with Guido's son, Buonconte, in Purgatory, as well as taking delight in showing how the deceiver was deceived; cf. *Inf.* XXVII, 61–6; *Purg.* V, 88, 97–108.

32 The same technique provides the first line of the *Inferno* ('nel *mezzo* del cammin') and informs the whole of the first canto (earlier events being narrated only in Canto II).

33 Horace, *Epist.* I, ii, 17–27. Boethius too (*Consolatio* IV, m. 3) lays the emphasis on Ulysses' *temperantia*. Horace's stress on Ulysses' indomitable spirit may have contributed ironically to Dante's imagining of the final shipwreck, for he says that Ulysses was 'adversis rerum *immersabilis* undis' (*ibid.* 22).

34 The *captatio benevolentiae* here is like an 'incantation' of the kind a necromancer might use to conjure up spirits from the dead. The opening phrase could almost be used in praise of the union of two Natures in Christ; and the repetition of a whole half line is very rare in Dante. The phrasing of the final question (line 84) shows that Virgil already knows the answer and understands its meaning. Ulysses became 'lost' both literally and metaphorically ('perduto' is from the same root as 'perdizione'). He also went to his 'death' both literally and metaphorically, for we are intended to think of what Dante called the '*second* death' of eternal damnation (cf. *Inf.* I, 117).

35 *Met.* XIII, 404–575 (Troy and the fate of Hecuba); 623–734 (Aeneas to Sicily); XIV, 75–157 (the voyage as far as Gaeta). The digression (XIII, 735ff.) deals with Circe and Scylla as well as Polyphemus and Galatea.

36 *Met.* XIII, 711–13, 730, 770–5; XIV, 70–1.

37 *Met.* XIV, 308, 435 (year's stay). The following lines in Macareus' long speech are relevant: XIV, 159–290, 435–44. It will be seen that Dante was able to read a reasonably full account of five adventures in the *Odyssey*.

38 The whole of this section of *De finibus* is relevant to Dante's interpretation of the myth of Ulysses. For example, in the very next paragraph, we read that Pythagoras, Plato and Democritus 'in their passion for learning travelled through the remotest parts of the earth' ('propter *discendi cupiditatem* videmus *ultimas terras* esse peragratas', xix, 50); and a little below we are told that the 'old philosophers imagine what the life of the wise would be in the islands of the blessed' ('veteres philosophi . . . in *beatorum insulis* fingunt qualis futura sit *vita sapientium*', xix, 53).

39 Horace probably made a contribution to the phrasing of both terzinas. The balanced separation of 'vices' and 'worth' in line 99 ('e de li *vizi* umani e del *valore*') seems to have been influenced by the placing of the nouns in Horace's translation of the third line of the Odyssey in the *Ars poetica* ('qui *mores* hominum multorum vidit et *urbes*'), while 'seguir *virtute* e *canoscenza*' echoes 'quid *virtus* et quid *sapientia*' from the Epistle, quoted on p. 246 above.

40 *Merchant of Venice* I, iii, 98. The quotation continues: 'An evil soul producing holy witness / Is like a villain with a smiling cheek, / A goodly apple rotten at the heart. / O, what a goodly outside falsehood hath.' Dante's Gerione, the 'sozza imagine di froda', has a 'faccia d'uom giusto' (*Inf.* XVII, 7–12).

41 'Pius Aeneas' is first referred to in the *Comedy* as 'quel giusto / figliuol d'Anchise' (*Inf.* I, 73–4). The phrase 'giusto e pio' is used by the corporate voice of the Eagle in *Par.* XIX, 13; cf. p. 214 above.

42 *Mon.* II, vii, 2–3, referring to *Ethics* I, ii, 8. It is significant that Dante uses *civitas* and *patria* as synonyms in this passage; and it may be remembered that Farinata recognised that he and his interlocutor were born in the same 'nobil *patria*' (*Inf.* x, 26).

43 Cf. Chapter 6 above, p. 140.

44 The sentence quoted provides another pertinent commentary on the adjective

'perduto' in the question Virgil put to Ulysses: 'dove, per lui, *perduto* a morir gissi', line 84; cf. note 34.

45 *Con.* IV, xxviii, 8; *Inf.* XXVII, 79–111.

46 Cf. Chapter 1 above, p. 11; *Perception and Passion*, pp. 177–80.

47 Cf. *Par.* XXXII, 57, quoted in Chapter 9 above, p. 207.

48 *In Ethic.* IX, *lect.* xii, §1913. The Greek proverb (*Ethics* IX, x, 1, 1170b 20) is really about guests and hospitality, not about travel and travellers.

49 *S.T.* 2a–2ae, 167. Cf. 'Desiderium eorum quae pertinent ad cognitionem . . . moderatur *studiositas*, quae opponitur *curiositati*' (*ibid.* 160, 2). 'Studium praecipue importat vehementem applicationem mentis ad aliquid' (*ibid.* 166, 1).

50 In this context 'mundum' probably refers to the universe, but the narrower meaning brings out the parallel with Dante's Ulysses.

51 *Ibid.* 167, 1. It is in fact the *third* species in order of treatment by Aquinas.

52 *Ibid.* On *inordinatio*, see p. 150 above.

53 *Con.* IV, xxx, 3; *Par.* XIV, 6.

54 *Par.* XIII, 97–102. Dante's examples are: whether a necessary major premiss coupled with a contingent minor premiss yields a necessary conclusion (logic); whether one can inscribe a triangle in a semi-circle such that it would not have one right angle (geometry); whether one may prove the necessity of a '*first* movement' (metaphysics); how many angels are deputed to move the physical heavens (theology).

55 *Par.* XIII, 109–35.

56 *Par.* II, 1–18.

57 Ecclesiasticus 3.21–2; 1.3.

58 *Par.* XIX, 40–69, 79–90; Genesis 3. 5; *Par.* XXVI, 115–17. See Chapter 8, p. 186, and Chapter 9, p. 220. We know from the fourth book of the *Convivio* that Dante found it hard to accept that mankind should have a natural desire for knowledge and yet lack the natural means to achieve it. It seemed a denial of the principles that 'Nature does nothing in vain', and 'Nature is not deficient in necessaries.' It seemed to make human happiness impossible. Nevertheless, he committed himself to the argument that (a) all the natural desires of a finite creature have a finite end or term; (b) our desire for knowledge is natural; and therefore (c) it is satisfied by a finite term: '(a) Li nostri desiderii naturali . . . sono a certo termine discendenti; (b) e quello de la scienza è naturale; (c) sì che certo termine quello compie' (*Con.* IV, xiii, 7). It is significant, however, that despite the syllogistic proof, he should add the afterthought: 'although very few people complete the journey because they travel badly' ('avvegna che pochi *per male camminare* compiano la giornata', *ibid.*). In the next-but-one paragraph he quotes Romans 12.3: 'E però Paulo dice: "Non più sapere che sapere si convegna, ma *sapere a misura*"' (*ibid.* 9).

59 See P. D. A. Harvey, *Medieval Maps*, London, 1991, pp. 39–48.

60 *Ibid.* pp. 19–37.

61 *Aeneid* I, 208–9.

62 There are no fewer than six balanced phrases, introduced by:'o socii', 'o passi'; 'vos . . . accestis', 'vos . . . experti'; 'revocate', 'mittite'; 'per', 'per'; 'fata', 'fas'; 'durate', 'servate'.

63 *Par.* XXVII, 82–3; *Inf.* II, 35; VIII, 91; *Purg.* XII, 43.

64 *Par.* VII, 78, 93; *Purg.* I, 59–63; *Inf.* V, 22.
65 The real and fictional geography is discussed at length in *Man in the Cosmos*, pp. 97–9, 107–11.
66 *Mon.* III, xvi, 7.
67 *Par.* XXVI, 118–23; XXXIII, 3; *Purg.* X, 35–6; cf. Chapter 5 above, p. 119.
68 *Purg.* XVII, 127–9.
69 *Par.* II, 19–21.
70 Cf. *Purg.* I, 130–3.
71 *Purg.* VII, 5; cf. I, 6; John 14.6.
72 Carducci, *Le rime nuove*, 'Dante', line 14.

Bibliography

Like its predecessors, this book aims to send its readers back to the *Comedy* and to promote the study of two of Dante's prose works, the *Monarchia* and the *Convivio* (especially Book IV). It is suggested that most of the questions arising from the text may be answered by going to the relevant passages and notes in the following editions and translations of these works: *Commedia*, ed. Annamaria Chiavacci Leonardi, 3 vols. (Bologna, 1999); *Monarchia*, ed. Bruno Nardi (Milan–Naples, 1979); trans. Prue Shaw (Cambridge, 1995); trans. with commentary Richard Kay (Toronto, 1998); *Convivio*, ed. Cesare Vasoli (Milan–Naples, 1988); trans. Christopher Ryan (Saratoga, 1989).

For a fuller treatment of individual names and terms, one would turn first to the *Dante Dictionary* by Paget Toynbee, revised by Charles Singleton, and the *Enciclopedia Dantesca*, which has full bibliographical details on all topics up to 1976 (see General Reference section below).

Many readers will have access to the Internet, and good recent bibliographies and search facilities are available on the three websites listed below.

The Bibliography itself is given in a single alphabetical list. At the head of each chapter will be found a list of works that are particularly relevant to its themes. These references take the form of short titles (consisting of author and date only). Specific references to these works in the notes are also given in this abbreviated form.

General reference

A Dictionary of Proper Names and Notable Matters in the Works of Dante. Paget Toynbee, revised by Charles Singleton. Oxford, 1968.

Enciclopedia Virgiliana. Francesco della Corte *et al.* (eds.). 6 vols., Rome, 1984–91.

The Cambridge History of Later Medieval Philosophy: From the Rediscovery of Aristotle to the Disintegration of Scholasticism, 1100–1600. Norman Kretzmann, Anthony Kenny and Jan Pinborg (eds.). Cambridge, 1982.

Enciclopedia Dantesca. Umberto Bosco *et al.* (eds.). 6 vols., Rome, 1970–6.

The New Jerome Biblical Commentary. Raymond E. Brown, S.S., Joseph A. Fitzymer, S.J., and Roland E. Murphy, O.Carm. (eds.). London, 1990.

The Cambridge Companion to Dante. Rachel Jacoff (ed.). Cambridge, 1993.

Dante e la 'bella scola' della poesia. Autorità e sfida. Amilcare A. Iannucci (ed.). Ravenna, 1993.

Websites

1. Società Dantesca Italiana (http://www.danteonline.it/).
2. DanteNet ('An Online Service for Dante Scholars Provided by the Dante Society of America') (http://www.princeton.edu/~dante).
3. Otfried Lieberknecht's Homepage for Dante Studies (http://members.aol.com/lieberk/welc_fr.html).

(It is, of course, likely that website addresses will be modified over the years.)

The Dartmouth Dante Project, which makes it possible to search more than fifty commentaries on the *Comedy*, and the Princeton Dante Project may both be accessed via the DanteNet.

Books and articles

AMBROSETTI, Giovanni. 'Giustizia e diritto in Dante', in *Lectura Dantis modenese 1988*, 113–32.

ANGELILLI, I. 'The Techniques of Disputation in the History of Logic', in *Journal of the History of Philosophy* 67 (1970), 800–15.

ARMOUR, Peter. 'Matelda in Eden: The Teacher and the Apple', in *Italian Studies* 34 (1979), 2–27.

The Door of Purgatory: A Study of Multiple Symbolism in Dante's 'Purgatorio'. Oxford, 1983.

'Dante's Virgil', in *Virgil in a Cultural Tradition: Essays to Celebrate the Millennium*. Richard A. Cardwell and Janet Hamilton (eds.), Nottingham, 1986, pp. 65–76.

Dante's Griffin and the History of the World. A Study of the Earthly Paradise ('Purgatorio', cantos XXIX–XXXIII). Oxford, 1989.

'Dante e l'imago mundi del primo Trecento', in Boyde and Russo (eds.) 1993, pp. 191–202.

'Gold, Silver, and True Treasure: Economic Imagery in Dante', in *Romance Studies* 23 (Spring 1994), 7–30.

AVALLE, D'Arco Silvio. 'L'ultimo viaggio di Ulisse', in *Studi Danteschi* 43 (1966), 35–68; now in *Modelli semiologici nella 'Commedia' di Dante*. Milan, 1975, pp. 33–63.

BARBLAN, G. (ed.). *Dante e la Bibbia*. Florence, 1988.

BARNES, J. *Aristotle*. Oxford, 1982.

BAROLINI, Teodolinda. *The Undivine Comedy: Detheologizing Dante*. Princeton, NJ, 1992.

BASILE, Bruno. 'Il viaggio come archetipo. Note sul tema della "peregrinatio"', in *Letture Classensi* 15 (1986), 9–26; now in *Il tempo e le forme. Studi letterari da Dante a Gadda*. Modena, 1990, pp. 9–36.

BELLOMO, Manlio. *Saggio sull'università nell'età del diritto comune*. Catania, 1979.

BOITANI, Piero. *L'ombra di Ulisse. Figure di un mito*. Bologna, 1992; *The Shadow of Ulysses: Figures of a Myth*, trans. Anita Weston. Oxford, 1994.

Sulle orme di Ulisse. Bologna, 1998.

BOSCO, Umberto. *Dante vicino*. Caltanissetta–Rome, 1966.

BOYDE, Patrick. *Dante's Style in his Lyric Poetry*. Cambridge, 1971.

Dante Philomythes and Philosopher: Man in the Cosmos. Cambridge, 1981.
'Predisposition and Prevenience: Prolegomena to the Study of Dante's Mind and Art', in *Proceedings of the British Academy*, London, 1983, 327–54.
Perception and Passion in Dante's 'Comedy'. Cambridge, 1993.
'Dante's Worlds', in *The Atlas of Literature*, ed. Malcolm Bradbury. London, 1996, pp. 12–15.
BOYDE, P. and Vittorio RUSSO (eds.). *Dante e la scienza*. Ravenna, 1997.
BREWER, Derek S. 'Honour in Chaucer', in *Essays and Studies* 26 (1973), 1–19; reprinted in *Tradition and Innovation in Chaucer*. London, 1982, pp. 89–109.
BRUGNOLI, G. 'Lo Stazio di Dante in Benvenuto', in *Benvenuto da Imola lettore degli antichi e dei moderni. Atti del Convegno Internazionale di Imola*, 26–27 May 1989, ed. P. Palmieri and C. Paolazzi with an introduction by G. C. Alessio. Ravenna, 1991, pp. 127–37.
BURROW, J. A. *The Ages of Man: A Study in Medieval Writing and Thought*. Oxford, 1988.
CAIRD, G. B. *The Language and Imagery of the Bible*. London, 1980.
CHIAVACCI LEONARDI, Annamaria. *La guerra de la pietate. Saggio per un'interpretazione dell' 'Inferno' di Dante*. Naples, 1979.
'Le beatitudini e la struttura poetica del *Purgatorio*', in *Giornale Storico della Letteratura Italiana* 161 (1984), 1–29.
COGHILL, Nevill. *Chaucer's Idea of What is Noble*. Presidential Address. London: English Association, 1971.
COLISH, Marcia L. 'The Virtuous Pagan: Dante and the Christian Tradition', in *The Unbounded Community: Papers in Christian Ecumenism in Honor of Jaroslav Pelikan*, ed. William Caferro and Duncan G. Fisher. New York, 1996, pp. 43–91.
COMPARETTI, D. *Virgilio nel Medioevo*. Florence, 2nd edn 1955.
CORTI, Maria. 'Le fonti del *Fiore di virtù* e la teoria della nobiltà nel Duecento', in *Giornale Storico della Letteratura Italiana* 136 (1959), 1–82.
Dante a un nuovo crocevia. Florence, 1981.
La felicità mentale. Nuove prospettive per Cavalcanti e Dante. Turin, 1983.
'Le metafore della navigazione, del volo e della lingua di fuoco nell'episodio di Ulisse (*Inferno* 26)', in *Miscellanea di studi in onore di A. Roncaglia*, 4 vols., Modena, 1989, 2.479–91; now 'On the Metaphors of Sailing, Flight, and Tongues of Fire in the Episode of Ulysses (Inferno 26)', in *Stanford Italian Review*, 9.1–2 (1990), 33–47.
Percorsi dell'invenzione. Il linguaggio poetico e Dante. Turin, 1993.
D'ONOFRIO, T. 'San Bonaventura nella concezione etica dantesca', in *Miscellanea Francescana* 75 (1975), suppl. 2, 351–7.
DI GIAMMARINO, G. *Il concetto dei beni in Dante*. Naples, 1977.
DISPENZA GRIMI, Erminia Maria. *'Cortesia' e 'valore' nella tradizione fino a Dante*. Rovito, 1993.
DRONKE, Peter. *Dante's Second Love: The Originality and Contexts of the 'Convivio'*. Occasional Papers no. 2, published by the Society for Italian Studies, 1997, pp. 51–71.
FORTI, Fiorenzo. 'Il limbo dantesco e i megalopsichoi dell'Etica Nicomachea', in *Giornale Storico della Letteratura Italiana* 138 (1961), 329–64; now in his *Fra le carte dei poeti*, Milan–Naples 1965, pp. 9–40.

Magnanimitade. Studi su un tema dantesco. Bologna, 1977.

FOSTER, Kenelm. 'Religion and Philosophy in Dante', in *The Mind of Dante*, ed. U. Limentani. Cambridge, 1965, pp. 47–78.

The Two Dantes, and Other Studies. London, 1977.

FOSTER, Kenelm (ed.) with Patrick BOYDE. *Dante's Lyric Poetry*, 2 vols. Oxford, 1967.

FRECCERO, John. 'Dante's Ulysses: From Epic to Novel', in *Concepts of the Hero in the Middle Ages and the Renaissance*, ed. Norman T. Burns and Christopher J. Reagan. Albany NY, 1975, pp. 101–19; now in Freccero, *The Poetics of Conversion*, ed. Rachel Jacoff. Cambridge, MA, 1986, pp. 136–51.

FUBINI, M. *Il peccato di Ulisse e altri scritti danteschi*. Milan–Naples, 1966.

GAUTHIER, R.-A. 'Introduction', in *Aristote. L'Ethique à Nicomaque. Tome 1, Première partie, Introduction*. Louvain, 1958, pp. 1–94.

GERI, V. *Giustizia divina e umana in Dante*. Perugia, 1977.

GILBERT, Allan H. *Dante's Conception of Justice*. Durham, 1925.

GILSON, Etienne. *L'Esprit de la philosophie médiévale*. Paris, 2nd edn 1948.

La Philosophie au moyen âge. Paris, 2nd edn 1952.

Dante et la philosophie. Paris, 2nd edn 1953.

Dante et Béatrice: Etudes dantesques. Paris, 1974.

GORNI, Guglielmo. *Lettera nome numero. L'ordine delle cose in Dante*. Bologna, 1990.

HASKINS, C. H. *The Renaissance of the Twelfth Century*. Cambridge, MA, 1927.

HAVELY, Nicholas R. 'Poverty in Purgatory: from Commercium to Commedia', in *Dante Studies* 114 (1996), 229–43.

HOLLANDER, Robert. *Il Virgilio dantesco. Tragedia nella 'Commedia'*. Florence, 1983.

Dante's Epistle to Cangrande. Ann Arbor, 1993.

JACKSON, M. '"Forse tu non pensavi ch'io loïco fossi": Traces of Formal Logic in the *Divine Comedy*', in *Romance Philology* 24.4 (1971), 563–72.

JACOFF, Rachel and Jeffrey SCHNAPP (eds.). *The Poetry of Allusion: Virgil and Ovid in Dante's 'Commedia'*. Stanford, 1991.

KATZENELLENBOGEN, A. *Allegories of the Virtues and Vices in Medieval Art*. Toronto, 1989.

KAY, Richard. *Dante's Christian Astrology*. Philadelphia, 1994.

KIRKPATRICK, Robin. 'The Principle of Courtesy in the *Convivio* and the *Comedy*', in *Italian Studies* 35 (1980), 25–30.

'Courtesy and Imagination: A Study of *Purgatorio* Canto XIV', in *Modern Language Review* 76 (1981), 67–80.

Dante's 'Inferno': Difficulty and Dead Poetry. Cambridge, 1987.

KNOWLES, David. *The Evolution of Medieval Thought*. London, 2nd edn 1988 (ed. D. E. Luscombe and C. N. L. Brooke).

KOLBERT, C. F. (trans.). *Justinian: The Digest of Roman Law: Theft, Rapine, Damage, and Insult*. London, 1979.

LAMPE, G. W. H. (ed.). *The Cambridge History of the Bible*. Cambridge, 1988.

LANGHOLM, Odd. *The Aristotelian Analysis of Usury*. Bergen–Oslo–Tromsø, 1984.

LEO, Ulrich. 'The Unfinished *Convivio* and Dante's Rereading of the *Aeneid*', in *Medieval Studies* 13 (1951), 41–64.

LIBERA, Alain de. *La Philosophie médiévale*. Paris, 3rd edn 1994.

LLOYD, G. E. R. *Polarity and Analogy: Two Types of Argument in Early Greek Thought*. Cambridge, 1966.

Aristotle: The Growth and Structure of his Thought. Cambridge, 1968.

LUSCOMBE, D. E. *The School of Peter Abelard: The Influence of Abelard's Thought in the Early Scholastic Period*. Cambridge, 1969.

Peter Abelard's Ethics. Oxford, 1971.

MCINERNY, R. *Ethica Thomistica: The Moral Philosophy of Thomas Aquinas*. Washington DC, 1982.

Aquinas on Human Action. Washington, 1992.

'Ethics', in *The Cambridge Companion to Aquinas*, ed. Norman Kretzmann and Eleonore Stump. Cambridge, 1993, pp. 196–216.

MAKDISI, G. 'The Scholastic Method in Education: An Inquiry into its Origins in Law and Theology', in *Speculum* 49 (1974), 640–1.

MANN, Jill. 'Price and Value in *Sir Gawain and the Green Knight*', in *Essays in Criticism* 36.4 (1986), 294–318.

MARENBON, John. *From the Circle of Alcuin to the School of Auxerre: Logic, Theology and Philosophy in the Early Middle Ages*. Cambridge, 1981.

MARENBON, John. (ed.). *Medieval Philosophy: Routledge History of Philosophy*, vol. 3. London, 1998.

MAZZONI, Francesco. 'Teoresi e prassi in Dante politico', in *Dante Alighieri: Monarchia, Epistole Politiche*, ERI. 1966.

Canto XI dell'Inferno (Lectura Dantis Neapolitana). Naples, 1985.

MAZZOTTA, Giuseppe. *Dante's Vision and the Circle of Knowledge*. Princeton, NJ, 1993.

MEYER-LANDRUT, Ehrengard. *Fortuna in Dantes 'Divina Commedia'*. Rheinfelden, 1987.

MINIO-PALUELLO, L. 'Dante's Reading of Aristotle', in *The World of Dante: Essays on Dante and his Times*, ed. C. Grayson. Oxford, 1980, pp. 61–80.

MINNIS, A. J. *Medieval Theory of Authorship: Scholastic Literary Attitudes in the Later Middle Ages*. Aldershot, 2nd edn 1988.

MOORE, Edward. *Studies in Dante*, 4 vols. Oxford, 1896–1917; 2nd edn 1969, with new introductory matter by Colin Hardie.

NARDI, Bruno. 'La tragedia di Ulisse', in *Dante e la cultura medievale*. Bari, 1949, pp. 89–99.

Dal 'Convivio' alla 'Commedia' (Sei saggi danteschi). Rome, 1960.

Saggi di filosofia dantesca. Florence, 1967 (1st edn 1930).

NICHOLAS, Barry. *An Introduction to Roman Law*. Oxford, 1969.

NOHRNBERG, James C. 'The Descent of Geryon: The Moral System of *Inferno* XVI–XXXI', in *Dante Studies* 114 (1996), 129–87.

PADOAN, Giorgio. *Il pio Enea, l'empio Ulisse. Tradizione classica e intendimento medievale in Dante*. Ravenna, 1977.

PANVINI, Bruno. 'La concezione tomistica della grazia nella *Divina Commedia*', in *Letture Classensi* 17 (1988), 69–85.

PERTILE, Lino. 'Dante e l'ingegno di Ulisse', in *Stanford Italian Review* 1 (1979), 35–65.

PETROCCHI, Giorgio. 'San Paolo in Dante', in *La selva del protonotario. Nuovi studi danteschi*. Naples, 1988, pp. 65–82.

PICONE, Michelangelo. 'La "viva speranza" di Dante e il problema della salvezza dei pagani virtuosi. Una lettura di *Paradiso* XX', in *Quaderni d'Italianistica*, 10. 1–2 (1989), 251–68.

RASHDALL, Hastings. *The Universities of Europe in the Middle Ages*, 3 vols. 2nd edn Oxford, 1936 (ed. F. M. Powicke and A. B. Emden).

RUSSO, Vittorio. '"Timor", "audacia", e "fortitudo" nel canto II dell'*Inferno*', in *Sussidi di esegesi dantesca*. Naples, 1966, pp. 9–32.

Il romanzo teologico. Sondaggi sulla 'Commedia' di Dante. Naples, 1984.

and Patrick Boyde (eds). *Dante e la scienza*. Ravenna, 1997.

RYAN, Christopher. 'Grace, Merit and "Buona volontade"', in *Italian Studies* 35 (1980), 6–11.

'Virgil's Wisdom in the *Divine Comedy*', in *Medievalia et Humanistica* n.s. 11 (1982), 1–38.

'*Inferno* XXI: Virgil and Dante: A Study in Contrasts', in *Italica* 59 (1982), 16–31.

'*Paradiso* VII: Marking the Difference between Dante and Anselm', in *Dante and the Middle Ages: Literary and Historical Essays*, ed. John C. Barnes and Cormac O' Cuilleanáin. Dublin, 1995, pp. 117–37.

SCOTT, John A. 'The Rock of Peter and *Inferno* XIX', in *Romance Philology* 23 (1970), 462–79.

Dante magnanimo. Studi sulla 'Commedia'. Florence, 1977; 'L'Ulisse dantesco' (pp. 117–93) previously published as '*Inferno* XXVI: Dante's Ulysses', in *Lettere Italiane* 33 (1971), 145–86.

'Dante, Boezio e l'enigma di Rifeo (*Par.* XX)', in *Studi Danteschi* 61 (1989, printed 1994), 187–92.

'Beatrice's Reproaches in Eden: Which "School" had Dante Followed?', in *Dante Studies* 109 (1991), 1–24.

'The Unfinished *Convivio* as a Pathway to the *Comedy*', in *Dante Studies* 113 (1995), 31–56.

Dante's Political Purgatory. Philadelphia, 1996.

SMALLEY, Beryl. *The Study of the Bible in the Middle Ages*. Oxford, 1954; 3rd edn 1983.

SOUTHERN, R. W. *St Anselm: A Portrait in a Landscape*. Cambridge, 1991.

Scholastic Humanism and the Unification of Europe. Oxford, 1995.

STANFORD, W. B. *The Ulysses Theme*. Oxford, 1954.

STULL, William and Robert HOLLANDER. 'The Lucanian Source of Dante's Ulysses', in *Studi Danteschi* 63 (1991, printed 1997), 1–52.

TOOK, John. 'Dante and the *Confessions* of Augustine', in *Annali d'Italianistica* 8 (1990), 360–82.

TRUSCOTT, J. G. 'Ulysses and Guido' (*Inf.* XXVI–XXVII)', in *Dante Studies* 91 (1973), 47–72.

VALENCY, Maurice. *In Praise of Love: An Introduction to the Love Poetry of the Renaissance*. New York, 1958.

VAZZANA, Steno. 'Chi sono gli ignavi?', in *L'Alighieri* 30.1 (1989), 3–14.

'Dov'è la "matta bestialitade"? (Ancora sulla struttura aristotelica dell'Inferno)', in *L'Alighieri* nuova serie, 9 (1997), 95–108.

WESTBERG, D. *Right Practical Reason*. Oxford, 1994.

WOODHOUSE, J. R. (ed.). *Dante and Governance*. Oxford, 1997.

Index

Abelard, Peter 29
absolute (*simpliciter*, without qualification) 47, 250
Achilleis 18
Achilles 241–2, 246
active life, *see vita activa*
actus (*in actu* opposed to *in potentia*) 83, 132, 139–40, 143
adaequatio rei et verbi 30, 56
Adam 104, 118–19, 120, 122, 136, 170, 185–6, 208, 212, 214, 259, 265–6
'adolescenza' (Age of Man) 140, 213, 271
Aeneas 19, 145, 222, 234–5, 236, 240, 247–8, 263, 265, 269
  contrasted with Ulysses 237, 263–4, 269
Aeneid 14, 18–19, 68, 144–5, 171, 214, 222, 235–6, 240, 246–7, 263, 269
  dramatis personae of 19, 145; *see also* Aeneas, Sinon, Ulysses
agere et facere (activities of practical intellect) 157
Ages of Man 59, 140–2, 144–5, 243, 252, 271
Ajax 240, 244
Albert, St 21, 79, 140
Alcmaeon 63
allegorisation 27, 63, 98, 145
  of justice as three ladies 212
ambition, proper (Aristotelian moral virtue) 93, 187
Ambrose, St 22–3, 35, 142
amor sui (*amor proprius*) 175, 187
Anchises 14, 145, 251
angels
  inequality of worth and bliss 65
  'neutral' 68
anima (as *forma* of a living being) 82
anima rationalis 131, 138
animal politicum, *see* human beings
'animo' (mind, mental powers) 84, 240
Anselm, St 117
Antepurgatory 70
apostasy (and *superbia*) 182, 259–60
Apostolic Creed 124, 275 n.1
Aquinas, St Thomas 21, 33, 34, 36–7, 51, 70, 79, 90, 95–6, 116, 120, 122, 135, 150–4, 169, 174–5, 185–7, 189, 192, 211, 241, 255, 258
  as character in *Comedy* 257
Arachne 185, 265
'arch-vices' (covetousness and pride) 149, 182
Argonauts 185, 234
Aristotle, Chapter 4 *passim*, 5, 13–16, 27, 30, 41–2, 45, 49, 53, 56, 59, 63, 68, 89, 103–4, 108, 125–6, 132, 134, 137–40, 142–4, 150, 158, 168, 170, 174, 185–6, 191–6, 198–200, 202, 206, 210, 213–14, 219, 233–4, 237, 251, 253, 255, 257
  his analysis of metaphor 4
  as 'the Philosopher' par excellence 28, 38
  Dante's reverence for 78
Arnaut Daniel 21
ars ('craft', *recta ratio factibilium*) 53, 90; *see also prudentia*
Ars amatoria 17
Ars poetica 245
Arthurian romances 129–30
articulus (part of *quaestio*) 33

Astraea 211
astrology 6, 61; *see also* influences
astutia 90, 243, 264
Athens 14, 209
auctoritas, *see* authority
Augustine, St 22–4, 59, 116, 209, 256
author, *see* authority
authority (in scholasticism) 12, 21, 28, 39, 125, 136, 143–4
 Dante's 'authors' Chapter 1 *passim*, 25, 159, 191, 268
auxilium (and divine grace) 120, 266
avaritia 153, 164–5
 compared with *cupiditas* 153
Averroes 79
aversio a Deo 152, 181–2, 190

banquet of learning (in simile) 39, 201
baptism 68, 120, 223–4
beatitude, Hebrew, its form and content 107
Beatitudes, the 70, 108–9, 120
beatitudo (happiness, blessedness) 34, 150, 236, 285 n.16; *see also beatus*, happiness, vision of God, *vita aeterna*
 as eternal vision of God 71, 236
 b. huius vitae 266
 b. inchoata, *imperfecta* 34, 70
 b. perfecta 21, 34, 89, 205, 266
 b. vitae aeternae 205, 266
 verus beatitudinis finis 267
Beatrice 15, 40, 47, 50, 88, 119, 124, 127, 132–3, 163, 182, 216–17, 254, 271
 as 'la gentilissima' 133
beatus 133, 205, 245
 as synonym for *felix* 107, 285 n.16
'bella scola' (of ancient poets) 17, 146, 227
Bernard of Chartres 22
Bernard, St 206–7, 239
Bible 16–17, 21, 23, 40–1, 70, 72, 104, 115, 126, 136, 153–4, 158, 198, 206, 216
 as divinely inspired 20
 read by Dante in Latin 100, 181, 200, 211
Bildungsroman (*Comedy* as) 232
blasphemy 69
blessedness, *see beatitudo*
bliss, *see beatitudo*
Boccaccio 102
Boethius 14–16, 24, 30, 35, 41, 144, 154, 160, 182, 267, 271
Bologna 16, 26, 29
Bonaventure, St 21
Boniface VIII, pope 31, 166, 167, 244
bonum 52, 84, 100, 127, 161, 182, 202–3, 234
 b. arduum 234, 271
 b. commune 202–3, 212, 215
Boyde, Dan 274 n.1
Briareus 185
building blocks (in simile) 26, 29, 36–7

Cacciaguida 145
Caelestis Hierarchia 66
camel (in simile) 101
Can Grande, see *Epistle to Can Grande*
canon law 28, 29, 115–16, 158, 168
Capaneus 183–4, 192, 270–1
Capital Vices (Seven) 61, 70, 149, 151, 153, 161, 168, 174, 182, 189
 as product of 'arch-vices' 153
 their 'children' 153, 161, 176
captatio benevolentiae 246, 261
cardinal virtues 13, 59, 60, 66–7, 142, 192, 234, 246, 253; *see also* virtue
Castel Sant'Angelo 26
Cato of Utica 13, 18, 23
Cavalcante de' Cavalcanti 195
Celestial Paradise 98, 271; *see also* Earthly Paradise
Celestial Rose 205–6
celestial spheres 65, 164, 206
charioteer (in simile) 90
charitas 106, 121, 124, 133–4, 168, 270; *see also* charity
charity (love, as theological virtue) 14, 64, 66, 115, 122, 237
 as ground of moral virtues 122–3
 see also charitas
charm (as Aristotelian moral virtue) 93
choler (in relation to vice) 59, 97
Christ 21, 23, 69, 70, 100, Chapter 5 *passim*, 144, 222–3, 234
 as 'Anointed', the 'Messiah' 100
 as Redeemer 118
 as Son of God 117, 119

his descent into Hell and Resurrection 21
his life as 'substantial form' of church 114
his life as pattern (to be followed) 20, 114
his obedience unto death 114
see also Beatitudes, Commandments, Crucifixion, Day of Judgement, Holy Spirit, Incarnation, Redemption, Sermon on the Mount
Christianity (in medieval Europe) 115
Ciacco 154, 169, 214
Cicero 14–15, 24, 42, 68, 88, 144, 160, 192, 199, 237, 249, 253, 257
Cimabue 189
Circe 231, 237, 246, 247–8, 252, 255
circumscription (Aristotelian preliminary sketch) 25, 79, 87, 199
civil law, *see jus civile*
classification of sins (in *Inferno*)17, 67–9, 157, 237–8
Clement V, pope 166–7
Co-elementationes 62
Columns of Hercules 260
Comedy 1, 3, 4, 7, 11, 15–16, 19, 21, 24, 43, 46, 49, 63, 65, 71, 102, 109, 116, 127, 144–5, Chapters 7–10 *passim*, 151, 156, 159, 216–17
as a 'road-movie' 232
as a *Bildungsroman* 232
as counterpart to Virgil's 'tragedìa' 19
Commandment, Great 105
commandments (*mandata, praecepta*) 20, 266
Commandments, Ten (*Decalogum*) 62, 102, 104, 110
majority in negative form 103
'distilled' in two only 105
commentary (importance in medieval education) 16, 27, 79
Convivio as 39
common good, *see bonum commune*
Confessiones 23, 24
Consolatio Philosophiae 15–16, 160, 267
Constantine 222
consuetudo (in relation to vice) 95–6
contemplative life, *see vita contemplativa*
contemptus (and *superbia*) 182; *see also despectus*
context (role in interpretation), Introduction *passim*, 78
of scholasticsm for Dante's works 3, 25–6, 250
in proportional comparisons 4
contradiction (law of non-c. in medieval logic) 31
contraries, the four, influence on character 59
convalescence (in simile) 177, 188
conversio ad Deum 152–3, 182, 189, 235–6; *see also aversio a Deo*
Convivio 5, 14–15, 24, 33, 38–9, 40, 46, 77–9, 81, 85–7, 89, 93–4, 97–9, 126, 134, 140–4, 146, 158–9, 192–3, 198, 201, 208, 213, 233, 243–4, 252–4, 257–8
'cor gentile' 127, 131; *see also* 'gentilezza'
Corpus juris civilis 16, 17, 29, 32, 59, 200, 208
Correlationes 62
cosmography (as modified in *Comedy*) 265
counsel (in relation to *prudentia*) 243–4, 252
courage (as Aristotelian moral virtue) 93, 268; *see also* cardinal virtues, 'magnanimitade'
court-room (in simile) 28, 270
covetousness, Chapter 7 *passim*, 271
modern synonyms 153
as *radix omnium malorum* 149; *see also cupiditas*
craft, *see ars*
Crassus 156
creation, direct, of individual human soul by God (consequences in Dante's thought) 5, 138, 193, 238
Crucifixion 124, 217, 235, 266
'cupidigia', *see cupiditas*
cupiditas 153, 162, 165, 167–8, 198, 215; *see also* covetousness
compared with *avaritia* 154
contrasted with *charitas* 168
opposed to *justitia* 168
c. scientiae 257
Cur Deus homo? 117
curiositas
philosophical critique 257–8
theological critique 255–6

curiosus 249, 258
custom (as becoming second nature) 95; *see also consuetudo*, *habitus*, *mos*
cutlery (in sustained simile) 79–81

Dante Alighieri
  as author, distinct from protagonist 11, 216, 220, 223, 263
  as protagonist, distinct from author 7, 179–80, 186, 195, 216, 219
   influences on characterisation 21, 146
  as victim of injustice 200–2
  as *vir praedicans justitiam* 201
  his affinity with Ulysses 271
  his exile 130, 155, 179, 200–1, 211
  his participation in politics 130
  his political thought 166, 202
  his vices 130, 174, 279 n.6, 291 n.2
  see also Comedy, *Convivio*, *De vulgari eloquentia*, *Epistle to Can Grande*, *Monarchia*, *Vita nuova*
Dante da Maiano 129
Darwin 6
David 20, 175–6
Day of Judgement, *see* Last Judgement
De amicitia 15, 88
De bello civili 18, 144
De civitate Dei 23
De doctrina christiana 23
De finibus bonorum et malorum 249
de jure, *see jus*
De officiis 68, 199
De senectute 253
Deadly Sins, Seven 61, 151; *see also* Capital Vices
Decretale 29, 32
definitions (importance in scholasticism) 42, 136; *see also* distinctions
Deidamia 241–2
deliberation (and free choice) 90, 208; *see also* counsel, freedom
Democritus 13
demonstration (logical proof) 32, 40, 42–3, 220, 222; *see also* persuasion
despectus ('dispitto') 179, 193
dialectic (contrasted with logic), 32, 42; *see also* persuasion
Didymus ('comma' of) 73
differentia 80–2, 84, 88
Digest 16–17, 28–9, 202, 209
digression (as recurrent feature of medieval commentary) 27, 39, 44–5, 143
Dionysius the Areopagite 35, 51, 66
'dirittura' ('drittura'), *see* righteousness
disobedience 186, 259
dispositio 91, 94, 98, 139, 150
  d. inordinata 151
disputation (in scholasticism) 29, 34–7
distinctions (importance in scholasticism) 32, 257
  between 'absolute' and 'qualified' meanings 32, 41, 47, 158, 234, 250–1; *see also secundum quid*
  between knowledge and appetite for the truth 255
  between fraud and violence 237
Divine Comedy, *see Comedy*
division (in scholastic thought) 50–2, 69, 190, 237
  and numeration 157
   in the *Comedy* 63, 64, 71–3
   in the *Inferno* 67–9
   in the *Paradiso* 65–7
   in the *Purgatory* 69–70
  and sub-division 51–2, 68–9, 237; *see also* tree
  attractions and dangers 56, 157
DNA 6
documenta
  philosophica 78, 167
  spiritualia 78, 115, 167
'Doglia mi reca ne lo core ardire' (canzone by Dante) 155
'dolce stil novo' 132–3
Dominic, St 21
'Donna gentile' (as image of philosophy) 40, 98, 134
Donne, John 7
doubt, *see* 'dubbio'
'drittura', *see* 'dirittura'
dualisms (of popular religion) 63
'dubbio' (*dubitatio*, perplexity leading to inquiry), 43–7, 205–6, 216, 218–19, 222, 270

as 'efficient' cause of reasoning 44
dwarf (in simile) 22, 32

eagle (as symbol of Roman Empire) 218
Eagle (of Justice, in Heaven of Jupiter) 218–22, 259
Earthly Paradise (Eden) 52, 70, 78, 98, 170, 185, 212, 259, 266, 271
figura of earthly happiness 70; *see also beatitudo*
'eccellenza' (pre-eminence) 189–91
Ecclesiasticus 181, 258
Eden, *see* Earthly Paradise
Einstein, Albert 57
embryology 5–6, 138, 193
Emperor (in relation to Pope) 41, 167; *see also monarcha*
Empyrean 63, 65–6, 71, 97, 217
envy, *see invidia*
Ephialtes 184
Epicurus 13–14
epistemology (Aristotelian) 254; *see also* sense-experience
Epistle to Can Grande 63, 204, 235
equator (of two hemispheres, in simile) 77
equity (in relation to justice) 209
Esau (and Jacob) 139, 207
esse (existence, as primary good) 83
ethics 68, 79, 86–9, 99, 137, 140, 142, 192, 198, 214, 251, 255
as a practical science 111
deals with choices leading to action 87
in relation to the natural sciences 5–6
modern and medieval approaches to 3, 6
richness of Dante's system, 6–7
uncertainty of subject matter v, 56, 79, 208; *see also* moral virtue, 'operazioni umane', vice, worth
Ethics (work by Aristotle)
its contents and character 78–9, 87,
dominated by *finis*, *principium* and *media* 233; *see also* Aristotle
ethos (trait of character) 95
Etymologiae 185, 199
etymology (and word-play) 155
Euclid 32, 40, 42–3, 234
exile, *see* Dante (his exile)
in Florentine politics 195–6
as *figura* of post-lapsarian existence 233
Exodus (of Israelites, as *figura* of deliverance) 235
experience
and practical wisdom 90
and sensation, *see* sense-experience
expiation (by blood sacrifice) 117
eyes (as 'windows of the soul') 40

Faith (as gift of God) 121, 220, 223; *see also* theological virtues
Fall (of Adam and Eve) 23, 119–120, 122, 153, 170, 185–6, 212, 214–15, 238, 244, 259, 265–6, 271; *see also* disobedience, Redemption, *superbia*
false friends (among medieval and modern terms) 7, 34
fama 34; *see also* vainglory
Farinata (degli Uberti) 179–80, 187, 191
his *magnanimitas* 194–6
'fatale andare' (Dante's God-willed journey) 236, 265
felicitas 202; *see also beatitudo*, happiness
feudalism 68, 128, 178
Fibonacci sequence 57
fides quaerens intellectum 117, 216
final goal (of human life) 8, 33, 78, 150, 152, 267, 271; *see also finis*, 'primo bene', vision of God
finis 44, 81–3, 85–6, 185; *see also forma*
Finnegans Wake 155
First Philosophy, *see* metaphysics
Florence 5, 197, 209; *see also* Dante (his exile), Farinata
'follia' (reckless presumption, of Adam, Dante and Ulysses) 264–5
forgiveness 106, 114, 119; *see also* Beatitudes
of sins, by Christ 117
forma (structure, essence) 44, 80–2, 86, 132, 185
in relation to *finis* 80
Fortune 172
Francis, St 21, 31, 169
Franco Bolognese 188
frankness (as Aristotelian moral virtue) 93

fraud
as sin of Ulysses 237
its two main species 68
sub-species of simple fraud 69; *see also* *astutia*, Guido da Montefeltro
freedom (of human will and actions) 96–8, 235
as greatest under Emperor 217
friendship (as Aristotelian value) 88
frui (contrasted with *uti*) 151

Gaeta (in relation to Ulysses) 231, 236, 247–8
Galileo 39
Garden of Eden, *see* Earthly Paradise
generatio (self-reproduction, as primary good) 83–4
generosity (as Aristotelian moral virtue) 93, 155
Genesis 6
'gentile' (noble) 127
applied to feudal upper class 127–8, 130, 136, 176–80
implying aspiration to refinement 128; *see also* 'gentilezza'
'gentilezza' (nobility of heart) 77, Chapter 6 *passim*, 213, 271
and 'amore' 131
and Aristotelian ethics 137
and *charitas* 132
and *magnanimitas* 193
as more comprehensive term than virtue 137
as 'seed of happiness' 138–9
Dante's full definition 139
in courtly literature 129
its essence 132
its 'signs' 139–42, 253; *see also* Ages of Man
its source 138
Ghibellines 130, 179, 244; *see also* Guelphs
giants (and *superbia*) 184
Giotto 189
'gioventute' (Age of Man) 140, 144, 213
gloria 34
glory 33–6, 188–9; *see also* vainglory
God
as 'Emperor' 215
as all goodness (*omne bonum*) 105
as Love 105
as the highest good (*summum bonum*) 122, 124–5, 221
as the primal good ('primo bene') 151, 159, 163, 191
as Three Persons 58, 71–2; *see also* Christ, Holy Spirit
Golden Age 169, 211
Golden Chain of Being 186
golden section 57
good (*bonum*)
as primary and secondary 83
as always specific 84; *see also* goodness, happiness
as arousing love 124
supreme, *see* God
good temper (*eutrapelia*, as Aristotelian moral virtue) 93
goodness, human
as state of character (*ethos*) 91
resides in voluntary power, 91; *see also* moral virtue
grace 37, 44,115, 122, 133, 139, 163, 206–7, 223, 235–6, 265–6, 271; *see also* *gratia*, Holy Spirit, infusion
as divine 'help', *see* *auxilium*
virtues infused by 120–1; *see also* theological virtues
grammatica (any artificial language, Latin) 2, 6
gratia (root meaning) 120; *see also* grace
Gratian 29
gravitas (in relation to *magnanimitas*) 194
Greek culture and language 2, 12; *see also* Aristotle, Homer
Gregory the Great, St 70, 102, 116, 182, 191
Guelphs 130, 180, 196; *see also* Ghibellines
guides (metaphorical) 11, 233
Guido da Montefeltro 31, 244, 254
Guinizzelli, Guido 21, 131–2
gula (gluttony, as Capital Vice) 169

habitus (settled disposition in the will, conferring inclination to action) 91–2, 94–8, 143, 149, 151, 170, 199, 202
as 'acquired' (by repetition) 96

as like a 'second nature', *de difficili mobilis* 95–6
h. operativus (in definition of vice and virtue) 149–50
Hadrian V, pope 165
happiness 79, 85, 202, 212; *see also beatitudo*
and moral goodness 91
and pursuit of knowledge 89, 250
and society 202
as supreme good 33
for Aristotle 14, 79, 88–9, 99,137
for Boethius 16
for Cicero 42
perfect 33, 40, 65, 89, 97, 99, 107–08, 124, 151, 236, 266–7
two distinct happinesses (for Dante) 88–9; *see also* Celestial Paradise, Earthly Paradise
Hartley, L. P. 2
hemispheres (in simile), *see* equator
Hercules 260
Hereford Map 260
heresy 68
Heroides 251
heterogeneity (of Dante's authors and values), Chapter 1 *passim*, 68
hierarchy 66, 123, 205
history (Jewish conception of) 19, 104, 235
Holy Spirit 20, 60, 71, 122, 150, 165, 205; *see also* grace, infusion, theological virtues
Homer 12, 17, 22, 145, 231, 235, 245–6, 249, 275 n.4
honour 33, 128, 181, 188–9, 196
desire for (as Aristotelian virtue) 93, 187, 192
hope 124; *see also* theological virtues
Horace 17, 18, 61, 145, 154, 245, 249
human beings
as 'rational animals' 85
as gregarious, 'companionable' animals 88, 93, 202
as 'political' animals 85, 88, 202, 210, 213, 251
as 'unstable' animals 2
in personal relationship with God 103–4, 118, 124
their 'confused' awareness of a supreme good 267
humilitas (as virtue opposed to *superbia*) 178, 185, 270
three examples of 175–6
Hyde, Mr (Ulysses as) 239, 272

Icarus 185
Iliad 231, 245
In exitu Israel de Aegypto (Psalm 113, allegorically interpreted) 235
inanis gloria, *see vanagloria*
Incarnation 119, 150, 235, 267; *see also* Christ
inclinatio (of the appetites and will) 91, 199, 239
inequality 203
of all parts of creation 161
of bliss 206–7
of human endowments 66
of natural and divine gifts received at birth 139
Inferno 7, 11, 17, 18, 31, 53, 68, Chapters 7, 8, 10 *passim*
influences, presumed, of planets and stars 61, 66, 91, 94, 97, 127, 139, 238
infundere 121; *see also* infusion
infusion (of theological virtues) 121, 150, 223, 266; *see also redundare*
ingenium ('ingegno', innate power of mind) 238, 240–1, 262
inordinatus 150–3, 161, 171, 186–7, 256–8, 270
inquisitio 43
insatiability (of desire for created goods) 159–60
Institutes (of Justinian) 16–17, 28; *see also Corpus juris civilis*
intellect
practical, contrasted with speculative 67, 85, 88, 257
speculative, seeks truth for its own sake 89, 254
intellection (immediate understanding, contrasted with ratiocination) 8, 41, 44
intellectual virtues 87; *see also ars, prudentia*
intellectus practicus and *speculativus* 85, 88

inversion (of expectations in Heaven) 110, 112, 222
invidia 161, 168, 191
Iphigenia 241, 252
irony (and *magnanimitas*) 193, 195
Isaiah 20
Isidore, St 185, 199
Ithaca 231, 235, 247

Jeremiah 20
Jerome, St 22–3, 100, 153
Jesus, *see* Christ
Jews (their history and sense of history) 19, 103–4, 235; *see also* Moses
Joachim of Fiore 58
Job 20, 107–8
John, St 105, 123–5, 165
John XXII, pope 169
journey
  of Dante and Ulysses 11, Chapter 10 *passim*
  etymology 233
  opposed to 'wandering' 233
  providential, of whole people 235
  symbolic meanings of, in Middle Ages 43, 232–4
Joyce, James 155
judicium Dei 216, 219, 221, 223, 270; *see also* justice
Julius Caesar 18, 57, 218
Jupiter (classical deity) 183, 211–12, 235–6, 270, 272
  as poetic name for Christian God 184, 260, 264
Jupiter (the planet) 217
jurisprudence v, 28, 213, 223–4
jus 200, 203
  ipsum jus (absolute, God-given standard) 221
  civile 28–9, 168
  gentium 211–13
  in rebus 221
  positivum (local laws) 211–13
  see also justice
justice 143, Chapter 9 *passim*
  and absence of passion 200
  and commensuration 205, 206
  and 'fittingness' 207
  and *judicium Dei* (*q.v.*) 204
  and judge on the bench 204
  and mercy 216
  and prayer 216
  and rulers ('Love j.') 315, 217; *see also* Solomon
  and Trajan 175
  apparent injustice of God 216, 219
  as 'consonance' with God's will (despite appearances) 216, 219, 221–2, 267
  as 'most human' virtue 200
  as Aristotelian moral virtue 213
  as concerned with reward and punishment 203–5
  as directed towards others 202, 213, 215
  as equity, not equality 203–4
  as giving what is due 203
  as moral virtue *tout court* 94
  as most illustrious virtue 198
  as supreme good of a community 202
  as triple emanation from God 212
  as virtue proper to Third Age 213
  consists in ordered relationships 117–18
  differences from other virtues 200, 202
  embraces all virtues 198, 214
  infallibility of God's j. 215
  loved even by its enemies 198
  metaphorically applied to the self 214
  natural, *see* natural law
justification (in theology, 'setting to rights') 120, 214, 265
Justinian 16, 20, 28, 29, 200, 202, 206, 215
justitia 7
  and *judicium* 215
  as 'righteousness' 200, 211, 214
  etymology 199
  see also 'dirittura', *jus*, justice
Juvenal 18

knowledge of good and evil 11; *see also* tree

ladder and rungs (in simile) 64
Laelius 15
language-learning 2–3
'larghezza' (as Aristotelian moral virtue), *see* generosity

Last Judgement 7, 20, 23, 31, 110, 120, 124, 171, 222
law
  and civilisation 209
  and common good 208
  and right reason 208
  as 'intellect without appetite' 213
  as 'ragione scritta' 17, 208
  as order 213
  Dante's reverence for 208
  of the nations 211
  see also *lex*, Roman law
law-court (in simile) 12, 28
'Le dolci rime d'amor' (canzone by Dante) 134–7, 139, 140–1, 193
legis latio et executio 17, 208, 209, 215
lex 208
  divina 20, 103, 208
  naturalis 103, 210, 212
Liberal Arts, Seven 23, 40, 52, 60
liberum arbitrium 97, 204; *see also* freedom
Limbo 14, 15, 19, 68, 89, 194, 267
liveliness (as Aristotelian moral virtue) 93
locomotio
  and journey (as paradigm for 'operazioni umane') 233
  as highest power of animal soul 84
logic 30, 42, 131, 167, 190, 220, 224, 257
  and dialectic 32
  'sins' against 41–2, 135
  as instrument to philosophise 31
  as reasoning (drawing valid inferences) 30
  prestige and role in medieval education 30
  underlying assumptions 30
  see also syllogism
logician (devil as) 32
Lombard, Peter 29
Lord's Prayer 60, 177, 183
love (and goodness) 124; *see also* charity, God
Lucan 17, 18, 144, 146
Lucifer 183–5, 265
Lucy, St 163
Luke, St 20
luxuria (lechery, as Capital Vice) 169
Macareus 247
Macrobius 12
'magnanimitade' (greatness of soul)
  as Aristotelian moral virtue 94, 142–3, 187, 192–4
  etymology 192
  in relation to Farinata 192–7
  in relation to Ulysses 268
  multivalency 192
magnanimus ('great-souled' man), characterised by Aristotle 192–4
malum 84, 191; *see also* *bonum*, sin, vice
Manes 24
Manzoni, Alessandro 196
mappa mundi 260
Marco Lombardo 96, 98
Mardocheus 214
Marlowe, Christopher 30
Marsyas 185
martyr ('witness' to the faith) 22, 111
marvel ('maraviglia'), *see* wonder
Mary, *see* Virgin Mary
materia 80, 132
Matthew 20, 100, 105, 108, 285 n.3
mean, doctrine of, in Aristotelian ethics 91–3, 137, 170, 186, 202; *see also* 'not too little'
means (in relation to ends) 90, 233; *see also* deliberation, *finis*, *principium*
merces, *see* reward
mercy (and justice) 119
'merito' ('proprio' and 'altrui') 206; *see also* justice
Messiah *see* Christ
Metamorphoses 17, 18, 144, 236, 240, 246–8, 261
metaphor
  as compressed comparison 4
  decoded by Dante 98
  for 'dubbio' 46, 48
  for giving of grace 121
  for Heaven and Hell 109
  for original sin and consequences 118
  for redemption 120
  of eagle's flight 218
  of eye of a needle 175
  of falcon and lure 164

metaphor (*cont.*)
of journey of human life 11, 159
of kissing 200
of law among animals 210
of Love as a sleeping lord 131
of moral health and diseases 149
of monuments 25, 28
of oars and wings 4, 264
of reins and spurs 145
of rungs on ladder 186
of smiling pages 189
of slavery to sin 118
of soul as bride 140
of sparks of vice 154
of straight and crooked 62; *see also* dualisms
of storm on entry to port 253
of swamping and drowning 162, 166
of whore 162
of withered fruit 162
metaphysics 5, 38, 40, 56
metre (of the *Comedy*) 71–2
Midas 156, 172
Milton, John 186
Minos 204
miser 156; *see also avaritia*, 'Doglia mi reca'
monarcha 17, 215, 217–18
Monarchia 12, 14, 21, 41–2, 44, 46, 78, 114, 144, 166–8, 202–3, 215, 217–21, 251
money (medieval perceptions of) 156
Montagues (and Capulets) 181
monuments, architectural and written 25, 28
moral virtue 87, 90, 92–4
acquisition of 94
as a disposition of the will 91, 95; *see also habitus*
as fruit of the seed of 'gentilezza' 134, 137, 140
as *habitus operativus* 91, 149
as human goodness 91; *see also* morality, 'operazioni umane'
as *recta habitudo animae* 177
cardinal ('pivotal'), *see* cardinal virtues
compared to health and beauty 95, 150
defined and divided by Aristotle 91–4, 137; *see also* mean
defined by Aquinas 122–3
distinguished from *ars* 90; *see also agere*
distinguished from virtues of intellect 37, 90–1; *see also intellectus*, *prudentia*
theological, *see* theological virtues
see also cardinal virtues, *dispositio*, 'gentilezza', *habitus*, theological virtues, vice
moralis (derived from *mos/moris*) 96
morality (as 'beauty of philosophy') 99; *see also* ethics, 'operazioni umane', vice, virtue, worth
mortar (in simile) 26, 36
mos (natural disposition or custom) 96; *see also ethos*
Mosaic Law 102, 105, 114, 207; *see also* Commandments
as fulfilled by Christ 102
Moses 20, 103–4, 116, 125, 235, 265
motion, rectilinear 233
motus localis, *see locomotio*
munificence (as Aristotelian moral virtue) 93, 142–3
musical theory, medieval, proportion in 57; *see also* Didymus, metre
myths, classical (Dante's attitude to) 18, 184, 260

Napoleon 196
natura
etymology of 179
scholastic axioms concerning 82
secundum naturam 157
Natura universalis, *see* universal nature
natural justice, *see* natural law
natural law 103, 210–12
its fundamental precept 103
see also justice
nature (contrasted with 'nurture') 91; *see also* embryology, influences, *natura*
Nero 18
New Testament 35, Chapter 5 *passim*
Nicaea (Council of) 23
Nicholas III, pope 166–7
Nicomachean Ethics, *see Ethics*
Nimrod 184–5
Niobe 184–5
'nobiltà di sangue' 130, 177, 193; *see also* 'gentilezza'

and Ovid's Ulysses 241
noble heart, *see* 'cor gentile'
non sequitur 30
'not too little and not too much' 82, 84, 91–2, 137, 170, 255; *see also* mean
notitia 34, 36
numbers (as 'elements of all things') 62
numeration, 57–62 *see also* division
nutrimentum 83–4

obedience 104, 114, 118, 142–3, 213
Oderisi da Gubbio 187–90
Odysseus, *see* Ulysses
Odyssey 231, 235–6, 245, 247, 249, 261
Oedipus 18
ogival arch (in image) 50
Old Testament 21, 35, 70, 102–4, 107, 116, 220, 235, 237; *see also* Bible, Exodus, Jews, New Testament
Omberto degli Aldobrandeschi 178–9, 183, 187–8
operatio 81–3, 121, 199, 206, 215–16
  and happiness 137
  ordinata 150
  propria 83–5, 137, 210
'operazioni umane' 81, 89, 111, 123, 144, 206, 208, 213, 233, 243, 252–4
  as subject to reason and will 87
order, Chapter 3 *passim*
  among all things in universe 8, 46, 51, 186, 205, 212
  among powers of the soul 214
  and form 51
  in system of Purgatory 98
    see also inordinatus, justice, tree
Ordinamenti di Giustizia 130
original sin 118, 120, 122, 186, 208, 212; *see also* Adam, Fall, grace
Orpheus 234
Ottimo commento 241–2
Ovid 17–18, 40, 144–5, 192, 212, 236, 240–3, 247–8, 251–2
Oxford 26

pact (God's, with Israelites) 103–4
pagans, virtuous, divine judgement of 218–24
Palladium 240–2
Pantheon (building in Rome) 26
parables (Christ's)
  character and history of 111
  inculcating need for virtuous action 111, 113
  of Good Samaritan 112–13, 116
Paradiso 8, 29, 33, 50–1, 66, 217–24, 257–8
Paris 12, 21, 26–8, 31, 59, 188
pars construens et destruens 135, 137, 143; *see also* scholasticism
pathos (transient emotion, contrasted with *ethos*) 95
patria 179–80, 251
  in p. contrasted with *in via* 233
Paul, St 18, 20–3, 35–6, 59, 115, 120–1, 125, 144, 153, 168, 234, 257
Pavia 2
peccatum 118, 150–2; *see also* sin
penalty, just, payment of 118–20
Penelope 250–1
perfect numbers 57
perfectio (maturity, fullness of being) 83
perfection (moral) 101–2, 106–7, 110
Peripatetics 14
perplexity, *see* 'dubbio'
persuasion (contrasted with demonstration) 41, 220, 222
Peter Lombard 124
Peter, St 18, 20–1, 31, 100, 123, 165–6
Petrus Hispanus (Peter of Spain, logician and pope) 31
Phaethon 184, 192, 270
Pharisees 102, 114–15, 117
philomythy (paired with philosophy) 132, 159, 184; *see also* metaphor, myth
philosopher (importance of etymology for Dante) 3, 41
philosophy, Chapters 2 and 4 *passim*; *see also* Aquinas, Aristotle, Boethius, Cicero, *documenta*, scholasticism
  as aid to faith 220
Piccarda de' Donati 47, 123–4, 205–6
'pie in the sky' 110
pietas 251
pilgrimage (in relation to Dante's journey) 232
Plato 13, 16, 22, 41, 219
plenitudo temporis 267, 270

politia (*recta* and *obliqua*) 210; *see also* justice, law
Politics (work by Aristotle) 202
polytheism 22, 104, 106
populus romanus (their mission and special gifts) 14, 19, 221, 235, 242; *see also* Aeneas, *Monarchia*
possessions (as 'tools' for living well) 92
potentia (contrasted with *actus*) 80–3, 86, 132, 139, 143
potentiae (faculties of the soul) 189, 271
poverty, evangelical 169
predestination 224
presumption 187
pride, Chapter 8 *passim*
  as *initium omnis peccati* 149, 182
  in art 188–9
  see also superbia, *vanagloria*
'primo bene', *see* God
primum mobile 50, 65
principium
  'beginning' and 'principle' 233
  in ethics, constituted by the *finis* 78, 234; *see also* deliberation
prodigality (as vice, collateral with avarice) 171
proof, *see* demonstration
property, private (as 'tool' for 'living well') 170
prophets (as forerunners of Christ) 117
proportional relationships 4, 6
Providence 53, 82
prudentia (virtue of the practical intellect) 90, 112, 213
  defined as *recta ratio agibilium* 90
  determines the means not the end 90
  leads to good counsels 243; *see also* Solomon
Ptolemy 234
Purgatorio 18, 52, 96–7, 174–8, 181, 271; *see also* Beatitudes
Purgatory 156
  its geographical co-ordinates in the *Comedy* 235, 265–6
  as 'reformatory' 97
  as site of Earthly Paradise 266
pusillanimitas 188, 195
puzzlement, *see* 'dubbio'
Pythagoreans 62–3, 73

Quadrivium 60
quaestio (vehicle of scholastic thought) 25, 33–5, 37, 43, 45–6, 135, 137, 192, 205, 207, 216, 219, 241–2, 255–6, 270
quest for knowledge 25, 49; *see also* 'dubbio'

ramification (of concepts) 51–5
ratio 39, 85, 103, 131, 135, 220; *see also* intellect, intellection, ratiocination, reason
  r. recta 208
  secundum rationem 85–6, 210
ratiocination (as laborious process) 43, 46
Ravenna 15
reclamation of materials (in simile)
Redemption 115, 118–9, 223–4, 235, 265–7
redundare (image of grace in soul) 122
regnum caelorum 101, 109–10, 120–3; *see also vita aeterna*
Remedium amoris 17
respondeo (section of a *quaestio*, *q.v.*) 36, 205, 207, 219–20, 270
Resurrection 124; *see also* Christ
retaliation (opposed to forgiveness) 106, 108
reward (proportionate to use made of talents) 66, 123; *see also* 'merito'
rhetoric, art of (Dante's attitude to) 262
Rhipeus 222–4, 267
riches 136, 154
righteousness 211, 214, 223–4, 236, 251; *see also jus*, *justitia*
'rime aspre' (matching subject matter)173
river, both deep and shallow (in simile) 102
Robert of Lisle 52
Roman de la rose 69
Roman law 16–17, 28, 59, 69, 107, 140, 142, 199, 200, 203
Rome 25–6
Romeo and Juliet 181
Salvation 102, 204, 207, 223–4, 234, 265
satisfaction (in theory of justice) 118–19, 152, 267
Scala Naturae 186

scholasticism 3, 5, 26–7, 40, 42, 50, 136, 157, 190, 220, 224, 237
and logic 30
as syncretist and systematic 12
assumptions challenged in Dante's lifetime 272
attractions and dangers 52–3
etymology (*schola*) 26
its ethics contrasted with modern ethics 3
its pervasive influence on Dante 3, 7, 38
its rigour and clarity 67
see also Aquinas, definitions, distinctions, 'dubbio', logic, *quaestio*
scientia (certain knowledge) 5, 38, 255
as dearer than one's native land 249–51
contrasted with modern 'science' 5
human pursuit of 89
perfecta 56
s. est universalium 88
Scipio Africanus 15
Scriptures (*Scripturae*)
allegorical interpretation of 23
as 'writings' par excellence 20
see also Bible
seafaring (in extended images) 252–4, 257–8
'secondi beni' 159, 163, 191; *see also* 'primo bene'
secundum naturam 157
secundum quid (in a qualified sense) 32, 41, 47, 158, 191, 250; *see also* distinctions, *simpliciter*
sed contra (section of a *quaestio*, *q.v.*) 35, 207, 271
self-control (*temperantia*, as Aristotelian moral virtue) 93
Semiramis 216
Seneca 192
'senettute' (Age of Man) 140, 213, 243, 252
'senio' (Age of Man) 140, 243, 252, 254
signs of 'gentilezza' in 252, 253
sense-experience
as source of *scientia* 11, 44, 254
contrasted with *scientia* 255
sensus moralis 236
sententia (verdict, pithy excerpt) 28
Sententiae (compilation by Peter Lombard) 29, 32, 124
Sermon on the Mount 70, 106, 110, 116, 177
seven (as symbolic number) 60
Shakespeare, William 186, 250
shame (as a 'laudable passion') 138
Sic et non (compilation by Abelard) 29
Simon Magus 165
simony 69, 165–6, 237
simpliciter (without qualification, *absolute*) 41, 47; *see also secundum quid*
sin
and charity 237
as 'offence against God' 152
defined by Aquinas 150
distinguished from vice 151
in Trojan War 245
mortal 151–2, 181–2, 244
venial (pardonable) 151–2, 182
see also Capital Vices, *malum*, 'operazioni umane', vice
Sinon 19, 240
Siren(s) 162–3, 172, 174, 246, 249
smile ('coruscation of the soul's delight') 40; *see also* persuasion
Solomon 20, 144, 197, 213, 215
and 'kingly prudence' 257
Sordello 181, 187
soul, *see anima*
'sovrasensi' ('higher meanings') 39, 235–6
spheres (celestial, in medieval universe) 39–40; *see also* influences
Statius 18, 19, 97, 144, 171, 183, 192
Stoicism 13–14, 16, 18, 59, 67, 142, 192, 196, 246; *see also* Cato
studiositas (opposed to *curiositas*) 256
studium (zeal) 255
suicide 69, 214
Summa contra gentiles 135
Summa Theologiae 34–6, 46, 49, 51, 116, 120, 182, 192, 205, 241, 255–7
structure of 52–3
subjects treated in second part 33, 37
Summulae logicales 31
summum bonum 150; *see also* God, happiness
superbia, Chapter 8 *passim*, 185, 270
and *amor proprius* 175
and Lucifer 183

superbia (*cont.*)
as apostasy (defiance of God) 182–3, 259
as 'arch-vice' 174
as 'beginning of all sin' 181–2, 187
as going beyond the mark 186, 260
as sense of superiority 177–8
etymology as guide to meaning 175, 185
in pursuit of knowledge 256, 258–9
its species ('children') 187, 189
the *superbus* characterised 190
see also magnanimitas, pride, *vanagloria*
suum cuique (tradere) 94, 203
swallow (in simile) 91
Swift, Jonathan 149, 152
syllogism 30, 32, 34, 39, 124, 157, 221, 261
faults ('sins') in 41–2
see also logic, demonstration, scholasticism
syncretism (as tendency of scholasticism, *q.v.*) 12, 64, 184, 191, 199, 237, 272
synthesis (desire for in scholasticism, *q.v.*) 64, 67, 70, 77; *see also* order
system-building (in medieval thought) 32, 37

Terence 3
'terza rima', *see* metre
Thebaid 18, 144, 183
theological virtues 59, 66, 98, 115, 120–3, 223; *see also* charity, faith, hope, infusion, Holy Spirit, moral virtue
Theseus 234
Trajan 175, 183, 215, 222
translation (Dante's confidence in) 2
'Tre donne intorno al cor mi son venute' (canzone by Dante) 201, 211
treachery 64, 68
tree
and leaves (in images) 50–1, 53, 65, 71, 140, 186; *see also* ramification, division
'of the knowledge of good and evil' (Genesis) v, 52, 104, 118, 259
Trees of the Vices and Virtues 52, 54–5 (Figures 1 and 2)
Trivium 60
Troy 12, 19, 231, 235, 240–1, 246, 252, 263, 266
tunnel-boring (in simile) 78

Ulysses 4, 11, 163, 186, 191, Chapter 10 *passim*
a circumscription of his voyages 4, 231
a summing up of his worth and vices 270–1
age at time of final voyage 252
and Aeneas 237, 263–4, 269
and Dante the protagonist 238–9
and Diomedes 240–2
and Guido da Montefeltro 244, 254
as 'Ithacorum dux' 257
as 'pattern of wisdom and virtue' 245–6, 249, 251
as 'perduto' 246, 253, 272
as traveller seeking knowledge 249
his 'ardore' as 'concreated thirst' for supreme good 268
his 'folle volo' (and 'varco folle') 232, 237, 264; *see also* 'fatale andare'
his conscious command of rhetoric 240–1, 261–2
his *superbia* as 'apostasy' 260
his use of subterfuge 240–2, 244
his vice of *astutia* 243
his vice of *curiositas* 256
his virtues of courage and self-control 246, 248
in Homer 231, 261
in Horace 245–6
in Latin literature, 239–41, 245–9
in Ovid 240, 246–8
in Virgil 240
the last voyage and Dante's journey 232, 235–6, 262
the last voyage as downward 'Fall' 260
the last voyage as quest for happiness 266
within the 'horned flame' 238, 246, 248
universal nature 53, 82
universities 26
usury 69, 157
usus 81; *see also operatio*
uti/*usus* (contrasted with *frui*) 151

vainglory 174, 188–9; *see also* pride, *superbia*
'valore' 105, 126–7, 135
as name of God 127

value judgements (in Aristotelian ethics) 81, 83–4, 88–9
vanagloria, *see* vainglory
Vanni Fucci 183, 271
Vestibule (area in Dante's Hell) 67; *see also* Antepurgatory
'via naturale' (ethics and empiricism) 77, Chapter 4 *passim*
'via teologica' (ethics and revelation) 77, Chapter 5 *passim*
vice (*see also* sin, *malum*, virtue)
  a circumscription 150
  as customary, ingrained 95, 97
  as *habitus operativus* 149
  as innate 95, 99
  as opposite of virtue 150
  contrasted with sin 151, 170
vices 92 (*see also* Capital Vices)
  collateral 92, 170, 192, 194, 195
  dispositions that Heaven does not want 92
  moral 'diseases' 103
videtur quod (section of a *quaestio*, *q.v.*) 34, 135, 205–6, 219, 272
'vile' (base-born)136, 139, 158; *see also* 'gentile'
'viltate' (baseness) of possessions 158
Virgil 14, 17–19, 40, 53, 68, 98, 144–5, 161, 163–4, 171–2, 175, 177, 183, 191, 211, 219, 222–3, 235, 239–40, 251, 267, 269
Virgin Mary 70, 119, 163, 176, 239, 267
virtue
  as acquired 122, 234
  as infused by God 120–2, 234
  see also cardinal virtues, moral virtue, theological virtues
virtuous pagans, fate of 267
virtus (faculty or property) 81, 86–7
vis concupiscibilis 122
vis irascibilis 122; *see also bonum arduum*
vis motiva (in ratiocination) 43; *see also* 'dubbio'
vis ultima (highest power of soul) 83, 86
vision of God 44, 64, 224, 236, 266–7; *see also* God, happiness, *vita aeterna*
vita activa 14, 66–7, 89; *see also* 'operazioni umane', virtue
vita aeterna 109, 120, 150, 266; *see also regnum caelorum*
vita contemplativa 66–7, 89
Vita nuova 3, 15–17, 24, 39, 124, 132, 140, 144
vitia capitalia, see Capital Vices
'vizi consuetudinarii' 95; *see also* vice
voluntas 85, 98, 200
vulgare (natural or spoken language) 2, 6; *see also De vulgari eloquentia*, *grammatica*
Vulgate (Latin Bible), *see* Bible, Jerome

wolf (as symbol of covetousness) 160, 172, 174
wonder (at new phenomenon as stimulus to inquiry) 45–6, 222; *see also* 'dubbio'
Wooden Horse 240, 242, 252
works, good 111, 113; *see also* 'operazioni umane'
worth v, 6, 11, 14, 24, 77, 85, 103, 115, 118, 123, 125, 144, 204, 224, 246, 251–2, 254
  and reward 65–6, 71–2
wrongs (*delicta*, in Roman law) 59

Zeno of Citium 13
Zodiac 61; *see also* influences